Constitutional Law and Constitutional Rights in Ireland

THIRD EDITION

BRIAN DOOLAN

GILL & MACMILLAN

Published in Ireland by
Gill & Macmillan Ltd
Goldenbridge
Dublin 8
with associated companies throughout the world
© Brian Doolan, 1984, 1988, 1994
0 7171 2047 3
Print origination by
Seton Music Graphics Ltd, Bantry, Co. Cork
Printed in Ireland by
ColourBooks Ltd, Dublin

A catalogue record is available for
this book from the British Library.

1   3   5   4   2

Contents

PREFACE TO THE THIRD EDITION

It is an axiom that constitutional law is the foremost legal subject within our system of laws. As a body of first principles it is rapidly expanding. In the ten years since the first edition of this book, which has become the standard comprehensive introduction to the subject, the case law has increased from 101 primary cases to just over 200. There have been a number of amendments to the Constitution and a number of statutes which have altered areas of the subject matter.

Our constitutional law lends itself to a natural division of the subject matter into political rights and personal rights. This division is emphasised in the scheme of this book. Part One considers such political and governmental matters, from a purely legal viewpoint, as the Nation, the State and the institutions of government. There have been major developments in this area as these aspects of the Constitution are subjected to judicial comment. Part Two concentrates, individually, on the various personal rights available to the individual.

A study of constitutional law would be incomprehensible without a working knowledge of the case law. Law reports are often inaccessible, time-consuming to read because of their length, confusing because of the differences of reasoning or conclusion of the judges on the same subject — even in the one case, and difficult to grasp because of their language, diffusion, and sheer breadth of topics covered. As a first step in the introduction to the case law, I have retained a feature, innovative in the first edition, which was universally welcomed by reviewers and readers alike. Part Three contains, in alphabetical order, a synopsis of the 200 or so cases of constitutional importance. When the case is reached in the text the reader is referred to that case by a distinctive number which provides a quick method of reference to the facts and decision, and the otherwise constant repetition of the facts of the case is thus avoided.

I have endeavoured to explain the law as it stood on 1 January 1994.

Brian Doolan
Dublin Institute of Technology
6 January 1994

AMENDMENTS OF THE CONSTITUTION

TABLE OF STATUTES

* denotes British statute

TABLE OF CASES

Chapter 1

THE NATURE OF THE IRISH CONSTITUTION

Meaning of Constitution

In political and legal affairs the word *constitution* is used in at least two differing senses: the wide and abstract sense and the narrow and concrete sense. The constitution of a state in the wider sense is the system of laws, customs and conventions which create and validate the organs of government and which regulate the interaction of those organs with one another and with the individual. Most of these rules are legal in the sense that courts of law will recognise and apply them where appropriate. Other rules, non-legal in nature, consisting of customs and conventions, will be adhered to, though not having the force of law; all combine to give a wide and abstract meaning to the word constitution. The more appropriate expression to encompass this meaning is *constitutional law*.

A constitution in its narrow and concrete sense means the document or documents in which the basic legal rules of the constitution are authoritatively declared. It is *the* source of law of the community. The law of the constitution is readily and easily ascertained by reference to one or a few documents which, by some legitimating means, have been given the stamp of approval. Such approval marks them down as being the *law* above all else, that by which all other legal norms and rules are to be judged.

On Constitutions in General

In a modern state there exists a readily identifiable document or collection of documents which embodies a selection of the most fundamental rules about the government of that state. A comparative study indicates a series of features common to all or most of these constitutions.[1] The most common characteristic is that a special process has been used to enact the constitution as distinct from the method used to enact ordinary laws. There are two effects flowing from this. In the first place it gives to the constitution a form of legitimacy not given to other forms of laws, while secondly the constitution is given a primary character as law: it is *the* fundamental law of the state over and above all other forms of law.

The second common characteristic of many constitutions is a provision granting the power to the courts to pronounce ordinary laws inconsistent with the constitution and therefore null and void. The courts decide on the compatibility of ordinary laws and administrative action with the provisions of the constitution and those found wanting are condemned and are bereft of authority. The word *constitutional* means *in conformity with the constitution* and the word *unconstitutional* means *in violation of the constitution*.

Since the constitution is the fundamental law of the state it follows that to retain this character it must be immune from easy and unconsidered amendment. This protection from mutilation is the third feature common to many constitutions. A special procedure is required before the constitution can be amended. If amendments were permitted by ordinary law the constitution would be denied this badge of speciality which it claims because of its special enactment and its fundamental character.

Having looked at the character of constitutions let us now examine the contents of constitutions. Constitutions are primarily about political authority or power. The constitution will usually locate, confer, distribute and limit authority and power among the organs of government of a state. More often than not it is concerned with procedure as much as substantive rules of law. The organs of government will interact with each other to prevent abuse, and all the organs will interface to form a system which will have, as their aim, good and just government. In a political society the individual must yield to government. How far the individual must submit will depend on the type of society which exists. Government and individual freedoms of an absolute nature are incompatible. Good government will permit the greatest freedoms. For freedom to flourish, government must be controlled. The purpose of a constitution, apart from establishing the State and its institutions, is to limit the powers of government. There cannot be unlimited power under a constitution: the word *constitution* denotes limitation. A study of constitutions will show how the various organs of government are limited and controlled. These restrictions are imposed to prevent tyranny and the individual, subjected to the least amount of control, can develop personality and assert individuality to the fullest.

Because a constitution signals a new political beginning, many constitutions contain explicit guarantees of rights and freedoms to be enjoyed by the individual. Remembrance will be made of the injustices that went before because of a colonial or dictatorial regime. A new political beginning demands a new attitude towards the individual. The individual is elevated into constitutional significance. The individual's role is not alone that of the governed but of the governing. As far as it is practicable the individual is allowed to exist, develop and be possessed of rights that cannot easily be negatived. Some constitutions will incorporate ideological pronouncements in the form of principles by which the community ought to be guided or to which it might aspire. These principles must be given effect when interpreting the constitution and when ordinary laws and actions are to be judged. Such ideas will depend on the political and moral beliefs of the community.[2] While a study of constitutions will exhibit an array of differing philosophies, a central feature of constitutions will be some idealistic foundation.

The Irish Constitution and Constitutional Law

Against this backdrop of constitutions in general we can approach the Constitution of Ireland with some preconceived expectations. The Constitution when enacted in 1937 marked a new political beginning in that it was a document drafted without reference to any other government[3] though it incorporated institutions which had been tried elsewhere. It was enacted by the People;[4] it established the State and the organs of government; it contained a statement of individual rights; it declared its objectives to be the attainment of stated social aspirations and it provided a special method of amendment. It thus contained many of the characteristics of other modern constitutions while it in turn exhibited these characteristics as the typical foundations of a modern constitution.

When we speak of the Irish Constitution we mean the document enacted by the People. This is the narrower meaning which can be given to constitutions. But a reading of the Constitution, worthwhile in itself, does not introduce the reader to the entire rules of our constitutional law. The Constitution as a basic document denotes the idea of a foundation upon which will be built a structure that must include other documents and customs. The Constitution is the legal framework upon which must be hung legal rules and interpretations which give it shape. This book attempts to examine the Constitution together with its implementing statutes and in the light of judicial interpretation. Such a study proves that constitutional law is a real and vital force in our law and society and leads to the conclusion that our constitutional law, more than any other branch of our law, has developed in a way peculiar to our own ideals, aspirations and needs.

The Legitimacy of the Constitution

For a measure to have the force of law it must have the appropriate legitimacy. Legislation is law because it was enacted by a competent authority. In what circumstances can a constitution claim to have this legal authority? By what criteria do those whose task it is to administer the law recognise that a certain document, described as a constitution, forms part of the law? The general rule, as already mentioned, is to seek a body competent to make law. But the difficulty is obvious: since the constitution itself creates the law-making body, can there exist another body competent to enact a constitution before the constitution itself is in being? To resolve this puzzle it becomes necessary to conceive of a body which can give the force of law to a constitution before the constitution itself authorises the establishment of a law-making body.

Where then are these original primeval lawgivers? To this question there are three possible answers. In the first type of case the original lawgiver will be an assembly specially constituted for that purpose. The assembly will be directly elected by the people though the latter do not take part directly in the acceptance or rejection of the constitution. In India a special constituent assembly was elected to frame the Constitution. The Constitution of Saorstát Éireann* was enacted by this method. Using the second possibility is the acknowledgment that the original lawgiver is another parliament. The Constitution of Australia is a statute of the British Parliament.

In the third type of situation the original lawgiver will be the People. The constitution will be voted on by popular franchise and the decision of a mere majority, or some weighted majority, will prevail. The People are the fountain-head of all authority. This method was adopted when the Constitution of Ireland was framed and proposed. It was put to the People in a plebiscite and enacted by them.[5] The first principle of our constitutional theory is that the People are the first and primary authority. The People are the first and primary lawmakers and are the sole entity under our constitutional law possessed of unlimited power. This fundamental principle pervades our legal system and has been accepted by judicial pronouncements regularly. This primary source of authority has been re-emphasised regularly by the necessity of ascertaining the will of the People before the Constitution can be amended: permission to alter has been both given and refused.

The Supremacy of the Constitution
The supremacy of the Constitution over other forms of law is achieved by giving it a quality of uniqueness against which all other laws are to be judged. If a law infringes the Constitution it is declared to be null and void and it is irrelevant how necessary, how good and how useful that law may be. The Constitution is our legal yardstick against which *all* other laws are to be judged. Many of our constitutional cases are concerned with that very issue as to whether some aspect of the ordinary law infringes the Constitution.

The Ethos of the Constitution
It can be expected, since the Constitution was enacted by the People, that the ethical values on which it is based will reflect the broad morals of this society. This society is undeniably Christian in character. It is therefore hardly surprising that the Constitution will reflect Christian values and virtues. The Preamble acknowledges the Christian God and seeks to promote the common

good with due observance of prudence, justice and charity.[6] To consider such sentiments as sectarian exhibits some level of intolerance. A constitution could not realistically give expression to the moral and ethical beliefs of every individual or group in society. Because this diversity cannot be attained within the pages of a constitution is not an argument for the complete absence of sentiments which have the broad support of the majority.[7] The majority are entitled to this consideration provided the sentiments expressed are not intended and used to persecute and alienate those who do not subscribe to such ideals. The tyranny of a minority can be as destructive as any majority persecution.

It is generally accepted that the Constitution is based on natural law teachings.[8] The natural law is based on value judgments which cite as their authority some absolute source such as, for example, God's revealed word. These absolute value judgments claim to reflect the essential character of the universe and purport to be immutable and eternally valid. They can be grasped and understood by the proper employment of human reason. When perceived, they must overrule all positive or man-made law. There are thus two kinds of law, the *natural law* and the *positive law*. Both are necessary in society but the positive law must always yield to the natural law. Some oppose the notion that natural law exists or that it should be used to measure positive law. If the notion that natural law does not exist is accepted it is difficult, if not impossible, to argue for the existence of natural rights. If only positive law exists then rights can be granted and abrogated by positive law. The Constitution and the courts refuse to countenance the proposition that rights are given by positive law.

Apart from the Christian nature of the Constitution there is another broad concept which pervades it. The People enacted the Constitution by popular vote and it can be amended only by popular vote. The role of the People in deciding issues of importance is evidence of the democratic nature of this society. Not alone do the People vote on what are directly constitutional issues, they vote from time to time in elections to decide who should exercise various constitutional functions. The People are an integral part of government: it is government by the People for the People.

Interpretation of the Constitution
A reading of the Constitution, like the reading of other material, leads to some conclusion as to its meaning. Because it is a legal document some legal terminology must be used though essentially the Constitution is a document that can be read and understood by the lay person.[9] The politician, the lawyer, the moralist, the sociologist and the lay person can, with differing emphases on different nuances, argue in favour of particular conclusions. This may appear to cause confusion. On the contrary, if the Constitution is to remain

vibrant and relevant it is imperative that it lends itself to differing and changing interpretations. When the Constitution loses this quality its importance
will fade.

Of course there must be some institution or person who can give the
Constitution an authoritative interpretation. The Constitution grants this power
to the courts and consequently the Constitution means what the superior
courts declare it to mean. The High Court has jurisdiction, having regard to
the provisions of the Constitution, to question the validity of any law, and the
Supreme Court has appellate jurisdiction* from such decisions (see page 118).
Walsh J* explained in *McGee v Attorney General* (1974) (Case 101):

> it falls finally upon the judges to interpret the Constitution . . . the judges
> must, therefore, as best they can from their training and experience interpret
> these rights in accordance with their ideas of prudence, justice and charity.

This is an acknowledgment that any interpretation of the Constitution is
subjective: it cannot be otherwise. While the judges interpret the Constitution
it does not follow that the People must accept such interpretations. A decision of the courts could be negatived by a referendum, or the People could
amend the Constitution by removing this power of interpretation from the
courts. An interpretation once given is not immutable in perpetuity. It can
subsequently be altered. Again Walsh J explained in the same case:

> it is but natural that from time to time the prevailing ideas of these virtues
> may be conditioned by the passage of time; no interpretation of the
> Constitution is intended to be final for all time. It is given in the light of
> prevailing ideas and concepts.[10]

Amendment of the Constitution

Constitutions are often classified as *flexible* or *rigid*.[11] A flexible constitution
can be changed with the same ease and in the same manner as ordinary law.
The unwritten British constitution is usually given as an example of a
flexible constitution. A rigid constitution is one which requires some special
procedure to effect an alteration. Amendment of the United States Constitution
requires either initiation by two-thirds of both Houses of Congress and ratification by the legislatures of three-fourths of the states or initiation by two-
thirds of the states and ratification by convention in three-fourths of the states.

Few constitutions require a referendum by the electorate. Since our Constitution was enacted by the People it is hardly surprising that amendments
to it must be enacted by the same method. The possibility of amendment is
controlled in that any proposal must be initiated in Dáil Éireann and be passed
or deemed to be passed by both Houses of the Oireachtas* (Article 46).[12]
An initiation by the electorate is not possible. An attempt was made, in

Roche v Ireland (1983), to prevent by injunction the *Eighth Amendment to the Constitution Bill 1983*, passed by the Houses of the Oireachtas, from being put to the People. It was argued that the wording of the amendment lacked meaning and precision and that it was open to conflicting and divergent interpretations. Dismissing the claim the High Court ruled that if a citizen was uncertain of the meaning to be given to the amendment the citizen could vote against it. Carroll J, in emphasising the supremacy of the People in the process of amending the Constitution, explained:

> it is clear that a constitutional amendment involves a particularly solemn legislative process. There must first be a Bill initiated in Dáil Éireann passed by both Houses of the Oireachtas, which is then submitted to the People for their approval. If a majority vote in favour, the Bill is signed by the President and promulgated as a law. It is not a question of there being just a legislative process in the Oireachtas. The people participate in passing an amendment to the fundamental law of the State. They are as much part of the legislative process as the proceedings in the Oireachtas and the signing by the President . . . It would be totally opposed to the separation of powers provided by the Constitution that the courts could prevent any particular wording, duly passed by the Oireachtas, from being put to the People of Ireland.

Another attempt to prevent the same amendment being put to the People was made in *Finn v Attorney General* (1983) (Case 67) where it was argued that the proposal was not a variation, an addition or repeal, but was the reiteration of a right already implicitly protected by the Constitution. The Supreme Court, adopting the reasoning of the High Court in *Roche*'s case, held that the courts had no jurisdiction to construe or to review the constitutionality of a Bill to amend the Constitution, whatever its nature. An attempt to injunct the holding of a referendum in relation to the *Tenth Amendment to the Constitution Bill 1986* also failed for the same reason. In *Mhic Mhathúna v Ireland* (1986) it was unsuccessfully argued that should the proposed amendment be carried by the People the plaintiff would be denied her constitutional right to have proceedings, which were then pending in the High Court, determined by the courts under the provisions of the Constitution pertaining when the proceedings were initiated. It was feared that the proposed amendment, if carried, could be used to defeat the pending proceedings.

The Supreme Court, in *Slattery v An Taoiseach* (1992), refused to injunct the holding of a referendum on the *Eleventh Amendment of the Constitution Bill 1992* holding that there was no constitutional obligation on the Government to provide funds for those opposed to the enactment of the amendment; nor was there an obligation on the Government to explain or attempt to explain the meaning or consequences of the proposed amendment.

Every proposal submitted to the People in a referendum is approved if a majority of votes cast are in favour (Article 47.1). Referenda, apart from deciding particular questions, give the People an opportunity to confirm their allegiance to the Constitution.

The Constitution provided in Article 51, now deleted, that the Constitution could be amended by the Oireachtas within a period of three years after the date on which the first President entered into office.[13] A proposal for the amendment of the Constitution by this method was not to be enacted into law if the President, after consultation with the Council of State, signified in a message addressed to the chairman of each of the Houses of the Oireachtas that the proposal was, in his opinion, a proposal to effect an amendment of such a character and importance that the will of the People ought to be ascertained by referendum before its enactment into law. Two amendments where enacted under this article: the *First Amendment of the Constitution Act 1939*,[14] and the *Second Amendment of the Constitution Act 1941*,[15] though neither was voted on by the People.

There have been sixteen proposals to amend the Constitution placed before the People. Eleven have been accepted and five were rejected. Three proposals were approved in 1972: entry into the EEC (see page 16);[16] extension of the franchise to eighteen-year-olds (see page 87);[17] and the deletion of a portion of Article 44 which gave mention to a number of churches.[18] Two were approved in 1979: a proposal for the redistribution of the university seats in Seanad Éireann (see page 92);[19] and a proposal that adoption orders made by An Bord Uchtála (the Adoption Board) were immune from challenge on the ground that the board was not a court (see page 262).[20] In 1983 the pro-life amendment was approved (see page 219),[21] and in 1984 a proposal to permit the Oireachtas to extend the franchise in Dáil Éireann elections to non-citizens was approved (see page 81).[22] In 1987 a proposal to permit the State to ratify the Single European Act was accepted by the People[23] (see page 17) and in 1992 a proposal to permit the State to ratify the Treaty on European Union, known as the Maastricht Treaty was approved.[24] Later in 1992 two proposals relating to the right to life of the unborn and the equal right to life of the mother were accepted. The first covered the freedom to travel[25] and the other concerned the freedom to obtain and make available information (see page 221).[26]

In 1959, a proposal to abolish proportional representation was defeated.[27] When the question was again put in 1968 it was again defeated (see page 88),[28] together with a proposal to permit a departure from the principle of uniformity of representation (see page 78).[29] A proposal in 1986 to delete the ban on divorce was defeated (see page 248).[30] In 1992 a proposed limitation on the application of Article 40.3.3 of the Constitution, which relates to the right to life of the unborn and the equal right to life of the mother, was defeated.[31]

Whether an amendment to the Constitution has merely prospective effect and not retrospective effect will depend on the wording of the amendment.

Text of the Constitution

The Taoiseach* shall from time to time cause to be prepared under his or her supervision a text of the Constitution as then in force embodying all amendments. A copy of every text so prepared, when authenticated by the signatures of the Taoiseach and the Chief Justice, shall be signed by the President and be enrolled for record in the office of the Registrar of the Supreme Court. The copy so signed and enrolled shall be conclusive evidence of the Constitution and supersedes all texts of the Constitution of which copies were previously so enrolled. In cases of conflict between the texts of any copy of the Constitution so enrolled the text in the national language, that is the Irish language, shall prevail (Article 25.5).[32]

Part One

THE NATION, THE STATE AND THE INSTITUTIONS OF GOVERNMENT

Chapter 2

THE NATION

The People are the Nation

In the first chapter the scheme on which our constitutional framework rests was laid out. As the primary lawmakers the People enacted the Constitution which established the State and the institutions of government. The Preamble speaks of the 'People of Éire'. This impersonal and imprecise subject is identified in Article 1 which declares that the People, the primary lawmakers and the ultimate source of authority, under God, are the Irish nation: so the People and the Irish nation are synonymous. A power reserved in the Constitution to the People can only be validly exercised by the Irish people. This view has received judicial approval. In *Article 26 and the Electoral (Amendment) Bill 1983* (Case 7), O'Higgins CJ,* in the Supreme Court, explained:

> Article 6 proclaims that all powers of government derive under God from the People and, further, that it is the People's right to designate the rulers of the State and, in final appeal, to decide all questions of national policy. There can be little doubt that *the people* here referred to are the people of Ireland by, and for whom, the Constitution was enacted. In short, this Article proclaims that it is the Irish people who are the rulers of Ireland and that from them, under God, all powers of government derive and that by them the rulers are designated and national policy decided. It is not possible to regard this Article as contemplating the sharing of such power with persons who do not come within the constitutional concept of the Irish people in Article 6.

Article 1 declares that the Irish nation affirms its inalienable, indefeasible and sovereign right to choose its own form of government, to determine its relations with other nations, and to develop its political, economic and cultural life in accordance with its own genius and traditions.

There are two possible definitions of a nation. First, a nation can be an aggregation of a people, or peoples, of one or more cultures or races organised into a single state. Applying this test, it can be positively seen that there is a state called Ireland, and within its borders is a people who share a common heritage and aspirations. Secondly, a nation can be a community of persons not constituting a state but bound by common descent, language, religion and history. When this definition is applied it can be said that the Irish nation spreads beyond the borders of the State to encompass persons who identify closely with the national territory. The Constitution seems to intend this definition to be the operative one. This will be seen when we examine the extent of the national territory a little later in the chapter.

An attribute of nationhood is a distinct language which need not be widely spoken by the People. It might rather be of historical importance, and while the possibility of restoring it to common usage might be remote, the sympathy shown towards it is sufficient to identify it as the national language. The Constitution declares Irish, which is not the regular language of the majority of the population, to be the national and first official language (Article 8). The English language, which is the regular language of the majority of the population, is recognised as a second official language. The Constitution was drafted, proposed and enacted in both languages. Both languages have played, and continue to play, an important role in the life and culture of the nation. The Constitution neither expressly, nor by implication, attempts or aspires to substitute one language for the other.

The National Territory
The Constitution declares that the national territory consists of the whole island of Ireland, its islands and the territorial seas (Article 2). This is a trenchant and unambiguous declaration that the Irish nation is the inheritor and the rightful possessor of the whole island of Ireland. The reality of the political division of the island does not in any way detract from that factual statement that the Irish nation possesses the whole island of Ireland.

This declaration is not a claim by the State, established under the Constitution, to exercise jurisdiction over the whole of the island. On the contrary, it is an unambiguous acknowledgment that the Irish nation as a whole, and not any particular state existing on the island, is entitled to possess the national territory.

Article 3 of the Constitution accepts the political division of the national territory by declaring that the jurisdiction of the State, established under the Constitution, has the like application as the laws of Saorstát Éireann. This is an acceptance that the State called Ireland, established under the Constitution, is composed of the same geographical area as was the Irish Free State, and no more. It is a *de facto** recognition that the national territory consists of more than one political entity.

Pending the reintegration of the national territory, Article 3 declares that the laws enacted by the Parliament established under the Constitution shall have the like extent and application as the laws of Saorstát Éireann 'without prejudice to the right of the Parliament and Government established by this Constitution to exercise jurisdiction over the whole of that territory'.

The Supreme Court, in *McGimpsey v Ireland* (1990) (Case 102), has given an authoritative definition to these articles. Finlay CJ explained:

1. The reintegration of the national territory is a constitutional imperative.
2. Article 2 of the Constitution consists of a declaration of the extent of the national territory as a claim of legal right.
3. Article 3 of the Constitution prohibits, pending the reintegration of the national territory, the enactment of laws with any greater area or extent of application or extra-territorial effect than the laws of Saorstát Éireann and this prohibits the enactment of laws applicable in the counties of Northern Ireland.
4. The restriction imposed by Article 3 pending the reintegration of the national territory in no way derogates from the claim as a legal right to the entire national territory.

   The provision in Article 3 of the Constitution contained in the words 'and without prejudice to the right of the Parliament and Government established by this Constitution to exercise jurisdiction over the whole of that territory' is an express denial and disclaimer made to the community of nations of acquiescence to any claim that pending the reintegration of the national territory the frontier at present existing between the State and Northern Ireland is or can be accepted as conclusive of the matter or that there can be any prescriptive title thereby created and an assertion that there can be no estoppel created by the restriction in Article 3 on the application of the laws of the State in Northern Ireland.

Article 3 does not define the geographical State established under the Constitution though it declares that the laws, and therefore the jurisdiction, are to have the same application and extent as the laws of Saorstát Éireann. This latter entity was not defined in the Constitution, or indeed in the Constitution of the Irish Free State, or even in the Treaty between Great Britain and Ireland. Recourse must be made to the *Government of Ireland Act 1920*. This statute of the British Parliament divided the island of Ireland for the first time into two political entities: Southern Ireland and Northern Ireland. Only Northern Ireland was defined in that statute. It was declared to consist of the parliamentary counties of Antrim, Armagh, Down, Fermanagh, Londonderry and Tyrone. Southern Ireland was to consist of the remainder of the island. This entity became Saorstát Éireann and is now the geographical extent of the State established under the 1937 Constitution.

In 1985 the governments of Ireland and the United Kingdom[1] signed an agreement which stated *inter alia*, in Article 1, that the two governments affirmed that any change in the status of Northern Ireland would only come about with the consent of a majority of the people of Northern Ireland. The Supreme Court, in *McGimpsey v Ireland* (1990) (Case 102), held that this statement constituted a recognition of the *de facto* situation in Northern Ireland without expressly abandoning the claim to the reintegration of the national territory.

Various statutes delimit the extent of the territorial waters of the State. There is a ribbon of water around the State over which exclusive jurisdiction is exercised. There are other areas of water over which the State exercises limited jurisdiction and the concept of extra-territorial jurisdiction is considered in the next chapter.

Chapter 3

THE STATE

Nature of a State

In international law the legal criteria of statehood, set out in Article 1 of the Montevideo Convention on Rights and Duties of States,[1] are permanent population, a defined territory, a government and the capacity to enter into relations with other states. The concept of independence is represented by the capacity to enter into external relations with other states. Guggenheim distinguishes the State from other legal orders by two tests.[2] First, the State has a degree of centralisation of its organs not found in the world community, and secondly, in a particular geographical area, the State is the sole executive, legislative and judicial authority. If an entity has its own organs of government and, according to Brownlie, a nationality law of its own,[3] there is prima-facie* evidence of statehood.

The Irish State

Applying these criteria to the circumstances existing in 1937, and currently pertaining, Ireland in international law has the status of a State. It has a permanent population, it occupies a defined territory, it has organs of government and it enters into relations with other states.

The People in 1937 had to decide the kind of State they wished to establish. A monarchy, a dictatorship or an oligarchy could have been established. The State could have been structured as a unitary state or a federation. In international affairs the State could have aligned itself with any other state or group of states. Instead, Article 5 of the Constitution declares Ireland to be a sovereign, independent, democratic State.

The Name of the State

According to Article 4 of the Constitution the name of the State is Éire, or in the English language, Ireland. The *Republic of Ireland Act 1948* states that the 'description of the State shall be the Republic of Ireland'. Speaking as to how this State should be described in *Ellis v O'Dea* (1990), an extradition case, Walsh J, in the Supreme Court, said:

In the English language the name of this State is 'Ireland' and is so prescribed in Article 4 of the Constitution. Of course if the courts of the United Kingdom or of other states choose to issue [extradition] warrants in the Irish language then of course they are quite at liberty to use the Irish language name of the State as prescribed in the Constitution. However they are not at liberty to attribute to this State a name which is not its correct name. It is quite clear from various warrants which have come before this court from time to time that this is a conscious and deliberate practice. In effect it is a refusal to recognise a provision of the Constitution of Ireland. Every court in this State and every member of the Garda Síochána is duty bound to uphold the Constitution and not to condone or acquiesce in any refusal to recognise the Constitution or any part thereof. If the courts of other countries seeking the assistance of the courts of this country are unwilling to give this State its constitutionally correct and internationally recognised name then, in my view, the warrants should be returned to such countries until they have been rectified. Hence it should be the concern and care of the requesting prosecuting and judicial authorities of another state not to ignore or brush aside the fundamental law of this State. It should be the concern and care of the Irish authorities not to permit the existence of any such situation. The name of the State is as provided for in Article 4 of the Constitution. In 1948 the Oireachtas* enacted Acht Phoblacht na hÉireann in both the Irish and English languages. In the latter language it is entitled 'the Republic of Ireland Act 1948'. It does not purport to change the name of the State nor could the Oireachtas do so even if it so wished. An amendment of the Constitution would be required for a change in name.

A Sovereign State

Despite the remark by Stark[4] that sovereignty is a term of art rather than a legal term admitting of precise definition, Schwarzenberger[5] defines sovereignty in the context of the constitutional theory of the unitary state as meaning omnipotence. Sovereignty may be external or internal. In international law the external sovereignty of a state reflects its autonomy or independence. It is positive in that power is exercised in pursuance of objectives such as the maintenance of status and power. It is negative in that it involves the absence of subordination to any foreign or exterior power. This view of external sovereignty accords with judicial thinking. According to Walsh J in *Byrne v Ireland* (1972) (Case 29):

the declaration as to sovereignty means that the State is not subject to any power of government save those designated by the People in the Constitution itself, and that the State is not amenable to any external authority.

In international law a sovereign state is possessed of rights and duties. It has the exclusive right to control its own domestic affairs and to admit or expel aliens. It exercises the sole jurisdiction over crimes committed within its territory. A state has the duty:

- not to perform acts of sovereignty over the territory of another state;
- to abstain and prevent agents and subjects from committing acts constituting a violation of another state's independence or territorial supremacy;
- not to interfere in the affairs of another state.

There is hardly a state in existence which has not accepted some restrictions on its liberty of action in the interest of the international comity of nations. Most states belong to the United Nations. Such membership limits the unfettered discretion of a state in matters of international policy. Sovereignty is lost, according to Brownlie, where foreign control overbears decision-making on a wide range of matters of high policy on a systematic and permanent basis. Since sovereignty is an attribute of statehood no organ of government can curtail it. This was decided by the Supreme Court in *Crotty v An Taoiseach* (1987) (Case 43) where the executive was injuncted from ratifying an international agreement which fundamentally restricted the sovereignty of the State in the conduct of its foreign affairs. The power to define and curtail sovereignty resides exclusively with the People.[6]

Does our membership of the European Community dent our sovereignty in a serious way? The answer must be in the affirmative and it could now be argued that applying the criteria of the Brownlie test this State is no longer sovereign. Ireland formally became a member of the EC in January 1972. For the laws of the community, made externally and not by the organs of government established under the Constitution, to have the force of law in this State it was necessary to amend the Constitution. This was done by the People on 10 May 1972.[7] This amendment to Article 29.4.3° was repealed in 1992. Its substitution is set out presently. The original provision limited our sovereignty in economic and legislative matters. A further restriction in matters of foreign relations was added to Article 29.4.3° of the Constitution by the *Tenth Amendment to the Constitution Act 1987* which provides:

the State may ratify the Single European Act (signed on behalf of the Member States of the Communities at Luxemburg on 17 February 1986 and at The Hague on 28 February 1986).

A further amendment was necessary when European Union was considered as an objective. On 18 June 1992 further provisions were added to Article 29.4.3° of the Constitution and read as follows:

29.4.4° The State may ratify the Treaty on European Union signed at Maastricht on the 7th day of February 1992, and may become a member of that Union.

5° No provision of this Constitution invalidates laws enacted, acts done or measures adopted by the State which are necessitated by the obligations of membership of the European Union or of the Communities, or prevents laws enacted, acts done or measures adopted by the European Union or by the Communities or by institutions thereof, or by bodies competent under the Treaties establishing the Communities, from having the force of law in the State.

6° The State may ratify the Agreement relating to Community Patents drawn up at Luxemburg between the Member States of the Communities and done at Luxemburg on the 15th day of December 1989.

The laws of the EC have found their way into domestic law in a number of ways. The *European Communities Act 1972* made the Treaties part of the domestic law and Ministers of State are empowered to incorporate further laws into domestic law by statutory instruments.* And the *European Communities Act 1986* enacted portion of the Single European Act, which amended the original Treaties, into law. This was permissible, according to the Supreme Court in *Crotty v An Taoiseach* (1987) (Case 43), because the amendments did not alter the essential scope or objectives of the Communities. Some statutes which have been enacted to give effect to Community law, in the nature of Regulations, automatically become the law of the State. The Community issues Directives which set out objects to be achieved while leaving it to each member state to choose its own method of achievement.

The State's membership of the EC has had a profound effect on the sovereignty of the State's law-making process. For instance, in *Meagher v Minister for Agriculture* (1994) (Case 115), the Supreme Court ruled that a power granted to the executive by statute to make laws by regulation or statutory instrument which included provisions either repealing, amending or modifying statute law enacted by the Oireachtas, was immune from constitutional challenge because such a measure was necessitated by our membership of the EC in that the power in the statute was provided for one purpose, and one purpose only, that of enabling the application of Community law to be binding on the State and to become part of the domestic law subject to the conditions laid down in the Treaties. On the other hand, the High Court held, in *Greene v Minister for Agriculture* (1990), that the conditions imposed on a scheme, contained in a Directive, designed to provide compensatory payments to persons farming in disadvantaged areas, by the executive were so far reaching and detached from the result to be achieved that it could not be said to have been necessitated by the obligations of membership of the EC and was therefore not immune from challenge by virtue of Article 29.4 of the Constitution.

Internal Sovereignty

What is the status of the State in domestic law? While it is sovereign in international affairs how far does this concept extend in the domestic forum? It was not until *Byrne v Ireland* (1972) (Case 29) that the status of the State with regard to internal sovereignty, and the extent of its rights and liabilities, were convincingly established. In that case when the State was sued for the wrongful acts of its servants the defence was raised that by reason of its sovereignty the State was not liable in its own courts and there was vested in the State an immunity from action, a prerogative formerly vested in the crown. The Supreme Court rejected these contentions by holding that the State was the creation of the People and consequently could only exercise powers granted to it by the People. In several articles of the Constitution the State was either under a duty to bestow rights on the citizen or was restricted on the exercise of powers. These restrictions tended to prove that the State was not sovereign. Had the Constitution intended the State to be possessed of immunity from action it would have declared so expressly. The concept of immunity from action was a medieval one based on feudal theories contained in the maxim that *the King can do no wrong*. These concepts were irreconcilable with modern ideas. Ireland was a State established in modern times and its Constitution was of recent enactment. The Crown was completely absent from the Constitution and gone with it was any idea of the Crown as the personification of the State.

Reiterating this principle that the prerogatives which may have attached to the Crown do not attach to the modern State of Ireland, the Supreme Court found in *Webb v Ireland* (1988) (Case 212) that the common law prerogative of the Crown to claim treasure trove — that is items of money, gold or silver found hidden in the earth and where the owner is unknown — was not part of our law. More importantly the Supreme Court stressed that a necessary ingredient of the sovereignty of a modern State was that the State should be the owner of objects which constituted antiquities of importance which are discovered and have no known owner. This right was an inherent attribute of a sovereign state.

Another aspect of internal sovereignty arose in *Howard v Commissioners of Public Works* (1993) (Case 81), where the courts had to consider whether the State was bound by statutes enacted by the Oireachtas. In that case the point at issue was whether a State agency was bound by the planning laws. Historically the Crown in England had a special position in relation to legislation in that laws made by the Crown, with the assent of the Houses of Parliament, were intended to bind subjects but not the Crown itself. The Supreme Court ruled that where the issue arose as to whether the State was bound by the provisions of a statute the court should, in accordance with the ordinary rules applicable to the interpretation of statutory provisions, and without any presumption in either direction, seek to ascertain whether the legislature intended the statute to apply to the situation under review.

The point arose in *Geoghegan v Institute of Chartered Accountants in Ireland* (1993) whether a body, which had been validly incorporated in the nineteenth century in the then United Kingdom of Great Britain and Ireland in pursuance of a charter granted in accordance with the royal prerogative, withered away or ceased to have the right to exercise the powers conferred on it by the charter on the coming into operation of the Constitution of Saorstát Éireann in 1922 or the Constitution of Ireland in 1937. It seemed to the High Court that the laws carried forward by both Constitutions comprised a full range of laws whether customary or statutory and however enacted subject only to their not being inconsistent with either Constitution. However, in that case, the matter was beyond doubt because the *Institute of Chartered Accountants in Ireland (Charter Amendment) Act 1966* provided that the charter shall be and remain in full force and effect.

Ireland, the State, is thus a juristic person possessed of rights and duties, capable of suing and being sued, though in *Pesca Valentia Ltd v Minister for Fisheries* (1985) the Supreme Court considered it inappropriate that an injunction should be issued against Ireland.

The Jurisdiction of the State

The sovereignty of a state in international law is essentially a negative concept: the *jurisdiction* of a state is its positive counterpart. Jurisdiction is concerned with legislative, executive and judicial competence and can be divided into *personal* and *territorial* jurisdictions.

Personal jurisdiction is the authority asserted over individuals on the basis of fidelity and loyalty. In the evolution of contemporary international law, personal jurisdiction preceded territorial jurisdiction. By virtue of this concept the subject of a sovereign was considered to remain under the sovereign's authority wherever the subject was. This concept of personal jurisdiction finds a place in our constitutional theory. The Constitution draws a distinction between the status of the citizen and that of the non-citizen. Fidelity to the nation and loyalty to the State are demanded of the citizen (Article 9.2). In return the State acknowledges that certain fundamental rights are available to citizens and not to others (see page 158).

The concept of personal jurisdiction was enforced by the common law on the basis of *domicile* (see page 26). Irish courts may apply Irish law to actions committed abroad provided the person has retained an Irish domicile. Conversely an Irish court might refuse to apply Irish law where the party has retained a foreign domicile. For example, Irish courts may recognise a divorce obtained by parties whose domiciliary law at the time of the divorce granted the divorce although there is no law of divorce available to persons, citizens or otherwise, domiciled within this State.[8]

The trend in international law has been away from personal jurisdiction and towards *territorial* jurisdiction. Sovereigns insisted on exclusive jurisdiction over all persons and every action performed within their borders. The most noticeable exception was diplomatic immunity. In Irish law territorial jurisdiction is the norm: all persons regardless of nationality are subject to the criminal and civil law of this State. This jurisdiction extends to Irish ships while on the high seas. A person was convicted of a crime, in *The People (AG) v Thomas* (1954), committed aboard an Irish-registered ship while on the high seas between Ireland and Britain.

Extra-territorial Jurisdiction

The principle of territorial jurisdiction which declares that the courts of a state in which a wrong is committed has sole and exclusive jurisdiction over the wrongdoer is one of almost universal application. This principle has a number of advantages including the convenience of the forum, the presumed involvement of the interests of the state where the wrong was committed and, adhering to the principle of statehood, that one state will not perform acts of sovereignty over the territory of another state.

Despite these reservations of a state's right to extra-territorial jurisdiction the possibility of its acceptance under our law has been mooted. Two judges of the former Supreme Court,* in *R (Alexander) v Circuit Judge for Cork* (1925), without citing authority, held that it could. Kennedy CJ said that if specific legislation of such a kind were passed without reciprocal enactment by the parliament within whose territorial sovereignty the persons to be bound were, it would prima facie offend against the conventions of international law by impinging upon the exclusive sovereignty and jurisdiction of that other state. FitzGibbon J declared that by the constitutional usage and the comity of nations and so-called international law the courts of one country did not, as a rule, exercise jurisdiction over the subjects or citizens of another. He was prepared to hold that an act of the Oireachtas which conferred on the courts of Saorstát Éireann jurisdiction over foreigners would be valid provided it was essential for the peace, order and good government of Saorstát Éireann.

The actual question of extra-territorial jurisdiction came up for decision in *Article 26 and the Criminal Law (Jurisdiction) Bill 1975* (Case 5) which provided for the trial in this State of certain offences committed elsewhere. The Supreme Court upheld the constitutionality of the Bill on two grounds. First, it held that Article 3 of the Constitution did not prohibit the Oireachtas legislating with extra-territorial effect provided the parliament of Saorstát Éireann had had the same power which the court ruled it had. Secondly, the court held that there was ample authority in international law for the proposition that every sovereign state has power to legislate with extra-territorial effect.

An Independent State

The word 'independent' as used in Article 5 of the Constitution may be a synonym with sovereign or it may imply something different. 'Sovereign' means free from external authority. 'Independent' could mean not affiliated or not reliant on other states. This interpretation would mean that this State must not take a partisan attitude to world affairs. Possibly the word indepen-dent implies neutrality.

A Democratic State

Democracy can be defined as government by the People or their elected repre-sentatives. The common people are the political force within such a state. Democracy must be more than the citizens having a periodic say in the election of their leaders: it must mean the correlative right to offer oneself for election. It must mean that the affairs of state be conducted fairly. There must be equity in the taxation system: one section of the community must not be overburdened with taxes; nor must another section reap all the benefits without contributing. Public funds must be evenly distributed. In a democratic state public service posts must be open to all in fair competition: the foster-ing of an elite must not occur.

Different regimes lay claim to the description of being democratic. Most countries in the western world claim to be democratic. In these pluralist regimes the most notable feature is peaceful political struggle which takes place openly and freely under the glare of publicity. There are several political parties: the struggle for power is open to public attention. Liberal concepts of freedom are accepted: there are freedoms to express opinions, to establish and join political organisations and to hold meetings and disseminate political beliefs and opinions.

It is a meaning the courts would probably adopt if called on to interpret the word 'democratic' in Article 5 of the Constitution. Such a definition prevents the establishment of a one-party state. Support for this proposition is not found among the political rights enumerated in the Constitution but rather in the personal rights. It seems that once there is a plurality of can-didates allowed in the election, the citizen's political rights are vindicated. The prevention of a one-party state is found in Article 40 which guarantees freedom of expression and association. The most fundamental method of exer-cising these rights is by the citizen running for elected offices established under the Constitution.

The spirit of the Constitution demands positive incentive towards political activity. While no constitutional or legal restriction exists on the establishment of a political party, the state through its existing political establishment may create a hegemony of its own: while not forbidding new activity it may create a climate in favour of existing order, thus preventing the dissemination of new ideologies and ideas. There is some evidence which suggests that such is the position in this State. A registered political party may place its name on the ballot papers of its candidates. To be registered a party must fulfil requirements set down by those already elected. The state-owned radio and television stations, while not bound by law to cover political activities, do so by giving the largest party represented in Dáil Éireann the greatest amount of coverage, while others are covered according to size in descending order of representation. A new party gets little or nothing. For Dáil Éireann elections a deposit is payable: this discriminates in favour of those in power who have the means by drawing earnings from the State, and against those seeking it. Existing political parties represented in Dáil Éireann are favoured by the payment to their leaders of sums of money from public finances. Elected representatives are favoured by the provision of travelling subsidies and free postage as against those seeking office. Do these restrictions prevent the State from being a true democracy, and what approach would the courts take should any of these restrictions be challenged?

A Republican State

The one political concept noticeably absent from Article 5 is the declaration that the State is a republic. A republic can be defined as a form of government in which the head of state is elected by the People, or by some body itself directly elected by the People. This republican form of government is evidenced by the presidential system, the most impressive examples being the American and French models. In the United States the People directly elect their head of state whereas in India it is the Congress, itself an elected body, which performs this function. Under our Constitution the head of state, the President of Ireland, is elected by the People (see page 63). Surprisingly, until 1948, the executive function in relation to external relations was performed by the British Crown on the advice of the government. This power was repatriated with the passing of the *Republic of Ireland Act 1948* which declares that the description of the State shall be the Republic of Ireland, whereas Article 4 of the Constitution declares the name of the State to be *Éire*, or in the English language 'Ireland' (see earlier this chapter at page 14).

In keeping with this concept of a republican state, Article 40.2 of the Constitution declares that titles of nobility must not be conferred by the State, nor may a title of nobility or of honour be accepted by any citizen except with the prior approval of the Government. The Constitution and the law are silent as to the consequences which follow from a citizen's failure to obtain such prior approval.

A Unitary State

Article 5 establishes Ireland as a unitary State. In such a state the legislature of the entire country is the supreme law-making body. It may permit other legislatures to function, but it retains the power in law to overrule them: they are subordinate to it. On the other hand, in a federal constitution the powers of government are divided between a government for the entire country and governments for parts of the country in such a way that each government is legally independent within its own sphere. The government of the entire country has its own areas of powers and it exercises these without any control from the governments of the constituent parts and these latter in turn exercise their powers without being controlled by the central government. Among examples of federal constitutions may be mentioned those of the United States, Switzerland and Australia. In each the constitution sets out the matters on which the legislature of the entire country can make laws and it reserves to the states or cantons a sphere in which their legislatures may operate in legal independence of the central government and of each other. The *Government of Ireland Act 1920* established a federal Ireland with institutions for each part of the island and all-Ireland institutions. One of the possible constitutional solutions to the partition of Ireland may be the establishment of a federal State similar to that provided in that statute.

Ownership of the State

Article 10 of the Constitution declares that all natural resources, including the air and all forms of potential energy, belong to the State, subject to all estates and interests, lawfully vested in any person or body. Does this declaration hold that all the natural resources, particularly land, in the State are held from the State as all the lands in the United Kingdom are said to be held from the crown? If this is the meaning to be accorded to the Article then the State has failed to vest the natural resources in itself as ultimate owner. Large tracts of Irish lands are owned by old feudal landlords who reside abroad and have little interest in the affairs of this State. It is even possible that rents leaving this country find their way from landlord to landlord ultimately to the British Crown. The placing of the State in the position of ultimate owner could probably be done without any interference with the right of private ownership. On the other hand, Article 10 can be construed as placing the State in the category of private owner together with other private individuals. The State cannot abrogate interests which existed in others at the time the Constitution was enacted: these continue to exist and can be alienated without hindrance. On this construction the State owns some of the land and the remainder belongs to others.

The Constitution of Saorstát Éireann prohibited the permanent alienation of state property and this limitation was not continued. The temporary or permanent alienation of State property is permitted: this power adds weight to the construction that the State should be classified as a private owner of property.

A Citizen of the State

Nationality is important in two respects. It is significant in international law in matters such as diplomatic protection abroad, immigration, deportation and the negotiation of treaties. Citizenship is the legal concept which binds the individual to a state. In constitutional law the distinction between citizen and non-citizen is relevant because the former is possessed of rights and the latter is subject to disabilities. Nationality and citizenship are founded on the doctrine of allegiance which is considered to bind the citizen to the state. The Constitution demands fidelity to the nation and loyalty to the State as political duties of the citizen, and in return the State protects and vindicates the citizen.

Article 9 of the Constitution confers citizenship on any person who was a citizen of Saorstát Éireann immediately before the coming into effect of the Constitution.[9] The further acquisition and loss of citizenship is to be determined by law, currently the *Irish Nationality and Citizenship Act 1956*, as amended, which provides for the acquisition of citizenship in a number of ways.

A person born in Ireland is a citizen from birth. A person is a citizen if his or her father or mother is a citizen at the time of his or her birth: the birth can take place anywhere and it is immaterial whether the child's parents are married. The child of a foreign diplomat accredited to Ireland is not a citizen. The High Court held in *Gomaa v Minister for Foreign Affairs* (1992) that a child born in Ireland of Egyptian parents was not an Irish citizen. His father had recently been employed as a chef at the Egyptian Embassy, and therefore entitled to enjoy certain diplomatic immunities, though the child was born after his parents had left for Egypt but returned to Dublin from London because of the illness of his pregnant mother. Because these immunities continued to apply for a reasonable period after the person who enjoyed the immunities had to leave the State the father had continued to retain his diplomatic status when the child was born.

Pending the reintegration of the national territory, a person born in Northern Ireland on or after 6 December 1922 is not a citizen unless that person makes a declaration as to citizenship. Where that person is not of full age his or her parent or guardian may make such declaration. In either case that person takes citizenship from birth. A person born of parents who themselves were born outside Ireland is not a citizen unless the birth is registered in a diplomatic or consular office or in the Department of Foreign Affairs.

Under the 1956 Act a woman, not a citizen at the date of her marriage to a citizen, did not become a citizen merely on marriage. She had to lodge a declaration either before or at any time after her marriage accepting citizenship as her post-nuptial citizenship. If the declaration was lodged before marriage citizenship dated from the marriage: in other cases it dated from the lodgment. There was no similar provision applying to non-citizen males who marry citizens, though they may apply for citizenship by naturalisation. This inequality was challenged in *Somjee v Minister for Justice* (1981) (Case 176) where the High Court in upholding the statute held that it was not the act of marrying which conferred citizenship but the law. The different methods of acquiring citizenship did not create an invidious discrimination but were merely a diversity of arrangement. The court ruled that even if the statute was unconstitutional it availed the non-citizen nothing because the court could not instruct the Oireachtas to legislate in a manner which would confer on the non-citizen the benefit sought.

The *Irish Nationality and Citizenship Act 1986* repealed the 1956 Act in this regard and now provides a uniform method of acquiring citizenship after marriage. Marriage does not of itself confer citizenship. The non-citizen may lodge, not earlier than three years from the date of the marriage, a declaration accepting Irish citizenship as post-nuptial citizenship. But the marriage must be subsisting at the date of the lodgment of the declaration, the couple must be living together as husband and wife and the spouse who is a citizen must submit an affidavit to that effect when the declaration is being lodged. A non-citizen who lodges a declaration becomes a citizen from the date of lodgment.

A child born posthumously whose father at the date of his or her death was a citizen acquires citizenship in the same manner as if his or her father was alive at the date of the birth. Every deserted infant first found in the State is, unless the contrary is proven, a citizen. On the making of an adoption order under the *Adoption Act 1952* the adopted child, if not already a citizen, becomes one if the adopter, or where the adopters are a married couple either spouse, is a citizen.

The President may grant citizenship as a token of honour to a person, or to that person's child or grandchild, when in the opinion of the Government that person has done signal honour or rendered distinguished service to the nation.[10]

Citizenship may be conferred on a non-citizen by means of a certificate of naturalisation granted by the Minister for Justice in his absolute discretion. Certain formalities must be complied with, and before it is granted the person must in open court before a District Judge, or in such manner as the Minister for special reasons allows, make a declaration of fidelity to the nation and loyalty to the State. A citizen by naturalisation has all the political and personal rights of a citizen by birth or descent except that his or her citizenship may be revoked.

A person not a citizen is an alien, and the *Aliens Act 1935* gives wide power of control over non-citizens. Whether or not a non-citizen can avail of the personal rights acknowledged in the Constitution is considered in Chapter 10 on page 158. One undoubted right not possessed by non-citizens is the right of entry to the State.[11] The non-citizen can be deported.[12] Some cases on this topic are considered in Chapter 16 on page 254 in the discussion of Family Rights though some of the non-citizens involved in those cases would now, under the 1986 Act, be able to acquire citizenship in the manner already noted.

On the other hand it seems that a citizen, unlike a non-citizen, cannot be deported from the State. In *The State (K. M.) v Minister for Foreign Affairs* (1979) (Case 190) the High Court in declaring for the citizen a constitutional right to leave the State must, by implication, have acknowledged the corresponding right of entry to the State by the citizen. If the citizen has a right to leave the citizen must have the right to return, which may be curtailed when the common good requires, though not in any arbitrary or unjustifiable manner.

Domicile

Domicile is the place in which a person has a fixed and permanent home, and to which, when absent, he or she has the intention of returning. The concept of domicile is used to determine questions of personal status. Domicile and citizenship are distinct legal concepts. A person may have Irish citizenship and, for example, a French domicile and vice versa. Domicile has three forms.

The first form of domicile is that of origin which is imposed by operation of law on a person at birth. It is conferred generally on the basis of parentage. The domicile of origin of a legitimate child, born during its father's lifetime, is the same as its father's domicile at the time of the child's birth. A legitimate child, born after the death of its father, takes the domicile of its mother at the date of its birth, as does an illegitimate child. This domicile of origin continues to operate until its owner either acquires a different domicile of dependence or acquires a domicile of choice. It is the accepted law that the burden of proving a change of domicile from a domicile of origin to a domicile of choice rests with the party claiming such change, and per Black J in *In re Joyce, Corbet v Fagan* (1946):

the domicile of origin persists until it is proved to have been intentionally and voluntarily abandoned and supplanted by another.

A domicile of choice, the second form of domicile, can only be acquired by a person of full age and capacity. No formal steps are necessary for the acquisition of a domicile of choice. The only requirements are (a) residence in the country of choice, and (b) an intention at the commencement or during the time of such residence to remain permanently in that country. The Supreme Court, in *T. v T.* (1982), held that a married man, with an English domicile of origin, who came to live in Ireland with his family and obtained permanent employment here, and who within two years had filed for divorce in England, had not acquired a domicile of choice in this country. The High Court held in *Rowan v Rowan* (1988) that an Irishman who had lived in France for most of his working life, married there, had a home there, and where his four children were born, had acquired a French domicile of choice despite having made a will on a visit to this country in which he described himself as having been domiciled in Ireland.

The third form of domicile is that of dependence, being the domicile conferred by operation of law on persons legally dependent. It applies particularly in the case of married women and minors. Until the end of 1986 the domicile of a married woman was treated as a form of domicile of dependence. Until that year a woman took the domicile of her husband once she married, and her domicile remained the same as his as long as the marriage lasted. Any domicile of choice she may have had at marriage was lost, and her domicile of origin ceased to operate. From 3 October 1986 married women have the full capacity to acquire a domicile of choice. The *Domicile and Recognition of Foreign Divorces Act 1986* abolished the wife's dependent domicile. It provides that in determining the domicile of a married woman the same factors are to be used as in the case of any other person capable of having an independent domicile. In many instances the domicile of a married woman will be the same as that of her husband but if that is so the domicile acquired, other than a domicile of origin, is acquired by choice and not by dependence. See page 249 and *W. v W.* (1992) (Case 209).

As a minor's domicile of origin acquired at the moment of birth depends on that of the parent on whom he or she is dependent, so his or her domicile will change during the period of dependence to correspond with any changes taking place in the parent's domicile. At birth a legitimate child takes the domicile of its father, and an illegitimate child that of its mother. A domicile of dependence thus imposed on a child will continue and change with that of its parent until it reaches the age of capacity for domicile when the child is able to acquire an independent domicile of choice on the basis of the factors of intention and residence.

The *Domicile and Recognition of Foreign Divorces Act 1986* makes provision for the instances where the child's parents are separated. Where the child lives with the father, his or her domicile is that of the father. This is the common law rule and is unchanged by the statute. The domicile of the child shall be that of the mother if the child has a home with her and no home with the father, or the child has, at any time, had the domicile of the mother and has not since had a home with the father. The domicile of a child whose mother is dead is that which the mother had before she died provided the child had that domicile and had not since had a home with the father.

THE SEPARATION OF POWERS

The Danger of Unlimited Powers
The ability or the capacity to perform, act or to exercise a choice may be limited or unlimited. In legal affairs the very meaning of the word 'law' denotes limitation. When something is done according to law we mean that only that which is permitted to be done is performed, and nothing more. In constitutional law when speaking of an act or power being *unconstitutional* we mean it was performed without any justification for it in the Constitution. It is clear from our constitutional framework that the State is the creation of the People. It has only limited powers and duties: the State is not all power-ful. In our constitutional law the sole entity possessed of unlimited power is the People. How does the Constitution ensure that limited powers only are conferred on the institutions of government? The answer is that it relies on the doctrine of the *separation of powers*. There is a maxim, the truth of which can be seen throughout history, that all power corrupts and that absolute power corrupts absolutely. The doctrine of the separation of powers accepts that maxim unquestioningly and attempts to frustrate its effect. Tyranny is inevitable if too much power is placed in too few hands. According to Montesquieu:

> personal liberty is to be found only where there is no abuse of power. But constant experience shows us that every man invested with power is liable to abuse it, and to carry his authority as far as it will go . . . To prevent this abuse, it is necessary from the nature of things that one power should be a check on another . . . There would be an end of everything if the same person or body, whether of the nobles or the People, were to exercise all . . . powers.[13]

Tripartite Division of Powers of Government
Montesquieu[14] divided the powers of government into three, and this division forms the basis of the present classification for most modern states. The legislative function is the making of new laws and the alteration or repeal of existing ones: in this country the legislative organ of the State is the Oireachtas. The executive function is the general administration of the State, including the framing of policy: this function is performed by the Government. The judicial function consists of the interpretation of laws and their application

to the facts of particular cases: this function within the State is exercised by independent courts. Of course a complete separation of powers in the sense of a distribution of the three differing functions among three independent organs of government with no co-operation would bring government to a halt. There must be some interaction if good and fair government is to flourish. The doctrine does not forbid co-operation provided that each organ operates as a check on the powers of the other institutions of government.

The Separation of Powers in Other Constitutions
The United States Constitution adopts this doctrine in a fundamental way. The executive power is vested in the President, elected directly by the People for a fixed term; the federal legislative power is vested in the Congress and the federal judicial power is vested in the Supreme Court. The President and his advisers cannot be members of Congress, nor are they responsible to Congress, nor can they initiate legislation though they can recommend it in a message to Congress. In Britain the separation of powers is not so clear. Parliament legislates and operates a check on the executive who are all members of parliament. The judges are independent though some judges are members of the House of Lords, one of the Houses of Parliament. The Lord Chancellor is a member of parliament, the cabinet and the judiciary.

These examples of how the doctrine operates in two very different constitutions both prove and disprove the doctrine. They contradict it in the sense that there is some contact between the organs of government, and they support the doctrine in that in both systems there are checks and balances which operate to prevent the concentration of all power in the hands of one organ of government.

The Separation of Powers in the Irish Constitution
Article 6 of the Constitution declares that all powers of government, legislative, executive and judicial, derive, under God, from the People. This is an emphatic direction that the powers of government be divided threefold and that limitations be placed on the institutions of government which exercise these powers. A study of the Constitution reinforces this directive which has been supported many times in judicial comment.

The Oireachtas can control the Government by refusing to enact its policies into law and Dáil Éireann can, by withdrawing its support, force the Government's resignation. The Oireachtas checks the courts by deciding the content of the law, legal procedures, the structure of the court system and by being empowered to remove judges from office. The Government balances the power of the Oireachtas by having the exclusive right to recommend the appropriation of public monies. The courts check the government by demanding that it acts *intra vires** the Constitution and checks the Oireachtas by denying it the ability to enact unconstitutional legislation. Apart from these general checks by one organ of government on the other two, there exists internal checks and balances within each organ of government which are considered in the appropriate places later.

Each organ of government must respect the sphere of influence of the other two so that the essential symmetry of the separation of powers which is inherent in Article 6 of the Constitution is preserved.

While a rigid separation of powers is not demanded by the Constitution, the courts have not hesitated to condemn actions or strike down measures on the ground that one organ of government has trespassed on the domain of another. There are three possible clashes. The first can be between the legislature and the executive, the second between the legislature and the judiciary, and the third between the executive and the judiciary.

Encroachment by the Legislature on the Executive Domain

In our constitutional framework there is no provision for the Oireachtas to exercise any of the functions of the executive. It is not constitutionally permissible for the Oireachtas to direct the government as to the manner in which it conducts its business. The government is collectively responsible to Dáil Éireann for all the decisions it takes or fails to take, but it is not responsible to Dáil Éireann as to the manner by which such decisions were arrived at. The Supreme Court, in *Attorney General v Tribunal of Inquiry into the Beef Industry* (1993) (Case 14), upholding the doctrine of the separation of powers, refused to permit a Tribunal of Inquiry established by the Houses of the Oireachtas, to inquire into discussions at government meetings on the ground that confidentiality was a necessary consequence of collective responsibility (see page 101).

The executive must not encroach in the legislative domain. The former Supreme Court ruled, in *Article 26 and the School Attendance Bill 1942* (Case 11), that it was for the legislature, and not the executive, to define the expression 'a certain minimum standard of education' contained in Article 42.3.2 of the Constitution. In the *East Donegal Co-operative Livestock Mart Ltd v Attorney General* (1970) (Case 61) the Supreme Court held that the Oireachtas could not confer on the executive a power to exempt a party from the provisions of a law. The Supreme Court decided in *Meagher v Minister for Agriculture* (1994) (Case 115) that a power granted by statute to the executive to make regulations which could amend or repeal statute law was not an invasion of the legislative domain.

Encroachment by Legislature in the Judicial Domain

There are a number of cases where it was alleged that the Oireachtas had trespassed into the judicial domain of government. In the first of these, *Buckley v*

Attorney General (1950) (Case 27), the Oireachtas passed a statute which covered matters which were then being litigated on in the courts. The High Court refused to stay the proceedings, in accordance with the provisions of the statute, because to do so would be to abdicate its proper jurisdiction to administer justice in a cause whereof it was duly seized. The former Supreme Court upheld that decision on appeal. O'Byrne J declared:

> in bringing these proceedings the plaintiffs were exercising a constitutional right and they were, and are, entitled to have the matter in dispute determined by the judicial organ of the State. The substantial effect of the [statute] is that the dispute is determined by the Oireachtas.

The Supreme Court, in *In re Haughey* (1971) (Case 77), when rejecting the claim that a committee of Dáil Éireann had tried and convicted a witness before it, warned, per Ó Dálaigh CJ:

> the trial of a criminal offence is an exercise of judicial power and is a function of the courts, not a committee of the legislature . . . The Committee of Public Accounts is not a court and its members are not judges . . . Trial, conviction and sentence are indivisible parts of the exercise of this power.

The Supreme Court accepted in *Desmond v Glackin* (1992) (Case 52) that the certification to the High Court of a refusal to answer a question put by an inspector investigating the affairs of a company under statutory powers was not an invasion of the judicial domain by the legislature.

The Supreme Court, in *Maher v Attorney General* (1973) (Case 112), struck down a statutory provision which gave a badge of conclusiveness to a certificate in a criminal trial. FitzGerald CJ said:

> the administration of justice, which in criminal matters is confined exclusively by the Constitution to the courts and judges set up under the Constitution, necessarily reserves to those courts and judges the determination of all the essential ingredients of any offence charged against an accused person.[15]

The prevention by statute of a person remanded in custody from being returned to the court on the remand day was, in *The State (C.) v Minister for Justice* (1967) (Case 184), found to be an unwarrantable interference with the administration of justice by the legislature. Ó Dálaigh CJ explained:

> in the year 1875 it was for an omnipotent parliament to determine what should be done . . . no question could arise as to whether the provision made by parliament was or was not an intrusion into the judicial domain. It is otherwise now because the Constitution effects a separation of legislative, executive and judicial powers . . . the provisions of the Act of 1875

... [are] about as large an intrusion upon a court's proceedings as one could imagine.

A challenge was made, in *The State (O'Rourke) v Kelly* (1983) (Case 197), to a statute which imposed a mandatory obligation on a court to issue a warrant once satisfied that certain facts had been proved. It was argued that by depriving the court of discretion there was an infringement of the judicial domain. The Supreme Court upheld the statute on the ground that the warrant could only be issued after the establishment of specified facts to the satisfaction of the court. Where these facts were not proved the court could not issue the warrant. The Supreme Court struck down portion of a statute in *The State (McEldowney) v Kelleher* (1983) (Case 192), which provided that judicial proceedings in a court were to be dismissed if a garda officer in the course of those proceedings gave sworn evidence that he had reasonable grounds for believing that a particular fact was true. It was held that the statute constituted an impermissible invasion of the judicial domain by requiring that justiciable* proceedings, within the competence of the courts established under the Constitution, were being determined by the legislature. The High Court ruled, in *Cashman v Attorney General* (1990) (Case 32), that a statute which limited the persons who might be heard or who might adduce evidence before a court amounted to an infringement of the judicial power by the legislature.

What the courts have objected to in these cases is the direct interference with actual litigation rather than the proper ordering of the judicial system. The Oireachtas can and does interfere, with due constitutional propriety, with the administration of justice without complaint from the courts. For example, statutes have declared and limited the civil jurisdictions of the courts;[16] created new procedures;[17] criminal offences[18] and torts;[19] granted new remedies;[20] abolished civil wrongs;[21] and created courts[22] and rule-making committees.[23] All these matters are vitally necessary if the legal system is to cater for the constantly changing needs of a modern society.

Encroachment by the Executive on the Judicial Domain

There have been instances when it was alleged that the executive power invaded the judicial domain. In the first of these the High Court considered the nature of the power given to a member of the executive to order the internment without trial of a person, in *The State (Burke) v Lennon* (1940) (Case 181). In striking down the function, Gavan Duffy J remarked:

the authority conferred . . . is an authority, not merely to act judicially, but to administer justice and condemn an alleged offender without charge or hearing and without the aid of a jury.[24]

The Oireachtas retaliated by changing the offending word in the impugned section from 'satisfied' to 'opinion' and re-enacting the section in an amending statute. The President referred the Bill to the former Supreme Court: *Article 26 and the Offences Against the State (Amendment) Bill 1940* (Case 10) which rejected the argument, and by implication the decision in *Burke*'s case, that the executive when making an internment order was hearing a criminal charge and imposing punishment.

Of the two judgments the High Court decision is to be preferred but the judiciary, particularly the Supreme Court, must have been aware when giving their decision that the Constitution could be amended by ordinary legislation and they may have feared some major curtailment of judicial functions if they appeared to challenge and frustrate the legislature and executive. The Oireachtas did in fact move to trim the judicial review sail. In the *Second Amendment of the Constitution Act 1941* the Oireachtas attempted to prevent a repetition of what happened in *Burke*'s case by providing an addition to Article 40.4.3° of the Constitution, under which the proceedings had been taken. Henceforth when the High Court considered that the statute, under which a person is detained is unconstitutional, it cannot adjudicate on the matter but must refer the question to the Supreme Court. This restriction has proved of little consequence (see page 219) though it is an indication as to how the legislature and executive felt at the behaviour of the High Court in *Burke*'s case.

The Supreme Court, in *Deaton v Attorney General* (1963) (Case 48), struck down legislation which permitted the executive to choose which of two penalties a court could impose. Ó Dálaigh CJ stated:

the selection of punishment is an integral part of the administration of justice and, as such, cannot be committed to the hands of the executive.

It must be noted that in *Conroy v Attorney General* (1965) (Case 38) the Supreme Court held that the mandatory disqualification from driving was not a punishment but the withdrawal of a privilege.[25] Can the Oireachtas constitutionally lay down in statute mandatory and minimum sentences? It might appear from the dictum of Ó Dálaigh CJ in *Deaton*'s case that it cannot. The issue in that case was the executive, as distinct from the legislature, choosing the form of punishment. There are instances of mandatory sentences to be found in our laws. For example, the *Criminal Justice Act 1964* provides penal servitude for life for murder and the *Criminal Justice Act 1990* provides a forty-year imprisonment term for treason and capital murder. Neither of these provisions has been challenged as to its constitutionality.

The courts were called on to decide in *Murphy v Dublin Corporation* (1972) (Case 124) whether the executive could claim privilege over documents which were considered essential in pending litigation. The Supreme Court was not enamoured with the common law* rule that once the claim of executive privilege* (see page 107) was made, the courts were bound to accept it. According to Walsh J:

> the division of powers does not give paramountcy in all circumstances to any one of the organs exercising the powers of government over the other ... it is, however, impossible for the judicial power in the proper exercise of its functions to permit any other body or power to decide for it whether or not a document will be disclosed or produced. In the last resort the decision lies with the courts so long as they have seisin* of the case.

The court acknowledged that different rules might apply where the vital interests of the State were involved.[26] The Supreme Court, in *Ambiorix Ltd v Minister for the Environment* (1992) (see page 108), refused to depart from the principles of law established in *Murphy*'s case.

The issue arose in *The State (Craven) v Frawley* (1980) (Case 186) whether a statute which permitted a member of the executive to commute, in certain circumstances, the unexpired residue of a term of detention, imposed by a court on a youthful offender, to a term of imprisonment, was an administration of justice. The High Court held that, since there was no essential difference between a term of imprisonment and a term of detention, there was no constitutional impediment to permitting the executive, under legislative authority, to alter the place of detention of a convicted person without the intervention of a court.

The courts will not permit the legislature to enact legislation and, when it is challenged as to its constitutionality, permit the executive to suspend its operation. This was decided in *Condon v Minister for Labour* (1981) (Case 37) where O'Higgins CJ explained:

> serious consequences could ensue if this court pronounced that temporary legislation ... should be immune from judicial review merely because it had expired before the question of its validity could be examined. All legislation passed by the Oireachtas is presumed to be valid. If the Oireachtas were free to enact temporary legislation ... and if that legislation, on its expiry, escaped examination in the courts, a form of legislative intimidation could be exercised.

It was argued, in *The State (Boyle) v Governor of Military Detention Barracks* (1980) (Case 178), that a statute which permitted a member of the executive to transfer a convicted prisoner from a civil prison to a military prison was an administration of justice in that the executive was authorised to select the form of punishment which was different to that imposed by the court. The Supreme Court ruled that the power was administrative, rather than judicial, in nature. In *Costello v DPP* (1984) (Case 40) the issue arose whether the power given to the Director of Public Prosecutions to return a person for trial, where a court has refused to do so, was an invasion of the judicial domain.[27] The Supreme Court held that the power under the statute was an interference by the executive in the judicial domain. But, on the other hand, the Supreme Court ruled in *O'Shea v DPP* (1989) (Case 149) that the statutory power which permitted the inclusion of counts in an indictment either in substitution for or in addition to counts for which an accused person had been sent forward for trial did not constitute an invasion by the Director of Public Prosecutions of the judicial domain. To do so was an administrative or executive function.[28] The case was made, in *Shannon v Attorney General* (1984) (Case 174), that a statute which empowered the endorsement and execution by the Gardaí of extradition warrants without the intervention of the courts constituted an administration of justice. The Supreme Court, in dismissing the claim, held that the mere execution of the warrant could not lead to extradition. Extradition could only occur as a consequence of the making of a court order.

The Supreme Court ruled, in *The People (DPP) v Gallagher* (1991) (Case 155), that a statute which confined to the executive the decision as to when to release a person who had been found guilty of murder but insane was not in breach of the separation of powers. It had been argued that this power was judicial. The High Court decided, in *Murphy v Wallace* (1990) (Case 126), that a statute which permitted the executive to determine the length of time a debtor should be detained in prison breached the separation of powers.

Courts Refuse to Trespass into Legislative and Executive Domains
The doctrine of the separation of powers demands that each organ of government stays within its own constitutional boundaries. Should one institution of government purport to exercise a power reserved to another organ of government the transgression must be checked. Equally the doctrine of the separation of powers demands that each organ of government should voluntarily refrain from straying into the domain of the other organs of government.

Bearing this principle in mind the courts have decided that they cannot interfere with the mere policy of the executive. The challenge to be entertained by the courts must be to some action which purports to transgress into the legislative or judicial domains. The making of executive policy is strictly for the Government and cannot be reviewed by the courts. This principle was clearly stated by the Supreme Court in *Boland v An Taoiseach* (1974) (Case 23). The courts refused to intervene on the ground that it was inappropriate for the judicial organ of government to transgress upon the policy decisions of the executive arm of government though a warning was given that actions *ultra vires** the Constitution by the executive may be halted. Griffin J warned:

> in the event of the Government acting in a manner which is in contravention of some provisions of the Constitution . . . it would be the duty and the right of the courts, as guardian of the Constitution, to intervene when called upon to do so if a complaint of a breach of any of the provisions of the Constitution is substantiated in proceedings brought before the courts.

The case of *Crotty v An Taoiseach* (1987) (Case 43) saw just such a judicial intervention when the courts injuncted the executive from ratifying a Treaty which materially restricted our sovereignty in foreign affairs on the ground that the Government was acting *ultra vires* the Constitution. While the People in a referendum permitted the State to ratify the Treaty, the principle is clearly established that the courts will restrain the executive from acting unconstitutionally.

The Supreme Court, in *McGrath v McDermott* (1988), held that the courts could not invade the legislative domain. Finlay CJ said:

> for this court to avoid the application of [the law] to these [tax avoidance schemes] could only constitute the invasion by the judiciary of the powers and functions of the legislature, in plain breach of the constitutional separation of powers.

The High Court in *D. v Ireland* (1992) (Case 47) ruled that the provision of a scheme of compensation for the victims of crime was a matter for the legislature or executive and was not a matter for the courts.

Chapter 4
THE OIREACHTAS

Nature of the Oireachtas

One of the three arms of government is the Oireachtas, created by Article 15.1 of the Constitution, and consists of a President and two Houses, a House of Representatives, called Dáil Éireann, and a Senate, called Seanad Éireann. The Oireachtas is the legislative institution of government. A feature of such institutions in many constitutions is that the legislative organ of government is generally popularly elected. While the making of laws is the central function of the Oireachtas the powers of this legislative body extend to exercising control over financial and international affairs.

Oireachtas within Constitutional Framework

The expression 'parliamentary government' means government by an executive in and through and under the control of the legislative organ of government. The doctrine of the separation of powers (see page 28) demands that there be some separation between the Oireachtas and Government and that there is an effective system of controls. Under the Constitution the Oireachtas supervises the Government's conduct by granting or withholding its approval and being responsible for the Government's continuation in office. The Oireachtas controls the judicial arm of government by possessing the power to make the laws, by limiting, subject to the provisions of the Constitution, the scope of the courts, by organising the system of courts and by having the power to remove judges from office. The Oireachtas in turn is controlled by the courts in that the judicial arm of government will not permit the Oireachtas in its laws to trespass into the other domains of government and can declare Acts of the Oireachtas unconstitutional which it has done on numerous occasions.

While exercising checks on the other branches of government the Oireachtas operates an internal system of balances on its component parts. Thus the President can request the Supreme Court's advice on the constitutionality of legislation passed by the Houses of the Oireachtas; and Dáil Éireann, with its greater powers, can check, and be checked, by the Seanad.

A study of the Oireachtas encompasses both these aspects: its role as one of the three organs of government, and the particular roles of its components. This chapter deals with the Oireachtas itself while the component parts, namely the President, Dáil Éireann and Seanad Éireann are given separate chapters.

Supremacy of the Oireachtas?

The legislative supremacy of a parliament means, in its positive sense, that the legislative arm of government could pass *any* law it desires and, negatively, that no legislative power of any person or body could override it. How far does the Constitution accept this principle of parliamentary supremacy? The constitutional framework does not acknowledge such a concept because to do so would result in the acceptance of the notion that unlimited power may reside in any one organ of government. One of the major functions of a constitution is to divide, and thus limit, the general power of government among different bodies or organs. It must follow that the Oireachtas, like the other organs of government, is confined to the functions assigned to it in the Constitution, and that the exercise of these functions must be limited or curtailed. In this chapter we examine the areas of government which the Constitution has assigned to the Oireachtas, and the limitations imposed on their exercise.

The Oireachtas must not enact any law which is repugnant to the Constitution (Article 15.4.1°). Unfortunately a declaration of constitutional invalidity generally comes after the law has been enacted and has been in operation for some time. Apart from the limited scope of Article 26 of the Constitution (see page 49) there is no constitutional machinery for ascertaining whether proposed legislation is constitutional or not before its enactment. In France legislation considered unconstitutional is referred before its enactment into law to a constitutional court. Should that court declare the proposal to be constitutional it may be enacted into law; if unconstitutional it cannot be enacted. Once laws are passed in France they cannot be challenged subsequently. In this country there are two ways of testing the constitutionality of legislation. After certain Bills have been passed by the Houses of the Oireachtas, the President may seek the advice of the Supreme Court before signing and promulgating the Bills as a law (see page 49). The second method is by an individual affected by the enacted legislation taking an action in the courts to have its provisions declared constitutionally invalid (see page 129).

Apart from this general direction the Constitution prohibits the Oireachtas from legislating on certain matters. The Oireachtas must not declare acts to be an infringement of the law which were not so at the date of their commission (Article 15.5). The Supreme Court, in *Magee v Culligan* (1992) (Case 111), per Finlay CJ, explained:

> the court is satisfied that the provisions of Article 15.5 of the Constitution are an expressed and unambiguous prohibition against the enactment of

retrospective laws declaring acts to be an infringement of the law, whether of the civil or the criminal law. It does not contain any general prohibition on retrospection of legislation, nor can it be by any means interpreted as a general prohibition of that description.

Thus the liability imposed by newly created criminal offences and civil wrongs cannot act retrospectively: such offences and torts can only apply prospectively on the ground that an individual should know at the time of performing an action whether it is lawful or unlawful. This constitutional provision does not mean that no law can act retrospectively. For example, the *Marriage Act 1972* regularised certain marriages celebrated abroad. Retrospective legislation, since it necessarily affects vested rights, has always been regarded as being prima facie unjust. For a statute to have retrospective effects its provisions, according to the Supreme Court in *Hamilton v Hamilton* (1982), must clearly displace the presumption of prospectivity. In that case the *Family Home Protection Act 1976*, which renders void a conveyance of the family home by one spouse without the consent in writing of the other spouse, was held not to apply retrospectively to a transaction begun before its enactment and not completed until after it became law, because to do so would frustrate contractual rights and thus constitute an unjust attack on the property rights of the purchaser contrary to Article 40.3.2° of the Constitution. Henchy J explained:

> the judicial authorities . . . make clear that, because there is a presumption that a statute does not intend to operate unfairly, unjustly or oppressively by trenching on rights or obligations lawfully acquired or created before the statute came into force, it should be construed as prospective in its application and not retrospective, unless there is a clear and unambiguous intention to the contrary expressed, or necessarily implied, in the statute . . .

A law cannot disqualify on the ground of sex any citizen from either membership of Dáil Éireann, or voting in Dáil Éireann elections (Article 16.1). A law cannot be enacted which provides that the number of members to be returned for a Dáil Éireann constituency can be less than three (Article 16.2.6°).

No law can be enacted which removes the appellate jurisdiction of the Supreme Court in cases which involve the question as to whether a law is invalid having regard to the provisions of the Constitution (Article 34.4.4°). No law can be enacted which permits divorce (Article 41.3.2°). The State guarantees to pass no law attempting to abolish the right of private ownership (Article 43.1.2°), and legislation providing state aid for schools must not discriminate between different religious denominations (Article 44.2.4°).

Apart from these expressed prohibitions on the enactment of legislation there are clearly numerous portions of the Constitution which could not be altered by statute. For example, Article 34.3.2° provides that the jurisdiction of the High Court shall extend to the question of the validity of any law having regard to the provisions of the Constitution. It is not possible to curtail this jurisdiction by statute. In reality, apart from the few expressed instances where no laws can be enacted, there are many more instances where laws could neither amend nor curtail the provisions of the Constitution.

Leaving these constitutional limitations aside, the Oireachtas is free to legislate as it pleases. It can pass unreasonable laws and could refuse to pass just laws. But an Oireachtas cannot fetter the freedom of its successors by enacting laws which claim to be unamendable or unrepealable.

Presumption of Constitutional Propriety

As with all institutions of government there is an onus on the Oireachtas to act within the ambit of the Constitution. Bearing this in mind the courts have ruled on occasion that there is a rebuttable presumption that the actions of the Oireachtas are constitutional: it would be absurd to presume the contrary. It has long been the rule that where the courts consider the constitutionality of a statute it is accepted as an axiom that a law passed by the Oireachtas, the elected representatives of the People, was presumed to be constitutional unless and until the contrary was clearly established (*Pigs Marketing Board v Donnelly (Dublin) Ltd*) (1939) (Case 165, see page 129). The statement of facts contained in the resolutions of the Houses of the Oireachtas which established a state of national emergency were presumed to be correct unless and until it was displaced (*Article 26 and the Emergency Powers Bill 1976*) (Case 8, see page 55). And resolutions of the Houses of the Oireachtas establishing a Tribunal of Inquiry enjoy a similar presumption of constitutionality (*Goodman International v Tribunal of Inquiry into the Beef Processing Industry*) (1992) (Case 73).

Having stated the obvious it must be emphasised that the courts are the institution of government fixed with the task of ensuring compliance with the Constitution. In exercising this function the courts have struck down laws which were enacted in contravention of the Constitution and declared actions of the executive to be invalid.

Duties and Powers of the Oireachtas

A distinction must be drawn between the duties and the powers of the Oireachtas. There are instances when the Oireachtas *must* act: it is placed under a mandatory duty. And there are instances where the Oireachtas *may* act: it is given a discretionary power. The functions of the Oireachtas will be considered under the headings of duties and powers. But it must be noted here that each House of the Oireachtas does not possess concurrent duties and powers. This difference of responsibilities stems from the fundamental fact that Dáil Éireann, directly elected by the People, is possessed of greater powers than Seanad Éireann, which is elected by a rather restricted electorate.

DUTIES OF THE OIREACHTAS

Nomination and Removal of Constitutional Officeholders
Some appointments to constitutional offices are made by one House of the Oireachtas. The Taoiseach is nominated by, and the other Government members are approved by, Dáil Éireann. All are appointed by the President (Article 13.1). The Comptroller and Auditor General is appointed by the President on the nomination of Dáil Éireann (Article 33.2). The Houses of the Oireachtas have the power, and the duty in the appropriate circumstances, to remove the President from office (Article 12.10, see page 67). The Houses of the Oireachtas may pass resolutions calling for the removal of a judge (Article 35.4, see page 116), and the Comptroller and Auditor General (Article 33) from office. In these instances the President formally executes such removals.

Meetings of the Houses of the Oireachtas
The Houses of the Oireachtas must hold at least one session every year though the Constitution does not provide for the length of such sessions (Article 15.7). Sittings are in public, but in special emergencies a private session may be held with the assent of two-thirds of the members present (Article 15.8).

Raising Defence Forces
The right to raise and maintain military forces is vested in the Oireachtas and no other military or armed force may be raised or maintained for any purpose whatever (Article 15.6). The constitutional practice in Britain of authorising the keeping of a permanent army for one year only was a device by parliament to force the crown to hold at least one annual parliamentary session. This practice was continued annually here after 1922 until the *Defence Act 1954* provided for the raising and maintaining of permanent defence forces.

Standing Orders
Each House of the Oireachtas must make its own rules and standing orders with power to attach penalties for their infringement (Article 15.10). The question whether this duty was fulfilled was raised in *In re Haughey* (1971) (Case 77). It was argued that the standing orders in operation were those of the former Dáil Éireann, the chamber of deputies, established under the Constitution of Saorstát Éireann and not those of Dáil Éireann established

under the Constitution of Ireland. There was considerable truth in this contention. Before the coming into force of the Constitution, the Committee of
Procedure and Privileges of the former Dáil Éireann met and recommended
certain amendments which were adopted by the new Dáil Éireann on 12
January 1938. Ó Dálaigh CJ remarked:

> this was a tacit adoption by the new Dáil Éireann of the standing orders of
> the former Houses, as amended, as the standing orders of the new House.

The added comment by the Chief Justice that 'taciturnity is uncharacteristic
of parliaments' remains true because, as yet, Dáil Éireann has not adopted a
new set of standing orders. The power of punishment for breach of standing
orders is considered later.

Chairman of Each House of the Oireachtas

Each House of the Oireachtas must elect from among its members a chairman and a deputy chairman. The Chairman of Dáil Éireann is known as the
Ceann Comhairle and the Deputy as the Leas-Cheann Comhairle. The
Chairman of the Seanad is known as the Cathaoirleach and the Deputy as
the Leas-Chathaoirleach. Apart from taking the chair and ordering the proceedings in each respective House these constitutional officers have other
functions under the Constitution: the chairmen of both Houses are members
of the Presidential Commission (Article 14, see page 74), and of the Council
of State (Article 31, see page 73). The law has conferred extra functions.
For example, both are members of the Appeal Board which hears appeals
arising from the refusal to register a political party (see page 80), and both
are members of the Appeal Board which hears appeals arising from the refusal
to register a body as a Seanad Éireann nominating body (see page 95).

Because the Ceann Comhairle of Dáil Éireann restricts his or her political
activities by not, for example, asking parliamentary questions, or contributing
to debates, or voting on issues, that officeholder is given a unique privilege
under Article 16.6 of the Constitution. This declares that provision may be
made by law to enable the Ceann Comhairle to be deemed, without any actual
election, to be elected a member of Dáil Éireann at the ensuing general
election. The *Electoral Act 1963* provides that the Ceann Comhairle is to be
re-elected for the constituency for which he or she was a member, or if a
revision of the constituencies has taken place the constituency declared to
correspond to that constituency. It can be argued with some force that those
who voted for a member of Dáil Éireann who is subsequently elected Ceann
Comhairle are denied proper representation by that member although in the
multi-seat constituencies this does not amount to complete non-representation.
A case can be made for appointing a Ceann Comhairle from outside the

membership of Dáil Éireann. This privilege of automatic re-election does not extend to the Cathaoirleach of Seanad Éireann.

Decision of Issues
All questions in each House of the Oireachtas, unless otherwise provided by the Constitution, are decided by a majority of the votes of the members present and voting. The Ceann Comhairle, or other presiding member, shall have and exercise a casting vote in the event of an equality of votes (Article 15.11). An example of a weighted majority is to be found in Article 12.10 on the impeachment of the President (see page 67).

Oireachtas and Financial Affairs of the State
The Government must prepare Estimates of the Receipts and Estimates of Expenditure in each financial year (Article 28.4.3°), and these must be presented to and be considered by Dáil Éireann. Presumably this constitutional requirement gives to each member a right to raise questions and debate its contents. Seanad Éireann has no power to consider these estimates. More attention is given to the finances of the State in Chapter 8 on page 101.

Right of Audience
Members of the Government have the right of audience in both Houses of the Oireachtas. Each member of the Government can attend to explain policy and answer questions and reply to debates. This provision (Article 28.8) clarifies the standing of a Government member in relation to the House of which he or she is not a member. In general there is no right of audience given to Oireachtas members to speak in the House of which he or she is not a member; nor is there a constitutional provision for the meeting of both Houses of the Oireachtas, though this does occur on ceremonial occasions with the agreement of both Houses.

Oireachtas and International Agreements
International agreements to which the State becomes a party must be laid before Dáil Éireann (Article 29.5). This rule seems to be for information purposes only because the expression 'laid before' is used. But the State cannot be bound by an international agreement involving a charge on public funds unless its terms have been approved by Dáil Éireann. An instance where the State attempted to implement a Treaty which was a charge on public funds without the prior approval of Dáil Éireann was *The State (Gilliland) v Governor of Mountjoy Prison* (1987) (Case 188). The role of the State in international affairs is fully considered in Chapter 8 on page 103.

POWERS OF THE OIREACHTAS

The Power to Legislate

Legislation is the laying down of legal rules by a competent authority. Generally these rules are purely for the future though occasionally past or present situations are legislated for. Thus some legislation applies retrospectively as well as prospectively. Law-making is the central function of the legislator and includes every expression of the will of the legislature irrespective of its purpose and effect. Legislation may be superior or subordinate. The former proceeds from the superior legislator in the State and is incapable of being repealed, annulled or controlled by another legislative authority. In this country a judicial act may declare legislation unconstitutional and thus devoid of effect. And it is possible that domestic legislation may offend the laws of the EC. On the other hand, subordinate legislation proceeds from an authority other than the superior authority and depends for its continued existence and validity on the superior authority.

Superior Legislation

The Oireachtas is the superior law-making authority: we have already noted that superior must not be confused with supreme. The Oireachtas is the sole and exclusive lawmaker (Article 15.2.1°). The law made by the Oireachtas may create and recognise subordinate legislatures (Article 15.2.2°). When this occurs the superior lawmaker grants to subordinate legislators the power to make rules which have the force of law although control over subordinate legislatures is maintained by the superior legislator. But the Oireachtas must be careful to prevent an unconstitutional delegation of legislative power. This point arose in *Article 26 and the School Attendance Bill (1942)* (Case 11) where the former Supreme Court ruled that it was the function of the legislature, and not the executive, to define the expression 'a certain minimum standard of education' contained in Article 42.3.2° of the Constitution. The Supreme Court, in *East Donegal Co-operative Livestock Mart Ltd v Attorney General* (1970) (Case 61), held that the Oireachtas could not confer on the executive a power to exempt a party from the provisions of the law. Walsh J explained:

> the constitutional right of the Oireachtas in its legislation to take account of difference of social function and difference of capacity, physical and moral, does not extend to delegating that power to members of the executive, to the exclusion of the Oireachtas, in order to decide as between individuals . . . which of them shall be exempted from the applications of [law].

The Supreme Court left open what would be the effect, if any, of the Oireachtas exempting named individuals from the application of the law. In

Cityview Press Ltd v An Chomhairle Oiliúna (1980) (Case 34) it was argued that a statute which permitted a body to impose a levy was an unconstitutional delegation of this power. While rejecting the claim, the Supreme Court, per O'Higgins CJ, gave some guidelines as to what, if any, delegation was permissible:

> the ultimate responsibility rests with the courts to ensure that constitutional safeguards remain, and that the exclusive authority of the National Parliament in the field of law making is not eroded by a delegation of power which is neither contemplated nor permitted by the Constitution. In discharging that responsibility, the courts will have regard to where and by what authority the law in question purports to have been made . . . the test is whether that which is challenged as an unauthorised delegation of parliamentary power is more than a mere giving effect to principles and policies which are contained in the statute itself. If it be, then it is not authorised: for such would constitute a purported exercise of legislative power by an authority which is not permitted to do so under the Constitution. On the other hand, if it be within the permitted limits — if the law is laid down in the statute and details only are to be filled in or completed by the designated Minister or subordinate body — there is no unauthorised delegation of legislative power.

The Supreme Court decided in *Harvey v Minister for Social Welfare* (1990) that a statutory instrument made under a statute was invalid because the Minister, by exercising the power of regulation vested in him by the statute in the manner he did so, negatived the express intention of the Oireachtas as stated in the statute and was an intervention in the legislative function in breach of Article 15.2 of the Constitution. The Supreme Court decided in *Meagher v Minister for Agriculture* (1994) (Case 115) that a power granted by statute to the executive to make regulations which could amend or repeal statute law was necessitated by our membership of the European Community and was beyond constitutional challenge on the ground of being an impermissible delegation of legislative power. An initial impermissible delegation of legislative power may be cured by the enactment of a subsequent law. That was accepted by the Supreme Court in *McDaid v Sheehy* (1991) (Case 99).

Provided the Oireachtas legislates *intra vires* the Constitution, an unqualified discretion rests with it as to the contents of the laws. The courts have no role in directing, or advising, the Oireachtas how to perform its legislative functions. The extent of the courts' jurisdiction was explained in *Somjee v Minister for Justice* (1981) (Case 176) by Keane J:

> the jurisdiction of this court in a case where the validity of an Act of the Oireachtas is questioned because of its alleged invalidity having regard to

the provisions of the Constitution, is limited to declaring the Act in question to be invalid, if that indeed be the case. The court has no jurisdiction to substitute for the impugned enactment a form of enactment which it considers desirable or to indicate to the Oireachtas the appropriate form of enactment which should be substituted for the impugned enactment.

Applying procedural criteria, legislation can be divided into four categories. Ordinary legislation is that which does not fall within the other three categories. Financial legislation is the second, abridged time legislation is the third, and legislation to amend the Constitution is the fourth.

Ordinary Legislation

Ordinary legislation can cover a multitude of subjects: a profession can be regulated,[1] conditions of employment controlled,[2] a new coinage created,[3] succession rights altered,[4] semi-state bodies established,[5] criminal offences created,[6] legal procedures provided,[7] and civil actions abolished.[8]

Every ordinary Bill initiated and passed by Dáil Éireann is sent to Seanad Éireann (Article 20.1). A Bill may lie on the order paper of Dáil Éireann indefinitely, but once passed to Seanad Éireann a time limit applies. Seanad Éireann has a maximum of ninety days, or any longer period agreed to by both Houses of the Oireachtas, to consider an ordinary Bill (Article 23.1.2°). When Seanad Éireann passes the Bill within the time limit allowed it proceeds to the next stage of the legislative process. There are two possible consequences where Seanad Éireann (a) rejects a Bill completely, or (b) amends it in ways not agreeable to Dáil Éireann, or (c) neither passes nor rejects the Bill within the ninety days or other agreed period of time. Dáil Éireann is given a constitutional option: either the Bill lapses or Dáil Éireann may insist on it becoming law. Where the second option is desired the Bill is deemed to have passed both Houses of the Oireachtas should Dáil Éireann so resolve within a 180-day period after the expiration of the ninety days (Article 23.1.1°).[9]

This legislative scheme prevents Seanad Éireann from thwarting the legislative programme of Dáil Éireann, the popularly elected House of the Oireachtas, by holding a Bill indefinitely, or by rejecting it in the hope of ensuring its permanent defeat. While Seanad Éireann is given a role in the vital constitutional function of legislating, it is in essence a consultative or secondary role

Where a Bill is passed by both Houses of the Oireachtas it must be passed separately by both Houses as there is no constitutional provision for a joint meeting of both Houses of the Oireachtas to consider and pass legislation even in times of emergency.

An ordinary Bill may be initiated in Seanad Éireann and when passed proceeds to Dáil Éireann. Should Dáil Éireann amend the Bill it is then considered to have been initiated in that House and must proceed again to Seanad Éireann after it has been passed by Dáil Éireann (Article 20.2).

This legislative scheme provides the general framework within which the Houses of the Oireachtas operate. While checks and balances are provided to prevent one House having excessive powers in the legislative process, the Houses of the Oireachtas do co-operate in enacting legislation within the permitted time period where legislation is urgently needed.[10]

Financial Legislation

Financial legislation is the second category of legislation with a different procedural process. A Bill containing a financial proposal, or a Money Bill to use its constitutional term, is one which *solely* contains any of the following: (1) the imposition, repeal, remission, alteration or regulation of taxation; (2) the imposition for the payment of debt or other financial purposes of charges on public money or the variation or repeal of any such charges; (3) supply; (4) the appropriation, receipt, custody, issue or audit of accounts of public money; (5) matters incidental to any of these matters (Article 22.1).[11]

The Ceann Comhairle certifies that a Bill is a Money Bill (Article 22.2).[12] A Money Bill can only be initiated in Dáil Éireann and when passed proceeds to Seanad Éireann for its recommendations which must be given within twenty-one days before the Bill is returned to Dáil Éireann which may accept or reject them. Where Seanad Éireann fails to return a Money Bill, or makes recommendations unacceptable to Dáil Éireann, the Bill is deemed to have passed both Houses at the expiration of the twenty-one days (Article 21).

Here is a further illustration of Dáil Éireann's greater prerogative powers though Seanad Éireann is not left bereft of redress. A challenge can be made to the certificate of the Ceann Comhairle. Seanad Éireann may pass a resolution at a sitting at which not less than thirty members are present requesting the President to refer the question as to whether the Bill is or is not a Money Bill to a Committee of Privileges. Should the President, after consultation with the Council of State, accede to this request, the President appoints a committee consisting of an equal number of members from each House with a judge of the Supreme Court as chairman, who has a casting vote only in the event of an equality of votes. Though the President must consult with the Council of State before acceding to the request, the President has a discretion as to the number of members on the committee and their choice. This committee must report within twenty-one days after the day on which the Bill was sent to Seanad Éireann. The decision of the committee is final and conclusive.

Where the President does not accede to Seanad Éireann's request, or where the committee fails to report within the time allowed, the certificate of the Ceann Comhairle stands confirmed (Article 22.2). Seanad Éireann has never challenged the certificate of the Ceann Comhairle in this regard.

Abridged Time Bills

The third category of Bills, known as abridged time Bills, has a different procedure from the first two categories. Article 24 states that where Dáil Éireann passes a Bill and the Taoiseach certifies in writing to the President and to the chairman of both Houses of the Oireachtas that, in the Government's opinion, the Bill is urgently needed for the preservation of the public peace and security, or by reason of a domestic or international emergency, then the time for the consideration of such a Bill by Seanad Éireann will, should Dáil Éireann so resolve and the President concurs, be abridged to such a period as Dáil Éireann specifies. The concurrence of Seanad Éireann to this abridgement is unnecessary though the President's role in this procedure offers some protection against abuse. Time for consideration can only be abridged and not abolished.

Where such a Bill is (a) rejected by Seanad Éireann, or (b) passed with amendments to which Dáil Éireann objects, or (c) neither passed nor rejected within the abridged time period, it is deemed to have passed both Houses of the Oireachtas at the expiry of that period. Abridged time legislation only remains in force for ninety days though this period can be extended by resolutions of both Houses. This procedure has never been resorted to, but is necessary because of the obvious need to act quickly in times of emergency.

Bills to Amend the Constitution

A Bill to amend the Constitution must be initiated in Dáil Éireann. It is then treated as if it were an ordinary Bill and proceeds through the Houses of the Oireachtas accordingly. A Bill containing a proposal to amend the Constitution must not contain any other proposal (Article 46).

Promulgation of Laws

The Taoiseach must present every Bill to the President for signature and promulgation as law as soon as it has passed, or deemed to have passed, both Houses of the Oireachtas (Article 25.1). A Bill is promulgated as law by the publication at the President's direction of notice in the *Iris Oifigiúil** that the Bill has become law. The President must sign a Bill between the fifth and seventh day after presentation though at the Government's request, and with Seanad Éireann's concurrence, a Bill may be signed earlier than the fifth day (Article 25.2). An abridged time Bill must be signed on the day it is presented to the President (Article 25.3). A Bill becomes law on the day it is signed though it may not come into operation until later (Article 25.4). While some Bills come into effect immediately, others contain a provision that they are to come into effect (a) at the term of some stated period, e.g. six months after enactment,[13] or (b) on some definite future date,[14] or (c) following the making of an order by the Government or a statutory instrument by a designated Minister.[15] Where the latter method is adopted it is entirely within the discretion of the party with the power as to when it is exercised. The Supreme Court refused, in *The State (Sheehan) v Government of Ireland* (1987), to order the Government to bring into effect a section of a statute, where the power to do so was reserved by the statute to the Government, despite the passage of over twenty-five years since the statute's enactment.

A Bill containing a proposal for the amendment of the Constitution is signed by the President forthwith on the President being satisfied that the provisions of Article 47 have been complied with and that such proposal was duly approved by the People. The President then promulgates the amendment as law.

Referral of Bills to the Supreme Court

The President has a duty to sign Bills into law though this duty is coupled with a singularly important discretionary power. The President may refrain from signing a Bill though for one purpose only: to obtain the views of others on the proposal, either the People in a referendum, or the opinion of the Supreme Court as to its constitutionality. This right to advice from the Supreme Court before the signing and promulgation of a Bill into law is unknown in other jurisdictions. It was expressly included in the Constitution because it was unforeseen when the Constitution was enacted that the courts would, on a regular basis, entertain actions brought by individuals challenging the constitutionality of laws which had been enacted by the Oireachtas.

The President may, after consulation with the Council of State, refer any Bill to the Supreme Court, other than a Money Bill, an abridged time Bill, or a Bill to amend the Constitution, for a decision as to whether it, or any of its specific provisions, is repugnant to the Constitution (Article 26).[16] The referral must be made not later than the seventh day after the Bill is presented for promulgation. Pending the Supreme Court's decision the President refrains from signing the Bill. The President may refer the entire Bill or merely part of it for decision. The Supreme Court may be asked the general question whether what is being referred offends the Constitution or the question of possible repugnance may be confined to specific articles of the Constitution.

A Supreme Court of at least five judges must consider the referral by hearing counsel on behalf of the Attorney General, who argue in favour of a constitutional construction, and counsel assigned by the court, who generally argue against a constitutional construction. A point never raised is whether these two parties are the exclusive parties that may appear and make submissions to the court. Has a party whose constitutional rights stand in real and imminent danger of being infringed, should the Bill become law, the *locus standi** (see page 124) to argue that case on a referral of the Bill to the Supreme Court?

The Supreme Court must pronounce its decision in open court within sixty days of a referral. To satisfy this constitutional requirement, a simple yes or no would suffice, but in keeping with judicial tradition a reasoned decision is given. The Constitution is silent as to the consequences of the Supreme Court failing or refusing to pronounce a decision within the sixty days.[17]

The decision of the majority of the judges is the decision of the Supreme Court and no opinion either assenting or dissenting is to be pronounced or even disclosed. It is difficult for a number of judges to agree on a unitary decision. Judges may disagree on the conclusion or agree on the conclusion but disagree on how to reach it. It is the judicial tradition to dissent. Article 26.2.2 of the Constitution when originally enacted did not prohibit the disclosure of whether the decision was unanimous or by majority. The former Supreme Court in its first referral, *Article 26 and the Offences Against the State (Amendment) Bill 1940* (Case 10), delivered a majority decision. This loophole was closed by the *Second Amendment of the Constitution Act 1941* which was passed as ordinary legislation within the three-year period in which such amendments could be made.

No court may question the validity of a law, or any provision of a law, or the provision of a law where the corresponding provision in the Bill for such law has been referred to the Supreme Court by the President (Article 34.3.3). The consequence of a referral is far reaching. That particular law, or more far reaching, a law which corresponds with a Bill which had been given a constitutional imprimatur* can never be challenged again no matter how long it remains on the statute book, no matter how circumstances in society change, or how judicial attitudes and developments have altered.[18] Of the four referrals which were held to be constitutional two statutes remain in force. The Supreme Court has ingeniously suggested that the referrals up to 1961, only one of which remains in force as law, may not be immune from further challenge because it was a decision of the former Supreme Court of Justice established under the Constitution of Saorstát Éireann which had not the jurisdiction to hear such referrals.[19] The present Supreme Court possessed of such jurisdiction was not established until late 1961.

In total only eight referrals have been made. The first was the *Offences Against the State (Amendment) Bill 1940* (Case 10) which was upheld by the former Supreme Court and remains in force.[20] The High Court had declared an identical provision unconstitutional in *The State (Burke) v Lennon (1940)*

(Case 181) and the Oireachtas enacted a new measure to cure the defect exposed in that case (see page 204). The President referred a single section of the *School Attendance Bill 1942* (Case 11) to the Supreme Court which advised that this second referral was unconstitutional (see page 258).[21]

Twenty years passed before the third referral, that of the *Electoral (Amendment) Bill 1961* (Case 6), which was found unobjectionable and has since been repealed.[22] The High Court, in *O'Donovan v Attorney General* (1961) (Case 141), had found the existing electoral law invalid (see page 78). The *Criminal Law (Jurisdiction) Bill 1975* (Case 5) was the fourth referral with the Supreme Court advising the President that it was constitutional (see page 20). This law remains in force.[23] The fifth referral was the *Emergency Powers Bill 1976* (Case 8) which was found to be constitutional.[24] This law has since lapsed.

The sixth referral was the *Housing (Private Rented Dwellings) Bill 1981* (Case 9) which was considered repugnant to the Constitution.[25] The Supreme Court, in *Blake v Attorney General* (1981) (Case 22), had ruled that certain rent restrictions provisions were unconstitutional and this Bill was enacted to deal with the consequences (see page 269). The seventh referral, the *Electoral (Amendment) Bill 1983* (Case 7), was deemed to be repugnant to the Constitution.[26] A constitutional amendment, the *Ninth Amendment to the Constitution (Extension of the Dáil Franchise) Act 1984*, which gave effect to proposals contained in the repugnant Bill, was passed by the People (see page 81).[27] The eighth referral, the *Adoption (No. 2) Bill 1987* (Case 4), which permitted the adoption of legitimate children in certain circumstances, was deemed to be constitutional (see page 262).[28]

The Presidential Commission, which acts in circumstances when the President is unable to act, has never referred a Bill to the Supreme Court though it has the power to do so.

In one referral, *Article 26 and the Housing (Private Rented Dwellings) Bill 1981* (Case 9), the Supreme Court commented on the usefulness of Article 26. It pointed out that its obvious shortcoming was that matters raised could only be dealt with as abstract problems in the absence of evidence and the court left open the question as to whether it could hear evidence in referral cases. On the general merit of the Article 26 procedure, O'Higgins CJ said:

> whether the constitutionality of a legislative measure . . . passed by both Houses of the Oireachtas is better determined within a fixed and immutable period of time . . . rather than by means of an action in which specific imputations of unconstitutionality would fall to be determined primarily on proven or admitted facts, is a question on which we refrain from expressing an opinion.

The conclusion from these comments is that the Supreme Court may be unhappy with the Article 26 procedure, as presently drafted, though of course it must operate this constitutional provision when called upon by the President. In another referral, *Article 26 and the Adoption (No. 2) Bill 1987* (Case 4), the Supreme Court ruled that documents by Éamon de Valera which attempted to elucidate the meaning of the words 'inalienable and imprescriptible' — which are used in Article 41 of the Constitution — were inadmissible as they merely reflected the views of a single individual.

The President must decline to sign a Bill which the Supreme Court has advised is unconstitutional. Where the court finds objection merely in part of a Bill it cannot be signed because there is no procedure which allows the President to delete the offending sections. The remaining sections may become law subsequently should the Oireachtas incorporate them in another Bill which is enacted. Should the Oireachtas persist in its intention to press on with such legislative proposals it has a number of options. It could propose an amendment to the Constitution — this it did when the Supreme Court advised the President that the *Electoral (Amendment) Bill 1983* (Case 7) was repugnant to the Constitution, or it could propose a more sweeping change, such as the abolition of the Supreme Court or the curtailment of its powers of judicial review, or it might enact the legislation under Article 28.3.3° of the Constitution, which is discussed later on page 54.

Referral of Bills to the People
When looking at the passage of Bills through the Oireachtas we noted that for a Bill to become law it need not be passed by both Houses of the Oireachtas (see page 46). A Bill rejected by Seanad Éireann will be deemed to have passed both Houses of the Oireachtas where Dáil Éireann so resolves. To balance this dominant role of Dáil Éireann in the legislative process Article 27 of the Constitution provides a procedure by which the views of the People may be ascertained before such a Bill becomes law.

A majority of the members of Seanad Éireann and at least one-third of the members of Dáil Éireann may jointly petition the President to decline to sign a Bill into law because it contains a proposal of national importance on which the will of the People ought to be obtained. The petition must be in writing, must be signed by the petitioners and must contain the reasons on which the request is based. It must be presented to the President within four days after the Bill has been deemed to have passed both Houses of the Oireachtas. This process cannot be invoked where the Bill is one to amend the Constitution because the view of the People must be obtained on such a measure.

The President must, after consultation with the Council of State, give a decision within ten days. Should the petition relate to a Bill which has been referred to the Supreme Court the President may defer a decision until after the court has delivered a judgment. Should the Supreme Court judge the Bill to be unconstitutional that ends the matter because even the People cannot approve of a Bill which offends the Constitution without amending the basic law.

Where the President concurs with the petition, the Taoiseach and the chairman of each House of the Oireachtas are so informed. The Bill is not signed until the proposals contained in the Bill are approved *either* by the People in a referendum or by a resolution of Dáil Éireann made after a general election, either of which must be performed within eighteen months of the President's decision. Every such proposal is vetoed by the People when a majority of the votes cast are cast against its enactment into law and where the votes so cast against its enactment amount to not less that 33⅓ per cent of the voters on the register of electors (Article 47.2). Where the People approve, or where the incoming Dáil Éireann resolves, the Bill must be signed by the President.

When the President dissents from the petitioners' request, the Taoiseach and the chairman of each House of the Oireachtas are so informed and the Bill is signed and promulgated as law not later than eleven days after it was deemed to have been passed by both Houses of the Oireachtas.

This valuable constitutional procedure for ascertaining the wishes of the People on a proposal for legislation before it is enacted into law is only of limited importance. It has never been used because it is very rare for Seanad Éireann to reject a Bill. There is no reason why Article 27 could not be broadened to apply to all legislative proposals. Some such proposals cause public controversy and a simple solution is to consult the electorate. Article 27 is a reiteration that the People are the supreme lawmaker. Should the procedures of Article 27 be resorted to, and should the People in a referendum vote for the measure, that is no constitutional bar to the provisions of the law being challenged in subsequent legal proceedings as to its constitutionality.

Authentication of Legislation

There must be some method by which a statute can be recognised as an Act of the Oireachtas. Article 25.4.5° declares that the text signed by the President must be enrolled in the office of the Registrar of the Supreme Court and is conclusive evidence of that law. The document enrolled is the law and no other document can prevail against it. All copies of the law must correspond exactly with the enrolled copy. Where the President signs a text in one official language an official translation must be issued in the other official language. Should the President sign texts in each official language, both must be enrolled, and in case of conflict the text in the national language prevails.

Procedural Invalidity

Can the courts look behind enacted legislation to ensure that the proper constitutional procedures have been observed? This question has never been litigated.[29] In Britain the courts refuse to concern themselves with the procedure of parliament. But in Ireland the role of the courts extends beyond merely accepting the laws laid down by the Oireachtas. The courts have a clear function in ensuring that the provisions of the Constitution are respected by the other institutions of government and by individuals. The courts presume that all things done are done in accordance with the Constitution. A litigant who could show some procedural indiscretion, for example, the fact that the Bill was not passed by Seanad Éireann, might be able to have that 'law' declared null and void. While the Oireachtas can enact laws it can only make law in the manner prescribed in the Constitution and not in any other way.

Judicial Power of the Oireachtas

The Houses of the Oireachtas exercise a judicial power when they remove certain constitutional officers from office. The President, judges, and the Comptroller and Auditor General can be so removed. Another possible judicial function is the punishing of outsiders for contempt of the Oireachtas, but as will be seen later in this chapter, it is unlikely that the Houses of the Oireachtas possess this power.

WAR AND STATE OF EMERGENCY

Declaration of War

War must not be declared, and the State must not participate in any war, without the assent of Dáil Éireann (Article 28.3.1°). In the event of actual invasion the Government may take whatever steps it considers necessary for the protection of the State. Dáil Éireann, if not sitting, must be summoned to meet at the earliest practicable date. The making of war is thus a legislative act. Similarly in the United States it is Congress and not the President that declares war, whereas in Britain the declaring of war is an executive function vested in the crown. The State has never declared war.

State of Emergency

The Houses of the Oireachtas may by resolutions declare a state of national emergency when an armed conflict is taking place in which the State is not a participant but which affects the vital interests of the State (Article 28.3.3°). This Article was more limited in scope when originally enacted, but was amended by the *First Amendment of the Constitution Act 1939* and the *Second Amendment of the Constitution Act 1941.*

Since 2 September 1939 a state of emergency has existed. On that date resolutions were passed by the Houses of the Oireachtas on account of the conflict in Europe. Despite pacification in Europe after 1945, the emergency was not revoked until 1 September 1976, and then only to be renewed. The Houses of the Oireachtas passed resolutions that 'arising out of the armed conflict now taking place in Northern Ireland a national emergency exists affecting the vital interests of the State'. These resolutions have not been revoked. Speaking in the Supreme Court, in *Article 26 and the Emergency Powers Bill 1976* (Case 8), O'Higgins CJ said:

> the last matter to be considered is the question of the existence of the state of affairs necessary to permit the application of Article 28.3.3° of the Constitution . . . these are the matters or statements of fact which are contained in the resolutions of the two Houses of the Oireachtas. Submissions were made as to the extent, if any, to which the court could examine the correctness of these statements. It was submitted by the Attorney General that there is a presumption that the facts stated in the resolutions are correct. The court accepts the existence of that presumption and the corollary that the presumption should be acted upon unless and until it is displaced. In this case it has not been displaced. The Attorney General submitted the general proposition that when the resolutions . . . have been passed this court has no jurisdiction to review the contents of them. When the consequences of this submission were pointed out to him he withdrew it as he said it did not arise in this case. The court expressly reserves for future consideration the question whether the courts have jurisdiction to review such resolutions.

Consequence of State of National Emergency

The consequence of the declaration of a national emergency may be serious and far reaching. Nothing in the Constitution can be invoked to invalidate any law enacted for the purpose of securing the public safety and the preservation of the State. The contents of such laws are beyond constitutional challenge. One of the essential safeguards existing in our constitutional law that the Oireachtas cannot pass any law which is unconstitutional may, depending on the contents of any law which is stated to be for the purpose of securing the public safety and the preservation of the State, stand suspended. While the Oireachtas, and in particular Dáil Éireann, may be answerable for enacting such laws to the electorate, in the intervening time constitutional rights may be interfered with.

Bearing in mind control by the electorate it is speculative the extent to which the Oireachtas would depart from the generally accepted standards of democratic behaviour. Under the protective umbrella of the 1939 resolutions some drastic departure from judicial norms took place. Military courts which could only impose the death sentence from which there was no appeal, and which could disregard the rules of evidence summarily tried a large number of persons who were then executed. In *In re McGrath and Harte* (1941) (Case 104) the ordinary courts acknowledged themselves incapable of reviewing the emergency laws. This was a period, now deliberately ignored, of which the legislature, the executive and the judicial arms of government must feel decidedly uncomfortable about.

Only one statute was passed on foot of the 1976 resolutions. The *Emergency Powers Act 1976* permitted the detention of persons without charge for seven days. This statute operated for a year and, while it could have been renewed, it was allowed to lapse.[30]

The effect of Article 28.3.3° is to remove from judicial review statutes passed under its provisions. The courts in earlier times tended to stand aside. This attitude was devastatingly explained in *The State (Walsh) v Lennon* (1942) by Gavan Duffy J:

> the function of the judiciary is to co-operate with the legislature and the executive in the government of the State for the People, and in the exercise of that function the judiciary may be called upon from time to time to pronounce a statute unconstitutional or to declare the act of an executive minister illegal. But in time of war or armed rebellion the apprehension of judicial intervention may at some delicate moment hamper the legislative or the executive authority when government needs all possible strength and freedom to steer the ship of State through the crisis, consequently the Constitution has placed in the hands of the Oireachtas, as lawgiver, special authority to suspend judicial control over the other organs of government during any such emergency.

This timid approach at that time is understandable because the judiciary may have feared that a more robust attitude would have jeopardised the continued existence of judicial review. The Oireachtas had responded to Gavan Duffy J's decision to strike down internment without trial, in *The State (Burke) v Lennon* (1940) (Case 181), not alone by amending the law which the President referred to the Supreme Court, *Article 26 and the Offences Against the State (Amendment) Bill 1940* (Case 10), but by amending the constitutional provisions relating to the courts. The fledgling Constitution could be amended by ordinary legislation for a period of three years and a confrontation at that time between the judiciary on the one hand and the legislature and executive on the other could have had only one conceivable result: the curtailment of judicial power to review statutes as to their constitutionality.

The courts by 1976, secure in the role of vindicator of constitutional rights against encroachment by the legislature and executive, gained in a series of trenchant decisions spanning twenty years, and having seen with hindsight the results of giving *carte blanche** to the other organs of government in the 1940s, reacted less generously when the issue came before the courts in *Article 26 and the Emergency Powers Bill 1976* (Case 8). The Supreme Court accepted that once the procedural requirements affecting a Bill to which Article 28.3.3° of the Constitution applied had been complied with, its provisions could not be invalidated by the courts. But as already noted it left open the crucial question as to whether the courts could look behind the resolutions of the Houses of the Oireachtas to ascertain whether the facts on which they were based existed.

This attitude suggests that had there been evidence which contradicted the facts on which the resolutions were based the Supreme Court might have held against the legislation. It follows from this that once the armed conflict in Northern Ireland is past, these resolutions are spent. It might also mean that the laws passed under the emergency must have some real connection with that emergency. The courts would probably not tolerate interference with constitutional rights under some colourable pretence that it was necessary under the emergency. An interesting dilemma for the courts would present itself if under a state of emergency legislation was passed which purported to abolish the Supreme Court. Could a court consider legislation which purported to abolish itself?

It was decided in *In re McGrath and Harte* (1941) (Case 104) that it was unnecessary to recite the resolutions of the Houses of the Oireachtas in a statute passed under Article 28.3.3° provided that statute was stated expressly to be for the purpose of securing the public safety and preservation of the State. It must be remembered that not all legislation passed during a time of national emergency falls within these provisions and thus be immune from judicial review. For example, the *Offences Against the State Act 1939* was not enacted under the provisions of Article 28.3.3° of the Constitution and is open to constitutional challenge in the usual way: see *The People (DPP) v Quilligan* (1992) (Case 163).

Armed Rebellion

There is no modern statute which defines, or deals with, the suppression of armed rebellion. Some indication as to how legally the organs of the State could respond to an armed rebellion must depend on the common law. This dependence on old unwritten law is hardly appropriate having regard to the existence of a Constitution and to the protection of constitutional rights afforded by that Constitution. In the absence of modern law the common law is all we have. In the past when an armed rebellion was alleged to exist a proclamation was issued by the executive arm of government which called on the armed forces to employ their facilities with the utmost vigour and decision for the immediate suppression of the rebellion and requiring the armed forces to punish all persons aiding the rebellion, according to martial law, either by death or otherwise as was considered expedient. Such a proclamation was issued by Lord Camden, the Lord Lieutenant of Ireland, during the 1798 Rebellion. Similar proclamations were issued during the War of Independence by the British authorities. It had been decided by the pre-1922 courts, in *Rex v Allen* (1921), that the civil courts have no jurisdiction *durante bello** to interfere with the decision of a military court sitting in a martial law area, provided the court was satisfied that a state of rebellion actually existed. Such military courts were not courts in the strict sense but merely committees formed for the purpose of executing the discretionary powers assumed by the executive.

During the Civil War a similar attitude was adopted by the courts, composed of the same judges who had heard the earlier cases during the War of Independence. In *R. (Childers) v Adjutant-General of the Provisional Forces* (1923), the law was explained by O'Connor MR:*

> for the purpose of suppressing this rebellion and restoring order, the Provisional Government has been obliged to employ its army. Force must be met with force, and violence by violence; and once an army is set in motion — once a state of war has been established — the rough and ready methods of warfare must be adopted, and take the place of the precise and orderly methods of civil government. The ordinary law is silenced by the sound of the pistol shot and the bomb. *Inter arma silent leges** is a maxim two thousand years old, and has come down to us from the Romans . . . Force then becomes the only remedy, and those to whom the task is committed must be the sole judges how it should be exercised.

Article 40.4.6° of the Constitution declares that this sub-article, which provides a speedy method of determining in the High Court whether a particular detention is lawful or not, cannot be invoked to prohibit, control, or interfere with any act of the Defence Forces during the existence of a state of war or armed rebellion.

THE PRIVILEGES OF THE OIREACHTAS

Freedom from Arrest

The members of the Houses of the Oireachtas are, except in the case of treason, felony* or breach of the peace, privileged from arrest while going to, within, and coming from the relevant House (Article 15.13). A member is free from arrest in civil and criminal matters. The exercise of this privilege may prevent members of the Houses of the Oireachtas from being charged with certain criminal offences. It has not been decided yet whether members of the Houses of the Oireachtas could maintain an action for damages for the breach of this constitutional privilege.

Freedom of Debate

Freedom of debate is an essential feature of every free legislative assembly. Members of the Houses of the Oireachtas are not amenable to any court, or other authority, for any utterances made within the House (Article 15.13). A member cannot be sued for slander where an individual is alleged to have been defamed in the course of debate. What is said is absolutely privileged.* Nor are members answerable to any tribunal of inquiry though that member is answerable to the House itself.[31] This provision is expressed in wide terms. It is desirable that it should be interpreted in such a way as to permit and encourage members of the Houses of the Oireachtas to engage in debate on matters of national interest without having to restrict their observations, or edit their opinions, because of the danger of being made amenable to any court or any authority at the suit of some person aggrieved by the statements made in the course of debate. Explaining the ambit of this privilege in *Attorney General v Hamilton* (1993) (Case 15) Finlay CJ said:

> the provisions of Article 15.12 and Article 15.13 of the Constitution are explicit and definite in their terms, though the application of them may be a matter of complexity in certain instances. They constitute a very far-reaching privilege indeed to members of the Houses of the Oireachtas with regard to utterances made by them in those Houses. They represent an absolute privilege and one which it is clear may, in any instances, represent a major invasion of personal rights of the individual, particularly with regard to his or her good name and property rights. In addition this immunity and this privilege constitutes a significant restriction on the important public right associated with the administration of justice of the maximum availability of all relevant evidence, a right which has been particularly emphasised in decisions of this court.

The issue in that case was whether Article 15.13 conferred on members of the Houses of the Oireachtas a privilege in respect of statements furnished to a Tribunal of Inquiry, which had been established by the Houses of the Oireachtas, such that they could not be compelled to disclose the sources of the information which formed the basis of the statements furnished to the Tribunal of Inquiry. The Supreme Court ruled that members of the Oireachtas could not be compelled to disclose the source of their information. Finlay CJ said:

Chapter 5

THE PRESIDENT OF IRELAND

THE OFFICE OF PRESIDENT

Head of State
In keeping with its republican nature the Constitution in Article 12 establishes the office of President of Ireland.[1] This office is more than a formal head of State. The President is cast by the Constitution, in a limited way, as the defender of the People's rights. The President is capable of exercising some restraint on the powers exercised by the other organs of government under the Constitution. But the powers of the President are so arranged as to prevent the holder of that office from becoming an overpowering constitutional figure.

In some countries, such as the United States and France, the President combines the roles of head of State and head of the executive. In Ireland the powers of the President are, under the Constitution, non-executive in nature. Other functions may be conferred by law but these, in so far as they are executive in nature, are limited and on the periphery of executive government.

Article 12 in establishing the President as head of State provides that the President takes precedence over all other persons in the State. This is not a declaration that the President is above the law. The notion that *le Roi ne peut mal faire*, which applied to the French kings before the Revolution of 1789 and to the Crown in Britain until 1947, has no application in our constitutional law. As the State created by the People cannot be equated to the feudal concept of the crown; neither can the presidency be identified with the feudal concept of the crown. The President is answerable for criminal and civil wrongs in the same way as other individuals.

Selection for Office
In western democracies the head of State can be selected in one of three ways. By the first method the Constitution permits a hereditary monarchy, as in Britain and Belgium. Secondly, the selection may be made by an elected body, as in Germany, where the President is chosen by parliament. Thirdly,

the head of State can be chosen directly by the People. In Ireland, as in the United States and France, the President's link with the People is forged by an election by popular franchise (Article 12.1).

Eligibility for Office

Every citizen who has reached his or her 35th year is eligible for election (Article 12.4). In this respect no distinction is made between natural-born citizens and citizens by descent and naturalisation. Only a natural-born citizen who has reached the age of 35 with a residency of at least fourteen years is eligible for the United States presidency. Apart from these qualifications the Constitution does not empower the Oireachtas to impose disabilities by statute. Should the President on election be a member of either House of the Oireachtas he or she is deemed to have vacated that seat (Article 12.6). But it is not a prerequisite of candidature that Oireachtas membership be resigned.

Nomination as Candidate

Article 12.4 provides the three methods by which a candidate for President may be nominated. The first method empowers nomination by not less than twenty Oireachtas members. To qualify as a nominating member the material date is that of nomination and not the later election date. The nomination paper must be signed by nominating Oireachtas members and be delivered to the presidential returning officer.

The second method is nomination by four administrative county councils, including borough corporations. The intention to propose a nomination resolution must be given in writing to every member of the council at least three days in advance. Should the resolution be passed, the nomination paper must be sealed with the seal of the council and delivered to the presidential returning officer. Nomination papers from county councils or corporations nominating the same person constitute a valid nomination. When a presidential election is declared, a county council or corporation may stand dissolved under the *Local Government Act 1941* and its powers transferred to another body or person. In that case the *Local Government (Nomination of Presidential Candidates) Act 1937* provides that such body or person does not have the power to nominate a presidential candidate.

A person or council is not entitled to nominate more than one candidate in the same election. Should an Oireachtas member sign two or more nomination papers the one first received by the returning officer is regarded as valid. Where two or more nomination papers are received from a county council or corporation the returning officer must declare invalid any two or more passed on the same day. Also deemed invalid is any other nomination paper passed on any subsequent day by the same council. Where one nomination paper is earlier in date than the others the returning officer may accept that one as valid and regard the remainder as invalid.

The third nomination method empowers a former or retiring President to nominate himself or herself. Such a nomination paper must be signed by the candidate and delivered to the returning officer.[2]

The nomination procedures are contained in the *Presidential Elections Act 1937*, as amended by the *Electoral Act 1963*. At noon on the last day for receiving nominations, the presidential returning officer must attend at the appointed place and rule on the nomination papers received. Every question relevant to the nomination of a candidate, such as citizenship and age, the sufficiency or correctness of the name, address or description, may be raised by the returning officer and any person entitled to take part in the proceedings. The President of the High Court acts as judicial assessor. Any matter referred to the judicial assessor must be immediately decided, and the decision given is final and cannot be reviewed by a court. Every candidate, or a representative, must attend and furnish all relevant information which is reasonably required by the returning officer or judicial assessor. Evidence, either oral or written, may be tendered and may if necessary be given on oath. The nomination may be disallowed where the candidate does not attend, or attending refuses to give relevant information. A candidate for the presidency, unlike candidates for Dáil Éireann, is not required to lodge a deposit with the nomination paper.

Necessity for an Election

Article 12.4.5° declares that no election is necessary where there is only one candidate. Where only one person stands nominated the returning officer declares such person elected, notifies the Taoiseach, and publishes that fact in *Iris Oifigiúil*. Where there is more than one candidate the returning officer adjourns the election for the purpose of taking a poll. Where no candidate stands nominated, the procedure must be recommenced. Where after the adjournment and before the taking of the poll a candidate dies the returning officer must countermand the poll and the procedure is recommenced.

Presidential Election

The election must be held not later than, and not earlier than, the sixtieth day before the expiry of the incumbent President's term of office. Where the President resigns, is removed, dies or is declared permanently incapacitated, the election for a successor must be held within sixty days of such event (Article 12.3.3°). The Minister for the Environment sets the date and appoints a fit and proper person as the presidential returning officer with the duty to conduct the election, count the votes cast, ascertain and declare the result. The country is divided into constituencies, use being made of the previous

Dáil Éireann general election constituencies. Local returning officers are appointed.

The President, the Taoiseach, the Chief Justice, the Chairman of Dáil Éireann, the Chairman of Seanad Éireann, the secretary to the President and the successful candidate must all be informed by the presidential returning officer of the result of the election.

Eligibility to Vote in Presidential Election

Every citizen possessed of the right to vote in Dáil Éireann elections has the right to vote at a presidential election.[3] The voting is by secret ballot on the system of proportional representation by means of the single transferable vote (Article 12.2).

Entering into Office by President

The President elect enters office on the day following the expiry of his or her predecessor's term. Where an immediate predecessor has resigned, has been removed from office, has died while in office, or has been declared permanently incapacitated, the President elect enters office as soon as may be after the election (Article 12.7).

The President enters into office by taking and subscribing publicly the constitutional declaration in the presence of members of the Houses of the Oireachtas, the judges of the Supreme Court and High Court, and other public personages. The President elect pledges to 'maintain the Constitution of Ireland and uphold its laws' (Article 12.8). The making of this declaration is mandatory. Where a judge fails to make a similar declaration it is expressly provided that the office is terminated (Article 34.5.4°). There is no similar provision to cover the situation where a President elect defaults in this regard. There has been no instance where a President elect has failed or refused to make the declaration. The declaration invokes the name of Almighty God and pleads for direction and sustenance. A problem might arise should a President elect object to making this declaration, or propose to make it in a modified form. A President elect might have conscientious grounds for such action. Whether a refusal simply prevents a President elect from taking office or amounts to misbehaviour is debatable. The President of the United States must make a similar declaration though an option to swear or affirm is given.

Term of Office of President

The President holds office for seven years, from the date of entering office, which is presumably the day on which the declaration is made. A person who holds, or who has held, office as President, shall be eligible for re-election to that office once, but only once (Article 12.3). This term is curtailed where the President dies or resigns. The death of a President sets in train a presidential election, but how does a President resign? The Constitution and statute law are silent in this regard. A President probably effects resignation by publicly announcing that fact, surrendering the seal of office, vacating Árus an Uachtaráin* and refusing to act as President, as the late President Ó Dálaigh, who resigned the office of President, did. A constitutional dilemma would arise should a President withdraw a resignation during a subsequent presidential election campaign or after a successor was elected.

Permanent Incapacity of President
The President may forfeit office on becoming 'permanently incapacitated'. Such incapacity must be established to the satisfaction of the Supreme Court consisting of not less than five judges. This expression is not defined in the Constitution so it falls to the Supreme Court to give it interpretation. The words are wide enough to cover physical and mental incapacity, though it must be of a nature which interferes with, and/or prevents, the President carrying out the functions of the office. Because the President must sign Bills into law, it seems implicit that the holder of the office must be able to read and write. Would any illness which affected either capacity, or the advance of senility, come within this expression? Mental disorder, more difficult to define and prove, must obviously fall within its ambit.

What meaning is to be given to the expression 'satisfaction' of not fewer than five judges of the Supreme Court? The law of evidence has two differing standards. In a criminal case, the standard of proof is beyond a reasonable doubt, while in civil proceedings the standard of proof is on the balance of probabilities. Because the consequences are so grave, the removal of a constitutional officeholder who may have been directly elected by the People, the standard of beyond a reasonable doubt seems the more appropriate one. It also seems that the decision of the five judges must be a unanimous one, though should there be more than five judges then a majority of at least five is necessary to remove the President from office. The Constitution is silent as to who may bring such a motion before the Supreme Court. In the absence of qualification it is fair to assume that any citizen may initiate and prosecute this procedure. Had the Constitution placed this initiative solely in specific hands, such as in the Government or the Houses of the Oireachtas, it might have been seen as a covert threat to the President.

Article 30 declares that all crimes and offences must be prosecuted by the Attorney General or other person authorised by law. The procedure under discussion is not a criminal one and is therefore not caught by this restriction. The hearing itself probably must be in open court though the Constitution does not expressly so provide. In keeping with the rules of fair procedures the President must be informed of the charge and the nature of the evidence to be presented, and must be given an opportunity to call rebutting evidence and to be professionally represented. Should it be alleged that the President is mentally ill, the preliminary question as to whether the President understands the proceedings and can give instructions in the matter, may have to be decided.

Impeachment of President

The second way a President can be removed from office is by 'impeachment' for stated misbehaviour (Article 12.10). Impeachment is an old English device for bringing formal charges against a public official with the intent of removing the holder from office. It was a judicial proceeding for a state offence beyond the reach of the law and is now considered obsolete in Britain. Impeachment is possible under the United States Constitution. In this State it is the function of the Houses of the Oireachtas to impeach a President and is one of the few instances in which the Houses of the Oireachtas administer justice, a function in general confined under the Constitution to the courts.

A President can only be impeached for stated misbehaviour, an expression not defined in the Constitution though it must be such as to render the President unfit to continue in office. Obvious examples of misbehaviour are the refusal to appoint a Taoiseach, and leaving the State without the consent of the Government. It cannot be misbehaviour to refuse an exercise of the discretionary powers, or to exercise any of these in a particular way. A more difficult decision concerns indiscretions of a President in his or her personal life. The conviction for a serious criminal offence probably amounts to misbehaviour in that the President's committal to prison would make it difficult to properly perform the functions of office. Matters of a domestic nature, such as matrimonial difficulties between a President and spouse, would not amount to misbehaviour. The American Constitution confines impeachment to treason, bribery or other high crimes and misdemeanours.[4]

A proposal for impeachment may be made in either House of the Oireachtas, on a notice of motion in writing, signed by not less than thirty members of that House, and can only be adopted by a resolution of that House if supported by not less than two-thirds of its total membership. It is not sufficient to gain the support of two-thirds of the members present and voting. After adoption by one House the resolution is passed to the other House for investigation, though it is not constitutionally obligatory for that other House to investigate the charge: any court, tribunal or body appointed or designated by either House of the Oireachtas may investigate the charge. The President has the right to appear and to be represented. Should, after investigation, a resolution be supported by not less than two-thirds of the total membership of that House, declaring that the charge has been sustained and that the behaviour was such as to render the President unfit to continue in office, such a resolution operates as a removal from office.

Can the courts exercise jurisdiction over the impeachment process? They can, but only in a limited way. While the courts could not be involved with the merits of the allegations they could intervene where the constitutional requirements were not met. The courts would probably insist that the rules of fair procedures be observed (see page 172). A clash between the courts and the Houses of the Oireachtas on issues relating to impeachment would be of high constitutional importance, as indeed would the impeachment process itself. The Houses of the Oireachtas might not welcome such intervention and might take action to curtail the powers of the courts. On the other hand, the courts could hardly shrink from their constitutional duty to protect the President from the unconstitutional actions of the Houses of the Oireachtas.

Consequence of Removal or Impeachment

The impeachment or removal of a President sets in motion a presidential election. Surprisingly, the Constitution does not prohibit a President removed from office in either of these ways for seeking re-election on his or her own nomination though this can only occur where one term of office has been served because a former President can be re-elected only once.

Seal of Office

The Constitution by implication provides that the President should have a seal of office though there is inconsistency in when it must be used. When removing a judge or the Comptroller and Auditor General from office the President must do so under hand and seal (Article 35.4.3° and Article 33.5.3°) whereas when a Government member is dismissed the appointment is terminated by the President (Article 13.1.3°). While the Constitution expressly provides for its use in a limited number of cases, in practice all proclamations, such as that dissolving Dáil Éireann, and all warrants of appointment, such as those appointing judges, have the seal affixed.

The *Presidential Seal Act 1937* provides that the President shall have an official seal which shall be in the President's custody while exercising and performing the powers and functions of the office. It is affixed to instruments made by the President and when affixed is authenticated by the President's signature. This seal must be officially and judicially noted and must be admitted in evidence in legal proceedings without further proof.

Duty to be Informed

The Taoiseach shall keep the President generally informed on matters of domestic and international policy (Article 28.5.2°).

Presidential Independence

For the President to carry out the discretionary constitutional functions it is essential for the Constitution to invest the President with protection from undue or improper influences. A President must be amenable to reasonable requests and approaches as to how to perform the functions of the office. For example, it is hardly improper for a citizen to request the President to refer a Bill to the Supreme Court. Such a request could not be considered to be undue pressure. But a request to act in a particular manner, made either openly or obliquely, by the Government might be more difficult to resist. To assist the President in preserving independence from the legislature and executive, which is in keeping with the doctrine of the separation of powers (see page 28), the Constitution provides two safeguards. Article 12.11.3° provides that the emoluments and allowances of the President must not be diminished during a term of office. Financial intimidation cannot be used as a lever of pressure against a President. These amounts may be increased and, of course, they may be reduced in the interregnum between Presidents.

The second safeguard is security of office. It is difficult to remove a President from office and no President has ever been removed. These procedures have already been explained earlier.

Presidential Immunity

The President is not answerable to either House of the Oireachtas, or to any court, for the exercise and performance of the powers and functions of the office (Article 13.8). The exception to this is the impeachment procedure. The failure by the President to perform the non-discretionary duties of the office would be misbehaviour, while the exercise or non-exercise of the discretionary powers are immune from action. The question arose in *The State (Walshe) v Murphy* (1981) (Case 205) as to the extent of the ambit of this sub-article. While it was accepted that the President was not answerable to a court the point arose as to whether the acts of the President were open to judicial review. In that case a criminal conviction was challenged on the ground that the judge who had heard the case, when appointed by the President, was not qualified as was required by law. In defending these proceedings the judge argued that his appointment by the President could not be reviewed, an argument rejected by the High Court which held that the ordinary meaning to be given to 'answerable' was that the person concerned could be made or forced to give account of the conduct under review. Since these proceedings did not involve the President being compelled to account for or explain in any way the performance of the function of appointing the judge the article could not be used as a defence. Indeed it would seem that this immunity is the sole property of the President and cannot be availed of by others, a point not discussed by the court.

An attempt to injunct the Taoiseach from advising the President to dissolve Dáil Éireann failed in *O'Malley v An Taoiseach* (1990) (Case 147). The High Court held that the courts had no jurisdiction to place any impediment between the President and the Taoiseach, the constitutional adviser in this important matter, which is solely the prerogative of the President.

As part of the Oireachtas the President's official papers are privileged (Article 15.10).

DUTIES AND POWERS OF THE PRESIDENT

Duty and Power Distinguished

As already mentioned when examining the Oireachtas (page 40) a distinction must be drawn between a *duty* and a *power*. A *duty* denotes obligation: it is *mandatory*. There is no discretion in the exercise of a duty; it must be performed. On the other hand, a *power* denotes discretion: there is a choice as to whether it is or it is not performed. Broadly speaking the functions of the President can be divided into duties *simpliciter* and powers *simpliciter* though there is also the hybrid of a duty coupled with a power. Each of these will be examined individually.

Duties of the President

In keeping with the doctrine of the separation of powers the President is prohibited from being a member of either House of the Oireachtas and from holding any other position of emolument (Article 12.6). These rules ensure that the impartiality so essential to the performance of the functions of the office is maintained. The President must not leave the State without the consent of the Government (Article 12.9). The President has an official residence in or near the City of Dublin (Article 12.11.1). While it is not expressly stated that the President must reside in, and perform the constitutional functions of the office in Árus an Uachtaráin, there is probably an implied duty to do so. The purpose of the State in providing an official residence and the prohibition on the President from leaving the State without the Government's consent is to ensure that the other organs of government have ready access to the President, particularly in a time of emergency.

The President appoints the Taoiseach on the nomination of Dáil Éireann (Article 13.1.1°), and appoints the other Government members on the nomination of the Taoiseach with the approval of Dáil Éireann (Article 13.1.2°). On the advice of the Taoiseach the President accepts the resignation, or terminates the appointment of, a Government member (Article 13.1.3°). The President appoints and accepts the resignation, or terminates the appointment of, the Attorney General on the advice of the Taoiseach (Article 30), an appointment which does not constitutionally require the approval of Dáil Éireann. The President appoints the Comptroller and Auditor General on the nomination of Dáil Éireann, and on the receipt of resolutions of both Houses of the Oireachtas that appointment is terminated (Article 33). The President appoints the judges to the courts established under Article 34 of the Constitution and on the receipt of resolutions of both Houses of the Oireachtas the President removes a judge of the Supreme Court or High Court from office (Articles 35.1 and 35.4).[5]

The supreme command of the Defence Forces is vested in the President though its exercise may be regulated by law (Article 13.4). The *Defence Act 1954* vests this exercise in the Minister for Defence.

The right of pardon and the power to commute or remit punishment imposed by a criminal court are vested in the President (Article 13.6), a duty solely exercisable on the advice of the Government. This is a judicial function and its scope can be judged from the language used. 'Commute' means to reduce and 'remit' means to relax. Any punishment can thus be mitigated. The President has altered a death sentence to one of forty years' penal servitude. This duty of commutation may, except in capital cases, be conferred by law on other authorities. Capital crimes were those for which the death penalty could have been imposed before its abolition by the *Criminal Justice Act 1990*. The *Criminal Justice Act 1951* confers this power to commute or remit punishment on the Government though it may be delegated to the Minister for Justice (section 23). There is no power, constitutionally or otherwise, to remit any order of a civil court which would extend to an order committing a person to prison for disobedience of a court order in a civil case (see Contempt of Court, page 238).

The President on the advice of the Taoiseach fixes the date on which Seanad Éireann first meets after a general election (Article 18.8).

Powers of the President

The President may at any time, after consultation with the Council of State, convene a meeting of either or both Houses of the Oireachtas (Article 13.2.3°). The President may, after consultation with the Council of State, communicate with the Houses of the Oireachtas by message or address on any matter of national or public importance (Article 13.7.1°). The President may, after consultation with the Council of State, address a message to the nation at any time on any such matter and every such message or address must have the prior approval of the Government (Articles 13.7.2° and 3°). To give such address or to issue such message without Government approval would amount to misbehaviour. The President of the United States is bound annually to address the Houses of Congress but it must be remembered that the President of the United States is the chief executive.

The President, exercising absolute discretion, may appoint and later dismiss, not more than seven persons to be members of the Council of State (Article 31).

Duties Coupled with Powers

The President must summon and dissolve Dáil Éireann on the advice of the Taoiseach. The High Court, in *O'Malley v An Taoiseach* (1990) (Case 147), refused to injunct the Taoiseach from advising the President to dissolve Dáil Éireann. The President may, exercising absolute discretion, refuse a dissolution on the advice of a Taoiseach who has ceased to retain the support of a majority of Dáil Éireann (Article 13.2). A dissolution has never been refused in such circumstances, probably in deference to the view that the will of the People in a general election, and not the President's own view, should prevail.

The President must sign Bills into law (Articles 13 and 25) but the President may, before signing a Bill into law, refer it to the Supreme Court for advice as to its constitutionality (Article 26, see page 49). The President may, on the petition of some members of the Houses of the Oireachtas, refer a particular Bill to the People in a referendum (Article 27, see page 52). The President must concur before the stated period of time in which Seanad Éireann may consider a Bill can be abridged (Article 24, see page 48). The President may accede to a request from Seanad Éireann to refer the question whether a Money Bill is such a Bill to a Committee of Privileges (Article 22, see page 47).

Absolute Discretionary Powers

As has already been noted, there are only two instances where the Constitution affords the President the right to exercise absolute discretion. The first permits the President to refuse to dissolve Dáil Éireann on the advice of a Taoiseach who has ceased to retain the support of a majority in Dáil Éireann (Article 13.2.2°). The second permits the President to appoint up to seven persons to be members of the Council of State (Article 31.3).

Powers Performable on the Advice of Government

Despite the fact that the President is part of the Oireachtas the Constitution creates a special relationship between the President and the Government, the executive arm of government. It will already have been noted that the President may only exercise certain powers on the advice of the Government. The powers and functions conferred on the President are exerciseable and performable only on the advice of the Government save where it is provided that the President shall exercise absolute discretionary powers or after consultation with the Council of State (see page 73) or on the advice or nomination of, or on receipt of any other communication from, any other person or body (Article 13.9).

Duties Conferred by Law

Statute law may confer extra powers and functions on the President (Article 13.10). The *Republic of Ireland Act 1948* provides that the President, on the advice and authority of the Government, may exercise the executive power or any executive function of the State in connection with its external relations (section 3). Thus the President accredits Irish diplomatic personnel abroad and accepts the credentials of foreign diplomats to this State. This function was performed by the British Crown until 1948 despite the enactment of the Constitution some eleven years earlier. The *Irish Nationality and Citizenship Act 1956* empowers the President to grant Irish citizenship as a token of honour (section 12). The President appoints the Ombudsman on resolutions passed by both Houses of the Oireachtas recommending such appointment: *Ombudsman Act 1980.*

OFFENCES RELATING TO THE PRESIDENT

The criminal law creates a number of offences relating to the protection of the person and office of the President. The *Offences Against the State Act 1939* provides that the prevention or obstruction by force of arms or other violent means, or the intimidation of the President in the exercise of the functions of the office is a felony (section 8). Should murder be done in the course or furtherance of such offences the convicted person must be sentenced to a minimum of forty years' imprisonment: *Criminal Justice Act 1990*, section 4.

THE COUNCIL OF STATE

Purpose and Composition
Established by Article 31 the Council of State is the body which aids and counsels the President in the exercise of certain of the functions of the office.[6] It is composed of three classes of members. The first class are *ex officio** members consisting of the Taoiseach, the Tánaiste, the Chief Justice, the President of the High Court, the Chairman of Dáil Éireann, the Chairman of Seanad Éireann and the Attorney General. The second class are former holders of certain offices, willing and able to act, such as those who have held the office of President, or Taoiseach, or Chief Justice. In the third class are not more than seven persons whom the President, exercising absolute discretion, may appoint as members.

A member must, at the first meeting attended, make a declaration to faithfully and conscientiously carry out the duties as a member of the Council of State. Members appointed by the President may resign at any time, and the President may for sufficient reason terminate such appointment. Such members hold office until the successor of the President by whom they were appointed shall have entered into office.

Functions of the Council of State

A meeting of the Council of State is convened at such time and place as the President determines. The President must convene the Council of State where the Constitution expressly so provides (Article 32). The President has a duty to explain the reason the meeting has been convened, which must include a duty to outline any proposed action, e.g. that consideration is being given to referring a particular Bill to the Supreme Court under Article 26. No constitutional right is granted to members to express an opinion or to be heard. Article 32 provides that the members present at such meeting shall be heard by the President. Obviously if the Council of State is to serve a useful role in aiding and counselling the President the members must be given an opportunity to state an opinion. The President is not obliged to accept any advice offered even where that advice is unanimous.

The President must convene the Council of State where it is intended to do any of the following:

1. convene a meeting of either or both Houses of the Oireachtas (Article 13.2.3°);
2. communicate with the Houses of the Oireachtas by message or address on a matter of national or public importance (Article 13.7.1°);[7]
3. address a message to the nation on a matter of national or public importance (Article 13.7.2°);
4. decide on a request from Seanad Éireann to refer the question of whether a Bill is or is not a Money Bill to a Committee of Privileges (Article 22.2);
5. concur in abridging the time for the consideration by Seanad Éireann of a Bill certified by the Taoiseach to be urgent (Article 24.1);
6. refer a Bill to the Supreme Court for a decision on its constitutionality (Article 26.1.1°);[8]
7. pronounce a decision on a petition from the members of Dáil and Seanad Éireann that a Bill be submitted to the People in a referendum (Article 27.4.1°).

This list is exhaustive. The Constitution does not empower statute law to authorise additional functions.

While the Council of State may have the appearance of being a constitutional trimming it can make provision for the exercise of the powers and functions of the President in any contingency which is not provided for in the Constitution (Article 14.4).

THE PRESIDENTIAL COMMISSION

Ireland, unlike the United States, has no office of Vice-President, to act when the President has died, is absent, has resigned, is incapacitated, has been removed from office or is refusing to perform the powers and functions of the office. Article 14 provides for the establishment of a Presidential Commission to perform the functions of a President in such circumstances because the affairs of State must continue.

The Commission consists of the Chief Justice, or if unavailable, the President of the High Court; the Chairman of Dáil Éireann, or if unavailable, the Deputy Chairman; and the Chairman of Seanad Éireann, or if unavailable, the Deputy Chairman.

The Commission may act by majority. The usual function performed by the Commission is the signing of Bills into law though the Commission has dissolved on one occasion. The Commission has never performed the other duties coupled with a power which the President has, such as referring a Bill to the Supreme Court.

Chapter 6

DÁIL ÉIREANN

A Popularly Elected Assembly

A forum of individuals elected by popular franchise with stated powers and functions is an integral part of government in modern democracies. Article 51.1.2° states that one of the two Houses of the Oireachtas shall consist of a House of Representatives to be called Dáil Éireann. In our constitutional framework, Dáil Éireann is such a forum. The Constitution emphasises the idea of elected government in two ways: any citizen may stand for election, and every citizen has the right to vote in such elections. It is mistakenly thought that the Constitution only acknowledges and protects personal rights, such as the right to liberty, freedom of association and freedom of expression. Political rights, such as the right to stand for elected office and the right to vote, are also acknowledged as rights and are protected. Such rights are as fundamental to the well-being of a democratic society as are personal rights.

Eligibility for Membership

Every citizen, without discrimination of sex, over the age of 21 and not placed under disability by the Constitution or by law, is eligible for membership of Dáil Éireann (Article 16.1.1°). Individuals holding specified constitutional offices are disqualified from membership: the President (Article 12.6.1°); a member of Seanad Éireann (Article 15.14); the Comptroller and Auditor General (Article 33.3); and a judge (Article 35.3). These restrictions conform with the application of the doctrine of the separation of powers. Together with the notion that different functions of government are confined to different organs of government is the principle that those exercising the various powers cannot perform more than one of them. The same individual cannot be a member of the legislative, executive and judicial arms of government: duality of office is prohibited.

While the Oireachtas may impose further disabilities by law, the Constitution, as already noted, prohibits such law from discriminating on the ground of sex. The *Electoral Act 1923* categorises individuals disqualified by law from election. These are: (1) persons serving a prison term of at least six months, or a sentence of penal servitude, imposed by a court within the State; (2) a person of unsound mind; (3) an undischarged bankrupt; (4) a member of either the Defence Forces or Garda Síochána on full pay; (5) a permanent, or temporary, civil servant of the State; and (6) a person convicted of an electoral offence by a court within the State. A number of statutes prohibit the directors of various semi-state bodies from membership of Dáil Éireann.[1] There are obvious, and inexplicable, anomalies in the list of those prohibited from such membership. Persons convicted outside the State can be members; those serving in foreign armies can be elected; members of foreign legislatures can stand for election; and an ex-director of a liquidated company, which may owe more in debts than any bankrupt, is under no disability. Clearly some classes of persons must be disqualified: Defence Forces and Garda personnel, for example, in that (a) those elected might not be able to carry out both tasks adequately, and (b) a legislature composed of some military or police personnel offends one basic tenet of civilian democratic government which is that those whose duty it is to preserve the State and the peace obey the law rather than make it.

Number of Members of Dáil Éireann
It was open to the People when enacting the Constitution to provide for an elected assembly with a static number of members, as was done with Seanad Éireann (see page 91). Instead, the Constitution provides a system of flexible numbers, which is periodically reviewed. The number of members is to be fixed by law, but the total number must not be less than one member for 30,000 of the population, and not more than one member for each 20,000 of the population (Article 16.2). The relevant figures are those of population and not merely the total number of persons eligible to vote.

The Oireachtas must revise the constituencies at least once every twelve years, with due regard to changes in distribution of the population, but any alterations in the constituencies shall not take effect during the life of Dáil Éireann sitting when such revision is made (Article 16.2.4°). The High Court held, in *O'Malley v An Taoiseach* (1990) (Case 147), that this constitutional obligation placed on the Oireachtas was not discharged by revising the constituencies once in every twelve years. The Oireachtas was obliged to revise the constituencies when a census return disclosed major changes in the distribution of the population. Consequently the total number of members to be elected to Dáil Éireann will change as the population increases or decreases.[2]

The former Supreme Court in *Article 26 and the Electoral (Amendment) Bill 1961* (Case 6) considered the meaning to be given to the words 'population' and 'census'. It was argued that the Oireachtas ought to have relied on the more accurate, if less precise, figures provided by either the electoral registers, or the most recent population estimates rather than on the detailed, but no longer accurate, figures provided by the last previously completed census. The court rejected this argument and held that the population must be taken to mean the population as ascertained at the last preceding census. Census meant the last completed census because no other method could calculate the population with the degree of certainty required to comply with the provisions limiting the total membership of Dáil Éireann by reference to the total population of the State.

Uniformity of Representation

It is a simple principle inherent in the broad concept of democracy that equal weight attaches to the vote of each individual: a system of weighted voting cannot be regarded as democratic. Should this equality be departed from, the result would be the gross abuse of valuing the vote of one individual in securing parliamentary representation either higher or lower than another individual. The slogan 'one person one vote' means more than the obvious, that every individual should have a vote: it implies the equally fundamental principle that there be uniformity of representation.

The ratio between the number of members to be elected for each constituency must, as far as is practicable, be the same throughout the country (Article 16.2.3°). Here the principle of uniformity of representation is constitutionally acknowledged and protected. It cannot be a rigid principle guaranteeing exactness. How far the Oireachtas can stray was considered in *O'Donovan v Attorney General* (1961) (Case 141) where it was argued that the relevant statute had not maintained the required ratio. To prove the case a great volume of figures was produced: some of these will illustrate the point that was made. The constituency of Galway South had one member per 16,575 of the population, whereas the Dublin South West constituency had one member per 23,128 of the population. Dun Laoghaire and Rathdown had a population of 69,071 while Galway South had 49,726: both returned three members though the difference in population was 19,345. The State defended these variations on the ground that members representing western constituencies had large geographical areas with sparse populations and difficult communications problems and time was spent travelling to and from Dublin where Dáil Éireann was situated. These difficulties were not faced by the members of Dáil Éireann representing constituencies on the eastern seaboard. It was admitted by the State that from the purely administrative standpoint a closer approximation to equality of ratio of members to population could have been obtained by grouping or planning the areas and boundaries differently.

The High Court held the statute unconstitutional because it contained substantial departures from the stipulated ratio thus causing grave inequalities of parliamentary representation, and because no circumstances were present which justified such departures. The Supreme Court, in *Article 26 and the Electoral (Amendment) Bill 1961* (Case 6), dealing with a statute passed to cure the defect disclosed in *O'Donovan's* case which was referred to that court by the President, agreed with this decision though that court refused to lay down a figure above or below which a deviation would be permitted.

In 1968 the *Third Amendment of the Constitution Bill* was introduced in Dáil Éireann and passed by the Houses of the Oireachtas. It would authorise a tolerance of up to 16 per cent of the national average in drawing constituencies. A plea was made for more latitude for the underpopulated west. The High Court in *O'Donovan's* case had rejected a tolerance of 19 per cent. This proposal was put to the People in a referendum and was rejected.[3]

Constituencies

Dáil Éireann is composed of members who represent constituencies determined by law.[4] We have already examined the constitutional requirement of uniformity of representation. With regard to constituencies the other constitutional requirement is that the number of members to be returned for a Dáil Éireann constituency must be at least three (Article 16.2.6°). The constituencies must be multi-seated. There is no maximum number, so in theory the usual upper limit of five members may be exceeded. There must be more than one constituency because the Constitution speaks in the plural. The minimum is therefore two, and in theory the country could be divided into two large geographical constituencies. This would, of course, cause problems for the electorate and the candidates. Ballot papers would contain hundreds of names, and the candidates would have large geographical areas, or large densely populated urban areas to canvass though this is exactly what candidates for the European Parliament must do. The Constitution gives no direction as to how the constituencies should be drawn. The High Court, in *O'Donovan v Attorney General* (1961) (Case 141), rejected the suggestion that the boundaries must be based on geographical and administrative counties.

Until 1979 the task of drawing constituencies was in the hands, under the law, of the Minister for the Environment[5] who would present proposals in the form of legislation placed before the Houses of the Oireachtas. The criticism of this system was that the proposals made were entirely to the advantage of the political party or parties then forming the majority in Dáil Éireann and in Government. In that year the Government established a non-statutory *ad hoc** electoral commission to advise and report on the formation of constituencies for the election of members of Dáil Éireann.[6] Its terms of reference provided that account be taken of geographical consideration, in that the breaching of county boundaries should be avoided. The commission reported in 1980 and their submissions were accepted, and included, in legislation for the subsequent revision of constituencies. This commission has become the settled method of revising the constituencies.

Registration of Political Parties

A candidate for election to Dáil Éireann is not required to be a member of a political party. Such a requirement would offend the democratic concept of every citizen having the opportunity to stand for elected office without unnecessary restriction. Would it be possible to curtail eligibility for election to political party members or, more sinister, to confine eligibility to one particular political party? There is nothing in the Constitution expressly prohibiting such a proposal though the courts would probably reject it as offending Article 5 which proclaims the State to be a democratic one.

The *Electoral Act 1963*, section 13, established a Register of Political Parties. The Registrar is the Clerk of Dáil Éireann whose duty it is to prepare and maintain the register in which political parties are registered. Two methods of registration were permitted, one of which is spent. When the register was first established the registrar had to include all the parties then represented in Dáil Éireann. Other parties had to apply for registration. Registration will only be effected where the registrar is of opinion that the applicant is a genuine political party and is organised to contest Dáil Éireann or local government elections. Where the application is refused appeal may be made to an Appeal Board consisting of a judge of the High Court, the chairman of Dáil Éireann and the chairman of Seanad Éireann.

The constitutionality of section 13 was challenged in *Loftus v Attorney General* (1979) (Case 93) where it was claimed that this procedure discriminated against a bona fide political party which had failed to secure registration and in favour of a registered political party in that it permitted the latter's candidates to have the party affiliation stated on the ballot paper. To be compelled to adopt instead the misleading description of 'Non Party', or to remain undescribed imposed an unconstitutional curb on the freedom of political action. The Supreme Court upheld the section in that it was reasonable for the Oireachtas to regulate such matters. The purpose of the section was to permit genuine political parties to be distinguished from the feigned and the spurious. According to O'Higgins CJ:

> if some control and regulation were not provided, genuine political action might be destroyed by a proliferation of bogus front organisations calling themselves political parties but with aims and objects far removed from the political sphere.

This subjective reasoning could be used to justify all kinds of restrictions on future political actions. Limitations imposed in this area by those practising the art of politics must be resisted because the natural dislike of the newcomer may result in a monopoly by those currently hogging the stage. The reasoning of the Chief Justice could be used to support a one-party state, or at least to limit the badge of orthodoxy to existing political parties on the ground that the electorate had a sufficiency of choice.

How are we to distinguish between the genuine and the bogus? According to the Supreme Court the existing political parties can legitimately do so. It would seem in a democracy that it is the electorate which is ideally placed to draw this distinction. Voters have the right to vote for candidates of their choice. This right of the electorate is underpinned in the Constitution and the law. The expression 'genuine political party' was considered to need interpretation in this case. The Supreme Court rejected the test, used when deciding previous applications for registration, of 'an existing party or group which has a sizeable public image and which has a visible organisation'. Finlay P* said that the expression 'genuine political party' meant that the group should be:

> bound together by the cohesion of common political beliefs or aims, and by being organised for electoral purposes into an entity to such an extent and with such distinctiveness as to justify its claim to be truly a political party in its own right.

The Register of Political Parties contains the name of the party, the address of its headquarters and details of the officers authorised to sign certificates authenticating the candidature of its candidates at elections. The registrar annually inquires whether the party desires to remain registered and unless an affirmative reply is received within twenty-one days to such inquiry the registrar cancels the registration.

The Right to Vote

Every citizen, and such other person in the State as may be determined by law, without discrimination of sex, who has reached 18 years of age, is not disqualified by law and has complied with the relevant electoral law, has the right to vote at an election for members of Dáil Éireann (Article 16.1.2°). The extension of the franchise to non-citizens was approved by the People in a referendum by the *Ninth Amendment of the Constitution Act 1984.*[7] The *Electoral (Amendment) Act 1985* extended the Dáil franchise to British citizens resident in the State. Similar voting rights may be extended, by statutory instrument, to citizens of member states of the EC provided reciprocal voting rights are extended to Irish citizens. There is currently no legal disqualification on the right to vote. A person convicted of corrupt practices under the *Prevention of Electoral Abuses Act 1923* was disqualified from voting for seven years but this restriction has been repealed.

To vote a person must be registered as a Dáil Éireann elector in a constituency. A person otherwise qualified must be ordinarily resident in the constituency in which that person wishes to be registered. It is the duty of each local authority to prepare, and publish, the register of electors each year. A period of time for corrections is allowed and an appeal can be made to the Circuit Court. The Supreme Court ruled in *Quinn v Waterford Corporation* (1991) that an individual may be ordinarily resident in more than one constituency and that a student who resides away from home while attending college was ordinarily resident, at least during the academic year, in the constituency in which the college was situated. Article 16.4 of the Constitution did not prohibit double registration. A separate postal voters' list, confined to members of the Defence Forces and the Garda Síochána, and a disabled persons voters' list are prepared. The voters' lists are also used, under the *Juries Act 1976*, to compile jury panels. No voter may exercise more than one vote at an election for Dáil Éireann (Article 16.1.4°).

A distinction must be made between the right to vote and the opportunity to vote. For example, if the law was structured in such a way which required a voter in Dublin to exercise the right to vote in a polling station in Kerry it could hardly be doubted that the constitutional right to vote would be infringed. It is implicit in the Constitution that the right to vote encompasses the reasonable opportunity to vote. Polling stations must be convenient to the voters. Prisoners, long-term hospital patients, merchant seamen abroad and Irish diplomats serving abroad all have the right to vote but do not have the opportunity to vote. The absence of a general postal vote was raised by a disabled person in *Draper v Attorney General* (1984) (Case 57). The Supreme Court held that the absence of postal voting was not an infringement of the Constitution. Following on from that obvious injustice the employment of a little imagination resulted in a special scheme for providing disabled voters with the opportunity to vote. A special register of disabled voters is maintained and, since the voter may not be able to attend the polling station, the polling station comes to the voter.[8]

Declaration of Election
When the President accepts the advice of the Taoiseach and dissolves Dáil Éireann (Article 13.2, see page 72), the President issues a proclamation to that effect and declares the date on which the incoming Dáil Éireann must meet, which must be not later than thirty days after the election (Article 16.3.2°), which itself must be held not later than thirty days after the dissolution (Article 16.4.2°). Thus the maximum permitted period when Dáil Éireann stands dissolved is sixty days. Under the state of emergency then in operation the *General Elections (Emergency Provisions) Act 1943* postponed the dissolution of Dáil Éireann until after the members of the

incoming Dáil had been elected. Dáil Éireann is dissolved completely: there is no provision for a partial dissolution. Under the Constitution of the United States the Houses of Congress are never fully dissolved: elections are held in rotation with each member serving a set period in office.

On the dissolution the Clerk of Dáil Éireann issues a writ to the returning officer of each constituency directing that an election be held for the full number of members of the Dáil to serve for that constituency. The returning officer is usually the sheriff, the under sheriff, or the county registrar, and that officeholder has the responsibility of conducting the election properly.

Provision can be made by law to enable the member of Dáil Éireann who is Ceann Comhairle immediately before a dissolution to be deemed without any actual election to be elected a member of Dáil Éireann at the ensuing general election (Article 16.6). The *Electoral Act 1963*, section 14, provides that where there is a dissolution and the outgoing Ceann Comhairle has not announced to Dáil Éireann before the dissolution that he or she does not desire to become a member of Dáil Éireann at the general election consequent on the dissolution, he or she shall be deemed without any actual election to be elected at such general election as a member for the constituency for which he or she was a member immediately before the dissolution or if a revision of constituencies takes effect on the dissolution the constituency declared on the revision to correspond to that constituency.

Nominations

To contest a general election the candidate must be nominated in writing. That nomination must be delivered to the returning officer before noon on the last day for receiving nominations. A person may nominate him or herself, or be nominated by a person registered as a Dáil Éireann elector in the constituency for which that individual intends to stand as a candidate. The returning officer rules on the validity of a nomination paper within one hour of its delivery in the presence of the candidate, any proposer, and one other person selected by the candidate. The nomination paper can only be declared invalid if improperly made out. Objection may be taken to the description of the candidate. The candidate must be allowed to make the appropriate alternations, or the returning officer may, where the alteration is unsatisfactory, amend it. The nomination paper must contain the name, address and description of the candidate. It may contain the name of a registered political party, if appropriate.

Deposit

The *Electoral (Amendment) Act 1992* requires a candidate in a Dáil general election to deposit £300 with the returning officer with the nomination paper. This deposit is returned provided the candidate receives a number of votes equivalent to one-quarter of the quota at the subsequent election. Failure to achieve this number of votes results in the deposit's forfeiture to the State. This statutory requirement of a deposit constitutes another restriction on the individual's right to stand for elected office. Is such a restriction permissible under the Constitution? The acceptance of the principle of a deposit may justify setting it at any level and may undoubtedly deprive many individuals of this valuable constitutional right.

The deposit of £300 is not large by present values. There are occasional calls, usually from established politicians, to increase this amount in line with inflation. Presumably the foremost justification for the requirement of a deposit is that it may discourage the bogus candidate from standing for election thus leaving the field free to genuine candidates. It is a poor excuse for the interference with a fundamental political and personal right. Whether the courts would uphold as constitutional the requirement of a deposit can only be guessed at, in the absence of authority, by analogy. In *Finnegan v An Bord Pleanála* (1979) it was argued that a compulsory £10 deposit to be lodged by a person appealing a planning decision, under the *Local Government (Planning and Development) Act 1976*, was a restriction contrary to the democratic nature of the Constitution, and a discrimination between those who had money and those who had not. The Supreme Court rejected these arguments. The requirement of a deposit was to prevent appeals without substance and the amount was not so high as to prevent genuine appeals. In addition the deposit was returnable when the appeal was heard, withdrawn or determined. According to O'Higgins CJ:

> a similar provision is made under the Electoral Acts in relation to candidates standing for Dáil and other elections.

This reasoning suggests that deposits are constitutionally permitted in Dáil Éireann elections. But there are fundamental differences between standing in a Dáil Éireann election and lodging a planning appeal. To stand for a Dáil Éireann election is the exercise of a constitutional right which cannot be withdrawn by statute, whereas the lodging of a planning appeal is merely the exercise of a legal right which could be abolished by statute. A deposit is not always returned after Dáil Éireann elections whereas in planning appeals it always is. The requirement of a deposit does not debar the bogus candidate: it merely prevents the penniless bogus candidate from indulging in whims. The bogus candidate with a fortune can indulge in elections to his or her heart's content.

Surely it should be for the electorate to decide between the bogus and the genuine and not for some administrative method, arbitrary in all events, which smacks of legal high-handedness. The bogus candidate can stand for the office of President or membership of Seanad Éireann without the requirement of a deposit. In favour of the unconstitutionality of deposits stands the decision in *de Búrca v Attorney General* (1976) (Case 49) where the Supreme Court struck down a statute which favoured persons with particular types of property over persons with no property, and persons with different types of property with regard to jury service. A cash deposit, such as the one required for Dáil Éireann elections, discriminates against persons with no property, and persons with other types of property such as land, premises, shares and personal possessions. One possible solution to this objectionable practice is to return the deposit to every candidate, a system supported by the Supreme Court in *Finnegan*'s case.

Necessity for Election

Should no more candidates stand nominated than there are vacancies in a constituency, the returning officer declares those candidates elected and returns their names to the Clerk of Dáil Éireann. Should more candidates stand nominated the election stands adjourned in order to conduct a poll. Where an outgoing Ceann Comhairle is deemed to be elected at a general election as a member of Dáil Éireann for a particular constituency the number of members actually elected at that general election for that constituency shall be one less than would otherwise be required.

Election Campaign

Because the Constitution requires an election to take place not later than thirty days after a dissolution there is by implication the notion that some type of election campaign should be conducted. This enables the candidates to canvass the electorate, and the electorate to canvass the candidates. The State, or the law, neither interferes with, nor supports, such a campaign. There is one exception. Under the *Prevention of Electoral Abuses Act 1923*, a candidate may send, free of charge through the post to each person on the register of electors, one postal communication containing electoral matter not exceeding two ounces in weight. A specimen copy of the material must be deposited in advance with the Department of Communications.[9] This statutory right came up for interpretation in *Dillon v Minister for Posts and Telegraphs* (1981) where a candidate's communication was rejected as ineligible because the sentence, 'today's politicians are dishonest because they are political and must please the largest number of people' was considered offensive. The Supreme Court ordered that this communication be accepted for free postage. Henchy J said:

> I venture to think that those who practise what is often dubbed the art of the possible would not feel grossly offended by such an expression which, denigratory and cynical though it may be thought by some, is no more that the small coinage of the currency of political controversy.

A second objection was made to the material on the ground that it contained a list of issues on which the voter was invited to propound a view in order of preference and return this to the candidate. It was argued that the inclusion of such material was not a matter relating to the election. It was held by the Supreme Court that a consultative canvass, which this was, was a matter relating to the election.

A candidate is not entitled as of right to broadcast on RTE, the state-owned and controlled broadcasting service, or on privately owned radio stations. This topic was explored in *The State (Lynch) v Cooney* (1982) (Case 191) when, during a general election campaign, an order was made by the executive prohibiting broadcasts of a certain political party on the ground that the broadcasts would be likely to incite to crime or would tend to undermine the authority of the State. Objection was made to the organisation and not to what the candidates had to say. The strange irony was that the State had to afford the same candidates the statutory free postage. While RTE and private radio stations broadcast political party messages at election time it is not under a statutory duty to do so.

The Poll

The poll at a general election must, as far as is practicable, take place on the same day throughout the country (Article 16.4.1°). The *Electoral Act 1963*, section 34, permits advanced polling on coastal islands and disabled persons may vote in advance of the general election. Each constituency is divided into polling districts and the poll is conducted by presiding officers and poll clerks appointed by the returning officer. The presiding officer keeps order at the polling station, regulates the number of electors to be admitted at one time and excludes all other persons, except the agents of the candidate, companions of infirm electors and members of the Garda Siochána on duty.

The poll is taken on the day nominated by the Minister for the Environment, and must continue for a period of not less than twelve hours between 8.30 a.m. and 10.30 p.m. At the close of the poll the presiding officer must return the ballot boxes, the unused ballot papers, the marked copies of the register of electors and the counterfoils of the ballot papers to the returning officer.

Secret Ballot

The voting at Dáil Éireann elections must be by secret ballot (Article 16.1.4°). The ballot consists of a paper which shows the names in alphabetical order, address, description and political parties, if appropriate, of the candidates. It was argued in *O'Reilly v Minister for the Environment* (1986) (Case 148) that the requirement to list the candidates in alphabetical order was unconstitutional in that it resulted in a bias in favour of those candidates whose surnames began with letters at the commencement of the alphabet. The High Court rejected this contention. Murphy J explained:

> the established propensity of the electorate in favour of candidates whose names appear towards the top of the ballot paper is not ... so much a defect in the present electoral system but rather it is a measure of some degree of indifference by the electorate or some part of it as to how their votes, and in particular their second and subsequent preference votes, are cast ... what is described as a bias in favour of the candidates whose names appear at the top of the ballot paper is not so much a defect in the system itself as a defect or a want of care or a want of interest by the electorate.

Immediately before a ballot paper is delivered to a voter it must be marked with an official embossed or perforated mark which must be visible on both sides of the paper. The name and address of the voter is called out and these details are crossed out in the register of electors to denote that that voter has applied for a ballot paper. The voter goes to a compartment in the polling station, marks the paper, folds it and places it in the appropriate ballot box. This process ensures privacy to the voter and is sufficient to fulfil the constitutional requirement of a secret ballot.

What constitutes a secret ballot was considered in *McMahon v Attorney General* (1972) (Case 107)[10] where it was asserted that by reassociating the ballot paper and the counterfoil through the identical number printed on both and then associating these with the voter through the number on the voters' register the way the voter voted could be ascertained. The State argued for the necessity of such a method in order to trace votes cast illegally: for example, the vote — if it was imperative to the outcome of the election — cast by a person convicted of personation could be traced and eliminated. This reason for the possible violation of the voter's right to secrecy did not impress the Supreme Court. Ó Dálaigh CJ explained:

> the fundamental question is: *secret to whom?* In my opinion there can be only one plain and logical answer to that question. The answer is: *secret to the voter.* It is an unshared secret. It ceases to be a secret if it is disclosed ... the Constitution therefore requires that nothing shall be done which would make it possible to violate that secrecy.

The court said that the problem of eliminating votes cast by personators could be dealt with by a limited repoll, which was already available if the votes in a polling station were destroyed. This procedure has since been altered in that the voter's number on the electoral register is no longer written on the counterfoil of the ballot paper.[11]

No voter may exercise more than one vote at an election for Dáil Éireann (Article 16.1.4°). It is an offence to apply for more than one ballot paper in such elections.[12] The *Electoral Act 1923*, section 38, provides that in legal proceedings to question an election no voter can be compelled to state how that vote was cast.

The presiding officer may, and must if so requested on behalf of a candidate, ask the voter for identification.[13]

Proportional Representation

Members of Dáil Éireann must be elected on the system of proportional representation by means of the single transferable vote (Article 16.2.5°). This is a method of voting which allows the voter to give some measure of support to all the candidates by marking the ballot paper in order of preference. The single transferable voting method had been in operation for many years, since before 1922 in fact, and was continued by the Constitution. To operate this voting system it is necessary to have multi-seat constituencies. When counting the votes a quota is fixed:[14] this is the number of first preference votes that can be obtained by as many candidates as there are seats to be filled but not more. The formula for ascertaining the quota is:

$$\frac{\text{total valid votes}}{\text{total seats} + 1} + 1 = \text{quota}$$

The logic of this formula can be seen by applying it to a hypothetical case where there are 1,000 valid votes cast for 4 seats. The quota is then:

$$\frac{1,000}{4+1} + 1 = 201$$

If four candidates each obtain 201, there can only be a total of 196 remaining for all the other candidates. Only four quotas are obtainable under this formula. Any candidate who, on the first count of the counting, has reached the quota is elected. If that candidate has obtained more first preference votes than the quota the surplus votes are redistributed among the other candidates in proportion to the respective second preferences shown on all the elected candidates' papers. These distributed votes count as first preference for the candidates benefiting from the transfer of the surplus. This may bring the total of votes cast for one, or more, of the other candidates above the quota. If so, each such candidate obtains a seat on the second count. Should no candidate exceed the quota, then the candidate with the lowest number of first preference votes is eliminated and each of these votes is credited to the candidate marked by the voter as the next preference among the remaining candidates. This process is continued until all the seats in the constituency are filled.

The electorate has a deep-seated love of the present system of proportional representation. This has been proved both in the intelligent way the voting system is used and by the fact that two separate proposals to amend the Constitution in this regard, in 1959 and 1968, were rejected, the second more heavily than the first.[15]

Term of Office

The returning officer, as soon as is possible, gives public notice of the names of the candidates elected. The total number of votes cast for each candidate, together with details of all transfers, must also be given. The returning officer, having completed the election, returns the writ to the Clerk of Dáil Éireann with the names of the successfully elected members endorsed thereon.

A newly elected member is notified by the Clerk of Dáil Éireann to attend and sign the roll of members, and at the first meeting of Dáil Éireann, the Clerk announces to the House the names and constituencies of the members returned to serve in it. Any particular Dáil Éireann must not continue in existence for a period longer than seven years, though a shorter period may be fixed by law (Article 16.5). The *Electoral Act 1963*, section 10, prescribes the maximum period of existence of five years. In times of emergency the period of a Dáil Éireann's continuance could be extended indefinitely, by virtue of legislation enacted under Article 28.3.3° of the Constitution, though it is worthy of note that during the Second World War two general elections were held.[16]

An individual elected as a member of Dáil Éireann is a member from the moment of election to the moment that Dáil Éireann is dissolved. On signing the roll the member is entitled to take a seat and to avail of all the other privileges attaching to membership. A member ceases to be a member should he or she die, resign, or be disqualified. A member may voluntarily resign from membership of Dáil Éireann by giving notice in writing to the Ceann Comhairle, which resignation takes effect from the moment it is announced to Dáil Éireann. A member may be disqualified from membership on grounds similar to those which render a person ineligible for election. The disqualification does not seem to be automatic: it must be executed by an application of the appropriate predecures.

Casual Vacancies

Casual vacancies are filled in accordance with law (Article 16.7). The *Electoral Act 1963*, section 12, provides that where a vacancy occurs the Ceann Comhairle, on the direction of Dáil Éireann, instructs the Clerk to issue a writ to the appropriate returning officer. The procedures are the same as those at a general election. The decision as to when a by-election is to be held is a matter exclusively for Dáil Éireann. There have been occasions, because it was politically inopportune to have a by-election, when vacancies were not filled, or where seats were left vacant for very long periods of time. This has the effect of reducing the voters' representation in that particular constituency. The aid of the courts might be successfully sought if a constituency was left without representation altogether. Such a situation would clearly be a denial of the voters' constitutional right to Dáil Éireann representation.

Disputed Elections

The *Parliamentary Elections Act 1868*, as amended, permits a person who has (a) voted or had the right to vote, or (b) claimed to have had the right to be returned or elected at an election, to petition the High Court, within twenty-one days, claiming that irregularities have taken place which render the election void. Two judges of the High Court constitute an election court and should they differ the election stands confirmed, though should they agree the election may be declared void. The problem is that this statute was passed in the time of the single seat constituency and any declaration that the election is void would mean, in present circumstances, another election in the constituency for all the seats. It is somewhat surprising that a statute in this regard, passed in the middle of the last century when constitutional and political matters were so different, should continue to govern such an important topic.

Chapter 7
SEANAD ÉIREANN

Nature of Second Chamber
Article 15.1 of the Constitution provides that the Oireachtas shall consist of the President and two Houses: a House of Representatives to be called Dáil Éireann and a Senate to be called Seanad Éireann. Apart from distinguishing the House of Representatives from the Senate, and setting out the powers of each, the Constitution gives no assistance in explaining the essential difference in character, if any, between the two Houses.

There are obvious, and easily explainable differences. Dáil Éireann is elected directly by popular franchise: Seanad Éireann is not. Any citizen over the age of 21 years may stand for election to Dáil Éireann: membership of Seanad Éireann is restricted. This absence of popular involvement has led the Constitution to limit both the number of members and the powers of Seanad Éireann. The extent of these limitations was discussed in Chapter 4. When comparing the roles of each House it must be noted that the role of Dáil Éireann is paramount while Seanad Éireann plays a secondary role.

Number of Members
Seanad Éireann is composed of the static number of sixty members (Article 18.1). This number bears no relationship to the shifts in population, and an alteration in this fixed number would require a constitutional amendment.

Eligibility for Membership
The Constitution declares that to be eligible for membership of Seanad Éireann a person must be eligible for membership of Dáil Éireann (Article 18.2), that is be a citizen and over the age of 21 years. A deposit is not required and there is no provision in law for having a candidate's political party included on the ballot paper.

Acquiring Membership
Membership of Seanad Éireann can be acquired in three ways. A person can be nominated a member by the Taoiseach; secondly, a person can be elected

by citizen graduates of the universities; and thirdly, a person can be elected from panels.

In general, the public are excluded from this process and may be unaware that a Seanad election is in progress. It is not in keeping with the concepts of democracy that public officeholders should be appointed or elected to office by elite groups. The basis on which Seanad Éireann's electorate is composed is arbitrary and unrepresentative. Even the wider scheme permitted in Article 19 which empowers direct election by functional groups and associations has never been tried.

Membership by Nomination

The Constitution confers on the Taoiseach, appointed after the reassembly of Dáil Éireann following a dissolution, the absolute discretion to nominate eleven persons to be members of the incoming Seanad Éireann (Article 18.3). These members hold office during the continuance of Seanad Éireann, despite the vacation of office by the Taoiseach who appointed them. Casual vacancies in the number of nominated members are filled by the Taoiseach (Article 18.10.2°). A nominated member's membership could be challenged on the ground of disqualification.

Election by University Graduates

Six members are elected by two named universities: three are elected by Trinity College and three are elected by the National University of Ireland (Article 18.4). This granting of an additional franchise to university graduates supports the rather dubious theory that university graduates have some particular insight into the selection of the ideal public representative. There might be some credence in that proposition if there did not exist an unanswerable discrimination against graduates of other third-level educational institutions. One example illustrates the incongruity of this scheme. A law graduate from a university, who is not entitled *per se* to practise law, has a vote, whereas a member of either of the professional law bodies, who may practise law without a university degree, has no vote. In 1979 the *Seventh Amendment to the Constitution (Election of Members of Seanad Éireann by Institutions of Higher Education) Act* was enacted by the People.[1] This permits a redistribution by law of these six seats among the existing universities and other institutions of higher education though to date no legislation has been passed.

The *Seanad Electoral (University Members) Act 1937* establishes the franchise and the method of election. Every citizen who has attained 18 years and has received a degree, other than an honorary degree, is entitled to vote. The governing body of each university must keep a register of electors which contains the name and address at which the voter is ordinarily resident and may contain another address to which the ballot paper should be sent. An appeal from the refusal to register a voter can be made to the Circuit Court. Graduates of these universities who are not citizens cannot vote.

The Minister for the Environment appoints the last day for receiving nominations, the day for the issue of the ballot papers and the day and time of the poll. The returning officers are the Provost of Trinity College for the Trinity College constituency and the Vice-Chancellor of the National University of Ireland for the National University constituency. It is the duty of the returning officers to hold the election, count the votes and ascertain the result.

Each candidate must be nominated in writing by two registered voters, as proposer and seconder, and eight other registered voters who assent to the nomination. A candidate need not be a graduate of that, or indeed of any, university. A voter may subscribe to as many nomination papers as there are vacancies. The returning officer rules on the nomination papers which must contain the name, address and description of the candidate. Should no more candidates stand nominated than there are vacancies, the returning officer declares those candidates elected and returns their names to the Clerk of Seanad Éireann. Where there are more candidates than vacancies the returning officer adjourns the election in order to take a poll.

On the date appointed for the issue of the ballot papers the returning officer sends by post to each voter a ballot paper with a form of declaration of identity. The voter marks the ballot and completes the declaration of identity and returns both by post. The Constitution declares that the poll must be by secret postal ballot (Article 18.5).

The members must be elected on the system of proportional representation by means of the single transferable vote (Article 18.5, see page 88). When the returning officer ascertains the result, a declaration to that effect is made and notice of the result is sent to the Clerk of Dáil Éireann and the Clerk of Seanad Éireann in a certificate setting out details of the votes cast and the transfers.

Whenever the Clerk of Seanad Éireann by direction of Seanad Éireann informs the Minister for the Environment that a vacancy has occurred in the membership of a university constituency the Minister must, not later than six months thereafter, direct a by-election to be held. A member for a university constituency may resign by notice in writing to the Chairman of Seanad Éireann. The resignation is effective when an announcement is made to Seanad Éireann. No current member of Seanad Éireann can be a candidate at a Seanad by-election: that member must resign in advance of lodging nomination papers.

Election to the Panels
Before a general election for panel members is held, five panels of candidates must be formed in accordance with law (Article 18.7). The panels demonstrate

the idea of drawing representation from functional or vocational groups. Thus forty-three seats in Seanad Éireann are filled with persons having knowledge and practical experience of various professions, trades or callings. These five panels, enumerated in Article 18.7, require further regulation by law which is contained in the *Seanad Electoral (Panel Members) Acts 1947* and *1954*. The guidelines in Article 18.7.2° provide that not more than eleven and not less than five members are to be elected from any one panel. Section 52 of the 1947 Act sets the number of members to be elected for each panel. The matter is further complicated by the panels being divided into two sections with members being elected from two sub-panels which are considered later. The panels and the numbers to be elected from each are as follows:

1. Five members from the Cultural and Education panel which includes persons having knowledge and practical experience of the interests and services of the national language and culture, literature, art, education, law and medicine including surgery, dentistry, veterinary medicine and pharmaceutical chemistry. Two members at least to be elected from each sub-panel.
2. Eleven members from the Agricultural panel which includes persons having knowledge and practical experience of the interests and services of agriculture and allied interests and fisheries. Four members at least to be elected from each sub-panel.
3. Eleven members from the Labour panel which includes persons having knowledge and practical experience of the interests and services of labour, either organised or unorganised. Four members at least to be elected from each sub-panel.
4. Nine members from the Industrial and Commercial panel which includes persons having knowledge and practical experience of the interests and services of industry and commerce, banking, finance, accountancy, engineering and architecture. Three members at least to be elected from each sub-panel.
5. Seven members from the Administrative panel which includes persons having knowledge and practical experience of the interests and services of public administration, social services and voluntary activities. Three members at least to be elected from each sub-panel.

Each of these five panels is divided into two sub-panels with different nominating procedures for each sub-panel.

To be eligible for nomination a candidate must, apart from the constitutional and legal requirements, satisfy the returning officer that the candidate has knowledge and practical experience to be on the panel to which election is sought. In *Ormonde v MacGabhann* (1969) the High Court ruled that a candidate must have a reasonable amount of knowledge of the problems which arise in our society between employee and employer and that if the candidate had a reasonable amount of practical experience with those problems it was sufficient to qualify the candidate for the Labour panel.

There are two methods of nomination: the first is by a nominating body. All candidates nominated by nominating bodies form one sub-panel. The second method is on the nomination of members of the Oireachtas and all candidates thus nominated form another panel known as the Oireachtas sub-panel.

Nominating Bodies

A register of bodies known as nominating bodies, entitled to nominate persons as candidates to the panels, must be established and maintained. To qualify for registration the body must have objects which relate to the interests and services mentioned in Article 18.7 of the Constitution, or represent persons who have knowledge and practical experience of such interests and services. Certain types of organisation are excluded from registration: any body formed to carry on trade or business for profit is excluded, as are bodies composed of persons in the employment of the State, or a local authority, whose objects include the advancement or protection of employment. Two bodies must be included in the register: the Irish County Councils General Council and the Association of Municipal Authorities of Ireland. An application to be registered must be made in writing to the Clerk of Seanad Éireann and an appeal is provided should the application be refused. The register must be revised annually. The bodies in the existing register include professional, academic and charitable bodies, together with bodies representing commercial groups and bodies representing trade unions.[2]

Within ten days of the dissolution of Dáil Éireann, the Clerk of Seanad Éireann, the Seanad returning officer, sends by post to every registered nominating body a nomination paper and a notice informing it of the number of candidates it may nominate. This number fluctuates depending on the number of nominating bodies then registered. The nomination paper must contain the name and qualifications of the candidate and must be sealed, should the nominating body be a corporate body, or signed by the proper persons, should the body be unincorporated.

Oireachtas Nomination

A nomination by members of the Oireachtas must be in writing, contain the name and qualifications of the candidate and be signed by not less than four members of the Oireachtas. An Oireachtas member can join in the nomination of only one candidate and members of the outgoing Seanad may nominate persons.

Nomination Procedures to Panels

The Seanad returning officer rules on the nomination papers, and issues of dispute are decided by a judicial assessor, a judge of the High Court. The returning officer then prepares the panels of candidates. Each panel is divided into the sub-panels: one list contains the names nominated by the members of the Oireachtas, and the other the names nominated by the nominating bodies.

General Election for Panel Membership

A general election for Seanad Éireann must take place not later than ninety days after a dissolution of Dáil Éireann (Article 18.8). Since a general election for Dáil Éireann must take place within thirty days of a dissolution, Seanad Éireann may continue in office for a further sixty days.

Electorate for the Panels

The electorate consists, according to the *Seanad Electoral (Panel Members) Act 1947*, section 44, of the members of the incoming Dáil Éireann, members of the outgoing Seanad Éireann and members of every county council and borough corporation. The Clerk of Dáil Éireann, within three days of receiving the returns to the writs for a Dáil election, sends to the Seanad returning officer a list of the names and addresses of the members of Dáil Éireann entitled to be members of the Seanad electorate.

The secretary of a county council, or the town clerk of a county borough, must, within fifteen days of a dissolution of Dáil Éireann, send to the Seanad returning officer a list of the names and addresses of the council members. Should a person qualify because of Dáil or Seanad membership and council membership that voter can only be entered once in the register of voters.

The Seanad returning officer sends by post to each person on the Seanad electorate register for information a copy of the five panels. Later, a ballot paper for each of the five panels is sent by registered post to each voter. There is another unique privilege granted to Seanad Éireann voters: a voter may, in certain circumstances, obtain duplicate ballot papers. The election is held on the system of proportional representation by means of the single transferable vote (Article 18.5, see page 88). The returning officer ascertains separately the results in respect of each panel and makes a declaration of the election result.

Where a casual vacancy occurs in the membership of the panels, the Clerk of Seanad Éireann informs the Minister for the Environment in writing of the vacancy and a by-election takes place. Where a person is elected to a university constituency and also to a panel, an unlikely event, that person must, before taking the seat, deliver to the Clerk of the Seanad in writing, a declaration as to whether that member sits as a university member or a panel member. Such a member, neglecting to make this choice within a month after the first sitting of Seanad Éireann, is deemed to sit as a university member and to have resigned the panel seat.

Term of Office of Seanad Éireann

When the President dissolves Dáil Éireann the Seanad is not then dissolved. Seanad Éireann continues in existence until the day before the polling day of the general election for a new Seanad Éireann. While Dáil Éireann stands dissolved, Seanad Éireann exists. Constitutionally it seems that an incoming Dáil Éireann and the outgoing Seanad Éireann could constitute the Houses of the Oireachtas. The first meeting of Seanad Éireann, after a Seanad general election, takes place on a date fixed by the President on the advice of the Taoiseach (Article 18.8).

Direct Election to Seanad Éireann

Provision may be made by law, according to Article 19, for the direct election by any functional or vocational group or association or council of so many members of Seanad Éireann as may be fixed by such law in substitution for an equal number of the members to be elected from the corresponding panels of candidates. There thus exists in the Constitution a method whereby a wider representation in Seanad Éireann is possible. Unfortunately no such law has been enacted.

Chapter 8

THE GOVERNMENT

Nature of Executive Power

The Oireachtas is the lawmaker and not the administrator or executive. The executive is that branch of government which is charged with carrying the laws into effect. According to Article 28.2 of the Constitution the executive power of the State is vested in, and exercised by, the Government. The constitutional powers of the Government are few though far reaching.

The executive or administrative function is the general and detailed carrying out of government according to the Constitution and the law. It includes the framing of policy and the choice and manner in which the law may be enacted to render the policy possible. Today, it involves the provision and administration of a vast system of social services such as public health, housing, social welfare and education. The supervision of defence and internal order, a function which spreads from the provision of legal aid to the building and maintenance of prisons, is within this executive domain. The State also plays a part in industry by creating and controlling semi-state companies and by assisting the private sector. The financing of government has become a complex and intricate art within the province of the executive. The executive is responsible for the international relations of the State. Many of the functions of the executive are outside the ambit of constitutional law though the last two, financial matters and international relations, are considered later.

The Government and the Constitutional Framework

The Government is one of the three institutions of government. While it is invested with constitutional powers it is not, like the other two organs of government, possessed of unlimited powers. The Government cannot act *ultra vires* the Constitution. Nor can the Government act *ultra vires* the laws though this topic is more appropriately covered under administrative law.

The Government must exercise its powers within the constitutional doctrine of the separation of powers (see page 28). As can be seen there are a number of cases which indicate that the Government will not be permitted to act in breach of the Constitution. A classic example is that of *Crotty v An Taoiseach*

(1987) (Case 43) where the courts injuncted the government from acting unconstitutionally. The government must only act within its own powers and can neither legislate, the role of the Oireachtas, nor adjudicate, the role of the courts. Equally the courts will not stray into the executive domain and will not permit the Oireachtas to exercise executive powers.

Responsibility to Dáil Éireann

The scheme of the Constitution is that Dáil Éireann, because it is directly elected by popular franchise, has the greater prerogative powers. The Government must, with two exceptions, be drawn from Dáil Éireann, and since Dáil Éireann nominates the Taoiseach and approves the other members of the Government, this control of the Government by Dáil Éireann is completed by Article 28.4.1 declaring that the Government is responsible to Dáil Éireann.

The Taoiseach, and the Government, must resign when the Taoiseach ceases to retain the support of the majority of Dáil Éireann (Article 28.10). The Government is not responsible to Seanad Éireann, and votes of no confidence, or the withdrawal of majority support by that House, cannot force the resignation of the Taoiseach.

This constitutional requirement that the Government is responsible to Dáil Éireann is the method by which the legislative organ of Government checks the executive under the doctrine of the separation of powers. While the political reality and the legal theory may not always coincide, the Taoiseach and Government have on occasions been forced to resign following a vote of no confidence passed by a majority of the members of Dáil Éireann. This control is very real indeed. Having regard to the provisions of Article 28.10 of the Constitution, the members of Dáil Éireann have the ultimate sanction and control over the Government. When the majority of its membership ceases to support the decisions and policies of the Government they may cause a new Taoiseach to be nominated for appointment by the President or, alternatively, to cause the dissolution of Dáil Éireann and the declaration of a general election.

The accord that exists between Dáil Éireann and the Government is that, once appointed, the Government is taxed with the responsibility of making decisions in the administration of the State. In respect of those decisions it is responsible to Dáil Éireann. If a majority of Dáil Éireann resolves that it does not agree with the Government then a motion of no confidence may be passed on the Government. But Dáil Éireann cannot possibly be concerned with the process of dialogue by which the Government evolves its policies or reaches its decisions. That would involve the legislature invading the sphere of the executive which is not permissible under the doctrine of the separation of powers.

Under the Constitution there is no provision for the Oireachtas to exercise any of the functions of the Government or for the Government to exercise any functions of the Oireachtas. It is not constitutionally permissible for the

Oireachtas to direct the Government as to the manner in which it conducts its business. The Government is collectively responsible to Dáil Éireann for all the decisions it takes or fails to take, but it is not responsible to Dáil Éireann as to the manner by which such decisions are arrived at.

Composition of the Government

The Taoiseach, the head of the Government, is appointed by the President on the nomination of Dáil Éireann (Article 13.1.1°). The other members of the Government, not less than seven and not more than fifteen, are appointed by the President on the nomination of the Taoiseach with the prior approval of Dáil Éireann (Article 13.1.2°). Members of the Government must be members of either House of the Oireachtas, though the Taoiseach, the Tánaiste and the Minister for Finance must be members of Dáil Éireann. A maximum of two senators may be members of the Government (Article 28.7).

The Tánaiste, a member of the Government nominated by the Taoiseach, acts in place of the Taoiseach if the latter should die, become permanently incapacitated, or be temporarily absent (Article 28.6). It may be constitutionally improper for both the Taoiseach and Tánaiste to be absent from the State at the same time.

The Taoiseach continues in office from the moment of appointment until he or she dies, resigns, or advises the President to dissolve Dáil Éireann. A Taoiseach must resign on ceasing to retain the support of the majority of the Dáil (Article 28.10). In any event the Taoiseach continues in office, as do other members of the Government, until their successors are appointed (Article 28.11). This rule applies to a member of the Government who loses his or her seat in Dáil Éireann in the general election.

There is no formal procedure for deciding upon the permanent incapacity of the Taoiseach, unlike the role given to the Supreme Court in deciding this question in relation to the President. Presumably, the Tánaiste would announce that fact to the Dáil, and the appointment by the President, on the approval of Dáil Éireann, of a successor would be sufficient to remove the incapacitated Taoiseach from office.

Other members of the Government may resign by placing their resignations in the hands of the Taoiseach for submission to the President. The Taoiseach may dismiss a Government member at any time for reasons which seem sufficient and should that member fail to resign, his or her appointment is terminated by the President on the Taoiseach's advice (Article 28.9). Dáil Éireann cannot remove a member of the Government from office: this can be done only by the Taoiseach.

The Government may, on the nomination of the Taoiseach, by virtue of the *Ministers and Secretaries (Amendment) (No. 2) Act 1977*, appoint not more than ten persons, who are members of either House of the Oireachtas, to be Ministers of State at designated departments of State.

Collective Responsibility

The Constitution is silent as to who summons meetings of the Government and how regular these meetings must be. Presumably this is the responsibility of the Taoiseach and, in his or her absence, the Tánaiste. The only constitutional direction given to the Government is that it meets and acts as a collective authority (Article 28.4.2°). The individual members must act in co-operation in reaching and implementing policy. The Government must appear unified though the various decisions are supported by majority and not unanimously. Each member of the Government must accept responsibility for all, and all must accept the responsibility for each individual member. The Government is collectively responsible for the departments of State. While an individual Minister may be the head of a particular department, all members of the Government are responsible for all departments of State. There is one constitutional exception to collective responsibility: the Taoiseach alone advises the President to dissolve Dáil Éireann (Article 13.2).

Despite the absence of an express provision contained in Article 28 the Supreme Court ruled in *Attorney General v Tribunal of Inquiry into the Beef Industry* (1992) (Case 14) that discussions at Government meetings were confidential. The court held that it was clear from the very nature of collective responsibility of the Government that discussions among its members at their formal meetings must be confidential, otherwise its decisions were liable to be fatally weakened by disclosure of dissenting views. There was sufficient precedent for the resignation of members of the Government who dissented and could not accept collective responsibility, but none for unauthorised disclosure of the discussions which led to the situation. The obligation to accept collective responsibility for decisions and presumably acts of Government involved as a necessity the non-disclosure of different or dissenting views held by members of the Government to the making of decisions.

A legal challenge to the Government must name all the members of Government. For example, in *Boland v An Taoiseach* (1974) (Case 23) it was necessary to cite all members of the Government as defendants* when a challenge was made to executive policy on the ground that it was unconstitutional. It was insufficient to sue the Taoiseach as representing the Government: success against the Taoiseach might not have bound the other Government members.

Financial Affairs of the State

One of the executive duties of the Government is to manage the financial affairs of the State. The Government must prepare Estimates of the Receipts and Estimates of the Expenditure of the State for each financial year and present them to Dáil Éireann for consideration (Article 28.4.3°). Dáil Éireann can only consider these estimates and cannot necessarily vote on them. Dáil Éireann and each member must be given adequate time to consider the estimates.

The Constitution declares that all State revenues from whatever source arising must, subject to such exceptions as may be provided by law, form one fund (Article 11). This is known as the Central Fund and Dáil Éireann must not pass any vote or resolution, and no law can be enacted, for the appropriation of revenue or other public monies unless the purpose of the appropriation has been recommended to Dáil Éireann by a message from the Government signed by the Taoiseach (Article 17.2).

When the estimates have been debated and agreed to, a Bill is introduced to appropriate, from the Central Fund, the total sum mentioned in the schedule to the Bill. Because the Appropriation Bill it is a Money Bill, Seanad Éireann has only twenty-one days to consider it (Article 21), and the President cannot refer it to the Supreme Court under Article 26 of the Constitution though it may be challenged as to its constitutionality after its enactment. For example, the *Finance Act 1983*, which was a Money Bill, was unsuccessfully challenged in *Madigan v Attorney General* (1986) (Case 110).

Where there is a delay in preparing, debating or enacting the Appropriation Bill into law, there is provision in the *Central Fund (Permanent Provisions) Act 1965* to authorise the Minister for Finance to issue from the Central Fund an amount not exceeding four-fifths of the amount appropriated for each particular service during the preceding financial year.

There is no constitutional requirement for an annual budget but the practice has been to have at least one, or more. The annual statement of the Minister for Finance outlines proposals for new taxation and indicates the proposed changes to the existing tax structure. Some of these proposals are reduced into financial resolutions because some taxation measures come into effect on budget day. These resolutions contain declarations that it is expedient that they should have statutory effect under the *Provisional Collection of Taxes Act 1927*, normally for a period not exceeding four months. The Finance Bill for that year, based on those financial resolutions, is introduced as soon as possible. Such a statute gives legislative effect to the budget.

There are three paramount features in the management of State finances. The executive initiates action, the legislature supervises these actions, and finally there is inspection and audit by an independent official. We have considered the first two stages in the procedure; now we examine the third.

The Constitution creates the office of the Comptroller and Auditor General (Article 33). Appointed by the President on the nomination of Dáil Éireann, the holder of that office cannot be a member of the Oireachtas, and cannot hold another position of emolument. Removal from office, for stated misbehaviour, requires a resolution of both Houses of the Oireachtas. The President, on receipt of copies of such resolutions from the Taoiseach, removes the Comptroller and Auditor General from office. Additional terms and conditions of the office shall be determined by law. In this regard the main statute, the *Exchequer and Audit Departments Act 1866*, has been amended and extended on a number of occasions by other statutes.[1]

As the title implies, the Comptroller and Auditor General has two tasks. As comptroller he or she sees that no money leaves the Central Fund without statutory authority and that such money is properly applied. As auditor he or she audits the accounts of income. A report is made annually to Dáil Éireann. Questions may be raised on matters on which there are doubts. The Comptroller and Auditor General has never resorted to law because such a procedure seems inappropriate: his or her function is discharged when irregularities are raised, thus leaving it open to Dáil Éireann to take appropriate action if it chooses.

Financial legislation may, like other categories of legislation, come before the courts for scrutiny on constitutional grounds. According to O'Higgins CJ in *Madigan v Attorney General* (1986) (Case 110):

> on such examination as to constitutionality of a taxation law the court does not enter into the area of taxation policy, nor concern itself with the effectiveness of the choices made by the Government and the Oireachtas; all such matters relating to the object and range of taxation are matters of national policy which cannot, as such, be considered by the courts. The courts' concern relates solely to the question whether what has been done affects, adversely, constitutional rights, obligations or guarantees.

In appropriate cases, such as *Murphy v Attorney General* (1982) (Case 123), the courts have struck down taxation legislation as unconstitutional.

International Affairs of the State

The Preamble to the Constitution directs that concord be established with other nations. One criterion of statehood is the capacity to enter into relations with other states. Ireland affirms its devotion to the ideal of peace and friendly co-operation amongst nations founded on international justice and morality (Article 29.1) and declares its adherence to the pacific settlement of international disputes by international arbitration or judicial determination (Article 29.2).

The executive power of the State with regard to external relations is exercised by or on behalf of the Government (Article 29.4.1°). It was decided in *Crotty v An Taoiseach* (1987) (Case 43) that the exercise of this power was subject to judicial review. The Supreme Court ruled that the State's right to conduct its external relations was part of what was described as inalienable and indefeasible in Article 5 which declares that the State is sovereign, independent and democratic. Any attempt by the government to make a binding commitment to alienate in whole or in part to other states the conduct of foreign relations was inconsistent with the Government's duty to conduct those relations in accordance with the Constitution. The ultimate source and limits of the Government's powers in the conduct of foreign relations were to be found in Article 6 of the Constitution. The common good of the Irish people was the ultimate standard by which the constitutional validity of the conduct of foreign affairs by the Government was to be judged. The ratification of the Single European Act, a Treaty, would result in each member state of the EC surrendering part of its sovereignty in the conduct of its foreign relations. The freedom of action of each state was to be curtailed in the interests of the common good of the member states as a whole. To be bound by a solemn international treaty to act thus was inconsistent with the obligation of the government to conduct its foreign policy relations according to the common good of the Irish people. This Treaty amounted to a diminution of Ireland's sovereignty which was declared in unqualified terms in the Constitution. According to Walsh J:

> in enacting the Constitution the People conferred full freedom of action upon the Government to decide matters of foreign policy and to act as it thinks fit on any particular issue or issues so far as policy is concerned and as, in the opinion of the Government, the occasion requires. In my view, this freedom does not carry with it the power to abdicate that freedom or to enter into binding agreements with other States to exercise that power in a particular way or to refrain from exercising it save by particular procedures, and so to bind the State in its freedom of action in its foreign policy. The freedom to formulate foreign policy is just as much a mark of sovereignty as the freedom to form economic policy and the freedom to legislate. The latter two have now been curtailed by the consent of the People to the amendment of the Constitution which is contained in Article 29.4.3° of the Constitution. If it is now desired to qualify, curtail or inhibit the existing sovereign power to formulate and pursue such foreign policies as from time to time to the Government may seem proper, it is not within the power of the Government itself to do so. The foreign policy organ of the State cannot, within the terms of the Constitution, agree to impose upon itself, the State or upon the People the contemplated restrictions upon freedom of action. To acquire the power to do so would, in my opinion, require a recourse to the People 'whose right it is' in the words of Article 6, '. . . in final appeal, to decide all questions of national policy, according to the requirements of the common good'. In the last analysis it is the People themselves who are the guardians of the Constitution.

The ink was hardly dry on the Supreme Court judgments when a proposal to amend the Constitution was passed by the Houses of the Oireachtas. The *Tenth Amendment of the Constitution Bill 1987* proposed that the following sentence be inserted into Article 29.4.3° of the Constitution: 'The State may ratify the Single European Act (signed on behalf of the member states of the Communities at Luxemburg on 17 February 1986 and at The Hague on the 28 February 1986).' This proposal was accepted by the People.[2]

The Supreme Court, in *McGimpsey v Ireland* (1990) (Case 102), held that the terms of the Anglo-Irish Agreement of 1985 did not fetter the power of the Government to conduct the external relations of the State because the Government when carrying out the functions which had been agreed under the agreement was entirely free to do so in the manner in which it, and it alone, thought most conducive to the achievement of the aims which it was committed to. By contrast the basis of the decision in *Crotty v An Taoiseach* (1987) (Case 43) was that the terms of the Single European Act could oblige the Government in carrying out the foreign policy of the State to make the national interests of the State, to a greater or lesser extent, subservient to the national interests of other states.

The State may not be bound by any international agreement involving a charge on public funds unless the terms of the agreement have been approved by Dáil Éireann (Article 29.5.2). In 1983 a treaty of extradition between Ireland and the United States of America was signed. It was laid before both Houses of the Oireachtas but was never ratified by Dáil Éireann. It was argued in *The State (Gilliland) v Governor of Mountjoy Prison* (1987) (Case 188) that the Treaty was invalid in that, since it involved a charge on public funds, it had not been approved by Dáil Éireann. The Supreme Court upheld that claim.[3]

No international agreement may become part of the domestic law of the State save as may be determined by the Oireachtas (Article 29.6). Legislation has enacted many international agreements into domestic law.[4] Can an individual avail of the provisions of an international agreement to which the State is a party but which has not been enacted into domestic law? This question arose in *In re Ó Láighléis* (1960) (Case 144) where a person interned without trial could not challenge the constitutionality of internment because this process had been declared constitutional by the former Supreme Court in *Article 26 and the Offences Against the State (Amendment) Bill 1940* (Case 10, see page 204) with the consequence that its constitutionality could never be challenged again (see page 50). Instead it was argued that internment offended the European Convention on Human Rights, which Ireland adopted in Rome on 4 November 1950 and which came into force on 3 September 1953. The failure of the Oireachtas to enact the Convention into domestic law was fatal. According to Davitt P in the High Court:

where there is an irreconcilable conflict between a domestic statute and the principles of international law or the provisions of an international agreement, the courts administering the domestic law must give effect to the statute. If this principle were not to be observed it would follow that the executive government by means of an international agreement might . . . be able to exercise powers of legislation contrary to the letter and spirit of the Constitution. The right of citizens of this State to be bound by no other laws than those enacted by their elected representatives in the Oireachtas assembled is one to be carefully preserved and jealously guarded.

A similar result occurred in *Hutchinson v Minister for Justice* (1993) where the Convention on the Transfer of Sentenced Persons was signed by the State but was not ratified by the enactment of an Act of the Oireachtas.

Where the State declares that it will act in a particular manner as a consequence of the State's signing of an international agreement a person may be able to assert that there was a reasonable expectation that the matter would be decided in that manner. For example, the State is a party to the United Nations Convention on the Status of Refugees 1957 and a Protocol on the Status of Refugees 1967. In furtherance of the obligations imposed by these international agreements the State agreed procedures with the United Nations High Commissioner for Refugees for dealing with persons claiming refugee status in this State. A person claiming such status, in *Fakih v Minister for Justice* (1992), secured an order of mandamus from the High Court to compel the consideration of his application in accordance with the agreed procedures despite the fact that these procedures did not have the force of law in the State.

According to Article 29.3 of the Constitution Ireland accepts the generally recognised principles of international law as its rule of conduct in its relations with other states. In the Supreme Court, in the *Government of Canada v Employment Appeals Tribunal* (1992), O'Flaherty J explained:

the 'generally recognised principles' of international law change from time to time, as the debate and research in this case has demonstrated. The Oireachtas is, of course, entitled to enact any legislation it pleases in accordance with the article but the courts, also, must make the appropriate declaration when called upon from time to time.

The Supreme Court accepted the proposition, in *Bourke v Attorney General* (1972), that extradition was not possible in international law for political offences or offences connected with political offences, a view endorsed by the Irish members of the Law Enforcement Commission[5] (for political offences see page 213). The same court accepted, in *Government of Canada v Employment Appeals Tribunal* (1992), that the doctrine of sovereign immunity, which holds that sovereign states and their rulers are immune from action in the courts of this State, is one of the generally recognised principles of international law though there now exists a much more restrictive rule of sovereign immunity than in former times. An action by a former employee of the Canadian Embassy for unfair dismissal was dismissed on the ground of sovereign immunity.

The High Court ruled, in *Hutchinson v Minister for Justice* (1992), that it was not a principle of international law that the State had an obligation to ratify an international convention which was signed on behalf of the State. In that case it was argued unsuccessfully that the principle of good faith required the State to submit a Treaty to the appropriate procedures for ratification and to refrain from doing anything which was inconsistent with its obligations under the Treaty. Ireland, it was argued, having signed the Convention on the Transfer of Sentenced Persons had a duty to ratify it and the Minister for Justice had an obligation to introduce legislation to have it ratified by the Oireachtas.

Can legislation be enacted which conflicts with an international agreement which has been ratified by the State? This point was touched on in *Murphy v Asahi Synthetic Fibres* (1986), a revenue case, where O'Hanlon J in the High Court supposed:

> it can ... be contended that Article 29 of the Constitution ... would preclude the Oireachtas from enacting legislation which ran counter to an international agreement to which the State was a party.

Executive Privilege
At common law there was a principle that the executive organ of government could, by its own judgment, withhold relevant evidence from the courts in the determination of the rights of litigants. A claim to executive privilege was made on two grounds: first, that production of the material would be contrary to public policy and detrimental to the public interest and service; and secondly, that in any event the document was within a class of documents which on grounds of public interest ought to be withheld from production and disclosure. The theory on which this principle was based was that the executive was answerable to parliament rather than to the courts. Two crucial interests clashed in such circumstances: one interest required that justice be done and the other required that certain evidence be suppressed. How did this principle of executive privilege survive the enactment of the Constitution?

The issue did not arise, in a constitutional context, until *Murphy v Dublin Corporation* (1972) (Case 124). In that case the Supreme Court, per Walsh J, explained the position thus:

> under the Constitution the administration of justice is committed solely to the judiciary in the exercise of their powers in the courts set up under the

Constitution. Power to compel the attendance of witnesses and the production of evidence is an inherent part of the judicial power of government of the State and is the ultimate safeguard of justice in the State . . . If the conflict arises during the exercise of the judicial power then . . . it is the judicial power which will decide which public interest shall prevail. This does not mean that the court will always decide that the interest of the litigant shall prevail. It is for the court to decide which is the superior interest in the circumstances of the particular case and to determine the matter accordingly. It is, however, impossible for the judicial power in the proper exercise of its functions to permit any other body or power to decide for it whether or not a document will be disclosed or produced. In the last resort the decision lies with the courts so long as they have seisin of the case.

The Supreme Court accepted that where the vital interests of the State might be adversely affected by disclosure or production, greater harm might be caused by ordering the production of the documents rather than by a refusal. In such a case the court would refuse the order on its own decision. The onus of proof in such instances was on the party claiming the privilege. The Supreme Court, in *Ambiorix Ltd v Minister for the Environment* (1991) (see next page), refused to depart from the reasoning and the decision in *Murphy*'s case because to do so would be, according to McCarthy J, 'to lessen or impair judicial sovereignty in the administration of justice'.

Thus it is for the judicial power to choose the evidence on which it might act in any individual case in order to reach a decision. The executive cannot prevent the judicial power from examining documents which are relevant to an issue in a civil trial for the purpose of deciding whether they must be produced. There is no obligation on the judicial power to examine any particular document before deciding that it is exempt from production, and it can and will in many instances uphold a claim of privilege in respect of a document merely on the basis of a description of its nature and contents which the judicial power accepts. There cannot be a generally applicable class or category of documents exempted from production by reason of the rank in the public service of the person creating them, or of the position of the individual or body intending to use them.

The principle laid down in *Murphy*'s case has been applied in a number of subsequent cases. The Supreme Court, in *Geraghty v Minister for Local Government* (1975), held that it was the duty of the trial court to examine each of the disputed documents and that the party resisting their production must justify the objection in respect of each individual document and not in respect of the class of document to which each document was alleged to belong. But the court decided that communications for the purpose of obtaining, or giving, legal advice between the Minister and officials on the one hand and legal advisers, even legal advisers who were permanent civil servants, on the other hand were privileged.

The High Court emphasised, in *Folens & Co. Ltd v Minister for Education* (1981), that not all communications which arose in the course of the administration of the public service were confidential. In *Hunt v County Roscommon VEC* (1981) the High Court pointed out, applying the decided cases, that unless a prima-facie case could be made that the documents were privileged the court could not inspect the documents to ascertain whether they should be produced. In the *Incorporated Law Society v Minister for Justice* (1987) the High Court ordered memoranda passing between Ministers to be produced.

In *Ambiorix Ltd v Minister for the Environment* (1991) a claim was made that a class or category of documents consisting of documents emanating at the level of not below assistant secretary in the public service and being documents for the ultimate consideration of Ministers of the Government or of the Government itself, relating to the formulation of policy or proposals for legislation, were absolutely exempt from production and should not be examined by a judge before privilege was granted to them unless the judge was dissatisfied with the accuracy of the description of the document. The Supreme Court rejected this claim and ruled that there could not be a generally applicable class or category of documents exempted from production by reason of the rank in the public service of the person creating them or of the position of the individual or body intending to use them.

On the criminal side, the issue arose in the *Director of Public Prosecutions v Holly* (1984) whether a Garda could claim privilege in respect of an original report made in respect of an incident, at the trial of a person charged in relation to that incident. The High Court held that, since the State had not advanced specific grounds of possible damage to the public interest which might have resulted from such disclosure the claim to privilege should be rejected. Had such grounds been advanced it would have been necessary for the trial judge to have read the document privately to determine its admissibility in accordance with the principles laid down in *Murphy*'s case.

The balance to be struck between the administration of justice and the public interest in the prevention and prosecution of crime came up for decision in *Breathnach v Ireland* (1991) where in civil proceedings for malicious prosecution discovery of various documents, mainly statements made by Gardaí in the possession of the Director of Public Prosecutions which had come into existence in the investigation of a crime, were sought by a party who had been charged, convicted but later had the conviction quashed on appeal. While the case law showed that the desirability of preserving confidentiality in the case of communications between members of the executive had been significantly eroded it was accepted that different considerations might apply to communications between the Gardaí and the Director of Public Prosecutions where the public interest in the prevention and prosecution of crime must be given due weight. The High Court ruled that the public interest in the administration of justice outweighed the desirability in general of preserving the confidentiality of such documents in the circumstances of the present proceedings. The court inspected the documents for the purpose of deciding whether any of them should be produced. While not all the documents were ordered to be produced the court ruled that a number of the statements made by Gardaí should be produced.

Chapter 9

THE COURTS

The Administration of Justice

In modern states the judicial function is the third arm of government. The judicial function consists of the interpretation of laws and their application by rule or discretion to disputes which arise between individual and individual, and between the State and the individual. The Constitution establishes courts of law or courts of justice to exercise the judicial function. Under the doctrine of the separation of powers (see page 28) the courts must be independent of the legislature and executive, and be capable of exercising some control over the other organs of government. Thus the courts exercise a fundamental control over the legislature by being empowered to declare a statute invalid should it infringe any provision of the Constitution. In matters of policy the courts refuse to interfere with the executive power, but where constitutional or legal powers are given, the courts insist that these are exercised *intra vires* (see page 98).

Justice shall be administered in courts established under the Constitution according to Article 34. The administration of justice and the administration of the law may, at first glance, appear to be identical, though on reflection it can be seen that the two, while related, are not synonymous. Justice is pursued through the law but there are many preceived injustices under the law because the law has not developed in such a way as to grant a remedy in every instance. However, the general idea of law without justice is repugnant. The purpose of law is to achieve justice: justice without law is an impossibility. Leaving aside the *moral* concept of justice our society, by its use of law, attempts to secure fairness for all. This is known as the rule of law.

This concept of the rule of law has a number of meanings all of which emphasise the one underlying ideal that justice is attainable solely through the law. The first meaning given is that everything must be done according to law, or that an action done without legal justification is illegal. This is also known as the principle of legality. The second meaning given is that law must, by recognised rules and principles, restrict unlimited power. Often a discretion given by law can be abused, so the law confines its exercise within certain boundaries. A third meaning of the rule of law is that tribunals before which disputes are heard must be independent of the other organs of government. A fourth meaning is that the law should apply to all persons and, while this may be impossible, some effort must be made to ensure some equality of treatment before the law, because otherwise some individuals may believe themselves to be immune from the law while others will feel oppressed.

Providing an acceptable and easy definition of the administration of justice has defied jurists and judges over the centuries. Kennedy CJ, in *Lynham v Butler* (1933), mapped out its scope admirably when he explained:

> the controversies which fall to it for determination may be divided into two classes, criminal and civil. In relation to the former . . . the judicial power is exercised in determining the guilt or innocence of persons charged with offences against the State itself and in determining the punishments to be inflicted upon persons found guilty of offences charged against them, which punishments it then becomes the obligation of the executive department of government to carry into effect. In relation to justiciable controversies of the civil class, the judicial power is exercised in a final manner, by definitive adjudication according to law, rights or obligations in disputes between citizen and citizen or between citizens and the State . . . and in binding the parties by such determination which will be enforced if necessary with the authority of the State. Its characteristic public good in its civil aspects is finality and authority, the decisive ending of disputes and quarrels, and the avoidance of private methods of violence in asserting or resisting claims alleged or denied.

A meaning of the administration of justice within a constitutional framework was identified in tests set out by Kenny J in the High Court in *McDonald v Bord na gCon* (1965) (Case 100). While these characteristics so stated have been criticised in minor ways they have been adopted by judges in later cases.

1. A dispute or controversy as to the existence of legal rights or a violation of the law.
2. The determination or ascertainment of the rights of parties or the imposition of liabilities or the infliction of penalties.
3. The final determination (subject to appeal) of legal rights and liabilities or the imposition of penalties.
4. The enforcement of those rights or liabilities or the imposition of a penalty by the court or by the executive power of the State, which is called in by the court to enforce its judgment.
5. The making of an order by the court, which as a matter of history, is an order characteristic of courts in this country.

It was held by the High Court, in *O'Mahony v Melia* (1989) (Case 146) that the power to remand in custody and to grant bail are judicial acts. The power vested in the Attorney General to direct the Commissioner of the Garda Síochána not to execute an extradition warrant on the ground of insufficiency of evidence was held, in *Wheeler v Culligan* (1989) (Case 213), to be procedural rather than judicial in nature. The Supreme Court, in *Goodman International v Tribunal of Inquiry into the Beef Processing Industry* (1992) (Case 73), that a Tribunal of Inquiry established by the Houses of the Oireachtas which was to report back to them was not administering justice because it could not impose liability or punishment. In *Keady v Commissioner* of *An Garda Síochána* (1992) (Case 84) the Supreme Court ruled that the dismissal of a garda did not constitute an administration of justice because there was no contest between the parties.

It would be unwise to draw the conclusion that under our constitutional framework justice is solely administered in courts of law. Justice may be administered elsewhere according to the provisions of Article 37 of the Constitution, a topic discussed towards the end of this chapter on page 147.

Public Justice

Justice must be administered in public (Article 34.1). Courts open to the public gaze and the scrutiny of a free press are less likely to abuse their powers than a system of courts in secret. Apart from first principle, there are advantages in having open courts. The individual becomes aware of aspects of the law, how it is applied and enforced and the consequence of its infringement. The individual stands protected from unsustainable accusation because, under our accusatorial system, those who allege wrongdoing must give evidence in open court and are subject to cross-examination. Justice in public identifies the anti-social in society. The disadvantage may be that a wronged party, because of the likely glare of publicity, may not seek redress, or that the individual acquitted of any wrongdoing may be tainted with the allegations.

The courts have recognised the need for, and welcomed, publicity. In *Beamish & Crawford Ltd v Crowley* (1969) (Case 19) Ó Dálaigh CJ declared:

> publicity, deserved or otherwise, is inseparable from the administration of justice in public; this is a principle which, as the Constitution declares, may not be departed from except in such special and limited cases as may be prescribed by law.

This point was emphasised again in *In re R. Ltd* (1989) in the Supreme Court, by Walsh J:

> the actual presence of the public is never necessary but the administration of justice in public does require that the doors of the court must be open

so that members of the general public may come and see for themselves that justice is done. It is in no way necessary that the members of the public to whom the courts are open should themselves have any particular interest in the cases or they should have had any business in the courts. Justice is administered in public on behalf of all the inhabitants of the State.

There are many instances permitted by statute where justice is administered either totally in private, or where some aspects of the case may not be disclosed.[1] Each of these instances must be examined carefully to ascertain whether the particular restriction is in the best interest of society. Some are and some clearly are not. For example, all our family law is now heard in private. This has given rise to the false impression that there are no, or at least not many, disputes in this vital area. Surely as an exercise in information it is possible for the facts of the cases to be disclosed without identifying the parties. The public would then be in a better position to appreciate what, if any, reforms of the law are necessary.

The Supreme Court ruled, in *In re R. Ltd* (1989), that where a statute conferred on a court a discretion to exercise justice otherwise than in public the court had to keep in mind the overriding consideration of doing justice. Before ordering that proceedings be heard otherwise than in public the court had to be satisfied that a public hearing of all or part of the proceedings would fall short of the doing of justice, it being a fundamental principle of the administration of justice in a democratic State that justice be administered in public.

The Judiciary

A judge is a person vested with authority to decide questions in dispute between parties and to award the appropriate remedy. Together with judicial functions a judge may be entrusted with administrative functions.[2] Article 34.1 of the Constitution declares that justice shall be administered in courts established by judges appointed in the manner provided in the Constitution. Judges appointed under Article 34 must be appointed by the President (Article 35.1). Not all judges are appointed by the President in that special courts may be established under Article 38.3 and the members of such courts are appointed in a different manner. This accounts for one of the distinctions between the ordinary and special courts, a matter considered more fully later in this chapter.

The Constitution is silent as to who recommends to the President persons for judicial appointment. This is done by the Government,[3] though this task could be given elsewhere. Criticism has been made that many, though not all, of the persons appointed are politically aligned to the Government making those appointments. This is a valid point though it must be emphasised that such appointees are not thereby subject to executive direction in their judicial functions. It is argued that such appointments are not made on merit or ability but on political affiliation and that those with different allegiances, and with none, are blandly ignored. This method not alone debases politics but denies to the judicial system, and to the public, the best legal talent. It might be time to consider other methods of judicial appointment.

Once appointed judges hold office until resignation, retirement or removal from office. Judges of the Supreme Court and the High Court enjoy considerable security of office, a privilege not necessarily enjoyed by judges of the other courts. The Supreme Court ruled, in *Magee v Culligan* (1992) (Case 111), that a law which provided for the appointment of judges of the District Court for fixed short periods was not inconsistent with the Constitution.

Provisions relating to the number of judges, their terms of appointment, their remuneration, age of retirement and pensions, are to be regulated by statute (Article 36). Many of these matters are regulated by a number of statutes and the effect of the non-observance of these regulatory controls has come before the courts for consideration. The High Court ruled in *The State (Walshe) v Murphy* (1981) (Case 205) that a purported appointment of a judge was invalid because the person in question did not possess the requisite qualifications required by the statute. This decision was tantamount to a declaration by the High Court that the person in question could no longer serve as a District Justice. Of course, when that particular person acquired the appropriate qualifications he could then be validly appointed to the District Court. In an earlier edition of this book it was stated that this principle could be invoked to invalidate decisions of a judge who had continued to serve in office after the date of his retirement had passed. This was precisely the point in *Shelly v Mahon* (1990) (Case 175) where the validity of a conviction was challenged on the ground that the judge making the order had continued to act after the age of retirement had passed. In *Glavin v Governor of Mountjoy Prison* (1991) (Case 72) an order returning a person for trial made by the same judge was declared invalid by the Supreme Court for the same reason. The Supreme Court held, in *Magee v Culligan* (1992) (Case 111), that the statutory provision for the appointment of judges of the District Court for fixed short periods was an exercise by the Oireachtas of the express power contained in Article 36 to regulate by law the number of judges and their terms of appointment.

Judicial Independence

The Constitution provides a number of ways in which the independence of the judiciary can be ensured and the common law complements these. A judge must not be a member of either House of the Oireachtas (Article 35.3), and by implication, of the Government. This preserves the basis for the separation of powers. Nor may a judge hold any other office or position of emolument (Article 35.3). This rule prevents a judge being placed in a position where personal interest might clash with the judicial function. It obliges a judge to devote all his or her talents to the profession. A judge who hears a case in which he or she has a pecuniary interest, such as being a shareholder in a defendant company, offends the rule of natural justice, *nemo judex in sua causa* (no one should judge in his own cause), and the party who appears to be prejudiced by the result in such a case could have that decision set aside. A judge must be seen to approach a case without bias though there are occasions when a judge may have a preconceived attitude towards a particular problem. For example, the Chief Justice is *ex officio* a member of the Council of State and may be called to aid and counsel a President who in considering whether to refer a Bill to the Supreme Court for a decision as to its constitutionality (see page 49). Should the President refer the Bill the Chief Justice may sit in the Supreme Court, and may appear to approach the question with some preconceived ideas.

The second way in which the Constitution ensures judicial independence is by making it difficult to remove a judge from office. Article 35.4 declares that a judge of the Supreme Court or High Court may only be removed for stated misbehaviour and then on resolutions passed by both Houses of the Oireachtas.[4] The Taoiseach notifies the President and forwards copies of each of the resolutions. On receipt of these the President removes the judge from office. From the inception of the State no judge has been removed from office. It is a drastic step though one which could not be evaded should circumstances so demand. The Supreme Court pointed out, in *Magee v Culligan* (1992) (Case 111), that the Constitution did not contain any guarantee to judges of the other courts of the particular method by which they can be removed from office. In that case there was no constitutional objection to the appointment of judges of the District Court for short fixed periods and such appointments neither interfered with nor limited the constitutional guarantee of judicial independence to the holders of such appointments.

The third constitutional guarantee of judicial independence is contained in Article 35.5 which declares that the remuneration of a judge cannot be reduced during continuance in office. The impartiality of the judiciary could be attacked should reductions in their incomes be threatened by a hostile Oireachtas or Government. A novel point was taken in *O'Byrne v Minister for Finance* (1959) (Case 136) where the widow of a deceased judge claimed that taxation deducted from his salary while in office was a breach of this constitutional guarantee. The former Supreme Court rejected the claim on the basis that the purpose of the article was to safeguard the independence of judges and that to require a judge to pay taxes on income on the same basis as other citizens and thus to contribute to the expenses of government could not be said to be an attack on judicial independence.

Article 34.5 of the Constitution provides the fourth guarantee. Every judge must make a declaration in the prescribed form that he or she will faithfully and to the best of his or her ability and power execute the office without fear or favour, affection or ill will towards any person, and that he or she will uphold the Constitution and the laws. This declaration must be made by the Chief Justice in the presence of the President, and every other judge must make it before the Chief Justice in open court. It must be made before taking up office and not later than ten days after appointment. Failure to do so results in the office being deemed vacated.

The common law developed two further protections which complement these constitutional guarantees just explained. The first is the law of contempt. Criminal contempt includes contempt in the face of the court, such as words or actions in the presence of the court that interfere or tend to interfere with the course of justice. A physical attack on a judge, juror, lawyer or witness, or the use of threatening language against any of them is contempt. Where proceedings have terminated it may be contempt to scandalise the court by publishing scurrilous personal abuse of a judge's conduct of the case. This was the allegation in *The State (DPP) v Walsh* (1981) (Case 187) where, after a conviction for capital murder, a newspaper published an item drafted by the defendant which referred to the verdict 'as particularly reprehensible because it was passed by the Special Criminal Court, a court composed of Government appointed judges having no judicial independence, which sat without a jury and which so abused the rules of evidence as to make the court akin to a sentencing tribunal'. The Supreme Court found this statement was calculated to undermine the reputation of the Special Criminal Court as a source of justice. The purpose of the law of contempt is not to buttress the dignity of the judges by protecting them from insult but to protect the rights of the public by ensuring that the administration of justice is not obstructed. Contempt of court is considered in detail later in this chapter under the Trial of Offences (page 135).

The second protection granted by the common law is that judges enjoy immunity from legal action when performing their judicial functions. The object of this is to uphold judicial independence. Without it decisions may be warped by fear of personal liability. This protection extends to acts done, or things said, maliciously and corruptly, which hardly seems appropriate. In *Macauley & Co. Ltd v Wyse-Power* (1943) a judge was sued for slander arising out of remarks made during a case that seriously assailed the character and reputation of the plaintiff company. The action was unsustainable because the High Court held that there was a long line of authority which established the proposition that no action lay against a judge. It was better that an individual should suffer than the course of justice be hindered and fettered by apprehensions on the part of the judge that words uttered in the course of proceedings might be made the subject of an action. That was generally called judicial privilege and is similar to the privilege enjoyed by members of the Oireachtas (see page 59). Since this immunity is available it requires judges to be circumspect in their remarks particularly where the remarks are aimed at a party not before the courts. Of course, a judge can sue should he or she be defamed while performing his or her judicial functions.

The System of Courts

A court is defined as a tribunal having power to adjudicate in a civil, criminal or military matter and must be distinguished from a courthouse which is the building in which justice is administered (where the law courts are held). The Constitution envisages a hierarchical system of courts which has many of the characteristics of the system in force both prior to 1922 and under the Saorstát Éireann Constitution. The Constitution declares that there must be a Supreme Court and courts of first instance to include a High Court, and courts of limited and local jurisdiction.

The system of courts envisaged in the Constitution was not formally established until the *Courts (Establishment and Constitution) Act 1961* was enacted and, though the system of courts in operation until that year is similar to the present one, it is not identical. For example, there was no provision similar to Article 26 in the Saorstát Éireann Constitution and it is doubtful whether the Supreme Court of Justice which continued in operation until 1961, and commonly referred to as the former Supreme Court, possessed the jurisdiction to advise the President on the constitutionality of Bills. A doubt must exist concerning the validity of the three referrals of Bills to the former Supreme Court. Should these referrals possess no constitutional validity, the question whether internment without trial permitted under the *Offences Against the State (Amendment) Act 1940* is or is not constitutional remains open for consideration by the present Supreme Court.

The Supreme Court

The Supreme Court stands at the pinnacle of our system of courts. Article 34.4.1° provides that the Supreme Court is the court of final appeal. The Constitution expressly confers a number of jurisdictions on the Supreme Court some of which cannot be curtailed without constitutional amendment while others may be curtailed by law.

The first jurisdiction constitutionally conferred is that under Article 26 the Supreme Court must advise the President whether any Bill referred to it, is or is not, constitutional (see page 49). The second such jurisdiction, stated in Article 34.4.4° is that the Supreme Court has specific appellate jurisdiction from decisions of the High Court in cases which involve the validity of any law having regard to the provisions of the Constitution (see page 124). The Supreme Court ruled in *Brady v Donegal County Council* (1989) that although it was a fundamental principle of the appellate jurisdiction of the Supreme

Court, it does not decide issues not raised in the court of trial. Nevertheless, where a challenge to the constitutional validity of an Act of the Oireachtas was involved, it was proper that the court should consider every relevant ground of appeal. The third of these jurisdictions is that under Article 40.4.3° the Supreme Court must answer any case stated for it by the High Court where the High Court is satisfied that a person is detained in accordance with law but that such law is invalid having regard to the provisions of the Constitution. These three jurisdictions granted by the provisions of the Constitution cannot be curtailed by ordinary law.

The Supreme Court, with such exceptions and subject to such regulations as may be prescribed by law, has appellate jurisdiction from all decisions of the High Court (Article 34.4.3°). The extent of this appellate jurisdiction has been considered in a number of cases by the Supreme Court. In the first of these, *The State (Burke) v Lennon* (1940) (Case 181), the former Supreme Court held an appeal could not be brought by the State against the granting of a habeas corpus* order granted by the High Court. The court applied the common law rule that no such appeal lay. The present Supreme Court, in *The State (Browne) v Feran* (1967) (Case 180), refused to adopt this common law curtailment of its appellate jurisdiction and permitted such an appeal in such circumstances. The Supreme Court decided in *The State (Trimbole) v Governor of Mountjoy Prison* (1985) (Case 204) that where the High Court ordered the release of a person under Article 40.4.2° of the Constitution, a stay on that release could not be ordered pending an appeal to the Supreme Court. Having heard the appeal the Supreme Court could order the re-arrest of the person released should the appeal be successful (see page 218).

In *The People (AG) v Conmey* (1975) (Case 151) the Supreme Court decided that an appeal could be made directly to the Supreme Court against a conviction of the Central Criminal Court, which is the High Court exercising its criminal jurisdiction, though statute permitted an appeal to the Court of Criminal Appeal. The court held that to exclude its appellate jurisdiction the language of the statute must be unambiguous and clearly intended to have that effect. Failing the intervention of statute this decision has had the consequence of granting to a person convicted in the Central Criminal Court an option of either appealing directly to the Supreme Court, which most convicted persons avail of, or to the Court of Criminal Appeal.

The question was canvassed, following *Conmey*'s case, whether the State had the similar right to appeal an acquittal, which was prohibited at common law. In *The People (DPP) v O'Shea* (1982) (Case 162) the question came very close to being answered. In that case the Supreme Court decided it had jurisdiction to hear an appeal where the trial judge in the Central Criminal Court had directed the jury to acquit an accused.[5] It can hardly be doubted that, in the absence of statutory prohibition, the Supreme Court will in an appropriate case hear an appeal from a jury acquittal. This may not be a welcome development. At present an acquittal by a jury in a criminal case is the only instance of a decision within the judicial system which is outside the scope of review by a higher court. The Supreme Court decided in *The People (DPP) v Quilligan* (1989) that the jurisdiction to hear an appeal did not *ipso facto* carry with it the jurisdiction to order a retrial.

In civil cases the Supreme Court has adopted the similar vigorous stance of protecting its appellate jurisdiction. The Supreme Court, in *In re Morelli* (1968) (Case 119), rejected the argument that in probate matters it was the practice not to appeal the question of costs. But in *Beechams Group Ltd v Bristol Meyers Co.* (1983) (Case 20) the Supreme Court refused to entertain an appeal from the High Court because such appeal was expressly prohibited by statute. It was argued, in *Holohan v Donohoe* (1986) (Case 80), that should the Supreme Court set aside a damages award from a High Court jury, its sole jurisdiction was to refer the matter back to that court rather than substitute its own verdict on the issue. The Supreme Court ruled that it had the jurisdiction, in the absence of statutory prohibition, to substitute its own verdict. In *Eamonn Andrews Productions Ltd v Gaiety Theatre Enterprises Ltd* (1973) (Case 60) the Supreme Court ruled that there was a statutory prohibition on a further appeal to that court from a decision of the High Court hearing an appeal from the Circuit Court. A similar point was litigated in *W. J. Prendergast & Son Ltd v Carlow County Council* (1990) with the Supreme Court reaching a similar conclusion. The Supreme Court ruled in *Minister for Justice v Wang Zhu Jie* (1991) (Case 118) that the statutory provision confining the right of further appeal to the Supreme Court to cases in which the High Court had granted leave to appeal was unambiguous and constituted an exception to the general right of appeal.

It was decided in *Campus Oil Ltd v Minister for Energy* (1983) that the appellate jurisdiction of the Supreme Court did not include an appeal from a determination made by the High Court, in exercise of the jurisdiction conferred on that court by Article 177 of the Treaty of Rome, to request the Court of Justice of the European Communities to rule on the interpretation of a provision of the Treaty. It was decided that when the High Court came to apply the Treaty provisions to the case a judgment had been made which could be appealed to the Supreme Court.

The Supreme Court may be granted additional appellate jurisdiction by law (Article 34.4.3°). At present it hears appeals from the Court of Criminal Appeal though that right of appeal is not automatic, and it is for this procedural reason that most persons convicted in the Central Criminal Court appeal directly to the Supreme Court. Some statutes confer a consultative jurisdiction* on the Supreme Court, but whether this is constitutionally permissible is doubtful because the only kind of extra jurisdiction which can be conferred is appellate. In a consultative case only a point of law is raised for consideration while the verdict of the lower court on the facts cannot be reviewed. The only original jurisdiction* possessed by the Supreme Court is under Article 12.3.1°, which confers on that court the jurisdiction to declare the President to be permanently incapacitated (see page 66), and Article 26, which empowers the President to refer a Bill to the Supreme Court (see page 49). It is doubtful whether the Supreme Court can be endowed with other original jurisdictions simply because it is a court of final appeal.

The decision of the Supreme Court in all cases is final and conclusive which means that no decision of that court can be appealed to any other court either domestic or international.

As already mentioned the Supreme Court has appellate jurisdiction from the decisions of the High Court in cases which involve the validity of any law having regard to the provisions of the Constitution (Article 34.4.4°), a jurisdiction which cannot be modified by law. The exercise of this jurisdiction depends on the willingness of the parties to appeal the decision of the High Court. The State usually appeals, though not always, and the private individual, probably because of the expense, is more likely not to. Because it is abundantly desirable that the views of the Supreme Court be obtained on such legislation, some method of alleviating the problem of costs must be found.[6] It seems peculiar that an individual who by conviction and action affords the Supreme Court the opportunity to state or clarify the Constitution and the law for the benefit of the political order and society as a whole should be penalised by the enormous burden of costs. The judges of the superior courts should remember that the status and standing of those courts, and in particular the Supreme Court, has been achieved and will be maintained by pronouncements and not by silence.

In this type of constitutional case the decision of the court must be pronounced by one of the judges as the court directs and no other opinion, whether assenting or dissenting, should be pronounced; nor should its existence be disclosed (Article 34.4.5°). The Supreme Court has given this sub-article a restrictive meaning. It was decided in *The State (Sheerin) v Kennedy* (1966) (Case 203) that this single judgment rule should only be applied to a law of the Oireachtas which had been established under the present Constitution. A pre-constitutional statute was not caught by this rule, because the case is considered under Article 50 of the Constitution which is not covered by this rule and is therefore likely to suffer as many judgments as there are judges. This single judgment rule is not applicable where it is alleged, as it was in *Crotty v An Taoiseach* (1987) (Case 43), that some unconstitutional action has been committed.

According to Article 34.4.2° of the Constitution the president of the Supreme Court is the Chief Justice which is an important constitutional office. The Chief Justice is a member of the Presidential Commission (Article 14, see page 74) and a member of the Council of State (Article 31.2, see page 73). The Constitution provides that the Supreme Court shall consist of not less than five judges when deciding on the capacity of the President (Article 12.3.1°, see page 66) and on hearing Bills referred to it by the President (Article 26.2.1°, see page 49). Statute provides that in cases involving the constitutionality of a statute the court must consist of five judges. Legal cases may be heard by a three-judge court. Statute provides that the court may not consist of four judges because an even division would result in confusion.[7]

The High Court

Article 34.3.1° provides that the courts of first instance* must include a High Court invested with full original jurisdiction in all matters and questions whether of law or fact, civil or criminal. It is difficult to determine with any exactness the scope of this jurisdiction, though it appears literally to mean unlimited jurisdiction in the civil and criminal fields. The Constitution itself limits this jurisdiction by permitting the exercise of limited functions and powers of a judicial nature in civil matters by those other than courts or judges (Article 37, see page 147), and offences may be tried summarily, in special courts and by military tribunal (Article 38). There is some judicial confusion as to the scope of this High Court jurisdiction as will be seen from the cases.

The question arose, in *Ward v Kinahan Electrical Ltd* (1984) (Case 211), whether a statutory provision which permitted the remitting of a case instituted in the High Court to another court against the wishes of one of the parties was constitutional. In holding it constitutional McMahon J explained:

> Article 34.3.1° cannot be construed as conferring a universal right of recourse to the High Court for the determination of all justiciable disputes ... because Article 36 enables laws to be made for the distribution of jurisdiction and business among all the courts which may be established under the Constitution, including courts of first instance other than the High Court. It follows, therefore, that business which falls within the full original jurisdiction of the High Court may be assigned, within the limits express and implied in the Constitution, to some other court.

It was queried, in *R. v R.* (1984) (Case 169), whether non-access to the High Court in family law matters breached Article 34.3.1°. While the answer again was in the negative the High Court adopted a different line of reasoning. It was not accepted that statute could exclude the jurisdiction of that court. The approach taken was that the High Court would, in certain circumstances, refuse to exercise its jurisdiction. Gannon J explained:

> the jurisdiction, authority and powers with which the High Court is invested by that article of the Constitution include all such functions, authorities,

duties and powers as are incidental to any and every part of its jurisdiction without any necessary intervention of the legislature . . . I would reject, as wrong in law, the contention . . . that under Article 36 of the Constitution the Oireachtas may confer upon and withdraw from the High Court, or confer upon other courts to the exclusion of the High Court, jurisdiction in matters . . . I am of opinion that, when and in so far as other courts of first instance established by law have jurisdiction in matters . . . it is competent for the High Court to decline to entertain applications for orders obtainable in such other courts, or to remit to such other courts for hearing such applications brought in the High Court as are included in the jurisdiction of such other courts.

This approach was also taken in *O'R. v O'R.* (1985). Murphy J said:

it seems to me that the only circumstances in which the court would be justified in departing from procedures envisaged by the legislature would be where the High Court was satisfied that in the circumstances of a particular case there was a serious danger that justice would not be done if that court declined to exercise the jurisdiction vested on it by the Constitution in relation to that particular case.

The Supreme Court, in *Tormey v Attorney General* (1985) (Case 207), seemed to suggest that legislation could exclude the jurisdiction of the High Court thus differing from, and casting doubt on, the previously decided High Court decisions on the topic. Henchy J explained:

the full original jurisdiction of the High Court, referred to in Article 34.3.1°, must be deemed to be full in the sense that all justiciable matters and questions (save those removed by the Constitution itself from the original jurisdiction of the High Court) shall be within the original jurisdiction of the High Court in one form or another. If, in exercise of its powers under Article 34.3.4°, Parliament commits certain matters or questions to the jurisdiction of [other courts], the functions of hearing and determining these matters and questions may, expressly or by necessary implication, be given exclusively to those courts. But that does not mean that those matters and questions are put outside the original jurisdiction of the High Court. The interrelation of Article 34.3.1° and Article 34.3.4° has the effect that, while [other courts] may be given sole jurisdiction to hear and determine a particular matter or question, the full original jurisdiction of the High Court can be invoked so as to ensure that justice will be done in that matter or question. In this context the original jurisdiction of the High Court is exercisable in one or other of two ways. If there has not been a statutory devolution of jurisdiction on a local and limited basis to a court . . . the High Court will hear and determine the matter or question, without any qualitative or quantitative limitations of jurisdiction. On the other hand, if there has been such a devolution on an exclusive basis, the High Court will not hear and determine the matter or question, but its full jurisdiction is there to be invoked — in proceedings such as habeas corpus, *certiorari*,* prohibition,* mandamus,* *quo warranto*,* injunction or a declaratory action — so as to ensure that the hearing and determination will be in accordance with law.

Article 34.3.2° of the Constitution declares that the High Court has jurisdiction to question the validity of any law having regard to the provisions of the Constitution. This fundamentally important power of judicial review was implied by the American Supreme Court in the landmark case of *Marbury v Madison* in 1803. Judicial review of an Act of the Oireachtas as to its constitutionality is firmly and unequivocally stated to rest with the High Court and on appeal with the Supreme Court (Article 34.4.4°). There are two exceptions to this power of judicial review. No court has the jurisdiction to question the validity of a law, the Bill of which was referred by the President under Article 26 to the Supreme Court (Article 34.3.3°, see page 50). And according to Article 28.3.3° nothing in the Constitution can be invoked to invalidate any law enacted by the Oireachtas which is expressed to be for the purpose of securing the public safety and the preservation of the State in time of war or armed rebellion (see page 54).

The High Court, under the provisions of Article 40.4 of the Constitution, must on complaint being made to it inquire into the detention of any person. This powerful and summary procedure — known as an application under Article 40 of the Constitution — is considered in detail on page 215.

Who may Challenge the Constitutionality of a Statute

On a number of occasions the question has arisen as to whether the party taking the action has the *locus standi* to exercise the right to challenge the constitutionality of the statute in question. There are two possible alternative solutions. These were explained by Walsh J in *East Donegal Co-operative Livestock Mart Ltd v Attorney General* (1970) (Case 61) when he said:

> with regard to . . . *locus standi* . . . the question raised has been determined in different ways in countries which have constitutional provisions similar to our own . . . at one end of the spectrum of opinion on this topic one finds the contention that there exists a right of action akin to an *actio popularis* which will entitle any person, whether he is directly affected by the Act or not, to maintain proceedings and challenge the validity of any Act passed by the parliament of the country to which he is a citizen or to whose laws he is subject by residing in that country. At the other end of the spectrum is the contention that no one can maintain such an action unless he can show that not merely do the provisions of the Act in question apply to activities in

which he is currently engaged but that their application has actually affected his activities adversely. The court rejects the latter contention and does not find it necessary in the circumstances of this case to express any view upon the former.

But the latter contention, rejected in that case, surfaced later to become the rule in constitutional actions. In *Cahill v Sutton* (1980) (Case 31) Henchy J declared in the Supreme Court:

> the primary rule as to standing in constitutional matters in that the person challenging the constitutionality of the statute . . . must be able to assert that, because of the alleged unconstitutionality, his . . . interests have been adversely affected, or stand in real or imminent danger of being adversely affected, by the operation of the statute.

This does seem an over-strict rule because the publicity, effort and cost of litigating constitutional actions are deterrents in themselves. The respect for constitutional rights, and thus for the courts which declare them, have been gained in large measure by individuals prepared to run this gauntlet. A party might be willing to suffer defeat on the merits of a case but will hardly be likely to proceed should the possibility exist that the action would be dismissed because of lack of standing. A study of many of our fundamental cases in constitutional law reveals the fact that had this strict *locus standi* rule been applied, most of them would never have reached decision.[8]

The difficulty of enforcing this strict dictum can be seen in subsequent cases. It was argued in *The State (Lynch) v Cooney* (1982) (Case 191) that the prosecutor* had no *locus standi* to challenge a prohibition order because it was directed not against him, but against RTE. Since he had no statutory right to broadcast it was urged that he had no right to complain. This was rejected by the Supreme Court because once RTE had agreed to broadcast his political contribution, the order prohibiting the broadcast gave the prosecutor sufficient standing to challenge its making. The Supreme Court in *Norris v Attorney General* (1984) (Case 130), where a challenge was made to statutes which prohibited certain sexual activities by an individual who had neither been prosecuted nor convicted under the statutes nor was likely to be prosecuted, ruled that as long as the legislation continued to proclaim as criminal the conduct the plaintiff asserted he had a right to engage in, the plaintiff had the standing to sustain the action. On the other hand the court ruled that he had no standing to challenge the statutes on the ground that they infringed marital privacy, because the plaintiff was unmarried.

In *King v Attorney General* (1981) (Case 88) a challenge was permitted to be made to statutory provisions under which the plaintiff had been convicted but was not permitted to challenge the provisions of the statute under which the plaintiff had not been charged. In *Madigan v Attorney General* (1986) (Case 110) it was held that the plaintiff had no *locus standi* to advance hypothetical arguments as to how the statute in question might operate in other situations and was restricted to proving how he was prejudiced by the impugned legislation. It was accepted that a different plaintiff with sufficient *locus standi* might in a future action make these arguments provided that person was so affected by the statute.

The Supreme Court ruled in *Crotty v An Taoiseach* (1987) (Case 43) that the plaintiff had the *locus standi* to challenge legislation, enacted but not in force, because the legislation when operative would affect every citizen notwithstanding his failure to prove the threat of any special injury or prejudice to him, as distinct from any other citizen arising from the statute. The point was raised, in *McGimpsey v Ireland* (1990) (Case 102), whether the plaintiffs, born and living in Northern Ireland with one possessed of an Irish passport, could maintain constitutional proceedings. On the finding by the High Court that both plaintiffs were born in Ireland and were therefore in contemplation of Irish law citizens of Ireland the Supreme Court assumed, without deciding, that each of the plaintiffs was an Irish citizen and entertained the case on its merits. But the court felt that as a general proposition it was considerably doubtful whether any citizen would have the *locus standi* to challenge the constitutional validity of an action of the executive or of a statute of the Oireachtas for the specific and sole purpose of achieving an objective directly contrary to the purpose of the constitutional provision invoked.

Challenging a Statute
Since there is no constitutional procedure for ensuring that proposed legislation is constitutional, apart from the limited provisions of Article 26, a decision as to a statute's constitutionality must be made in hindsight, after it has been in operation, possibly for some years, and only when its operation is alleged to have infringed an individual's rights. What procedure should be used to mount such a challenge? The courts themselves will not initiate such an inquiry, which seems a failure by the judges to honour their declaration to uphold the Constitution. Since the Oireachtas is under the duty not to pass unconstitutional laws, surely the courts possess the corresponding duty not to apply such laws. The courts will not act until an individual seeks their assistance. Why should the onus of proving a statute unconstitutional rest on an individual? Surely the individual should be able to rest assured that the Oireachtas will not enact, and if it does, that the courts will not enforce, unconstitutional laws.

The challenge to a statute may be *direct* or *collateral*.* It is a direct challenge when the originating proceedings seek a declaration that particular sections of the statute are invalid having regard to the provisions of the Constitution, a claim made where the statute is of post-constitutional enactment

(Article 34.3.2°). Where the challenged statute is of pre-constitutional origin the claim is made that the particular sections are inconsistent with the provisions of the Constitution (Article 50).

The essence of a declaratory judgment is that it states the rights, or legal position, of the parties and once the court declares the statute unconstitutional, that settles the point. Because these statutory provisions have been stripped of their legality the individual is no longer bound by that law. The declaratory action is a common method of attacking legislation on constitutional grounds: it was used, for example, in *McGee v Attorney General* (1974) (Case 101) where a pre-constitutional statute was successfully challenged, and in *O'Donovan v Attorney General* (1961) (Case 141), a post-constitutional statute was successfully challenged.

In the successful cases to date no claim for a declaration has been coupled with a claim for damages, though there seems no reason why this could not be done. In some cases the plaintiff would not have suffered loss and would not then be entitled to compensation. For example, the plaintiff in *de Búrca v Attorney General* (1976) (Case 49) suffered no loss because she successfully challenged the jury law in advance of her trial. On the other hand, in other cases such as *McGee v Attorney General* (1974) (Cases 101) where because of statutory prohibition artificial contraceptives were not available to a married woman, damage might well have resulted to the health and welfare of the plaintiff. A question never considered by the courts is whether damages could be awarded in lieu of a declaration. For example, the result in *Blake v Attorney General* (1981) (Case 22) effectively ended rent control in an action taken by landlords who were denied a fair return in rent from their properties. Temporary legislation was enacted to cater for the intervening period until permanent legislation could be drafted.[9] When the latter was enacted it was referred by the President to the Supreme Court, which rejected it: *Article 26 and the Housing (Private Rented Dwellings) Bill 1981* (Case 9). Further legislation was then enacted which provided new procedures for assessing rents which may in certain cases be subsidised by the State.[10] It would have been administratively easier to have financially compensated the landlords who had suffered at the hands of the legislation and either leave the legislation intact or repeal it.

Statutes may be indirectly challenged as to their constitutionality, in collateral proceedings, by challenging a decision made under a statute. The argument will be made that the decision itself was *intra vires* the law but that the law itself is unconstitutional. Such a challenge is made by judicial review. *Certiorari*, which is commonly used, is used to quash a decision already made, on the ground that the deciding authority acted *ultra vires* the Constitution though it may have acted *intra vires* the statute. For example, in *The State (Nicolaou) v An Bord Uchtála* (1966) (Case 195) it was sought to quash a valid adoption order made under the *Adoption Act 1952* on the ground that the statute was unconstitutional. It was restated by the Supreme Court, in *The State (McEldowney) v Kelleher* (1983) (Case 192), that a party was entitled to challenge, *in certiorari* proceedings, the constitutionality of a statute.

Injunction proceedings have been used in a similar way. For example, in the *ESB v Gormley* (1985) (Case 65) a successful challenge was made to a statute when an injunction was sought to enforce its provisions.

The commonest method of challenging a statute, in collateral proceedings, is by way of an application under Article 40.4.2° of the Constitution, which obliges the High Court to inquire into a detention and order a release where the detention is unlawful (see page 215). Should the detention be lawful but the High Court is of opinion that the law under which the detention is effected is unconstitutional it must refer the question to the Supreme Court for its decision on the matter. It was decided in *The State (Sheerin) v Kennedy* (1966) (Case 203) that this duty of referral applied only to post-constitutional statutes, and in cases where a pre-constitutional statute was in question the High Court had jurisdiction to decide the issue. In that case the prosecutor was released because the statute under which he was detained was held to be inconsistent with Article 50 of the Constitution.

The High Court suggested in *Minister for Labour v Costello* (1989) that it was not permissible to raise the issue of the constitutionality of a statute by way of a Case Stated* from the District Court.

Should a Challenged Statute be Observed Pending Decision

The injunction is a weapon in the hands of the executive in the enforcement of the law. Where the fine for a breach of the law is trivial the injunction becomes a handy tool to enforce the law because a breach of its terms is a contempt of court. An example of its use to prevent a repetition of an offence which carried a trivial penalty is *Attorney General v Paperlink Ltd* (1984) (Case 12). But can the injunction be used to compel a party to observe the provisions of a law which that party has challenged and a hearing is awaited or a decision is pending? That was the issue in *Campus Oil Ltd v Minister for Energy* (1983) where a statutory instrument imposed an obligation on importers of petrol to purchase a portion of their requirements from the State. The plaintiff refused pleading that the law was in contravention of the Treaty of Rome and a case was stated by the High Court for the opinion of the European Court of Justice on the issue.* Pending the outcome of the case the defendant sought by injunction to compel compliance with the law. The Supreme Court, granting the injunction, held that the statutory instrument which was challenged had been made under the provisions of an Act of the Oireachtas which must be regarded as valid and part of the law of the land unless and until its invalidity was established.

In *Nova Media Services Ltd v Minister for Posts and Telegraphs* (1984) the question was whether a challenged statute had to be obeyed pending a decision of the courts on the matter. The plaintiff, broadcasting without a licence, had its equipment seized, challenged the constitutionality of the statute and sought an injunction, pending the determination of the action, to restrain interference with its ability to broadcast and to return the seized equipment. The High Court refused the injunction though it held that in certain circumstances the courts in the proper exercise of their discretion might refuse to grant an injunction on the application of the executive to secure compliance with a statutory provision by members of the public pending a decision of the courts as to the constitutionality of the particular statute, but it would only be in the most extraordinary circumstances that the courts would intervene to prevent the executive from exercising a function conferred by the express terms of a statute made for the control of a public resource and for the benefit of the public good.

But that is exactly what the courts did in *Pesca Valentia Ltd v Minister for Fisheries* (1985) where the owner of sea-fishing vessels registered in the State was granted licences on condition that 75 per cent or more of the crew were Irish or nationals of the member states of the EC. When one of the vessels was arrested and the master charged with fishing in breach of the licence the plaintiff challenged the law as to its constitutionality and that it offended EC law, and sought an injunction to restrain the Minister from withdrawing the licence pending the hearing of the action. The Supreme Court held, notwithstanding the presumption of constitutionality which attached to the statute, that the plaintiff had clearly established that there was a fair question to be tried and that the balance of convenience lay in favour of granting the injunction, notwithstanding that that course of action lead to the suspension of the statute. Finlay CJ explained:

> it is . . . the duty of the courts to protect persons against the invasion of their constitutional rights or against unconstitutional action. It would seem wholly inconsistent with that duty if the court were to be without power in an appropriate case to restrain by injunction an action against a person which found its authority in a statutory provision which might eventually be held to be invalid having regard to the Constitution.

Approach of Courts when Statute Challenged
In exercising the power of judicial review the courts have adopted a number of rules which have not the force of law but are merely guidelines to assist the courts in the task of interpreting whether a particular statute infringes the Constitution. The first of these rules states that where the court has to consider the constitutionality of a law it must be accepted as an axiom that a law passed by the Oireachtas, the elected representatives of the people, is presumed to be

constitutional unless and until the contrary is clearly established (*Pigs Marketing Board v Donnelly (Dublin) Ltd*) (1939) (Case 165). The onus of proof is, as in all other civil cases, on the plaintiff.

The second rule is that all laws in force on the date immediately prior to the coming into operation of the Constitution enjoy no such presumption in respect of the present Constitution (*The State (Sheerin) v Kennedy*) (1966) (Case 203). Where parts of a pre-constitutional statute are substituted with parts of a post-constitutional statute those substituted parts enjoy the presumption of constitutionality (*O'Callaghan v Commissioners of Public Works*) (1985) (Case 138).

The third rule is that the courts will only exercise this jurisdiction to strike down a statute where such action is unavoidable. The Supreme Court ruled in *McDaid v Sheehy* (1991) (Case 99) that it was not appropriate to pronounce on the constitutional validity of a statute when such pronouncement could be of no benefit to the plaintiff. Equally where the relief which a plaintiff seeks is argued on two distinct grounds — a constitutional ground and a legal ground — the court as a general rule should consider first whether the relief sought can be granted on a legal ground which does not raise a question of constitutional validity. If it can, then the court ought not to rule on the larger question of the constitutional validity of the law in question (*M. v An Bord Uchtála*) (1977).[11]

The fourth rule is that an Act of the Oireachtas will not be declared to be invalid where it is possible to construe it in accordance with the Constitution. It is not only a question of preferring a constitutional construction to one which would be unconstitutional where they may both appear to be open, but it also means that an interpretation favouring the validity of an Act should be given in cases of doubt (*East Donegal Co-operative Livestock Mart Ltd v Attorney General*) (1970) (Case 61).

The fifth rule ordains that the Constitution must be read as a whole, its several provisions must not be looked at in isolation, but be treated as interlocking parts of the general constitutional scheme. It follows from such global approach that, save where the Constitution itself otherwise provides, all its provisions should be given due weight and effect and not be subordinated one to the other. The true purpose and range of a Constitution would not be achieved if it were treated as no more than the sum of its parts (*Tormey v Attorney General*) (1985) (Case 207).

Consequence of a Declaration of Invalidity

What is the effect on a statute of declaring a section or sections of it to be unconstitutional? Prospectively those impugned sections are null and void: they are without legal effect and cannot impose legal liability or attract legal sanction. Should the Oireachtas wish those impugned sections to be re-enacted as law, it must initiate a proposal to amend the Constitution in line with the thrust of the impugned legislation. Ordinary legislation cannot negative such a decision of the courts on a constitutional point. This was emphasised in *Muckley v Ireland* (1985) (Case 121) where legislation enacted to cure a defect in the law, exposed by the decision of *Murphy v Attorney General* (1982) (Case 123), was struck down because it suffered from the same defect.

We have resorted to a constitutional referendum to attempt to tailor the Constitution in the fashion of impugned legislation. One such attempt was the proposal put to the People to accept a tolerance of up to 16 per cent of the national average in drawing up the constituencies, after the High Court in *O'Donovan v Attorney General* (1961) (Case 141) had rejected a tolerance of 19 per cent laid down by statute (see page 79). The People rejected the proposal.[12] This process is also seen in *Article 26 and the Electoral (Amendment) Bill 1983* (Case 7) where the Supreme Court advised the President that a Bill, which proposed to confer voting rights on no-citizens, was unconstitutional. Subsequently a proposal was put to the People to amend the Constitution in this regard, and it was carried.[13]

What consequence has the impugning of legislation on proceedings or actions in progress when the court's decision is announced? This was at issue in *The State (Byrne) v Frawley* (1978) (Case 182) where a criminal jury trial was in progress when the Supreme Court declared, in *de Búrca v Attorney General* (1976) (Case 49), that the relevant jury law was unconstitutional (see page 141). The accused neither objected to the continuance of the trial, nor did he raise this objection on appeal. When he did so, some months later, the Supreme Court held it was fatal to his attempt to have his conviction quashed that he had objected neither during the trial nor at the appeal despite his knowledge at the relevant time of the court's decision in the *de Búrca* case. The Supreme Court did point out that should a judge, or other person, implementing a statute become aware that its provisions have been declared unconstitutional they should abandon the proceedings or actions.

A more complex question is: from what date is the impugned legislation null and void? The question arose, in *Murphy v Attorney General* (1982) (Case 123), whether income tax paid under the impugned statute could be recovered. The Supreme Court drew the distinction between pre-constitutional and post-constitutional statutes and held that, in a case involving a pre-constitutional statute, inconsistency dated from the coming into operation of the Constitution which was 31 December 1937. As regards a post-constitutional statute it was void *ab initio*,* that is retrospectively from the date of its enactment and not merely from the date of the court's judgment. Does it then follow that all the seemingly valid actions done under the impugned legislation are null and void? In that case Henchy J responded thus:

> for a variety of reasons, the law recognises that in certain circumstances, no matter how unfounded in law certain conduct may have been, no matter

how unwarranted its operation in a particular case, what has happened has happened, and cannot or should not be undone. The irreversible progressions and by-products of time, the compulsion of public order and of the common good, the aversion of the law from giving a hearing to those who have slept on their rights, the quality of legality — even irreversibility — that tends to attach to what has become inveterate or has been widely accepted or acted upon, the recognition that even in the short term the accomplished facts may sometimes acquire an inviolable sacredness, these and other factors may convert what has been done under an unconstitutional, or otherwise void, law into an acceptable part of the *corpus juris.** This trend represents an inexorable process that is not peculiar to the law, for in a wide variety of other contexts it is either foolish or impossible to attempt to turn back the hands of the clock.

The Supreme Court permitted income tax to be reclaimed from the year the proceedings were instituted and confined this benefit to the individuals who had taken the successful action. Other persons who had been taxed under the impugned law received no retrospective benefit from the plaintiffs' successful action: any benefit which flowed could only be enjoyed prospectively.

Does a Declaration of Invalidity have Permanent Effect?
It is a principle recognised by the courts that an unsuccessful challenge to a statute is not a bar to a further challenge. It has happened that a statute declared valid in one case has been declared invalid in a subsequent case. For example, in *Costello v DPP* (1984) (Case 40) the Supreme Court declared invalid a section of a statute whose identical counterpart in another statute was deemed to be constitutional in a previous challenge some twenty years earlier.[14] What has never been decided by the courts is whether a declaration of invalidity relating to some sections of a statute has permanent effect, or do the impugned sections go to a sort of constitutional limbo, so to speak, there to await a possible resurrection by some future judicial decision. This problem was adverted to, but not decided, by the Supreme Court in *Moynihan v Greensmyth* (1977) (Case 120). The court reserved for a future case in which the point was duly raised and argued whether the section of the statute declared invalid in *O'Brien v Keogh* (1972) (Case 134) had been correctly decided. This judicial dictum seems authority for the proposition that a party who could claim the benefit of a section of a statute, which had been successfully impugned in previous proceedings, could argue that the previous decision was wrong. If successful the effect of that fresh determination would be to restore the impugned section to full legal effect. This is a proposition which must await further judicial pronouncement.

Severing the Impugned Law

A dilemma faces a court when a law is successfully impugned as to its constitutionality. In the successful cases to date the courts have found that either a single section or a number of sections offend the Constitution. There has never been a case where a complete statute was declared unconstitutional.

As a consequence of a declaration of unconstitutionality the court must ensure that the decision which is given does not result in the court straying into the legislative domain thus breaching the doctrine of the separation of powers (see page 35), a possibility adverted to in *McGrath v McDermott* (1988). The court when deleting the offending section, expressions or words, whichever the case may be, must be alert to the possibility that the law which remained may be a measure never intended by the legislature. The removal of the one offending word impugned in *Maher v Attorney General* (1973) (Case 112) would have left a section with a meaning never intended. The Supreme Court refused to remove the word and instead impugned the whole section. On the other hand, in *O'Mahony v Melia* (1989) (Case 146), the High Court was able to delete the offending words: section 15 of the *Criminal Justice Act 1951* read:

> (1) A person arrested pursuant to a warrant shall on arrest be brought before a justice of the District Court having jurisdiction to deal with the offence concerned [or, if a justice is not immediately available, before a peace commissioner in the district of such a justice as soon as practicable].

The unconstitutional words, which were deleted, are those within the brackets. The Supreme Court exercised its power of severance in *Desmond v Glackin* (1992) (Case 52).

Courts of Limited and Local Jurisdiction

The courts of first instance must include courts of limited and local jurisdiction with a right of appeal as determined by law (Article 34.3.4°). *Limited* must mean that courts so established may have such jurisdictions as are determined by law but must have lesser jurisdictions than the High Court. The word *local* was considered in *The State (Boyle) v Neylon* (1987) (Case 179) where it was claimed that the transfer of a criminal trial from the locality where the offences were committed to another area was in breach of Article 34.3.4° of the Constitution. The Supreme Court rejected the claim. Walsh J explained:

> it is quite clear that the whole structure of the [Circuit] Court is based upon the exercise of its jurisdiction locally, the localities being the circuits which are themselves created by statute and the boundaries of which have from time to time been altered by statute . . . It does not follow that for a legitimate reason the Oireachtas may not provide that in certain cases another locality would be properly available for the trial of a case whether civil or

criminal, as may be provided for by an Act of the Oireachtas. Experience has shown that justice itself would require a provision of this kind to avoid the risk of an injustice to one party or another by reason of local circumstances or conditions. The ability to transfer the trial of a case from one locality to another does not alter the essential local exercise of a jurisdiction of the Circuit Circuit.

As already noted, statute has established the Circuit Court and also the District Court, both of which are local and limited. The Court of Criminal Appeal, also established by statute, is limited though it is not local.

The Constitution envisages a system of appeals from courts of limited and local jurisdiction. Does this mean that a right of appeal must be available in every case? This point arose in *The State (Hunt) v O'Donovan* (1975) where an accused, having signed a plea of guilty in the District Court, was sent forward for sentence to the Circuit Court and could not appeal the sentence to the Court of Criminal Appeal because there had not been a conviction on indictment. The argument that the absence of a right of appeal was unconstitutional was rejected. The High Court ruled there was a very large gap between the interpretation that the article prohibited the establishment of a court of local and limited jurisdiction from which there was no appeal at all and the interpretation which excludes the right of the law to determine from which precise decision an appeal should lie.

Our System of Laws

It would have been impossible to invent a new system of laws for the State on the day the Constitution came into force, on 31 December 1937. Apart from the question of desirability it would have been impossible to achieve without great turmoil and confusion. The simple solution of continuing the system of laws then in force was adopted. The enactment of the Constitution, while important politically and legally, went almost unnoticed in the system of laws and in the courts. Article 50 declares that the laws in force in Saorstát Éireann were to continue to have full force and effect until amended or repealed by the Oireachtas, provided they were not inconsistent with the Constitution. There are many instances of statutes, for example, part of a 1935 statute in *McGee v Attorney General* (1974) (Case 101), and rules of the common law, for example, in *S. v S.* (1983) (Case 173), the prohibition on admission of evidence by a wife that a child born to her during wedlock was not the child of her husband, being declared inconsistent with the Constitution.

While it is not a central issue in constitutional law, it is a useful exercise to consider the nature of our legal system. It is not an indigenous one but imported, and has all the characteristics of the common law. Essentially it is judge-made law complemented by legislative intervention by a number of parliaments. It was almost fifty years after the achievement of political independence before the judiciary, and the legislature, felt confident to follow a unique direction in either law-making or in judicial interpretation. In the first edition of this book it was pointed out that, except in constitutional law, and then only because our basic legal document has no counterpart in the law of our nearest neighbour, our legal system has little to show for sixty years of independence. Our legislators despairingly plagiarised British statutes, our judges slavishly applied British precedents, our academic lawyers failed miserably to produce a written jurisprudence and our law reform was instigated by changes in British law and the fear that we would be out of step. There are now many hopeful signs that this dependence has weakened though a new outsider, the European Community has stepped into place. Our judges are, in various areas of the law, taking an independent attitude and there is now a considerable body of Irish legal books and writings. Regrettably our legislators still tend to hanker after our nearest neighbour when it comes to drafting new laws. It's easy and it's cheap, but it is hardly the badge of an independent State that it copies the laws of its nearest neighbour.

THE TRIAL OF OFFENCES

Due Process on a Criminal Charge
Article 38.1 of the Constitution declares that no person shall be tried on any criminal charge save in due course of law. Four methods of trial are provided, namely summary trial, trial by jury, trial by special court and trial by military tribunal. In addition the courts claim an inherent jurisdiction to try certain types of contempt summarily. Each method of trial is considered later but some consideration must be given firstly to the nature of a *criminal charge*, and then to the meaning of *due process*. Every person, and not merely citizens, can be tried and *person* includes both natural and artificial persons.*

Nature of Criminal Charge
The precise definition of a criminal charge has been much discussed among jurists for generations without general agreement on a definition. For example, in *Melling v Ó Mathghamhna* (1962) (Case 116) the matter was discussed in the context as to whether smuggling was criminal or civil in nature with the Supreme Court concluding that it was criminal. Kingsmill Moore J enumerated the *indicia* of a crime: (1) it is an offence against the community at large; (2) the sanction to be imposed is punitive; (3) failure to pay involves imprisonment; and (4) *mens rea** is a requirement. While not strictly accurate, it is a useful guideline. Lavery J looked to procedure in search of a definition and thought that proceedings

which permit the detention of the person concerned, the bringing of him in custody to a Garda Station, the entry of a charge . . . the searching of the person detained and the examination of papers and other things found upon him, the bringing of him before a District Justice in custody, the admission to bail to stand his trial and the detention in custody if bail is not granted or is not forthcoming, the imposition of a pecuniary penalty with the liability to imprisonment if the penalty is not paid has all the *indicia* of a criminal charge.

Proceedings commenced by summons are equally criminal. The High Court held, in *The State (McFadden) v Governor of Mountjoy Prison* (1981) (Case 193), that extradition proceedings are ancillary to criminal proceedings because the procedures for executing an extradition warrant were identical to those used when arresting for an offence. In *McLoughlin v Tuite* (1986) (Case 106) a statute which imposed penalties for failure to prepare and make income tax returns was challenged as being the imposition of punishment in a criminal matter without a criminal trial. The High Court, applying the reasoning laid down by the Supreme Court in *Melling*'s case, held that these penalties were non-criminal in nature and were recoverable only in civil proceedings. The High Court ruled, in *Downes v DPP* (1987), that an income tax statute which imposed a fixed penalty for the non-compliance with statutory obligations created a civil liability enforceable by civil proceedings and was not an offence capable of being prosecuted by the Director of Public Prosecutions. The High Court ruled, in *O'Keeffe v Ferris* (1993) (Case 143a), that a remedy for fraudulent trading in company law was civil in nature.

The Supreme Court ruled, in *Goodman International v Tribunal of Inquiry into the Beef Processing Industry* (1992) (Case 73), that a Tribunal of Inquiry established to inquire into matters of public importance and to report to the Oireachtas was not investigating a criminal charge because the essential nature of a trial of a criminal offence is that it was heard before a court or judge which had the power to punish in the event of a guilty verdict.

Due Course of Law
The expression 'due course of law' means that there must be basic fairness in procedures provided at a criminal trial. It is impossible to give a comprehensive list of each element of fair procedures and to discuss in detail many matters which are more pertinent to a textbook on the law of evidence. The right to basic fairness or due course of law includes the right to be adequately informed of the nature and substance of the charge, to hear and test the evidence offered by cross-examination, to be allowed to give and call evidence in rebuttal, to have the case heard by an impartial and independent tribunal, to have legal aid available if needed and to be granted bail. The High Court in

O'Leary v Attorney General (1991) (Case 145) ruled that every accused in every criminal trial had a constitutionally protected right to the presumption of innocence, a principle reiterated by the Supreme Court in *Hardy v Ireland* (1993) (Case 76). The right to due process requires that the burden of proof should be on the prosecution and that the standard of that proof should be beyond a reasonable doubt; it affords a defendant the right not to be put in double jeopardy, and the right to have the verdict and sentence reviewed on appeal.

In *Abbey Films Ltd v Attorney General* (1981) (Case 1) the Supreme Court held that a statute could impose on an accused the onus to establish a limited and specified matter in a criminal case, whereas in *King v Attorney General* (1981) (Case 88) the Supreme Court struck down a statute which permitted the guilt of an accused person to be proved by reference to previous convictions. The Supreme Court in *The State (O'Connell) v Fawsitt* (1986) (Case 196) held that an accused person was entitled to have criminal charges tried with reasonable expedition having regard to the circumstances of the charges, and in *Hannigan v Clifford* (1990) the Supreme Court ruled that an eighteen-month delay between the initial arrest and the bringing of the charge was not such that would prejudice the right to a fair trial. The High Court ruled in *C. v DPP* (1992) that a nine-year delay in making a complaint of sexual assault was unreasonably long and that the accused had been prejudiced in the preparation of a defence. *The State (McGlinchey) v Governor of Portlaoise Prison* (1982) decided that an accused person should have all criminal charges outstanding disposed of at the same time.

The High Court decided, in *Curtis v Attorney General* (1985) (Case 46), that all facts relevant to a particular prosecution must be determined by the court of trial. And in *The State (McCormack) v Curran* (1987) the Supreme Court held that an individual facing extradition proceedings to Northern Ireland could not demand to be tried in this jurisdiction under the *Criminal Law (Jurisdiction) Act 1976*. The Supreme Court suggested in *Goodman International v Tribunal of Inquiry into the Beef Processing Industry* (1992) (Case 73) that where a person charged with a criminal offence could for any reason establish that due to pre-trial publicity a fair trial was impossible the courts had jurisdiction to prevent an injustice occurring. The Supreme Court ruled, in *D. v DPP* (1993), that the test in such cases was whether there was a real risk of preventing the jury from giving an impartial verdict. The court in that case refused to prohibit the trial because of the nature of the publicity itself, a long and confused interview with the complainant in a sexual case on the front page of a Sunday newspaper, and because of the deserved confidence the judicial system had in juries to act responsibly. The Supreme Court ruled in *Glavin v Governor of Mountjoy Prison* (1991) (Case 72) that an accused person had a constitutional right to have any necessary preliminary examination in the District Court conducted by a judge duly appointed in accordance with the provisions of the Constitution.

Classification of Crimes

The common law divided crimes into felonies, misdemeanours* and statutory offences. The Constitution has departed from that classification. Article 38.2 divides crimes into minor and non-minor offences. In the absence of a constitutional definition as to what constitutes either a minor or non-minor offence the principles for deciding this crucial question have been laid down by the courts and applied in a number of cases. The first case is *Melling v Ó Mathghamhna* (1962) (Case 116) where the former Supreme Court stated the criteria for determining this issue: (1) how the law stood when the statute which created the offence and set out the punishment was enacted; (2) the severity of the penalty; (3) the moral quality of the act; and (4) its relation to common law offences. By and large in the subsequent cases the courts have determined that the punishment which may be imposed on conviction is the most important consideration and that the relevant criterion is the severity of penalty authorised and not the penalty actually imposed.

In all of the following cases those convicted of offences in the District Court, a court of summary jurisdiction (see below), argue in the High Court, and on appeal in the Supreme Court, that they have not been tried in accordance with the Constitution in that they should have been given a right to trial by jury. Those successful parties may as a result escape any punishment either because there was no statutory mechanism for providing a trial by jury or because for procedural reasons the time for bringing such proceedings had elapsed.

Three broad types of cases have come before the courts: 1) those where imprisonment features as a penalty; 2) those where the only penalty is the imposition of a fine; and 3) those where the loss of a licence follows conviction.

Why is this Distinction so Important?

The distinction between minor and non-minor offences is critical because it determines the method of trial which must be accorded the offence. Article 38.2 of the Constitution declares that minor offences may be tried in courts of summary jurisdiction whereas Article 38.5 provides that no person may be tried on any charge without a jury and this, by excluding minor offences, must apply to non-minor offences.

Crimes with Imprisonment as a Punishment

Many crimes carry imprisonment as a penalty. In *The State (Sheerin) v Kennedy* (1966) (Case 203) the District Court had imposed a two-year period of detention in a place, run as part of the prison service, which detained young adults only and in which training and instruction were given with a view to rehabilitation. The Supreme Court held that such a penalty took the offence out of the category of a minor offence on the ground that the deprivation of liberty was the real punishment and there was no material difference between suffering that loss of liberty in such a place and in a prison. But in *J. v Delap* (1989) (Case 83a) a period of three years in a reform school imposed on a 15-year-old was held by the High Court not to be analogous to a period of imprisonment and an offence carrying such a consequence was a minor offence.

The Supreme Court, in *Conroy v Attorney General* (1965) (Case 38), held that an offence which attracted a punishment of six months' imprisonment and/or £100 was not so severe as to exclude it from the category of minor offences. On the other hand, in *In re Haughey* (1971) (Case 77) the same court ruled that the offence in question was non-minor by reason of the unlimited nature of the imprisonment penalty authorised on conviction. Applying the reasoning of the *Haughey* case the Supreme Court in *The State (DPP) v Walsh* (1981) (Case 187) held that, generally speaking, the offence of contempt of court was a non-minor offence. Contempt of court, which carries the risk of a fixed but unlimited term of imprisonment or an unlimited fine on conviction, required the determination by a jury. The Supreme Court again applied the reasoning in *Haughey*'s case to *Desmond v Glackin* (1992) (Case 52) where the offence in question was contempt of court.

From these decided cases some guidelines can be drawn as to what constitutes a minor offence in contradistinction to what constitutes a non-minor offence where the crime carries imprisonment as a penalty. An offence which carries a sentence of six months' imprisonment or less is obviously minor, whereas an offence which carries two years or more is non-minor. Somewhere between lies the real borderline between the two. Further judicial pronouncements are necessary to indicate precisely where exactly that line settles.

Crimes with Monetary Punishments

Some crimes carry the possibility of the imposition of a monetary penalty only on conviction. In *Melling v Ó Mathghamhna* (1962) (Case 116) the former Supreme Court held that a smuggling offence which attracted a penalty of £100, or treble the value of the goods being smuggled provided they were valued at less than £100, was a minor offence. The imposition of an unlimited fine in lieu of damages for negligent driving was held by the High Court in *Cullen v Attorney General* (1979) (Case 45) to be non-minor. In *Kostan v Ireland* (1978) (Case 89) the penalty authorised by law on conviction for a fishing offence, apart from a nominal fine, was the forfeiture of the catch and fishing gear. The High Court, in holding the offence to be non-minor, declared that no one could deny that a punishment which involved the loss of property to the value of £100,000 was severe.

The penalty for the unlawful possession of salmon, a £25 fine and £2 for each fish, was challenged in *O'Sullivan v Hartnett* (1983) on the ground that the illegal possession of 900 salmon would have attracted a penalty of £1,825. In holding the offence to be non-minor, the High Court rejected the novel argument that salmon to the value of £7,862, in the unlawful possession of a defendant, should count as part of the penalty. The court ruled that a person in unlawful possession of property could not be said to be penalised in the sense of being fined when the property is confiscated in the course of enforcing the law.

A revenue offence, in *The State (Rollinson) v Kelly* (1984) (Case 202), which carried a mandatory fine of £500, which could be mitigated, was held by the Supreme Court, having regard to the contemporary value of £500, to be minor. Whether an offence is minor or non-minor cannot be determined by having regard to the cumulative effect it may have when tried with other offences. This rule was stated in *Charleton v Ireland* (1984) where the effect of the 64 summonses would be to expose the plaintiff to fines totalling something over £30,000. The High Court refused to accept that the nature of the offence could be gauged by reference to the cumulative effect of different (albeit allied) offences. In the view of the court the gravity of every offence must be considered separately. This point was emphasised again in *The State (Wilson) v Neylon* (1987) where the High Court held that in determining this issue each offence must be looked at separately and the gravity of each offence determined separately. An offence which was a minor offence could not change into a non-minor offence merely because a person was charged with a number of similar offences.

Loss of Licence on Criminal Conviction

Apart from the imposition of imprisonment and/or a fine on conviction a third possible consequence is the loss of a licence. Whether such loss is a punishment and should be calculated when determining whether an offence is minor or non-minor, was first raised in *Conroy v Attorney General* (1965) (Case 38). A mandatory driving disqualification was in issue in that case. The Supreme Court held that the disqualification was the regulation of a statutory right rather than a penalty. The court ruled that in so far as it may be classed as a punishment at all it was not a primary or direct punishment but rather an order which may, according to the circumstances of the particular individual concerned, assume, however remotely, a punitive character. Though it may have punitive consequences, disqualification could not be regarded as a punishment in the sense in which that term was used in considering the gravity of an offence by reference to the punishment it may attract on conviction such as imprisonment or a fine, but rather it was a finding of unfitness to hold the particular licence.

The reasoning in *Conroy*'s case was applied in two similar subsequent cases. In *The State (Pheasantry Ltd) v Donnelly* (1982) (Case 198) the High

Court held that the forfeiture of a liquor licence, on a third conviction, was not a primary punishment and not relevant when considering the gravity of an offence when deciding whether an offence under the licensing laws was minor or non-minor. Applying the precedent set by these cases, the High Court, in *Cartmill v Ireland* (1987), held that the forfeiture of a gaming machine, following a conviction for unlawful gaming, was a secondary punishment and not relevant in determining whether the offence was minor or non-minor. The machines were of considerable value, and this decision seems to ignore the case of *Kostan v Ireland*, discussed earlier. A further difficulty with this case was that no conviction had taken place and the High Court was asked to consider the issue in advance.

Summary Trial

Minor offences may, though not must, be tried in courts of summary jurisdiction (Article 38.2) A court of summary jurisdiction is one which gives judgment forthwith, by hearing and disposing of the case, and is often used in criminal procedure in contradistinction to trial by jury on indictment. Apart from providing for summary trial the Constitution is silent as to where, and how, this method of trial should be administered. The probability is that minor offences should be determined in a court of local and limited jurisdiction (Article 34.3.4°). The Constitution leaves the establishment and procedural aspects of summary trial to statute. At present the only ordinary court exercising summary jurisdiction is the District Court, which is presided over by a judge sitting alone without a jury, and who is a full-time lawyer paid from State funds. This court must try minor offences and may, in certain circumstances, try and punish non-minor offences. The punishment in such cases may be greater than those permitted for minor offences.[15] The District Court decides all issues of law and fact and its decisions of conviction and sentence can be appealed to the Circuit Court by aggrieved defendants and not by the prosecuting party. Its decisions are open to judicial review by the High Court, and on appeal in certain cases to the Supreme Court.

Trial by Jury

Apart from minor offences, special courts and military tribunals, no person shall be tried on any criminal charge without a jury according to Article 38.5 of the Constitution. The purpose of a jury is to interpose between the State and the accused an impartial body of the accused's fellow citizens to try the issue joined between the prosecution and the accused. A jury is a body of persons sworn to inquire of a matter of fact and to declare the truth on such evidence as is before them. The value and role of a jury was explained in *The People (DPP) v O'Shea* (1982) (Case 162) in the Supreme Court by Henchy J when he said:

this important personal right, commonly referred to as the right to trial by jury, is indicated in Article 38.5 to be a right to a 'trial with a jury', presumably to make clear . . . that what was being delineated was essentially a right to the evolved and evolving common law trial by jury, that is . . . a trial before a judge and jury, in which the judge would preside, ensure that all conditions necessary for a fair and proper trial of that nature are complied with, decide all matters deemed to be matters of law, and direct the jury as to the legal principles and rules they are to observe and apply; and in which the jury, constituted in a manner calculated to ensure the achievement of the proper exercise of their functions would, under the governance of the judge, be the arbiters of all disputed issues of fact, and in particular, the issue of guilt or innocence.

The basis for jury composition was considered in *de Búrca v Attorney General* (1976) (Case 49) by the Supreme Court. Henchy J explained:

the jury must be drawn from a pool broadly representative of the community so that its verdict will be stamped with the fairness and acceptability of a genuinely diffused community decision. The particular breadth of choice necessary to satisfy this requirement cannot be laid down in advance. It is left to the discretion of the legislature to formulate a system for the compilation of jury lists and panels from which will be recruited juries which will be competent, impartial and representative.

Following that decision the *Juries Act 1976* provides the current law on the subject. Jury panels are drawn from citizens aged between 18 and 70 years who are registered on the Dáil Éireann register of electors with certain persons excluded.

The *Criminal Justice Act 1984*, section 25, provides that the verdict of a jury in criminal proceedings need not be unanimous in a case where there are not fewer than eleven jurors if ten of them agree on the verdict. This departed from the common law which required a unanimous verdict of the twelve jurors. The Supreme Court found in *O'Callaghan v Attorney General* (1993) (Case 137) that a requirement of unanimity was not essential and rejected a constitutional challenge to the section.

As already noted trial by jury means trial by judge and jury. The judge supervises the conduct of the trial and decides and directs the jury on all questions of law. The Supreme Court decided in *The People (DPP) v Conroy* (1988) that the practice since the foundation of the State of having the issue of the admissibility of all evidence determined by the trial judge in the absence of the jury was required by Article 38 of the Constitution, since if such issues were determined as a preliminary matter by a jury there was a possibility of prejudice to the accused.

While the trial judge may advise the jury as to the facts, the jury decides the verdict and must be free to consider its verdict alone without the intervention or presence of the judge or any other person during its deliberations. There is an element of secrecy in so far as the members of the jury cannot be compelled to disclose which way they voted if, for example, the verdict is by majority. On the confidentiality of the jury's deliberation O'Flaherty J, in the Supreme Court in *O'Callaghan v Attorney General* (1993) (Case 137), noted:

> the court would wish to reiterate that the deliberations of a jury should always be regarded as completely confidential. The course of the deliberations of a jury should not be published after a trial.

The jury has no function in the imposition of punishment on a guilty verdict. In criminal matters jury trials are available in the Circuit Court and the Central Criminal Court (the High Court). Appeals from the former go to the Court of Criminal Appeal and from the latter either to the Court of Criminal Appeal or to the Supreme Court at the election of the appellant.* This appellate jurisdiction of the Supreme Court, in this regard, was considered earlier in this chapter on page 119.

Article 30.3 provides that all indictable offences prosecuted in any court constituted under Article 34 shall be prosecuted in the name of the People and at the suit of the Attorney General or some other person authorised in accordance with law to act for that purpose. Currently this task falls to the Director of Public Prosecutions (see page 146).

Special Courts

Article 38.3 of the Constitution permits the establishment of special courts and their constitution, powers, jurisdiction and procedure are to be prescribed by law. According to Article 38.6 the provisions of Articles 34 and 35 do not apply to special courts, which means that members of special courts need not be appointed by the President as are the judges of the ordinary courts, can be removed from office by methods other than the resolutions of both Houses of the Oireachtas, can have their salaries regulated and reduced while in office, and are not required to make a declaration to uphold the Constitution and the law. The traditional protections which ensure judicial independence are not given to members of special courts. It was argued in *Eccles v Ireland* (1985) (Case 62) that the apparent lack of judicial independence of members of a Special Criminal Court rendered a trial by that court void as not being in due course of law. The argument was rejected by the Supreme Court. Finlay CJ concluded:

> the non-application of these guarantees [in Article 35 of the Constitution] to persons sitting as members of the Special Criminal Court does not of

itself resolve the issue as to whether that court is so deprived of judicial independence as to render a trial before it of a person on a criminal charge otherwise than in due course of law.

But the Supreme Court did accept that any attempt by the executive to interfere with the independence of that court would frustrate the constitutional right of a person accused before it, and any such attempt would be prevented or corrected by the ordinary courts. This decision suggests that the onus of proving influence by the executive lies on the accused, which would of course be almost impossible. The intention of granting guarantees of independence to the judiciary under Article 35 of the Constitution was that justice would be seen to be done.

The mere possibility of establishing special courts is a dangerous threat to equality of treatment of those accused of crime. Once the concept of special courts is accepted it is impossible to defend the continued existence of the ordinary courts and this is particularly so if it is argued that special courts and ordinary courts administer the same standards of justice. A critical study of special courts is impossible because of the vigorous use of the law of contempt against those venturing to do so.

Special courts are only permitted when the ordinary courts are inadequate to secure the effective administration of justice and the preservation of the public peace and order. This crucial decision is made in a manner prescribed by law. The current law, the *Offences Against the State Act 1939*, vests this power in the executive arm of government, and was given judicial approval in *In re MacCurtain* (1941) (Case 98), in the High Court, by Gavan Duffy J when he said:

> the Government, in declaring itself satisfied . . . of the inadequacy of the ordinary courts and of the necessity to set up special courts cannot be said to be acting either in a judicial or in a legislative capacity.

Part V of the 1939 Act which sets out the constitution, powers, jurisdiction and procedure of special courts has been brought into force on numerous occasions, the last in May 1972. The essential feature of such courts is the absence of a jury. Membership of this court may be drawn from existing judges of the High Court, Circuit Court and District Court, or from barristers or solicitors of seven years' standing, or officers of the Defence Forces not below the rank of commandant. It was held in *In re MacCurtain* (1941) (Case 98) that the composition of the court by all army officers did not of itself convert the court into a military tribunal. Many judges of the ordinary courts serve as members of the Special Criminal Court though resort has been made to lawyers because it seems that not all the judges of the ordinary courts are willing to serve as members. Members of the court are appointed and removable at the will of the government and are paid such sums as the Minister for Finance decides. A Special Criminal Court must contain an uneven number of members, never less than three, and a verdict is that of the majority. In order to suffer conviction only two persons need be satisfied as to the guilt of an accused, whereas in a trial by jury generally all twelve jurors must be satisfied or in certain circumstances at least ten must agree on the verdict.

Ordinary criminal courts and special courts operate together; so who decides, and on what basis, by which court a person should be tried? This task rests with the Director of Public Prosecutions and it was decided in *Savage v Director of Public Prosecutions* (1982) that a certificate of the Director of Public Prosecutions that the ordinary courts were not adequate to secure the effective administration of justice and the protection of public peace and order could not be reviewed by the courts. Superficially it seems that 'subversive' crimes are dealt with by the Special Criminal Court and 'ordinary' crimes are disposed of by the ordinary courts. But even if it were possible to distinguish between crimes on this basis it is impossible to discern any pattern from the decisions of the Director of Public Prosecutions in this regard. Presumably a decision is made on the basis of garda reports and it is to be hoped these are of a better quality than those used to intern persons without trial. In *In re Ó Láighléis* (1960) (Case 144) the commission reviewing an individual's continued internment was furnished with a file marked 'Secret and confidential' which contained, *inter alia*,* carbon copies of certain documents with no originals, unsigned and anonymous reports from unspecified persons, and at least one report emanating from the 'Special Branch'.

Following conviction by the Special Criminal Court a person in the employment of the State or paid by funds coming from the State would forfeit that employment and pension rights. This was successfully challenged on constitutional grounds in *Cox v Ireland* (1991) (Case 42).

A consequence of the establishment of the Special Criminal Court in 1972 has been the enactment of statutes which depend for their operation on the existence of such a court. For example, much of the *Criminal Law (Jurisdiction) Act 1976* can only operate when a Special Criminal Court is in existence.

Military Trials

The Constitution in Article 38.4 provides for two kinds of military trials. The first, termed military tribunals, may be established to try offences against military law committed by persons subject to military law, and to deal with a state of war or armed rebellion.[16] The second, termed courts martial, may be established for the enforcement of military discipline within the defence forces. The *Defence Act 1954* sets out the constitution, powers, jurisdiction and procedure of courts martial. An appeal lies to the Courts-Martial Appeal Court.

Trial of Contempt of Court

Apart from the four methods of trial enumerated in Article 38 of the Constitution the courts themselves assume the power to punish for any act which plainly tends to create a disregard for the authority of the courts. Contempt of court is discussed fully in Chapter 15 on page 238 when examining the restrictions which are placed on the exercise of freedom of expression.

Contempt *in facie curiae* (in the face of the court) may be punished summarily by the court before which the contempt was committed but it must, as decided in *Keegan v de Búrca* (1973), be for a definite period of imprisonment. *The State (DPP) v Walsh* (1981) (Case 187) decided that the contempt of scandalising a court was, in general, triable by jury. The Supreme Court divided on the issue. The minority held that justice could only be protected by swift action and that summary disposal was constitutionally permissible. The majority held there was prima facie a right to trial by jury where there were live and real issues of fact to be decided. In cases where there are no live issues of fact to be tried the matter may be disposed of summarily by the High Court.[17]

With regard to the trial of civil contempt the High Court decided, in *The State (Commins) v McRann* (1977) (Case 185), that the matter can be disposed of summarily and that trial by jury is not available. The period of imprisonment may be of indefinite duration. That decision was approved by the Supreme Court in *The State (H.) v Daly* (1977).

Prosecution of Offences

Article 30.3 of the Constitution provides that all crimes and offences prosecuted in any court constituted under Article 34, other than a court of summary jurisdiction, shall be prosecuted in the name of the People, at the suit of the Attorney General, or some other person authorised in accordance with law to act for that purpose. The Office of the Director of Public Prosecutions was established by the *Prosecution of Offences Act 1974*. The Director, while a civil servant, is independent in the exercise of his or her functions. The functions of the Director are those capable of being performed by the Attorney General in relation to criminal matters. The exact scope of these powers was considered in *The State (Collins) v Ruane* (1984). In that case a Garda, acting as a common informer, initiated proceedings in a summary criminal matter and the question arose whether the Director of Public Prosecutions could withdraw such proceedings. The Supreme Court held that the Director of Public Prosecutions could not withdraw such proceedings.

As regards the general right to prosecute criminal matters the position, following from that decision, appears to be this: Article 30 vests the right to prosecute, in courts other than summary courts, in the Attorney General; this power may also be entrusted by statute to others, as it has to the Director of Public Prosecutions, but not to the exclusion of the Attorney General; the

Attorney General, the Director of Public Prosecutions and others, such as members of the Government, have the power to prosecute in courts of summary jurisdiction, conferred by various statutes; a common informer, that is a private prosecutor, can bring and conduct summary proceedings and that nothing in the Constitution or statute law has altered this rule; should summary proceedings be initiated by a Garda in the name of the Director of Public Prosecutions, the director has full control of such proceedings and can withdraw them; and, where a Garda, or other person, as a common informer, initiates summary proceedings, that complainant is completely independent of the Director of Public Prosecutions in the conduct of those proceedings.

The Supreme Court decided in *The State (Ennis) v Farrell* (1960) that a common informer could initiate, and manage, a complaint of an indictable offence during its summary stages, but that once the defendant was returned for trial the prosecution must be continued beyond that point by the Attorney General, and now the Director of Public Prosecutions. The court suggested that a private prosecutor who had adduced sufficient evidence to effect a return for trial could, as a general rule, rest assured that the Attorney General, or the Director of Public Prosecutions, would carry the case to trial before a judge and jury. The Supreme Court ruled, in *Cumann Luthchleas Gael Teo v Windle* (1993), that a body corporate could not institute criminal proceedings for an indictable offence by way of common informer.

ADMINISTRATION OF JUSTICE OTHERWISE THAN BY COURTS

Administrative Powers
The Constitution permits the exercise of limited functions and powers of a judicial nature by persons or bodies who are not judges or courts established under the Constitution (Article 37). It cannot therefore be said that all justice must be administered by judges in courts established under the Constitution. This article acknowledged the existing, and expanding, practice of permitting administrative tribunals to decide issues of conflict. These administrative tribunals are now an accepted part of our legal apparatus and are active in a wide variety of areas. The courts control these tribunals in various ways, for example, by insisting that they act *intra vires* and by applying the rules of fair procedures.

Criminal Matters Exclusive Domain of Courts
There are constitutional limitations on the extent of these powers. First, only courts can exercise jurisdiction in criminal matters, though what precisely a criminal matter is may cause some difficulty of definition. This occurred in

The State (Murray) v McRann (1979) (Case 194) where an assault was punished as a breach of prison discipline. A criminal offence was defined as an offence against the State or the public. According to Finlay P:

> a criminal matter within the meaning of Article 37 can be construed as a procedure associated with the prosecution of a person for a crime.

This decision is at variance with the view of Kingsmill Moore J, in the former Supreme Court, in the case of *In re O'Farrell* (1960) (Case 142) when he said:

> a characteristic feature of criminal matters is the infliction of penalties, a consideration which gives weight to the submission that a tribunal which is authorised to inflict a penalty, especially a severe penalty, even in cases where the offence is not strictly criminal, should be regarded as administering justice.

Limited Judicial Powers

The second limitation on the administration of justice by persons or bodies other than courts or judges, is that the function or power must be limited. How is this direction to be applied? The first dilemma, which we met at the beginning of this chapter, is either how to define a *judicial* power, or failing that, at least to be able to distinguish a *judicial* power from an *administrative* power. In this approach, taken in some of the cases on Article 37, it is a condition precedent that the power in question be judicial. Only if this question is answered in the affirmative does the second question arise as to whether the power is limited in nature.

This was the approach taken by the former Supreme Court in *Fisher v Irish Land Commission* (1948) (Case 68) where it was held that the resumption for specific purposes of land vested in the Land Commission, but let to a tenant, was purely an administrative act. This position was adopted by the present Supreme Court in *McDonald v Bord na gCon* (1965) (Case 100) where a distinction was drawn between an administrative power and a judicial power without any great attempt at a definition of either terms. In that case Kenny J in the High Court held the power in question to be judicial in nature and not a limited one. This decision was overruled by the Supreme Court which held that the power was administrative in nature. A like result was achieved by the High Court in *Madden v Ireland* (1980) (Case 109) where the power to compulsorily acquire land was considered administrative. The High Court, in *McCann v The Racing Board* (1983), came to a similar conclusion. The Supreme Court, in *O'Brien v Bord na Móna* (1983) (Case 133), concluded that the power of compulsory acquisition, obviously drastic in effect, was administrative rather than judicial in nature. The dismissal of a Garda from office was considered by the Supreme Court, in *Keady v Commissioner of An Garda Síochána* (1992) (Case 84), not to be an administration of justice.

Having decided that the power in question is administrative rather than judicial in nature the function of the courts is at an end. Only if the courts find that the power is judicial in nature does the second question arise — is it limited? In *In re O'Farrell* (1960) (Case 142) Kingsmill Moore J, in the former Supreme Court, suggested:

> the test as to whether a power is or is not *limited* . . . lies in the effect of the assigned powers when exercised. If the exercise of the assigned powers and functions is calculated ordinarily to affect in the most profound and far-reaching way the lives, liberties, fortunes or reputations of those against whom they are exercised, they cannot properly be described as *limited*.

The court held invalid, as not being a limited power or function, the striking off from the roll of solicitors of two solicitors by the Incorporated Law Society, the professional body for solicitors.[18] This test was applied in *Cowan v Attorney General* (1961) (Case 41) where it was decided that a local election court presided over by a practising barrister would not exercise powers of a limited nature. The High Court in *Madden v Ireland* (1980) (Case 109) held that the power to fix a price at which land could be compulsorily acquired was limited in nature. In *M. v The Medical Council* (1984) (Case 95) the various powers and functions of the Medical Council, the professional body for the medical profession, and its various committees, were challenged in this regard. The statute confined the power to strike a doctor from the medical register to the High Court. It was held that other powers, such as the publication of a finding by one of the committees and the power to advise, admonish, or censure a doctor by the council, were limited powers and functions of a judicial nature.

There are many powers exercisable by persons or bodies who are not judges or courts. Each must be examined in the light of decided cases to determine firstly, whether the power is judicial, as distinct from administrative; and if it is, then secondly, whether it is limited in nature.

Part Two
CONSTITUTIONAL RIGHTS

Chapter 10

CONSTITUTIONAL RIGHTS IN GENERAL

Constitutional and Legal Rights Distinguished

Under the common law pertaining prior to 1922 an individual had legal rights and legal duties. A right, according to Salmond, was an interest recognised and protected by a rule of right, or a principle or rule enforced by the courts.[1] This definition has all the hallmarks of legal positivism which postulates law as the command of the sovereign and which excludes moral values from the definition of legal rights. Legal rights are granted by human laws and can be withdrawn or curtailed in the same manner. The law, however iniquitous or unjust, must be obeyed. The enactment of two constitutions has changed utterly this philosophy. The enumeration of a collection of express rights in a document which was given a superior status as a source of law inevitably involved the theory that these rights were of a different character than mere legal rights. Two classes of rights were then acknowledged to exist: *constitutional rights* and *legal rights*.

The courts were slow to grasp this shift in emphasis probably because the judges of that early era after independence had been educated in the positivist school and because the significance of a written constitution, which contained expressions of rights, was simply not understood. The clash between the two kinds of rights, and the philosophical basis of each, can be clearly seen in *The State (Ryan) v Lennon* (1935), which was concerned with an amendment of the Constitution of Saorstát Éireann. The positivist view, held by the majority of the former Supreme Court, was expounded by FitzGibbon J thus:

> [counsel] . . . assert that there are certain rights, inherent in every individual, which are so sacred that no legislature has authority to deprive him of them. It is useless to speculate upon the origin of a doctrine which may be found in the writings of Rousseau, Thomas Paine, William Godwin, and other philosophical writers, but we have not to decide their theories and those of Delolme and Burke, not to mention Bentham and Locke . . . as we are concerned, not with the principles which might or ought to have been adopted by the framers of our Constitution, but with the powers which have

actually been entrusted by it to the legislature and executive which it set up. When a written Constitution declares that 'the liberty of the person is inviolable' but goes on to provide that 'no person shall be deprived of his liberty except in accordance with law' then if a law is passed that a citizen may be imprisoned indefinitely upon a *lettre de cachet* signed by a Minister ... the citizen may be deprived of his 'inviolable' liberty, but, as the deprivation will have been 'in accordance with law' he will be as devoid of redress as he would have been under the regime of a French or Neapolitan Bourbon.

But Kennedy CJ, in a minority judgment, looked to some higher source than mere man-made law:

it follows that every act, whether legislative, executive, or judicial, in order to be lawful under the Constitution, must be capable of being justified under the authority thereby declared to be derived from God. From this it seems clear that, if any legislation of the Oireachtas (including any amendment to the Constitution) were to offend against that acknowledged ultimate *source* from which the legislative authority has come through the people to the Oireachtas, as, for instance, if it were repugnant to the natural law, such legislation would be necessarily unconstitutional and invalid, and it would be, therefore, absolutely null and void.

Here was the first judicial attempt to mark rights, expressed in the fundamental legal document of the State, with a characteristic distinctively different from mere legal rights and the source was the natural law.

Natural law is perceived as deriving from some absolute source such as God's revealed word. Its precepts, it is claimed, reflect the essential character of the universe; they are immutable and eternally valid and can be grasped and understood by the proper employment of human reason. When perceived, these precepts of the natural law must overrule all positive law.[2]

The first effort at introducing the notion that the Constitution of Ireland, whatever about the Constitution of Saorstát Éireann, by expressly and clearly stating certain robust sentiments, was laying down ideal propositions against which ordinary law was to be judged was made in *The State (Burke) v Lennon* (1940) (Case 181). In the High Court, Gavan Duffy J explained:

the saving words in the declaration that 'no citizen shall be deprived of his liberty save in accordance with law' cannot be used to validate an enactment conflicting with the constitutional guarantees. The opinion of FitzGibbon J in *Ryan*'s case is relied on but it does not apply ... to a Constitution in which fundamental rights and constitutional guarantees effectively fill the *lacunae** disclosed in the polity of 1922. The Constitution, with its most impressive Preamble, is the charter of the Irish People and I will not whittle it away. There is nothing novel in the solemn recognition of the right to personal freedom as an essential basis of the social structure of a society of free men.

But the former Supreme Court, some two months later, again paid homage to the supremacy of positive law. In *Article 26 and the Offences Against the State (Amendment) Bill 1940* (Case 10), Sullivan CJ reaffirmed:

> the phrase 'in accordance with law' is used in several Articles of the Constitution, and we are of opinion that it means in accordance with the law as it exists at the time when the particular Article is invoked and sought to be applied ... A person in custody is detained in accordance with law if he is detained in accordance with the provisions of a statute duly passed by the Oireachtas.

The natural law basis for the fundamental rights enumerated in the Constitution had to wait until the mid-1960s before it came into its own and then with a vengeance. A new era in constitutional law dawned. It began with *Ryan v Attorney General* (1965) (Case 171) and has continued unashamedly since. It has fundamentally altered our attitude to the Constitution, to the law, to administrative action, and to constitutional rights. The words, few in number but of immense significance, by Kenny J, which brought about this transformation were:

> there are many personal rights of the citizen which follow from the Christian and democratic nature of the State which are not mentioned in Article 40 at all.

Constitutional rights are not alone superior to positive law but there are actually many natural rights to which the individual is entitled which are not expressed in the Constitution. Since the Constitution was not the source of these rights, then inescapably it must be the natural law. Following this decision the concept of natural law as a source of our fundamental, human, natural, civil, personal — entitle them as one may — rights, swept across judicial thinking and the consequences were far reaching. The summit was reached in *McGee v Attorney General* (1974) (Case 101) when Walsh J, in the Supreme Court, declared:

> Articles 41, 42 and 43 emphatically reject the theory that there are no rights without laws, no rights contrary to the law and no rights anterior to the law.

Source of Constitutional Rights

The Constitution is not the source of natural rights because if it were, then by an amendment, fundamental rights enumerated therein could be negatived. The

Preamble acknowledges that the aim of the Constitution is to seek to promote the common good, with due observance of prudence, justice and charity. According to Walsh J in the *McGee* case:

> natural rights or human rights are not created by law but the Constitution . . . confirms their existence and gives them protection. The individual has natural and human rights over which the State has no authority.

A novel point was raised by Murnaghan J in *The State (Ryan) v Lennon* (1935) when he warned:

> the view contended for . . . must go to this extreme point, viz. that certain Articles or doctrines of the Constitution are utterly incapable of alteration at any time, even if demanded by an absolute majority of the voters.

Such alteration has indeed occurred on one occasion, but as yet has not been subject to judicial review on constitutional grounds. In *G. v An Bord Uchtála* (1980) (Case 70) the Supreme Court declared that the mother of an illegitimate child has a constitutional right to the custody of that child. The following year the People added a provision to the Constitution, Article 37.2, by the *Sixth Amendment to the Constitution (Adoption) Act 1979*, which declared that no adoption order made under legislation enacted after the enactment of the Constitution could be invalidated on the ground that the body making the adoption order was not a judge or a court.[3] Effectively this prevents mothers of illegitimate children, who have been adopted, from asserting their constitutional rights to the custody of their children, at least on this ground, though other grounds would be open to them.

The individual is also the possessor of legal rights though legal rights may be curtailed or negatived by legislation. While constitutional rights may be regulated by law in furtherance of the common good a safeguard exists in that such regulation is open to review by the courts. While constitutional rights can be regulated by law they cannot be totally abrogated by law.

No Absolute Constitutional Right

An individual stranded on a desert island is, within environmental limitations, possessed of every right. That individual can go as he or she pleases, say what he or she wants and do as he or she likes. In a sense, that individual can exercise rights in an absolute way without any restrictions whatsoever. But once joined on the island by another human person a surrender of some of those rights must be made in order to live in community together. The obvious needs of society demand that the rights of each individual must be limited for the common good, which is, in simple terms, the equal needs of others. For example, an absolute right to personal liberty means that a wrongdoer could not be imprisoned, and an absolute right to freedom of expression residing in one individual would mean that a right to one's good name could not exist for other individuals. Should absolute rights exist it follows that only one individual could be possessed of them. That individual would be free and all others would be slaves. According to Kenny J in *Ryan v Attorney General* (1965) (Case 171):

> none of the personal rights of the citizen are unlimited: their exercise may be regulated by the Oireachtas when the common good requires this . . . the Oireachtas has to reconcile the exercise of personal rights with the claims of the common good, and its decision on the reconciliation should prevail unless it is oppressive to all or some of the citizens or unless there is no reasonable proportion between the benefit which the legislation will confer on the citizens or a substantial body of them and the interference with the personal rights of the citizen.

While regulation is necessary the extent of that regulation must not be such as to abrogate the exercise of constitutional rights completely. While the reconciliation of personal rights with the common good is a matter primarily for the Oireachtas it was accepted in *Abbey Films Ltd v Attorney General* (1981) (Case 1) by Kenny J in the Supreme Court:

> there is nothing to prevent the legislature from investing the courts with the sole jurisdiction to determine whether a particular act is or is not required by the exigencies of the common good.

Many of the constitutional law cases are disputes as to whether the legislature has in caring for the common good infringed too restrictively into personal freedoms. For example, in *McGee v Attorney General* (1974) (Case 101), the question for settlement was whether the restrictions placed on the availability of artificial contraceptives to married couples went far wider than was necessary for the protection of the common good. It was never claimed that there should be unrestricted access. The courts in striking down the legislation held that the restriction strayed unnecessarily into the area of personal freedoms.

Constitutional Duties

The possessor of an absolute right, presuming that such were possible, is under no duty to another as to its exercise. A 'duty', according to Salmond, is an obligatory act, the opposite of which is a wrong. When the law recognises an action as a duty it commonly enforces the performance of it, or punishes the disregarding of it. Some jurists argue that duties, and not rights, alone exist. An individual receives the benefit of a right when another refrains from acting in a particular way towards him or her, or is punished for such an action. Rights and duties are reverse sides of the one coin. This concept of duty is another method of limiting the performance of a right. The possessor of a right is limited as to its exercise: it cannot be used to the detriment of another. According to Ó Dálaigh CJ, in the *Educational Co. of Ireland v Fitzpatrick* (1961) (Case 63):

> liberty to exercise a right, it seems to me, prima facie implies a correlative duty on others to abstain from interfering with the exercise of such a right.

A Hierarchy of Rights

Has each constitutional right the same status and value? Taking each one in isolation, the answer must be yes. Each constitutional right must be given a quality and must consist of characteristics which are neither inferior nor superior to other constitutional rights. When one right is weighed against another in the scales of justice equality is the result.

The difficulty arises where the exercise of constitutional rights collide. In other words, the exercise of two constitutional rights in a head-on collision in a given situation must result in the advancement and recognition of the right of one individual to the exercise of one constitutional right and the denial of the right of the other individual to exercise another constitutional right. This dilemma is illustrated by the facts of *The People (DPP) v Shaw* (1982) (Case 164) where the constitutional right to life of one individual clashed with the constitutional right to personal liberty of another individual. In the Supreme Court Griffin J said:

> where such a conflict arises, a choice must be made and it is the duty of the State to protect what is the more important right, even at the expense of another important, but less important, right. The State must therefore weigh each right for the purpose of evaluating the merits of each, and strike a balance between them, and having done so to take such steps as are necessary to protect the more important right.

Other cases in which this balancing of rights was necessary are *Attorney General (Society for the Protection of Unborn Children Ltd) v Open Door Counselling* (1989) (Case 16a) where the clash was between the right to life of the unborn and the right to disseminate certain information, and in *Attorney General v X.* (1991) (Case 16) where the conflict was between the right to life of the unborn and the mother's right to life. Each case must be judged on its particular facts and it cannot follow, as a general rule, that any one right will always take precedence over other rights.

The Availability of Implied Constitutional Rights

A reading of the Articles on fundamental rights quickly establishes that only a handful of expressed rights are acknowledged. Are these then the only rights to which the individual is entitled? In other words, is this list exhaustive and can other rights only be acknowledged by constitutional amendment, as happened when the People enacted the *Eighth Amendment of the Constitution (Pro-Life) Act 1983*?

The courts have firmly rejected the notion that the only rights from which the individual can benefit are those ones expressly acknowledged. The courts have been inventive and flexible by interpreting the Constitution in such a way as to acknowledge the existence of other constitutional rights which are not expressly enumerated. This path was first charted in *Ryan v Attorney General* (1965) (Case 171) where Article 40.3 was minutely considered. It declares that the State guarantees in its laws to respect, and as far as practicable, by its laws to defend and vindicate the personal rights of the citizen, and the State shall, in particular, by its laws protect as best it may from unjust attack and, in the case of injustice done, vindicate the life, person, good name, and property rights of every citizen. In the High Court Kenny J reasoned that the use of the words 'in particular' related to rights connected with the life and good name of the individual and, as mere examples, did not exhaust the category of personal rights:

> it follows that the general guarantee. . . must extend to rights not specified in Article 40. Secondly, there are many personal rights of the citizen which follow from the Christian and democratic nature of the State which are not mentioned in Article 40 at all.

This conclusion was accepted by the Supreme Court on appeal and it paved the way for one of the most innovative features of our constitutional law. Who should declare the existence of these constitutional rights? Kenny J, again in the same case, stated:

> in modern times this would seem to be a function of the legislative rather than of the judicial power but it was done by the courts in the formative period of the common law and there is no reason why they should not do it now.

This function is not exclusive to the courts: it can and should be exercised by the Oireachtas. It is a rather unfortunate consequence of the great development in constitutional rights in recent years that the Oireachtas is wrongly cast as the whittler away of rights while the courts are seen as the exclusive protector of rights. A more positive role by the Oireachtas in this respect might recover for it some of the ground lost to the courts.

There is no universally accepted way of describing these rights. They are referred to differently by different jurists. Descriptions such as 'implied', 'unspecified', 'unenumerated' and 'latent' are frequently used to distinguish this collection of rights.

But Ó Dálaigh CJ, in the Supreme Court on appeal in *Ryan*'s case, warned that any attempt to list all the rights which may properly fall within the category of 'personal rights' would be difficult. This difficulty has not deterred the courts from declaring these constitutional rights to exist when the occasions arise in appropriate cases.

Because this collection of rights forms an amorphous group without any clear connection with each other apart from the fact that they are not expressly stated in the Constitution and because each such right can be connected, sometimes loosely, to an expressed right, a separate chapter is not given to them. Instead, each such right is examined when considering the expressed right most similar to it.

Surrender or Waiver of Constitutional Rights

An adult free from duress or undue influence is permitted to waive a legal right. Individuals constantly waive or surrender constitutional rights on a temporary basis. For example, a person taking employment waives the constitutional right to personal liberty in that presence in a particular place is usually required, the right to freedom of expression in that confidentiality may be demanded and freedom of association in that fellow employees will be chosen by the employer. The surrender of these rights is of a temporary duration and the restrictions cease when the employment is terminated.

The question whether an individual can irrevocably surrender or waive a constitutional right has been alluded to in a number of cases. According to Murnaghan J in *Murphy v Stewart* (1973) (Case 125):

> a person *sui juris** may agree to surrender or to waive all or part of his constitutional right . . . Before a court could decide that such a person had in fact made such a surrender or waiver it would have to be satisfied that the person involved, with a clear knowledge of what he was doing, deliberately decided to make such a surrender or waiver.

This view was largely accepted by the Supreme Court in *G. v An Bord Uchtála* (1980) (Case 70) where the question arose whether the mother of an illegitimate child could abandon her constitutional right to guardianship and custody of her child. According to O'Higgins CJ:

> this requires a free consent on the part of the mother given in the full knowledge of the consequences which follow upon her placing her child for adoption.

Walsh J, in the same case, was satisfied that, having regard to the natural rights of the mother, the consent, if given, must be such as to amount to a fully-informed, free and willing surrender or an abandonment of such rights. It can be concluded from these dicta that a constitutional right can be waived, surrendered or abandoned provided the individual concerned not alone knows what is being done, but understands the consequences of that act.

As already noted, a distinction must be made between a permanent and a temporary surrender, abandonment or waiver. Where the surrender, abandonment or waiver is of a temporary nature the individual may be able to reassert the right. Thus in *In re Doyle, an infant* (1955) (Case 56) a parent who consented to the placing of a child in an industrial school where his circumstances made it impossible to care for the child was able successfully to challenge a statute which prohibited the return of the child when his circumstances improved.

Who Can Avail of Constitutional Rights?

Some fundamental rights are expressly declared to attach to *citizens* while others are expressed to attach to *persons*. For example, no citizen can be deprived of personal liberty (Article 40.4.1°) and the dwelling of every citizen is inviolable (Article 40.5) whereas any person can make an application to the High Court under Article 40.4.2° and no person can be tried on any criminal charge save in due course of law (Article 38.1). While citizens are persons, not all persons living within the State are citizens (see page 24). These long-standing categories have been added to by two further classes of persons as a result of the *Eighth Amendment of the Constitution (Pro-Life) Act 1983*. The 'unborn' and the 'mother' are acknowledged as possessors of a particular constitutional right.

The question as to who can avail of and litigate on constitutional rights has been canvassed in some cases and ignored in others. This topic can be considered under a number of headings.

The first point for consideration is whether constitutional rights expressly acknowledged to be conferred on citizens are available for the protection of non-citizens. In *The State (Nicolaou) v An Bord Uchtála* (1966) (Case 195), the first case in which this question arose, a British citizen challenged a statute as to its constitutionality. The three judges of the High Court held differing views on this issue. Murnaghan J refused to express an opinion; Henchy J held that Article 40.3 could not apply though other provisions such as those relating to the family did; and Teevan J held that where there was no conflict between the common good and the right to be asserted by the non-citizen, the court should not refuse to hear the issue. The Supreme Court expressly reserved for another, and more appropriate, case consideration of the effect of non-citizenship on the interpretation of the Articles in question and also the right of a non-citizen to challenge the validity of an Act of the Oireachtas. In *The State (McFadden) v Governor of Mountjoy Prison* (1981) (Case 193) the High Court, on procedural grounds, granted the right to fair procedures to a British citizen. According to Barrington J:

> where the Constitution prescribes basic fairness of procedures in the
> administration of the law it does so, not only because citizens have rights,

but also because the courts in the administration of justice are expected to observe certain forms of due process . . . Once the courts have seisin of a dispute, it is difficult to see how the standards they should apply in investigating it should, in fairness, be any different in the case of [a non-citizen] than those to be applied in the case of a citizen.

In *Somjee v Minister for Justice* (1981) (Case 176), where a Pakistani citizen challenged a statute, the High Court followed the line taken by Walsh J in *The State (Nicolaou) v An Bord Uchtála* (1966) (Case 195) holding that it was unnecessary for the purpose of deciding the case to express any opinion on the submission, advanced on behalf of the State that, in any event, the plaintiff was precluded from asserting such rights because of his non-citizenship.

The Supreme Court, in *The People (DPP) v Shaw* (1982) (Case 164), ignored the fact that it was a British citizen who was pleading the constitutional right to personal liberty and considered the case on the basis that the constitutional right could be availed of. That approach was followed in *The State (Trimbole) v Governor of Mountjoy Prison* (1985) (Case 204) except McCarthy J who remarked:

it is not easy for anyone, particularly those outside the courts, to disassociate legal principles from the facts of any given case; it is important, therefore, to emphasise that the application of such legal principles must be the same for an Australian citizen on a temporary visit to Ireland as they would be for an Irish citizen, permanently resident in Ireland, when either of them is sought by a requesting State with which State Ireland has an extradition treaty or arrangement.

The High Court, in *Northampton County Council v A.B.F.* (1982) (Case 131), afforded to a British father the constitutional family rights under Article 41.

A number of non-citizens have availed of Article 38.1 which provides that no person shall be tried on any criminal charge except in due course of law. In *Kostan v Ireland* (1978) (Case 89) a Bulgarian citizen challenged a statute and in *L'Henryenat v Ireland* (1983) (Case 92) a French citizen did likewise.

Next for consideration is whether artificial persons, as distinct from human persons, can claim the protection of fundamental rights. The first consideration of this question was made by O'Keeffe P in *East Donegal Co-operative Livestock Mart Ltd v Attorney General* (1970) (Case 61) where he suggested that artificial persons may possibly not be entitled to rely on the constitutional guarantees, although they have been held to be so entitled in the United States. In *Quinn's Supermarket Ltd v Attorney General* (1972) (Case 168) Walsh J, referring to Article 40.1, said:

. . . it need scarcely be pointed out that under no possible construction of the constitutional guarantee could a body corporate or any entity but a human person be considered to be a human person for the purposes of this provision.

This view was followed in *Abbey Films Ltd v Attorney General* (1981) (Case 1) where the High Court ruled that a company was not a citizen within the meaning of the Constitution. It also appears to be very doubtful whether, having regard to the expression 'human persons' in Article 40.1 that personal rights could be attributed to a company for the purposes of the application of the Constitution. On appeal to the Supreme Court the question was left open for futher decision. Clearly, should a company be prosecuted the provisions of Article 38.1 would apply, if for no other reason that it would be impossible to afford one standard of justice to human persons and a different standard to artificial person.

In many constitutional actions a company is but one of the parties asserting the right: the others may be directors or shareholders. Examples of this joinder of parties are *Private Motorists Provident Society Ltd v Attorney General* (1983) (Case 167), and *Attorney General v Paperlink Ltd* (1984) (Case 12). In such cases constitutional rights may be afforded to individuals and not to the artificial person.

The next categories have arisen because of the amendment of the Constitution which accorded a constitutional right to life to the unborn and the equal right to life of the mother. Because the unborn cannot be possessed of citizenship the guarantee must be available to all unborn under the jurisdiction of the Irish courts. The expression 'mother' is wide enough to include all mothers, both those who are citizens and those who are non-citizens.

Who is to Vindicate Constitutional Rights?

As a general rule the proper person to vindicate constitutional rights is the person alleging infringement of the right. This strict rule as to *locus standi* governs the instance where the constitutionality of a statute is at issue (see page 124). There are obviously cases where the courts will permit one person to vindicate and protect the constitutional rights of another. One such instance is where parents may litigate to protect the constitutional rights of their children: see *O'Donoghue v Minister for Health* (1993) (Case 140, page 259). The Constitution permits an application to be made to the High Court, in Article 40.4.2°, by or on behalf of a person who is allegedly detained unlawfully.

Of necessity the right to life of the unborn can only be vindicated by another. The Supreme Court decided in *Attorney General (Society for the Protection of the Unborn Children (Ireland) Ltd) v Open Door Counselling Ltd* (1989) (Case 16a) that the Attorney General, as the holder of a high constitutional office, was an especially appropriate person to invoke the jurisdiction of the courts to vindicate and defend the constitutionally guaranteed right to life of the unborn. The same court decided in the later case of *Society for the Protection of Unborn Children (Ireland) Ltd v Coogan* (1990) that the Attorney General did not have an exclusive right to commence proceedings seeking to enforce compliance with Article 40.4.3° of the Constitution. Any citizen showing a bona-fide concern and interest in the right to life of the unborn may initiate an action seeking to enforce compliance with Article 40.3.3° of the Constitution.

Can the Courts Direct the Oireachtas to Provide Rights in Laws?
In the majority of constitutional cases claims were made that some statutory provision infringed some express or implied constitutional right. Where that claim was upheld the statutory provision was null and void, and the litigant and others were not bound to observe the provision which had been declared unconstitutional (see page 130). But in a small number of cases a very different claim has been made. The argument in these cases is that the absence from statute law of some particular provision rendered the statute constitutionally unsound. For procedural reasons the challenge had to be made that some existing law was unconstitutional though the kernal of the complaint was that the presence of some particular provisions would render it constitutionally more sound. For example, in *Dennehy v Minister for Social Welfare* (1984) (Case 51), while the challenge made to a statute was on the ground of discrimination there was no real objection to deserted wives receiving a special allowance. The essential grievance was that the non-availability of such allowance to deserted husbands rendered the statute unconstitutional. In *O'B. v S.* (1984) (Case 132) a challenge to the law relating to intestate succession was made not because it was objectionable in itself but because the absence from that code of provision for illegitimate children was discriminatory. In *Somjee v Minister for Justice* (1981) (Case 176) the claim was made that a statute which granted citizenship to a non-citizen woman who married a citizen was invalid because it did not grant the same right to a non-citizen male who married a citizen. While there was no begrudging non-citizen women this privilege the exclusion of non-citizen men from a like scheme was claimed to be unfair.

The hope of the litigant in such cases is that should the challenge be successful the Oireachtas will, when legislating for the defect exposed by the case, enact a law which would confer on the individual the benefit sought. This may or may not happen. The Oireachtas might leave well enough alone and refrain from legislating. For example, had the High Court struck down the deserted wives' allowance in *Dennehy*'s case, the Oireachtas might have been content to make the savings from not having to pay anyone such allowance rather than extending it to deserted husbands. In other words, a successful challenge may not confer any tangible benefit on the unsuccessful party. However it must be noted that in the three cases illustrated, unsuccessful though the challenges were, the Oireachtas when subsequently legislating did redress matters. There is now a single lone parents' allowance which can be claimed by deserted husbands; similar succession rights are available to all children and there is a common method of acquiring citizenship on marriage.

But the duty of the courts in such situations must be noted. In *Somjee*'s case Keane J in the High Court explained that had the challenge been successful:

> ... that would confer no benefit whatever on the plaintiffs: it would not redress any injustice ... or in any sense known to the law vindicate their personal rights ... The jurisdiction of this court in a case where the validity of an Act of the Oireachtas is questioned ... is limited to declaring the Act in question to be invalid, if that indeed be the case. The court has no jurisdiction to substitute for the impugned enactment a form of enactment which it considers desirable or to indicate to the Oireachtas the appropriate form of enactment which should be substituted for the impugned enactment.

Courts may Provide Rights by Declaring the Common Law

While the role of the courts is limited in instances where a successful challenge to a statute may bring no apparent benefit to the litigating party a different approach has been adopted by the courts where a common law rule is under attack. The case of *McKinley v Minister for Defence* (1992) (Case 105) clearly illustrates this approach. In that case it was argued that where it was shown that the absence from the common law of a right accruing to a wife which was available to her husband the correct approach was to extend the right to the wife rather than removing the right from her husband. McCarthy J explained:

> the simpler solution is to make the common law conform to the Constitution by declaring that the established right of the husband still exists and to deny such a right to the wife would be an infringement of Article 40.1.

While the Supreme Court acknowledged that the evolution of common law remedies by judicial interpretation was a well-established procedure it must give way to reform by an Act of the Oireachtas.

Remedies for Breach of Constitutional Rights

The remedy sought for a breach of constitutional rights will plainly depend on the particular circumstances of the litigant. Consequently there are a number a distinct remedies available for breach of constitutional rights.

The first of these, the challenge to the constitutionality of a statute, has been resorted to by litigants in a large number of cases. An individual feeling aggrieved by the operation of a particular statute, be it a pre-constitutional statute or rule of common law, or a post-constitutional statute, may seek a declaration to have it declared invalid or inconsistent. The result of a successful declaratory action is that the impugned provisions of that law are null and void and cannot operate against any individual in future (see page 130). Thus, following the decision of the courts in *McGee v Attorney General* (1972) (Case 101) the plaintiff, and other married persons, were entitled to have access to artificial contraceptives.

Another remedy which an individual may seek is to be set free from detentional restraint because either the law under which such detention is provided for is unconstitutional or because some constitutional procedure has not been observed. For example, in *The State (Sheerin) v Kennedy* (1966) (Case 203) a convicted prisoner was released following the decision that the law under which he was imprisoned should have afforded him the constitutional right to trial by jury (see page 138). And in *The State (Gilliland) v Governor of Mountjoy Prison* (1987) (Case 188) an extradition order was quashed because the State had not observed the constitutional requirement of having the Extradition Treaty approved by Dáil Éireann (see page 105).

An aggrieved individual may complain to the High Court under Article 40.4.2° of the Constitution, that his or her detention is not in accordance with law. An unlawful detention may also amount to a breach of the constitutional right to personal liberty. The classic illustration of this remedy is the case of *The State (Trimbole) v Governor of Mountjoy Prison* (1985) (Case 204) where the provisions of a law were abused to detain an individual who was ordered to be released, and a subsequent extradition order, valid in itself, could not retrieve the situation because it was tainted with the original illegality (see page 195).

A rule which the courts have long enforced is that evidence obtained in conscious and deliberate breach of constitutional rights is inadmissible in civil and criminal trials. This topic is discussed on page 195. Or an individual may escape being put in jeopardy of conviction on a criminal charge because there has been excessive delay in proceeding with the trial. This was the reason the Supreme Court, in *The State (O'Connell) v Fawsitt* (1986) (Case 196), prohibited a trial from proceeding and as a consequence an individual did not stand trial for offences of which the State alleged he was guilty (see page 137).

Another remedy for breach of constitutional rights is an action for damages for the unlawful interference with a constitutional right. This relief was first acknowledged in *Meskell v CIE* (1973) (Case 117) where an award of damages was made against an employer for conspiracy to deprive an individual of the constitutional right to dissociate. An award of exemplary damages was made in the cases of *Kennedy v Ireland* (1987) (Case 87), for breach of the constitutional right to privacy, and *Conway v INTO* (1991) (Case 39) for the breach of the constitutional right to free primary education. Such damages are awarded where there has been wilful and conscious wrongdoing in deliberate disregard of another's rights. The object of awarding exemplary damages is to punish the wrongdoer for the outrageous conduct, to deter such conduct in the future and to mark the court's detestation and disapproval of such conduct. But this remedy of damages must be sought against the party breaching the right. The High Court, in *D. v Ireland* (1992) (Case 47), refused to award damages against the State to a victim of crime.

The final remedy which may be awarded for a breach of constitutional rights is the injunction the essence of which is to prevent a continuance, a repetition or a threatened breach of constitutional rights. An injunction was granted in *Educational Co. of Ireland v Fitzpatrick* (1961) (Case 63) to prevent picketing, which was lawful in itself, because its purpose was to compel employees to refrain from exercising their constitutional right to dissociate (see page 224). In *Attorney General (Society for the Protection of Unborn Children (Ireland) Ltd v Open Door Counselling Ltd* (1989) (Case 16a) an injunction was granted to prevent assisting in the destruction of the life of the unborn.

Chapter 11

EQUALITY BEFORE THE LAW

Constitutional Right to Equality

Article 40.1 declares that all citizens shall, as human persons, be held equal before the law. This statement of high moral intent cannot be taken or applied literally. The law is peppered with inequalities both in its enacted laws and by the failure to legislate. Inequalities are often just. For example, it is just and equitable that minors be protected in contractual matters from certain sexual exploitation and be incapable of exercising certain civil liberties such as the right to vote. The taxation and social welfare codes are grounded in complicated and inexplicable inequalities. Positive inequalities are necessary in a civilised society. If Article 40.1 is to have any real substance it must seek out, and be used as a constitutional weapon against, something more than mere inequality. The courts in interpreting and applying this constitutional guarantee have suggested that legislation which *invidiously discriminates* offends the article. Invidious discrimination has been defined to mean unjust, unreasonable or arbitrary. It has been extremely difficult to formulate some accepted test by which legislation in this regard can be judged because of the subjective nature of each opinion given. But one worthy of consideration was suggested by Walsh J in *Quinn's Supermarket Ltd v Attorney General* (1972) (Case 168):

> this provision is not a guarantee of absolute equality for all citizens in all circumstances but it is a guarantee of equality as human persons and . . . is a guarantee related to their dignity as human beings and a guarantee against inequalities grounded upon an assumption, or indeed a belief, that some individual or individuals or classes of individuals, by reason of their human attributes or their ethnic or racial, social or religious background, are to be treated as the inferior or superior of other individuals in the community.

The scope of Article 40.1 extends only to citizens as human persons. It was held in the *Quinn's Supermarket* case that this guarantee did not extend to artificial persons.[1] Additionally this guarantee refers to human persons for what they are in themselves rather than to any lawful activities, trades or pursuits which they may engage in or follow. The High Court in *Madigan v*

Attorney General (1986) (Case 110) held (the Supreme Court was silent on the point) that the impugned law did not discriminate between the plaintiff and the rest of the community by reference to any attributes as human persons but merely by the reference to the value of premises occupied and by reference to the level of income. In *Heaney v Minister for Finance* (1986) (Case 78) the High Court ruled that Article 40.1 could not be called in aid because the complaint arose out of some activity in which the plaintiff was engaged rather than any attack on his dignity as a human person. This point was again emphasised in *Brennan v Attorney General* (1984) (Case 25) where O'Higgins CJ said:

> a complaint that a system of taxation imposed on occupiers of land which has proved to be unfair, even arbitrary or unjust, is not cognisable under the provisions of Article 40.1. This section deals, and deals only with the citizen as a human person and requires for each citizen as a human person, equality before the law ... the inequality ... in this case does not concern [the plaintiff's] treatment as human persons. It concerns the manner in which as occupiers and owners of land their property is rated and taxed.

Article 40.1 has been considered in many cases and a study of these will give some indication of how the courts have interpreted and applied this guarantee. It must be remembered that a decision which favours constitutionality, on one set of facts, may be impugned in the future and that some existing laws are likely to fall foul of the guarantee: it is an ongoing process.

Instances of Invidious Discrimination

Article 40.1 was successfully raised in a number of cases, the first of which was the *East Donegal Co-operative Livestock Mart Ltd v Attorney General* (1970) (Case 61) where a section of a statute which empowered the executive arm of government to grant exemptions from the application of a statute was impugned because the Supreme Court ruled that the Oireachtas could not constitutionally delegate such a function. The Supreme Court struck down a law which restricted jury service to persons with certain types of property in *de Búrca v Attorney General* (1976) (Case 49). O'Higgins CJ explained:

> this is a discrimination based not only on property but necessarily on a particular type of property ... if service [on a jury] be regarded as a right, then this means the exclusion of many thousands of citizens merely because they do not possess a particular type of property ... Without question, this is not holding all citizens as human persons to be equal before the law.[2]

A statute which permitted the proving of current criminal conduct by previous convictions was struck down in *King v Attorney General* (1981) (Case 88) because the citizens mentioned in Article 40.1 must include those who have been previously convicted when acting in any capacity which was not directly concerned with their previous criminal convictions. A provision which prohibited a widower, in certain circumstances, from adopting a child already in his custody fell foul of this guarantee in *O'G. v Attorney General* (1985) (Case 143). In the High Court, McMahon J concluded:

> widowers as a class are not less competent than widows to provide for the material needs of children and their exclusion as a class must be based on the belief that a woman by virtue of her sex has an innate capacity for parenthood which is denied to a man and the lack of which renders a man unsuitable as an adopter. This view is not supported by any medical evidence adduced before me and the fact that [the section] permits a widower who has already custody of a child to adopt another appears to be an admission that a man may acquire skills and capacities necessary to be an adopter.[3]

Rules of the common law may equally be scrutinised under Article 40.1 of the Constitution. The common law rule which stated that should a wife commit a crime in the presence of her husband it was presumed she committed it under his coercion was held not to have survived the enactment of the Constitution in *The State (DPP) v Walsh* (1981) (Case 187). In the Supreme Court Henchy J explained:

> a legal rule that presumes even on a prima facie and rebuttable basis that a wife has been coerced by the physical presence of her husband into committing an act prohibited by the criminal law, particularly when a similar presumption does not operate in favour of a husband for acts committed in the presence of his wife, is repugnant to the concept of equality before the law . . . therefore, the presumption contended for must be rejected as being a form of unconstitutional discrimination.[4]

The Supreme Court ruled in *W. v W.* (1993) (Case 209) that the common law rule that the domicile of a married woman was the same as that of her husband, the so-called dependent domicile rule, was contrary to Article 40.1 of the Constitution and did not survive its enactment (see pages 27 and 249). The Supreme Court also ruled in *McKinley v Minister for Defence* (1992) (Case 105) that the common law rule which granted to a husband the right to sue a third party for the loss of consortium of his wife and refused a similar remedy to a wife for the loss of the consortium of her husband offended Article 40.1 of the Constitution.

Instances of No Invidious Discrimination
More of the decided cases uphold various legislative measures on the ground that no invidious discrimination exists than there are cases where such a discrimination was acknowledged. In *O'Brien v Keogh* (1972) (Case 134)[5] the statutory provisions, according to Ó Dálaigh CJ in the Supreme Court:

far from effecting inequality would appear to attempt to establish equality between the two groups . . . Article 40 does not require identical treatment of all persons without recognition of difference in relevant circumstances. It only forbids invidious discrimination.

The High Court in *Landers v Attorney General* (1975) (Case 91) was not persuaded that a law which prevented a child of unusual musical talent from singing in a dance hall or similar place of public entertainment until it had reached the age of 14 years could fairly be described as invidious discrimination. The Supreme Court in *O'Brien v Manufacturing Engineering Co. Ltd* (1973) (Case 135) ruled that a statute which limited the bringing of an action by a workman who had accepted compensation to a period shorter than those who had not accepted compensation was not discrimination but a diversity of arrangements.

In *Somjee v Minister for Justice* (1981) (Case 176) a statute which conferred citizenship on non-citizen females who married citizens without a reciprocal arrangement for non-citizen males who married citizens[6] was upheld by the High Court. Keane J said:

> it is only in the case of [non-citizens] becoming married to Irish citizens that a distinction is drawn, and . . . the distinction is more properly regarded as conferring a form of privilege on female [non-citizens] rather than as being invidiously discriminating against male [non-citizens] . . . the provisions of the sections . . . do no more than provide a diversity of arrangements which is not prohibited by Article 40.1.

The Supreme Court in *Norris v Attorney General* (1984) (Case 130) rejected the argument that because statutes prohibited certain sexual conduct between males and failed to prohibit the same conduct between females offended Article 40.1. O'Higgins CJ said:

> the legislature would be perfectly entitled to have regard to the difference between the sexes and to treat sexual conduct . . . between males as requiring prohibition because of the social problems which it creates, while at the same time looking at sexual conduct between females as being not only different but as posing no such social problems.[7]

Dennehy v Minister for Social Welfare (1984) (Case 51) upheld a provision which granted a special allowance to certain deserted wives which could not be claimed by deserted husbands. In the High Court Barron J explained:

> the evidence adduced . . . indicates that the sections which are impugned were originally enacted to meet what was then an increasing problem of wives being deserted by their husbands and being left without proper provision. Similar provision was not made for husbands because the

desertion of husbands by their wives was not causing any problem which required to be resolved.[8]

Discrimination Constitutionally Permitted

Article 40.1 declares that the guarantee of equality before the law shall not be held to mean that the State shall not in its laws have due regard to differences of physical and moral capacity and of social function. This is a clear direction that inequalities are permissible on the grounds of capacity and of social function.

Difference of capacity justified legislation which interfered with the right to personal liberty. This was decided by the former Supreme Court in *In re Philip Clarke* (1950) (Case 36). O'Byrne J explained:

> the impugned legislation is of a paternal character, clearly intended for the care and custody of persons suspected to be suffering from mental infirmity and for the safety and well-being of the public generally. The existence of mental infirmity is too widespread to be overlooked, and was, no doubt, present to the minds of the draughtsmen when it was proclaimed in Article 40.1 of the Constitution that, though all citizens, as human persons, are to be equal before the law, the State may, nevertheless, in its enactments, have due regard to differences of capacity, physical and moral, and of social function. We do not see how the common good would be promoted or the dignity and freedom of the individual assured by allowing persons, alleged to be suffering from such infirmity, to remain at large to the possible danger to themselves and others.

In *The State (Nicolaou) v An Bord Uchtála* (1966) (Case 195) a provision which excluded the natural father of an illegitimate child from being consulted before its adoption was justified. In the Supreme Court Walsh J concluded:

> when it is considered that an illegitimate child may be begotten by an act of rape, or by a callous seduction or by an act of casual commerce by a man with a woman, as well as by the association of a man with a woman in making a common home without marriage . . . and that, except in the latter instance, it is rare for a natural father to take any interest in his offspring, it is not difficult to appreciate the difference in moral capacity and social function between the natural father and the several persons described in the sub-section.[9]

Certain provisions of the income tax code were upheld by the Supreme Court in *Murphy v Attorney General* (1982) (Case 123) on the ground of social function.[10] According to Kenny J:

> in so far as unequal treatment is alleged as between, on the one hand, married couples living together and, on the other, unmarried couples

living together, the social function of married couples living together is such as to justify the legislature in treating them differently from single persons for income tax purposes. Numerous examples could be given from the income tax code of types of income tax payers who are treated differently, either favourably or unfavourably, because of their social function. This particular unfavourable tax treatment of married couples living together, set against the many favourable discriminations made by the law in favour of married couples, does not, in the opinion of the court, constitute an unequal treatment forbidden by Article 40.1 particularly having regard to the vital roles under the Constitution of married couples as parents, or potential parents, and as heads of a family.

The inability of the District Court to award costs against a Garda was upheld by the Supreme Court in *Dillane v Attorney General* (1980) (Case 53) on the ground of social function. According to O'Higgins CJ:

when the State, whether directly by statute or mediately through the exercise of a delegated power of subordinate legislation, makes a discrimination in favour of, or against, a person or a category of persons, on the express or implied ground of a difference of social function, the courts will not condemn such discrimination as being in breach of Article 40.1, if it is not arbitrary, or capricious, or otherwise not reasonably capable, when objectively viewed in the light of the social function involved, of supporting the selection or classification complained of.

The High Court in *O'G. v Attorney General* (1985) (Case 143) rejected the claim that a law which discriminated against widowers was justified on the ground of social function. McMahon J explained:

the culture of our society has assigned distinct roles to father and mother in two parent families in the past . . . but this is a feature of our culture which appears to be changing as the younger generation of married people tend to exchange roles freely. No medical or psychological evidence has been adduced to explain the difference between these roles and its significance for the welfare of the child or to establish that the roles are mutually exclusive or that both are essential for the proper upbringing of children or to establish that there is any difference in capacity for parenthood between a widow and a widower.

The Supreme Court held in *O'B. v S.* (1984) (Case 132) that the discrimination in succession law between legitimate and illegitimate individuals could not be justified as being due to any of the differences of capacity or social function.[11] But the Supreme Court, in an innovative statement, held that the discrimination may be justified by some other provision of the Constitution, in this case Article 41. Walsh J explained:

the object and the nature of the legislation concerned must be taken into account, and . . . the distinctions or discriminations which the legislation creates must not be unjust, unreasonable or arbitrary and must, of course, be relevant to the legislation in question. Legislation which differentiates citizens or which discriminates between them does not need to be justified under the proviso if justification for it can be found in other provisions of the Constitution. Legislation which is unjust, unreasonable or arbitrary cannot be justified under any provision of the Constitution. Conversely, if legislation can be justified under one or more articles of the Constitution, when read with all the others, it cannot be held to be unjust within the meaning of any article.

Consequence of Law Found to be Discriminatory

A section of a statute which is found to offend Article 40.1 is null and void and without legal effect (see page 130). An individual who might have derived some benefit under the impugned statute is left without a remedy. The effect of the judgment is to extinguish the benefit granted by the law: it essentially has a negative consequence. The court cannot extend the benefit of the law to the claimant. The dictum of Keane J, given in *Somjee v Minister for Justice* (1981) (Case 176), is worth noting:

the jurisdiction of [the High] Court in a case where the validity of an Act of the Oireachtas is questioned . . . is limited to declaring the Act in question to be invalid, if that indeed be the case. The court has no jurisdiction to substitute for the impugned enactment a form of enactment which it considers desirable or to indicate to the Oireachtas the appropriate form of enactment which should be substituted for the impugned enactment.

That also appeared to be the rule where the discrimination had a common law origin. Thus in *The State (DPP) v Walsh* (1981) (Case 187) the Supreme Court ruled that a particular common law rule offended Article 40.1. The consequence was this decision was to extinguish a benefit which accrued to a class of persons, namely wives. But the case of *McKinley v Minister for Defence* (1992) (Case 105) saw the Supreme Court switch from this negative approach to a positive approach. Instead of extinguishing the common law benefit which accrued to a particular group, namely husbands, the court extended its application to both spouses. The more traditional approach would have been to withdraw the benefit from husbands and since the benefit could not be enjoyed by either spouse there would be no discrimination. The newer approach of extending the benefit to both spouses cured the complaint of discrimination and left the original legal benefit intact.

RIGHT TO FAIR PROCEDURES

Equality Under the Legal System

We have examined one meaning which has been accorded by the courts to the expression 'equality before the law'. We now turn to a possible second meaning which may be afforded to Article 40.1. Instead of interpreting Article 40.1 to mean equality in our laws it could be taken to encompass the concept of equality of treatment by the legal system. Equality before the law may mean equality before the system which adjudicates on legal disputes. This was the interpretation employed in *McMahon v Leahy* (1985) (Case 108) where, in the Supreme Court, Henchy J explained:

> if the order of extradition . . . were to be made, it would patently result in unequal treatment, at the hands of the courts, of citizens who, as human persons, are in equal condition in the context of the law involved. That unequal treatment would mean that the four fellow-escapers would have been judicially held (with at least the tacit approval of the State) to be entitled to escape extradition on the ground of political exemption while the plaintiff, whose entitlement to that exemption cannot be differentiated on the basis of any relevant consideration, would have been invidiously chosen (at the instance of the State . . .) for extradition . . . I am unable to see how such inequality of treatment could be said to be in conformity with the implicit guarantee in Article 40.1, that like persons must be treated alike by the law.

Sometimes the nature of the inquiry may be such that a person summoned before it must, of necessity, be afforded legal aid supplied by the State. Serious criminal charges are an instance where fair procedures demand that the accused be represented at the expense of the State. In *The State (Healy) v Donoghue* (1976) (Case 189), Henchy J, in the Supreme Court, explained:

> a person who has been convicted and deprived of his liberty as a result of a procedure which, because of his poverty, he has had to bear without legal aid has reason to complain that he has been meted out less than his constitutional due. This is particularly true if the absence of legal aid is compounded by factors such as a grave or complex charge; or ignorance, illiteracy, immaturity or other conditions rendering the accused incompetent to cope properly with the prosecution; or an inability, because of detentional restraint, to find and produce witnesses; or simply the fumbling incompetence that may occur when an accused is precipitated into the public glare and alien complexity of courtroom procedures, and is confronted with the might of a prosecution backed by the State. As the law stands, a legal-aid certificate is the shield provided against such an unjust attack.

The High Court held, in *Cahill v Reilly* (1992), that when a custodial sentence becomes probable or likely after conviction or on a plea of guilty in a situation where it may not have been likely before then at the sentencing stage the court should inform the accused, if it had not been done before, of the right to be legally represented or the right to apply for legal aid in relation to the sentence.

In criminal matters, because it is the State that prosecutes, it is the State, in the appropriate case, that must supply the legal aid. May an individual put to the expense of obtaining legal representation to defend his or her good name recoup those expenses from the party who initiates the inquiry? This question arose in *Condon v CIE* (1984) where a court of inquiry was held into a train disaster. The plaintiff, an employee of the company, claimed that since he was singled out as the person principally responsible for the disaster, his good name, his employment and even his liberty were in jeopardy, and because he was of humble means a constitutional duty rested on the State to defray his legal expenses. The High Court held that no such duty lay on the State.

The High Court held in *The State (McFadden) v Governor of Mountjoy Prison* (1981) (Case 193) that in extradition proceedings, which are akin to criminal proceedings, a person arrested should be given a copy of the warrant and should, when brought before the District Court, be given the opportunity of a remand in order to prepare a case, or to obtain legal advice or representation. Anything less amounted to an unfair procedure.

The rules of evidence of procedure should not be such as to create inequality. The High Court, in *S. v S.* (1983) (Case 173), held that the common law rule, which prohibited the admission of evidence by a wife that a child born to her during wedlock was not the child of her husband, was inconsistent with the right to fair procedures guaranteed by the Constitution.

Protection from Abuse of Exercise of Discretionary Power

The notion that an individual, when enmeshed in the legal system, should be treated fairly is an ancient one. Over time this concept has been applied outside the strict ambit of the judicial system to a myriad of instances where decisions are taken which affect the individual in some crucial way.

The exercise of discretionary power by the executive or other domestic tribunals may lead to abuse. To control this likelihood the courts have evolved a number of procedural rules which attempt to balance the scales of justice in favour of the person against whom the power is exercised. For generations the courts have insisted that those bodies or persons making administrative decisions which affect the welfare of an individual should apply a number of rules which implanted the generally accepted standards of judicial fairness.

Fair Procedures, Constitutional Justice and Natural Justice

This principle of fairness has surfaced under a number of different descriptions. At common law the topic was considered under the heading of *natural justice.* In more recent times with the development of constitutional principles it is more commonly referred to as *fair procedures* though in some cases it had been referred to by judges as *constitutional justice.*

The Right to be Heard

The first of the common law rules of natural justice is *audi alteram partem*: hear both sides. It is fundamental to fair procedures that those exercising powers should hear both sides before a decision is reached. The courts are not concerned with the merits of the decision but with the method by which it is reached. For example, in *The State (Gleeson) v Minister for Defence* (1976) the Supreme Court found the dismissal from the army of a soldier was invalid on this ground. Henchy J explained:

> the requirements of natural justice imposed an inescapable duty on the army authorities . . . to give [the soldier] due notice of the intention to discharge him, of the statutory reason for the proposed discharge, and of the essential facts and findings alleged for the proposed discharge; and to give him a reasonable opportunity of presenting his response to that notice.

The revocation of a taxi licence was declared invalid in *The State (Ingle) v O'Brien* (1977) because the person charged with the task had not notified the person to be affected in advance of the intended action. In *O'Brien v Bord na Móna* (1983) (Case 133) the bord's resolution of the intention to make a compulsory purchase order was void because the owner of the land in question had not been given adequate opportunity to present a case against the making of the order.

The adjudication by the courts that fair procedures have not been observed is not a bar which prevents a reconsideration of the matter afresh. A fresh determination will stand provided fair procedures are observed.

The Right to an Unbiased Decision

The second of the common law rules of natural justice is *nemo judex in sua causa*: never be a judge in one's own cause. This principle means that the person making the decision should be without bias in relation to the matter at issue. In *O'Donoghue v Veterinary Council* (1975) the High Court quashed a decision because the complainant later sat as a member of the council which heard the complaint. A decision to dismiss a trade union official was declared invalid, in *Connolly v McConnell* (1983), on the ground that those with financial interests in the outcome of the decision should not have taken part in the process to dismiss the official. The High Court quashed a decision in *O'Neill v Irish Hereford Breed Society Ltd* (1991) because participation by members in more than one stage of the investigation and decision-making process amounted to conduct which constituted bias consisting of re-judgment.

One final and oft repeated word on the subject of natural justice: once the procedural requirements are properly observed the courts are not concerned with the merits of the decision.

The Duty to Act Judicially
A person or body making an administrative decision must act judicially which essentially means to act fairly. The ambit of this duty was stated in the Supreme Court in *East Donegal Co-operative Livestock Mart Ltd v Attorney General* (1970) (Case 61) by Walsh J:

> all the powers which are granted . . . which are prefaced or followed by the words 'at his discretion' or 'as he shall think proper' or 'if he so thinks fit' are powers which may be exercised only within the boundaries of the stated objects of the Act; they are powers which cast upon the Minister the duty of acting fairly and judicially in accordance with the principles of constitutional justice, and they do not give him an absolute or an unqualified or an arbitrary power to grant or refuse at his will.

This duty, that those who make decisions which affect the welfare of the individual must act fairly, was again emphasised by the Supreme Court in *The State (Lynch) v Cooney* (1982) (Case 191), per O'Higgins CJ:

> the court is satisfied that [section 31 of the *Broadcasting Authority Act 1960*] does not exclude review by the courts and that any opinion formed by the Minister thereunder must be one which is bona fide held and be factually sustainable and not unreasonable.

Protection of One's Good Name
While an individual may not be directly affected by the outcome of a decision, should the possibility exist that the individual's good name might be tarnished, that individual must be given some opportunity to vindicate his or her good name. This point arose in *In re Haughey* (1971) (Case 77) where a witness before a committee of Dáil Éireann was neither allowed to cross-examine another witness who had given prejudicial evidence against him nor allowed to address the committee in his own defence. The Supreme Court declared that since the individual's good name was in issue the absence of these two requirements was a failure to vindicate the individual's good name which was protected by Article 40.3.2° of the Constitution.

DISCRIMINATION AND RELIGION

Religious Liberty

Article 44.2.3° of the Constitution declares that the State shall not impose any disabilities or make any discrimination on the ground of religious profession, belief or status. This restriction, against religious discrimination, is placed on the State and not on other bodies or persons. In an action for wrongful dismissal, in *McGrath v Trustees of Maynooth* (1979) by laicised members of the teaching staff of a Catholic seminary, the claim was made that since public funds were received by the seminary, the dismissals were unlawful as a discrimination on religious grounds. As was explained in the Supreme Court by O'Higgins CJ:

> the discrimination complained of is discrimination not by the State but by the defendants.

The Supreme Court in *Quinn's Supermarket Ltd v Attorney General* (1972) (Case 168) held that a statutory order, which exempted kosher meat shops from its application, was a discrimination on the ground of religious profession, belief or status. In *Mulloy v Minister for Education* (1975) (Case 122), a scheme which excluded certain secondary schoolteachers, because they were members of religious orders, was struck down by the Supreme Court. According to Walsh J:

> the present case concerns the disposition of public funds on a basis which, if sustainable, enables a person who is not a religious to obtain greater financial rewards than a person who is a religious and is otherwise doing the same work and is of equal status and length of service ... if that were constitutionally possible it would enable the State to prefer religious to lay people, or vice versa, in a manner which is in no way concerned with the safeguarding or maintenance of the constitutional right to free practice of religion.

A statute which prohibited adoption where the parties were not of the one religion was struck down by the High Court in *M. v An Bord Uchtála* (1975) (Case 94) as unconstitutional on this ground.[12]

Chapter 12

PERSONAL LIBERTY

A Fundamental Freedom

Probably the single most important attribute of a human person is personal freedom. The badge of a free human is that his or her life be subject to as few restraints as possible. The right encompasses much more than mere freedom of movement. In exercising this right the individual is free to choose his or her destiny and to pursue that goal without let or hindrance from the State or other individuals. An adult individual can live where and as he or she chooses, can marry, can work, can alter occupations, can pursue leisure activities and can do all the many things that are the essence of a free human spirit.

The Constitution in Article 40.4.1° expresses this right to personal liberty in a negative form. It declares that 'no citizen shall be deprived of his liberty save in accordance with law'. Most of the legal restrictions, and of necessity the case law, are concerned with the rather narrow aspect of arrest for a criminal, or related, offence. While this feature of law is important, it must not be allowed to overshadow the very wide extent and scope of the right to personal liberty. Many of the other personal freedoms, such as those of association, assembly and expression are extensions of this most crucial freedom. Not alone is liberty guaranteed but the quality of that liberty has been declared by the courts on occasion. The right to bodily integrity and the right to travel outside the State are examples of judicial pronouncements which extend the meaning of personal liberty.

The most likely interference with the individual's right to personal liberty will be at the hands of an organ of the executive, generally the Garda Síochána — the police force charged with the task of detecting criminal suspects as a prelude to the courts exercising their constitutional function to try the alleged offender. In the context of constitutional rights two public interests must be balanced: the necessity to ensure that those who commit crime are apprehended, and the right of individuals to conduct their affairs without undue interference. This chapter will attempt to outline the occasions on which the law, either common law or statute, permits infringements of the individual's liberty: it cannot be exhaustive for reasons of space, though the main restrictions are discussed at some length. Examples will be given to illustrate each such occasion, and it can be assumed that other similar restrictions apply.

Constitutional Right to Privacy

In the exercise of the constitutional right to personal liberty the courts have acknowledged that there are a number of unspecified constitutional rights in the area of privacy which fall to be protected. The constitutional right to be free from unlawful surveillance was recognised in *Kane v Governor of Mountjoy Prison* (1988) though the surveillance was considered justified in that instance. And in *Kennedy v Ireland* (1987) (Case 87) it was held that the deliberate and unjustified interference with private communications, both written and telephonic, was a breach of the right to privacy.

Powers to Stop and Demand Information

In general the Gardaí can ask an individual any question and, with a few exceptions, the individual is under no legal obligation to answer. Since it is beneficial for society to be free of crime the social obligation to assist the Gardaí will generally outweigh any reluctance to answer questions and provide information. The individual does not commit a criminal offence by a refusal to answer. The individual holds a discretion as to whether or not to co-operate.

Under various statutes a Garda can demand a person's name and address, and a refusal to furnish such information is an offence which may lead to the arrest of the person. Under the *Road Traffic Act 1961*, section 107, a garda may demand the name and address of a person whom he or she suspects of having committed a specified offence while using a motor vehicle. The *Misuse of Drugs Act 1977* empowers a Garda to arrest without warrant if he or she has reasonable doubts as to a person's identity or place of abode where he or she has reasonable suspicion that that person has committed an offence under the Act. Where members of the Gardaí, or the Defence Forces, are acting under a search warrant issued under the *Offences Against the State Act 1939*, section 29, as amended, they may demand the names and addresses of persons found where the search takes place. These three instances show that a demand for information can only be made in particular circumstances. Usually the Garda officer must have first formed the prior opinion on reasonable grounds that a particular criminal offence has been committed.

Demands of Other Sorts

Statutes permit other demands to be made. Where a Garda officer has reasonable grounds for believing that a motor vehicle has been used in a public place on a particular occasion he or she may, under the *Road Traffic Act 1961*, section 69, demand of the person using the vehicle to produce a certificate of insurance. Under section 40 of the same Act a Garda can demand the production of a driving licence from a person driving in a public place, or who is accompanying the holder of a provisional licence while the latter is driving in a public place. Under section 42, a Garda may request a specimen of signature from a person driving in a public place, or when that person produces his or her driving licence at a garda station. Where a Garda has reasonable grounds for believing that a road traffic offence has been committed he or she may demand the vehicle's owner to say who was driving the vehicle at a material time. This power, under section 107, was curtailed in *The People (AG) v Gilbert* (1973) where admissions made after such a demand were ruled inadmissible, on a charge unconnected with road traffic offences, on the ground that the answers given were not voluntary. Under the *Road Traffic Act 1978*, section 12, whenever a garda is of opinion that a person in charge of a motor vehicle, in a public place, has consumed alcohol he or she may require that person to provide a sample of breath by exhaling into a special apparatus. A litter warden, under the *Litter Act 1982*, may request a person's name and address and, on reasonable grounds, may request such information to be verified.

Powers of Search before Arrest

There is no general power residing in a garda officer or other officer of the executive to search an individual. Although less drastic in its effect than a power of arrest such an action does amount to a substantial and significant interference with the liberty of the individual. These powers must be carefully exercised if the constitutional guarantee of liberty is to be adequately defended and vindicated. A collection of statutes grants this power of search and like demands. It can only be exercised on reasonable suspicion that some specified crime has been, or is about to be committed. A refusal to be searched may either amount to an offence, or may constitute the more general offence of obstruction of a garda in the execution of his or her duty. An acquittal must follow should the garda fail to satisfy the court, where a person is charged with such an offence, that there was reasonable grounds of suspicion.

Section 29 of the *Dublin Police Act 1842* empowers a police officer to stop, search and detain any person who may be reasonably suspected of having or conveying in any manner anything stolen or unlawfully obtained. The High Court ruled, in *DPP v Rooney* (1993), that before this power of search can be lawfully exercised the suspect was entitled to be informed of the nature and description of the statutory power which was being invoked though it was not necessary to arrest the suspect prior to exercising the power of search. Section 23 of the *Misuse of Drugs Act 1977* empowers a garda, who has reasonable cause for suspecting that a person is in possession of certain drugs, to search that person, to detain that person for such time as is reasonably necessary for making the search, and may require that person to accompany him to a garda station for that purpose. This section survived a constitutional challenge in *O'Callaghan v Ireland* (1993) (Case 139). The Supreme Court ruled that a condemnation of the section would leave no alternative to the Gardaí except to arrest a suspected person which was a less desirable alternative from the citizen's point of view to the power of search. In a sense this power to search was in ease of the citizen rather than an invasion of rights. The *Criminal Law Act 1976*, section 8, empowers a garda who has reasonable suspicion that certain offences have been, or are about to be committed, to stop and search a vehicle and its occupants. The *Misuse of Drugs Act 1984* allows the Gardaí to search a vehicle, and to take it to a suitable place in order to do so. And under the same statute a garda may require a person, whom he suspects of having committed an offence, to accompany him or her to a garda station for the purpose of being searched.

Arrest

An arrest is a formal procedure whereby a person is detained, usually for the purpose of being brought before a court. According to Hederman J, in the Supreme Court, in *DPP v McCreesh* (1992):

> an arrest consists in or involves the seizure or touching of a person's body accompanied by a form of words which indicate to that person that he is under restraint. Whilst the older cases held that words alone would not suffice to constitute an arrest, nowadays words alone *may* amount to an arrest if, in the circumstances, they are calculated to bring, and do bring, to the person's notice that he is under restraint and he submitted to the compulsion.

For an arrest to be effective the garda, or other person effecting the arrest, must make clear to the person to be arrested that he or she is compelled to remain, and accompany the person making the arrest. A mere request to accompany the person authorised to make the arrest is not sufficient. Generally the person making the arrest will touch the arm of the person being arrested though reasonable force is permitted in effecting an arrest. The use of force cannot be justified where the person to be arrested neither resists nor attempts to escape. Where an escape is attempted the degree of force which may be used is measured by the amount of force used in the resistance or escape attempt. The use of excessive force is unlawful. The force must be used by the person effecting the arrest in the execution of his or her duty. In *Dowman v Ireland* (1986) a 13-year-old boy accompanied by two young children was caught stealing a bag of potatoes from a supermarket. When the Gardaí arrived they arrested the boy and when putting him into the patrol car he became concerned that the two children were being left behind. A scuffle took place in which the boy was injured. He successfully sued the Gardaí. The High Court held that the Gardaí were not acting in the course of their duty either to effect an arrest or to maintain one. The injury was caused when denying the boy the right to be concerned with the welfare of the two young children.

To resist a lawful arrest is an offence. An individual is legally entitled to resist, using reasonable force, an unlawful arrest. Discretion probably dictates submission to an unlawful arrest, with the availability of both civil and criminal remedies against the culprit at a later stage. The danger in resisting an unlawful arrest is that excessive force may be used, and that may be an offence. In *The People (AG) v White* (1947) armed detectives surrounded a house in which two men were staying. The Gardaí knew the identity of one man, whom they wanted to arrest, but not of the defendant. A gun battle took place. At the appeal against a conviction for the murder of one of the detectives, the Court of Criminal Appeal, per Gavan Duffy J, explained:

> since there was no lawful authority for the intended arrest it was man-slaughter even if [the defendant] was forearmed to resist an attempted arrest with a lethal weapon.

At common law a garda can arrest a person, without a warrant, whom he or she reasonably suspects of having committed a felony whether in fact a felony has, or has not, been committed. A garda may arrest for a breach of the peace committed in his or her presence. It was held in *Connors v McLaughlin* (1921) that although it was the duty of a police officer to take all reasonable steps to prevent a breach of the peace, including, where the circumstances demanded it, the arrest and detention of an innocent person, it was no defence to an action for false imprisonment that the officer bona fide believed the innocent person so arrested and detained to be in danger at the hands of wrongdoers and that the detention was for the protection of the person detained.

A varied collection of statutes authorises arrest without warrant. Some examples will illustrate the extent of this power though a common feature is that the person effecting the arrest must first have formed some prior opinion or suspicion. The *Larceny Act 1916*, section 41, empowers a garda to arrest without warrant any person found lying, or loitering in any highway, yard or other place during the day and of whom he or she has good cause to suspect of having committed, or being about to commit an offence under the Act, or certain other offences. The *Road Traffic Act 1961* permits arrest, with-out warrant, for a number of offences including drunken driving, dangerous driving, failing to allow a garda to read a produced driving licence or certificate of insurance, taking a vehicle without the consent of the owner, and interfering with the mechanism of a vehicle. The *Misuse of Drugs Act*

1977 empowers the arrest without warrant of persons suspected of certain drugs offences. The *Road Traffic Act 1978*, section 12, permits arrest without warrant for failure or refusal to give a specimen of breath. By virtue of the *Casual Trading Act 1980*, section 12, a garda may arrest without warrant a person whom he has reasonable cause to believe is contravening the Act. Under the *Family Law (Protection of Spouses and Children) Act 1981*, section 7, the Gardaí may arrest without warrant a spouse in breach of a barring order. The *Litter Act 1982*, section 6, empowers a Garda who is of opinion that a person is committing, or has committed an offence under the Act, to arrest that person, without warrant.

At common law a lay person has limited powers of arrest. A lay person may arrest, without warrant, a person whom he or she suspects of having committed a felony, though an action for damages may be instituted against the lay person where in fact no felony has been committed. A lay person may arrest for a breach of the peace. Some statutory powers of arrest are conferred on 'persons' and are not entrusted solely to the Gardaí. For example, the *Criminal Law (Jurisdiction) Act 1976*, section 19, empowers any person to arrest without warrant, anyone whom he or she, with reasonable cause, suspects of having committed certain offences in Northern Ireland.

What are the consequences of a person effecting an arrest without the requisite reasonable suspicion? The answer is simple: the arrest is unlawful. This was the central issue in *The State (Trimbole) v Governor of Mountjoy Prison* (1985) (Case 204), where the arrest was executed under section 30 of the *Offences Against the State Act 1939* on the suspicion of being in possession of a firearm and ammunition. In the High Court, Egan J held:

> I was satisfied after hearing evidence that no genuine suspicion could have been formed by the Gardaí in relation to possession by [Trimbole] of any firearm or ammunition and I found as a fact that the evidence as to the genuineness of the suspicion was most unconvincing. I accordingly found that the detention ... was illegal and made an order for his release.

Where a statute provides that for an activity to be unlawful it must be committed in a public place, then if a power of arrest without warrant is granted, the arrest to be lawful must not breach any constitutional or legal right of the suspect. The defendant, in *DPP v Gaffney* (1988), suspected of having committed a number of road traffic offences, was arrested without warrant at his home, the Gardaí having followed him there. The Supreme Court held that the arrest was unlawful because the power granted by the statute did not give authority to enter a private dwelling without the permission of the owner or occupant of the dwelling. Since the entry was unlawful it also constituted an unconstitutional invasion of the dwelling of a citizen protected by Article 40.5 of the Constitution. A similar situation occurred in

DPP v McCreesh (1992) though the defendant in this case immediately informed the Gardaí who had followed him there and entered his driveway that they were trespassers and should leave the premises. The Supreme Court ruled that in those circumstances the arrest of the suspect on the suspect's own premises was not a lawful arrest. But in *DPP v Forbes* (1993) the Supreme Court ruled that an arrest without warrant on other property not owned or controlled by the suspect was lawful. In that case the suspect, suspected of drunken driving, drove into the driveway of a private house where he was arrested. The court held that the Gardaí could not be regarded as trespassers because the owner of that property was held to have given an implied authority to the Gardaí to come on to the property to secure the enforcement of the law.

An arrest, otherwise than for a felony at common law, or without a warrant under an expressed statutory power, must be made by warrant, which is a written document, signed by a judicial officer, directed to a member of the Gardaí to arrest a named person. An arrest warrant cannot be issued to a lay person. To obtain a warrant the Gardaí must give details of the case on sworn evidence to the court, and it is for the court to decide whether or not to issue the warrant. It was held by the High Court, in *Byrne v Grey* (1988), that for a search warrant to be valid there must be an independent decision by the judicial authority issuing the warrant that its issue was justified over and above the decision made by the Gardaí of their suspicion that an offence had been committed. The warrant must include the name of the person and a description of the offence. The person to be arrested should, generally, be given an opportunity of perusing the warrant in order to ascertain whether it is lawful or not. In *The State (McFadden) v Governor of Mountjoy Prison* (1981) (Case 193), the High Court suggested that it would be appropriate and fair that a garda officer executing a foreign extradition warrant should not only produce and read the warrant to the person being arrested but should also hand him a copy of the warrant. There the court was considering the lack of fair procedures in extradition proceedings and there seems no logical reason why this rule should not apply to domestic warrants.

Helping the Police with their Inquiries
It is common practice for a person under suspicion of being involved in an offence to be questioned at a garda station without being under arrest. That person is said to be 'helping the police with their inquiries'. Unless the person voluntarily goes to, and remains in, the garda station, which that person is perfectly entitled to do, the question may arise whether in fact that person is in reality under arrest. Whether an individual is under arrest is a question of fact, irrespective of what the various parties involved believe. This question arose in *The People (DPP) v Lynch* (1982) (Case 159) where the defendant

went to a garda station voluntarily, remained there for twenty-two hours, was subjected to sustained questioning, was not given the opportunity of communicating with his family, and was not permitted to rest or sleep until he made an admission of guilt. The Supreme Court ruled that the evidence pointed coercively to the fact that the defendant was under arrest in the sense that he was not at liberty to leave the station. *Lynch*'s case was applied in *The People (DPP) v Coffey* (1987) where the High Court ruled that while the defendant went voluntarily to the garda station in the first instance, when the Gardaí had returned from checking his account he had become a very real suspect in respect of the crime under investigation and at that stage he should have been told he was free to go if he so wished. Failure to inform the defendant that he was free to go rendered his detention unlawful.

The onus is on the State to prove that a person in such a situation is aware of the right to leave the station and that the person refused to exercise that right.

Can Surveillance Amount to Detention?

It is a common police activity to mount surveillance operations against particular individuals. The question whether this surveillance amounts to the invasion of the constitutional right to privacy has already been considered (page 176). Here we examine the specific question whether the surveillance amounts to detention. An unlawful surveillance would amount to an unlawful detention which would have the consequence of rendering any subsequent arrest unlawful. This problem was encountered in *Kane v Governor of Mountjoy Prison* (1988) where the plaintiff had been arrested and detained under section 30 of the *Offences Against the State Act 1939*. He was later released but was kept under close overt surveillance by the Gardaí on the ground that an extradition warrant was expected. On his subsequent arrest under the extradition warrant it was argued that the plaintiff had never been truly released, that the nature and extent of the surveillance was unlawful and was an invasion of his constitutional right to privacy and complete freedom of movement, and that it vitiated the legality of the subsequent arrest. The Supreme Court ruled that the surveillance was not unlawful in that the State had a very clear interest in the expeditious and efficient discharge of the obligations reciprocally undertaken between it and other states for the apprehension of fugitive offenders and that it was the duty of the Gardaí to take reasonable steps to speedily execute the extradition warrant when it was obtained.

Reasons for Arrest to be Given

Since the personal liberty of an individual is at stake, and in order to decide whether the arrest is lawful or unlawful, the individual should be told the reasons for the arrest. From the decided cases a number of rules can be firmly stated:[1]

1. If a police officer arrests, without a warrant, on reasonable suspicion of felony, or of another crime of a sort which does not require a warrant, he or she must in ordinary circumstances inform the person arrested of the true ground of arrest. The garda is not entitled to keep the reason to himself or herself, or give a reason which is false.
2. This requirement naturally does not exist if the circumstances are such that the person must know the general nature of the alleged offence for which the arrest is made.
3. The arrested person cannot complain that he or she has not been supplied with the above information as and when it should be given if he or she produces a situation which makes it practically impossible to give the information, e.g. by immediate counter-attack or by running away.
4. Technical or precise language need not be used once the substance of the offence is stated.

Whether the failure to inform a person of the reasons for arrest at the moment of arrest amounted to an unlawful arrest was considered in *The People (DPP) v Walsh* (1980) by the Supreme Court. The defendant, arrested in a crowded pub one evening on suspicion of having committed a burglary five months previously, was not told the reason for his arrest at the time though he was so informed later in the garda station. It was held that informing the defendant of the reason for the arrest within a reasonable time of the arrest was sufficient. O'Higgins CJ explained:

> I conclude that there is nothing ... which would suggest that [the Gardaí's] failure at the moment of the arrest to inform the [defendant] of the reason for it rendered the immediate succeeding imprisonment in ... the garda station unlawful. The [defendant's] right to be informed was not questioned. It simply was not exercised by him. Since the [defendant] immediately acquiesced in the arrest no question concerning the authority for the arrest arose. In any event shortly afterwards the [defendant] was informed in the garda station the reason for the arrest in words which must have conveyed to him that he was suspected of being involved in the crime.

The Purpose of Arrest

The sole purpose of a lawful arrest at common law is to bring the arrested person before a court of law as soon as is practicable. O'Higgins CJ, in the Supreme Court, in *The People (DPP) v Walsh* (1980), explained this rule clearly:

an arrest and subsequent detention is only justified at common law if it is exercised for the purpose for which the right exists, which is the bringing of an arrested person to justice before a court. If it appears that the arresting Gardaí have no evidence on which to charge the person arrested, or cannot justify the suspicion on which he was arrested, he must be released.

It is commonly believed that the Gardaí are entitled to detain a suspect for a reasonable time during which inquiries can be made, and that such detention does not amount to an arrest. The courts have both repeatedly rejected such a notion and condemned such a practice. In the first of these cases, *Dunne v Clinton* (1930), two brothers, suspected of having committed a felony, went voluntarily to the garda station and were detained from Tuesday afternoon until Wednesday night before being charged. Subsequently the charges were dismissed, and the brothers sued the Gardaí for false imprisonment, accepting their arrests were lawful, but their detentions were not. They were awarded damages by the High Court. Hanna J restated the principle:

in law there can be no half way house between the liberty of the subject, unfettered by restraint, and an arrest ... a practice has grown up of 'detention', as distinct from arrest. It is, in effect, keeping a suspect in custody, perhaps under as comfortable circumstances as the [garda station] will permit, without making any definite charge against him, and with the intimation in some form of words or gesture that he is under restraint, and will not be allowed to leave ... this so called detention amounts to arrest, and the suspect has in law been arrested and in custody during the period of his detention. The expression 'detention' has no justification in law in this connection, and the use of it has in a sense helped to nurture the idea that it is something different from arrest and that it relieves the guards from the obligation to have the question of the liberty of the suspected person determined by ... a court.

This principle was again emphasised, and applied, in *The People (DPP) v O'Loughlin* (1979) (Case 161) by the Court of Criminal Appeal, per O'Higgins CJ:

apart from the special situation specified in [section 30] of the *Offences Against the State Act 1939*, there is no procedure under our law whereby a person may be held in a garda station without charge.[2] In particular our law does not contemplate or permit the holding of a person for questioning. It makes no difference whether the offence for which he is so held is an entirely separate matter to the one with which he is finally charged. 'Holding for questioning' and 'taking into custody' and 'detaining' are merely different ways of describing the act of depriving a man of his liberty. To do so without lawful authority is an open defiance of Article 40.4.1° of the Constitution.

This rule was again applied by the Supreme Court in *The People (DPP) v Higgins* (1985) (Case 157). Finlay CJ said:

> the [defendant] was held in custody and the only possible inference that could be drawn from the evidence ... is that he was held not for any purpose associated with charging him with that offence but specifically for the purpose of making him available for interrogation by other members of the Garda Síochána in respect of other crimes ... At the time he was alleged to have made the verbal admissions the [defendant] was not being detained for the purpose of being charged or brought before a court but specifically for the purpose of being interrogated. He was therefore detained unlawfully to the knowledge of the Gardaí concerned and, consequently, in conscious and deliberate violation of his constitutional rights.

Detention Permitted by Law

There are occasions when detention is allowed by either the common law or by statute. Under the common law every person, in whose presence a breach of the peace is being, or reasonably appears about to be, committed, has the right to take reasonable steps to make that other refrain. Those reasonable steps include detaining the other against his or her will, though the person doing so must release, or arrest, the culprit once there is no longer a danger to the public peace.

A statutory exception exists where a person arrested for driving with excess alcohol is requested by a member of the Gardaí, acting under section 13 of the *Road Traffic Act 1978*, to provide either a specimen of his breath or a blood or urine sample. Failure to respond to such a request is a criminal offence.[3] The High Court ruled, in *The People (DPP) v Greely* (1985), that this procedure was invalid where the defendant went voluntarily to the garda station instead of having been arrested. This detention period clearly exists for the purpose of allowing the Gardaí to acquire evidence which may subsequently be used in a prosecution against the arrested person.

Another statutory exception to the rule that the only purpose of an arrest is to bring the arrested person before a court is section 30 of the *Offences Against the State Act 1939*, which empowers a garda to arrest a person whom he or she suspects of having committed, or being about to commit, certain offences and detain that person for a period of twenty-four hours, which may be extended to forty-eight hours. This section is regularly used and its frequent abuse has had to be corrected by the courts (see *The State (Trimbole) v Governor of Mountjoy Prison*, page 195). The notion that section 30 can only be used for 'subversive' type crimes was rejected by the Supreme Court in *The People (DPP) v Quilligan* (1986). There it was argued that the arrest of the defendant under the section in respect of malicious damage to property was unlawful on the ground that the section was directed against subversive crime as distinct from ordinary crime. Walsh J explained:

> the object of the powers given by section 30 is not to permit the arrest of people simply for the purpose of subjecting them to questioning. Rather is it for the purpose of investigating the commission or suspected commission of a crime by the person already arrested and to enable that investigation to be carried on without the possibility of obstruction or other interference which might occur if the suspected person were not under arrest. Section 30 is part of the statute law of the State permanently in force and it does not permit of any departure from normal police procedure save as to the obligation to bring the arrested person before a court as soon as possible.

In *The People (DPP) v Quilligan* (1992) (Case 163), where a constitutional challenge failed, the Supreme Court ruled that a person arrested pursuant to section 30 had the following protections:

1. If the arresting garda does not have a bona-fide suspicion based on reason of one or other of the matters provided for in the section the arrest is unlawful and the person may be released by an order pursuant to Article 40.4.2° of the Constitution (see *The State (Trimbole) v Governor of Mountjoy Prison* (1985) (Case 204) page 195).
2. At the time of the arrest the suspect must be informed, if he does not already know, of the offence of which he is suspected otherwise his arrest is unlawful (see *The People (DPP) v Walsh* (1980) page 184).
3. The person detained has during his detention a right to legal assistance, and the refusal to grant it to him when reasonably requested can make his detention unlawful (see *The People (DPP) v Healy* (1990) (Case 156), page 192).
4. The right to medical assistance.
5. The right of access to the court under Article 40.4.2° of the Constitution.
6. The right to remain silent and the associated right to be told of that right.
7. The Judges' Rules with their provision in regard to the giving of cautions and the abstention from cross-examination of a prisoner apply to a person in detention under section 30 (see page 193).
8. A person detained under section 30 must not be subjected to any form of questioning which the courts would regard as unfair or oppressive, either by reason of its nature, the manner in which it is conducted, its duration or the time of day or its persistence to the point of harassment, where it is not shown that the arrested person has indicated clearly that he is willing to continue to be further questioned.

9. If the detention of a person arrested under section 30 is extended by a chief superintendent for a further period after the first period of twenty-four hours, he must entertain also the necessary bona-fide suspicion of the suspect that justified his original arrest and must be satisfied that the suspect's further detention is necessary for the purposes provided for in the section.

Another major exception to this rule that the sole purpose of arrest is to be charged is found in the *Criminal Justice Act 1984*, section 4. This empowers detention without charge where a person has been arrested without warrant on suspicion, with reasonable cause, of having committed an offence which is punishable by five years' imprisonment. Detention is only permitted if the member of the Gardaí in charge of the station, to which the arrested person has been brought, has, at the time of that person's arrival at the station, reasonable grounds for believing that such detention is necessary for the proper investigation of the offence. Detention is for six hours though this period may be extended in certain circumstances for a further six hours. The hours between midnight and 8 a.m., during which questioning, in general, may not take place, are excluded when calculating the period of detention.

If at any time during the detention there are no longer reasonable grounds for suspecting that the detained person has committed an offence to which the section applies, that person must be released forthwith. Where the Gardaí have enough evidence to prefer a charge the detained person must be charged without delay unless the detained person is suspected of another offence to which the section applies. This detention provision cannot apply to a person below the age of 12 years.

The Supreme Court ruled in *Keating v Governor of Mountjoy Prison* (1990) that it was not the role of the District Court to carry out an inquiry whether the provisions of section 4 had been observed when a person detained under the section is subsequently charged before that court. To permit that court to determine the validity of the detention would clearly be an unwarrantable and unlawful usurpation of the constitutional role of the High Court if any inferior court were to embark on such an inquiry with a view to holding that a person was being unlawfully detained and ordering a release. Where such an issue does arise the proper course is for the District Court to remand the person concerned thus enabling that person to make an application to the High Court under Article 40.4.2° of the Constitution (see page 215).

Courts' Response to Detention Provisions
While the courts must accept and enforce these statutory provisions relating to detention as is their constitutional duty unless and until found to be unconstitutional, they are not powerless in curtailing any abuses of these

powers. The courts supervise these measures in a number of ways. One method is to construe strictly these provisions. Speaking for the Supreme Court in *Article 26 and the Emergency Powers Bill 1976* (Case 8), a provision which permitted seven-day detention without charge, O'Higgins CJ stated:

> a statutory provision of this nature, which makes such inroads upon the liberty of the person, must be strictly construed. Any arrest sought to be justified by the section must be in strict conformity with it. No such arrest may be justified by importing into the section incidents or characteristics of an arrest which are not expressly or by necessary implication authorised by the section.

This detention provision was strictly applied in *The State (Hoey) v Garvey* (1978) where a person, arrested and detained for seven days, was released and re-arrested some days later on the same suspicion. The High Court ordered that person's release because the statute did not authorise the arrest and detention of a person on a second occasion if the second arrest was grounded on the same suspicion as had justified the first arrest, even though the Gardaí had acquired further information between the dates of the two arrests.

The common practice of detaining a person for forty-eight hours under section 30 of the *Offences Against the State Act 1939* and on release re-arresting that person for a further forty-eight hours, has ceased since this decision. And the Oireachtas was mindful of this potential abuse when it enacted the *Criminal Justice Act 1984*. Section 10 provides that where a person detained under section 4 of the Act is released without charge that person may not be arrested again for the same offence or for any other offence of which, at the time of the first arrest, the garda by whom he was arrested suspected him or ought reasonably to have suspected him except on the authority of the District Court which must be satisfied on information supplied on oath by a member of the Gardaí not below the rank of superintendent that further information has come to the knowledge of the Gardaí since the person's release as to that person's suspected participation in the offence for which the arrest is sought.

The courts have supervised detention provisions, particularly section 30, in an additional way. The courts have refused to admit evidence, usually confessions, obtained in breach of the section. For example, in *The People (DPP) v Madden* (1977) (Case 160), the detained person began to make a confession which was being reduced into writing by Gardaí shortly before the twenty-four hour period was due to expire. It was not finished until three hours after this period expired. A conviction for murder was quashed. In *The People (DPP) v Farrell* (1978) (Case 154) the detained person made a confession during the second twenty-four hour period which had not been extended properly in accordance with the statute. The conviction was quashed.

Both these cases will be considered later when examining the rules relating to unconstitutionally obtained evidence (see page 195).

The Place of Detention

Invariably an arrested person is taken to, and detained in, a garda station, though the particular statute may permit the detention in some other place. For example, section 30 of the *Offences Against the State Act 1939* provides that a person arrested under that section may be removed to and detained in custody in a Garda Síochána station, a prison, or some other convenient place. The Supreme Court ruled, in *The People (DPP) v Kelly* (1983), that the provisions of that section and section 11 of the *Interpretation Act 1937* authorise the detention of a suspect in garda stations, prisons and other convenient places. In that case the suspect had been held in three different garda stations over a period of forty-eight hours. In the Court of Criminal Appeal, Finlay P warned:

> if the removal of a person detained under section 30 ... from one garda station, or other place, to another was mala fides and was done for the purpose either of harassment or of isolating him from assistance or access to which he would properly be entitled, then that fact, of itself, would clearly render his detention unlawful.

The reasoning in this case was applied by the High Court in the *Director of Public Prosecutions v Sheehy* (1987) where a person arrested under section 13 of the *Road Traffic (Amendment) Act 1978* (see page 187 for a discussion of the section) was moved from one garda station to another because of the absence of the necessary equipment to carry out the statutory tests in the first garda station. The court ruled that a member of the Garda Síochána, acting bona fide, may bring a person to a succession of garda stations for the purpose of carrying out all the statutory procedures under that statute.

Procedure after Arrest

On arrest a suspect may be searched and certain property seized. The law was explained by O'Keeffe J in *Jennings v Quinn* (1968):

> ... the public interest requires that the police, when effecting a lawful arrest, may seize, without a search warrant, property in the possession or custody of the person arrested when they believe it necessary to do so to avoid the abstraction or destruction of that property and when that property is (a) evidence in support of the criminal charge upon which the arrest is made, or (b) evidence in support of the criminal charge against that person then in contemplation, or (c) reasonably believed to be stolen property or to be property unlawfully in the possession of that person ...

In general there is no obligation on a person, in custody or otherwise, to give his or her fingerprints when requested by the Gardaí. A person who does so does it voluntarily. A person arrested under section 30 of the *Offences Against the State Act 1939*, and under section 3 of the *Criminal Justice Act 1984* must give fingerprints and palm prints if demanded. Where these prints are taken under the latter statute and no charge is instituted or a charge is instituted and an acquittal follows, the prints must be destroyed.

As a rule there is no legal restriction on the taking of another person's photograph particularly in a public place. The Gardaí are possessed of no particular power to compel those in custody to be photographed, but a person arrested under section 30, or section 4, may be photographed, though these, like prints, must be destroyed as already explained.

There is no legal obligation on a person in custody to take part in an identification parade though that person may do so by agreement. There are internal garda guidelines for the holding of identification parades in order to ensure fairness.[4] A person about to be put on parade should be informed: (1) that the person will be placed among a number of other persons who are, as far as possible, of similar height, age and general appearance as the person; (2) that the person may have a solicitor or a friend present at the parade; (3) that the person may take up any position he may choose in the parade and that, after a witness has left, he may change his position in the parade before the next witness is called; (4) that the person may object to any of the persons on the parade or the arrangements and that such objection be made to the garda conducting the parade.

A person arrested under section 30 of the *Offences Against the State Act 1939* and section 4 of the *Criminal Justice Act 1984* must submit to any test designed for the purpose of ascertaining whether he or she has been in contact with firearms, or any explosive substance, and for that purpose may have swabs from his or her skin and samples of his or her hair taken. For these tests to be taken, in other cases, consent must be given.

A person in custody cannot be ill-treated while in custody.

Right of Access to Legal Advice
The Supreme Court ruled in *The People (DPP) v Healy* (1990) (Case 156) that the right of access to a lawyer when requested by a detained person, or by that person's family, must be deemed to be a constitutional right. A right of a detained person to reasonable access to a lawyer meant in the event of an arrival of the lawyer at a garda station in which that person was detained an immediate right of that person, to be told of the arrival and, if so requested, immediate access. Failure to grant this right may render confessions obtained inadmissible as evidence (see page 198).

Where a person is detained in a garda station pursuant to section 4 of the *Criminal Justice Act 1984* the Garda in charge of the station must inform that person without delay of an entitlement to consult a solicitor and must cause that solicitor to be notified as soon as practicable.

Notification of Detention
Section 5 of the *Criminal Justice Act 1984* provides that where a person is detained in a garda station under section 4, the Garda in charge of the station must inform the detained person of the entitlement to have the detention and station notified to one person reasonably named by the detained person and shall cause that named person to be notified as soon as practicable. Where the detained person is under the age of 17 years that Garda must as soon as practicable inform a parent or guardian.

The Right to Silence
A person in custody is under no obligation, in general, to answer any question. At present under our law a person in custody on suspicion of having committed a crime may remain silent though he or she may choose to answer questions or make a written statement. Legal rules have been formulated, for various reasons, to protect the person in custody. The atmosphere of a garda station may make it difficult for the arrested person to give a coherent explanation of his or her conduct. Experience has shown that persons in custody do confess to crimes they could not have committed.

One of the sets of rules laid down to protect persons in custody from oppressive questioning, known as the *Judges' Rules*, was first formulated in 1912 by the judges in England at the request of the Home Secretary and was added to in 1922. These rules have been applied in our courts since then, though they do not have the status of rules of law.[5] They are administrative directions, though statements obtained in breach of the Rules *may* be rejected as evidence. The trial judge has a discretion whether to accept, or reject, statements obtained in breach of the *Judges' Rules*, which are as follows:

(1) When a police officer is endeavouring to discover the author of a crime there is no objection to his putting questions in respect thereof to any person or persons, whether suspect or not, from whom he thinks that useful information may be obtained.
(2) Whenever a police officer has made up his mind to charge a person with a crime, he should first caution such person before asking him any questions, or any further questions as the case may be.
(3) Persons in custody should not be questioned without the usual caution being first administered.

(4) If the prisoner wishes to volunteer any statement, the usual caution should be administered. It is desirable that the last two words of such caution should be omitted, and that the caution should end with the words 'be given in evidence'.

(5) The caution to be administered to a prisoner when he is formally charged should therefore be in the following words: 'Do you wish to say anything in answer to the charge? You are not obliged to say anything unless you wish to do so, but whatever you say will be taken down in writing and may be given in evidence.' Care should be taken to avoid the suggestion that his answers can only be used in evidence against him, as this may prevent an innocent person making a statement which might help to clear him of the charge.

(6) A statement made by a prisoner before there is time to caution him is not rendered inadmissible in evidence merely because no caution has been given, but in such a case he should be cautioned as soon as possible.

(7) A prisoner making a voluntary statement must not be cross-examined, and no question should be put to him about it except for the purpose of removing ambiguity in what he has actually said.

(8) When two or more persons are charged with the same offence and their statements are taken separately, the police should not read these statements to the other persons charged, but each of such persons should be given by the police a copy of such statements and nothing should be said or done by the police to invite a reply. If the person charged desires to make a statement in reply the usual caution should be administered.

(9) Any statement made in accordance with these rules should, whenever possible, be taken in writing and signed by the person making it after it has been read to him and he has been invited to make any corrections he may wish.

There are a number of occasions when statute excludes this right to silence. Some we have mentioned when examining what demands a garda can make of a person (see page 178). Another is worthy of mention. The *Offences Against the State Act 1939*, section 52, empowers a garda to demand of a person detained under section 30, a full account of that person's movements and actions during any specified period. Failure to give such account is an offence. The *Criminal Justice Act 1984* does not alter the right to silence but section 16 allows a court to draw an inference if a person at the trial offers an explanation which could reasonably be expected to have been mentioned to the Gardaí when being questioned or charged. An inference can also be drawn where a person fails, or refuses, to account for any object, substance or mark, or for his or her presence in a particular place at or about the time the offence was committed, which the Gardaí reasonably believe may be attributable to his or her participation in the offence.

Consequence of an Unlawful Arrest or Detention

There are a number of consequences of an unlawful arrest or detention. The first is a common law action for damages for assault and false imprisonment (see *Dunne v Clinton* (1930), page 186). The second is that the person may be released by order of the High Court where an inquiry into the detention has been conducted under Article 40.4.2° of the Constitution (see page 215).

Where a release is ordered a problem may arise as to what becomes of any valid proceedings which are inextricably connected with the original unlawful arrest. This was at issue in *The State (Trimbole) v Governor of Mountjoy Prison* (1985) (Case 204) where the initial arrest was held by the High Court to be unlawful but extradition proceedings, which resulted in an extradition order being made, were initiated while the arrested person was in unlawful custody. Was the extradition order tainted with the original illegality and thus void, or could it be severed, and thus saved, from the original unlawful arrest? The High Court held that the object of the arrest was to ensure that the arrested person would be available for the extradition proceedings, that such arrest amounted to a deliberate and conscious violation of constitutional rights, that there were no extraordinary excusing circumstances, that the detention in the subsequent extradition proceedings were tainted by the illegality of the original arrest and accordingly the person had to be immediately released. The Supreme Court, on appeal, upheld this view. Finlay CJ explained:

> the courts have not only an inherent jurisdiction but a positive duty: (i) to protect persons against the invasion of their constitutional rights; (ii) if invasion has occurred, to restore as far as possible the person so damaged to the position in which he would be if his rights had not been invaded; and (iii) to ensure as far as possible that persons acting on behalf of the executive who consciously and deliberately violate the constitutional rights of citizens do not for themselves or their superiors obtain the planned results of that invasion.

Another consequence of an unlawful arrest or detention is that evidence obtained as a result of the illegality may not be admitted in evidence, thus denying the executive the benefit of such illegality. That topic is considered next.

Unconstitutionally Obtained Evidence

The courts must strive to reconcile two highly important interests which are likely to come into conflict in the investigation of crime: on the one hand the interest of any suspect may need protection from unconstitutional and illegal invasions of liberties by the investigating authorities, and on the other hand the interest of the State in securing evidence bearing on the commission of crime must be upheld. Neither of these objectives can be insisted on to the uttermost. The protection of the individual is primarily protection for the innocent individual against unwarranted and high-handed interference. The protection is not intended as a protection for the guilty individual against the efforts of the executive to vindicate and protect the constitutional and legal rights of others. On the other hand, the interest of the State cannot be magnified to the point of causing all the safeguards for the protection of the individual to vanish, and to present positive inducement to the authorities to proceed by irregular methods.

We have already seen that evidence obtained in breach of the *Judges' Rules* may be excluded from evidence. How should the courts respond to requests to admit unconstitutionally and illegally obtained evidence? There are three possible solutions currently obtaining in other jurisdictions. The courts could, as in England, admit an illegally obtained evidence, except confessions, so obtained: *R. v Sang* (1979). Or the other extreme position could be adopted, as in the United States, where evidence obtained unconstitutionally and illegally is excluded: *Mapp v Ohio* (1961). Or the courts could adopt some measure which falls between these extremes, as is done in Scotland, where a discretion is given to the court to admit illegally obtained evidence: *Lawrie v Muir* (1950).

Our courts have adopted a modified version of the Scottish rule. The rule in this regard was laid down by the Supreme Court in *The People (AG) v O'Brien* (1965) (Case 152). Walsh J stated:

> the vindication and the protection of constitutional rights is a fundamental matter for all courts established under the Constitution. That duty must not yield place to any other competing interest . . . The defence and vindication of the constitutional rights of the citizen is a duty superior to that of trying such citizen for a criminal offence. The courts in exercising the judicial powers of government of the State must recognise the paramount position of constitutional rights and must uphold the objection of an accused person to the admissibility at his trial of evidence obtained or procured by the State or its servants or agents as a result of a deliberate and conscious breach of the constitutional rights of an accused person where no extraordinary excusing circumstances exist, such as the imminent destruction of vital evidence or the need to rescue a victim in peril.

This is the standard rule adopted since that case and has survived despite some minor judicial hesitancy. In applying this test in any particular case the court must proceed through three stages: (a) was there a breach of constitutional rights? If there was no breach the inquiry ceases, though other issues may arise such as a breach of legal rights. Had there been a breach of constitutional rights then, (b) was it deliberate and conscious violation? If the answer is no, the evidence is admissible. If the answer is yes, then prima facie the evidence must be excluded unless (c) there are extraordinary excusing circumstances, which render the evidence admissible.

The courts have applied this test in many cases. In the *O'Brien* case itself the Supreme Court ruled that the breach of constitutional rights, which had occurred, was not a deliberate and conscious one but happened due to inadvertence. Kingsmill Moore J said:

> the mistake [in the search warrant] was a pure oversight and it has not been shown that the oversight was noticed by anyone before the premises were searched. I can find no evidence of deliberate treachery, imposition, deceit or illegality; no policy to disregard the provisions of the Constitution or to conduct searches without a warrant; nothing except the existence of an unintentional and accidental illegality to set against the public interest of having crime detected and punished.

The Court of Criminal Appeal ruled, in *The People (DPP) v Madden* (1977) (Case 160), that a confession should have been excluded at the trial because, as O'Higgins CJ explained:

> the statement was taken by a senior Garda officer who must have been aware of the lawful period of detention which applied ... it was taken in circumstances which suggest that he deliberately and consciously regarded the taking and completion of the statement as being of more importance than according to the defendant his right to liberty ... The court of trial appears to have sought an element of wilfulness or mala fides in the conduct of the Garda officers and not finding such to have concluded that the deprivation of constitutional rights was not deliberate and conscious ... What was done or permitted by [the Gardaí] may have been done or permitted for the best of motives and in the interests of the due investigation of the crime. However, it was done or permitted without regard to the right to liberty guaranteed ... by Article 40 of the Constitution and to the State's obligation under that Article to defend and vindicate that right.

In *The People (DPP) v Farrell* (1978) (Case 154) the Court of Criminal Appeal held that confessions admitted at the trial should have been excluded because, according to O'Higgins CJ:

> the result is that the second period of detention ... in the garda station has not been shown to have been authorised under the [statute]. Therefore, it appears to have been an interference with ... liberty which cannot be shown to have been authorised and to have been lawful ...These statements were made at a time when [the defendant] was being detained ... without any authorisation. This was in breach of his rights and this court

feels bound to apply in his case the principles already laid down ... in *The People (DPP) v Madden*. This is a case in which evidence has been obtained in circumstances in which the rights of the person concerned have been frustrated.

The Court of Criminal Appeal yet again, in *The People (DPP) v O'Loughlin* (1979) (Case 161), ruled that a confession admitted in evidence at the trial which resulted in a conviction should have been rejected. According to O'Higgins CJ:

> the Gardaí chose not to charge the [defendant] when they ought to have done so. Instead, in effect they held him further for questioning for many hours. This could not have been due to either inadvertence or oversight. It was done by experienced Garda officers who must have had a special knowledge of citizens' rights in such circumstances. It could only have been the result of a deliberate decision by those officers who were aware of the [defendant's] rights. These rights were disregarded and swept aside because of the concern to continue the investigation ... It would ill serve respect for the Constitution and the laws if this court, by allowing evidence so obtained, were to indicate to citizens generally that the obligation on the State to safeguard and vindicate constitutional rights could be dispensed with or erased in the circumstances of a criminal investigation.

Two years later the Supreme Court ruled, in *The People (DPP) v Lynch* (1981) (Case 159), that on facts similar to *O'Loughlin's* case, confessions should be excluded. O'Higgins CJ explained:

> once the Constitution has been violated for the purpose of securing a confession on that ground alone, the fruits of that violation must be excluded from evidence.

The Supreme Court ruled yet again, in *The People (DPP) v Higgins* (1985) (Case 157), that confessions ought to have been excluded at the trial. Finlay CJ said:

> at the time he was alleged to have made the verbal admissions the [defendant] was not being detained for the purpose of being charged or brought before a court but specifically for the purpose of being interrogated. He was therefore detained unlawfully to the knowledge of the Gardaí concerned and ... in conscious and deliberate violation of his constitutional rights.

The Supreme Court, in *The People (DPP) v Healy* (1990) (Case 156), held that the postponement of access to a lawyer by a detained person making a confession until after the completion of the confession rendered the confession inadmissible. Finlay CJ explained:

it is clear on the evidence in this case that the accused should have been informed ... of the arrival of the solicitor, and if he had asked to see him at that time, should have been permitted to see him. The failure to follow that course and the postponement of the access to the solicitor and the informing of the accused of the presence of the solicitor until after the completion of the statement was ... both a deliberate and conscious violation of the accused's constitutional right and also a complete failure to observe reasonable standards of fairness in the procedure of interrogation.

This rule has been applied also in civil cases. In *C. v C.* (1981) a husband and wife had entered into a separation agreement, a term of which prohibited the wife from visiting the husband's home or interfering with him. While the husband was on holiday the wife went to his home and removed letters and photographs which she tended as evidence in maintenance proceedings. The High Court ruled that these items were inadmissible as evidence because they had been obtained in fragrant violation of the husband's constitutional right to the inviolability of his dwelling.

Except in *O'Brien*'s case where the breach of constitutional rights was inadvertent and the evidence was admissible, the cases indicate that the conduct engaged in was a deliberate and conscious breach of constitutional rights, thus the evidence was inadmissible. What should a court do where the action is deliberate but those performing it are unaware of any illegality in what they do? While they intend to do the act in question they do not intend to breach constitutional rights. This was the problem faced in *The People (DPP) v Kenny* (1990) (Case 158) where the Gardaí executed a search warrant by breaking into a premises having obtained the warrant under a procedure which had been in almost universal use throughout the State for many years and which had never been challenged as to its legality but which subsequently turned out to be unlawful (see *Byrne v Grey*, page 276). It was argued that the breach of constitutional right as to the inviolability of the dwelling was not deliberate and conscious unless the Gardaí knew or ought reasonably to have known that they were infringing such right and that the evidence obtained as a result of the search should have been admitted. The Supreme Court rejected that argument. Finlay CJ said:

as between two alternative rules or principles governing the exclusion of evidence obtained as a result of the invasion of the personal rights of the citizen the court has ... an obligation to choose the principle which is likely to provide a stronger and more effective defence and vindication of the right concerned. To exclude only evidence obtained by a person who knows or ought reasonably to know that he is invading a constitutional right is to impose a negative deterrent. It is clearly effective to dissuade a policeman from acting in a manner which he knows is unconstitutional or from acting in a manner reckless as to whether his conduct is or is not unconstitutional. To apply ... the absolute protection rule of exclusion whilst providing also that negative deterrent, incorporates as well a positive encouragement to those in authority over the crime prevention and detection services of the State to consider in detail the personal rights of the citizens as set out in the Constitution and the effect of their powers of arrest, detention, search and questioning in relation to such rights.

To be inadmissible it must be shown that the evidence was obtained as a result of the violation of a constitutional right and not merely after a breach of constitutional rights had occurred. That was the issue in *Walsh v Ó Buachalla* (1990). A person arrested for driving with excess alcohol, while in the garda station awaiting the arrival of a doctor to take a blood or urine specimen, requested a solicitor, which request was ignored. At the trial the question arose as to whether the certificate proving the analysis of the specimen of the blood should have been admitted because the constitutional right of access to a solicitor had been infringed. The High Court ruled that since there was a statutory obligation to give a specimen no advice from a solicitor could have altered that. Since no advice could have prevented the specimen being obtained the non-access to a solicitor in no way affected its being obtained. Accordingly, despite the breach of a constitutional right there was no causal connection between such violation and the giving of the specimen and the certificate was correctly admitted into evidence.

In each of the cases so far discussed there was no extraordinary excusing circumstance which would have permitted the unconstitutionally obtained evidence to be admitted in evidence. In each case, except *O'Brien*'s case, the interest of the individual prevailed over the interest of the State in prosecuting a crime. But in *The People (DPP) v Shaw* (1982) (Case 164) there was a real dilemma in that the defendant was kept in custody longer than was legally permitted because it was believed by the Gardaí that the victim of the crime was alive. The Supreme Court accepted that an extraordinary excusing circumstance existed. Griffin J said:

in my opinion, where such a conflict arises, a choice must be made and it is the duty of the State to protect what is the more important right, even at the expense of another important, but less important, right. The State must therefore weight each right for the purpose of evaluating the merits of each, and strike a balance between them, and having done so take such steps as are necessary to protect the more important right. Although the right to personal liberty is one of the most fundamental rights, in my view, in any civilised society, if a balance is to be struck between the right to personal liberty, for some hours or even days, of one person, and the right to protection against danger to the life of another, the latter right must ... prevail.

Illegally Obtained Evidence

Where the complaint is a breach merely of a legal right as distinct from a constitutional right the courts, according to another aspect of the decision in *The People (AG) v O'Brien* (1965) (Case 152), have discretion to admit or exclude such evidence. According to Kingsmill Moore J:

> we can do no more than ... lay down that, in future cases, the presiding judge has a discretion to exclude evidence of facts ascertained by illegal means where it appears to him that public policy, based on a balancing of public interests, requires such exclusion.

An example of a breach of legal, as distinct from constitutional, rights is exhibited in the case of the *Director of Public Prosecutions v McMahon* (1987) where plain clothes Gardaí entered licensed premises for the specific purpose of ascertaining whether breaches of the gaming laws were being committed. A search warrant was necessary, which had not been obtained, and the question arose whether the observations by the Gardaí could be admitted in evidence. The Supreme Court held that the Gardaí could not enter such premises except with the agreement or by the invitation of the owner for the purpose of ascertaining whether a gaming offence was being committed unless they complied with the statute. In law, the Gardaí were trespassers. There was no breach of constitutional rights because the public portion of a licensed premises which is open for trade is not constitutionally protected under Article 40.5, which is confined to dwellings. The Supreme Court held that the rule in such cases was that evidence obtained by illegal means, not involving conscious and deliberate violation of constitutional rights, should be admissible in evidence unless the trial court, in its discretion, excludes it. The case was referred back to the District Court to apply the principles set down by the Supreme Court.

The High Court ruled in *Minister for Justice v Wang Zhu Jie* (1991) that where Gardaí entered premises in the course of routine inquiries they could give evidence of breaches of the law which they observed. In such circumstances the Gardaí were not trespassers because members of the public who own property impliedly consent to permit Gardaí to enter to make inquiries in the enforcement of the law. Where the owner objects to the entry or objects to the continued presence the Gardaí become trespassers (see page 277).

The distinction between these two cases is that in *McMahon*'s case the Gardaí entered premises to investigate whether a specific offence was being committed, whereas in *Jie*'s case the Gardaí entered to make routine inquiries.

The Right to Bail

Once the judicial process begins on the preferring of a charge the question of bail arises. It was held by the High Court, in *O'Mahony v Melia* (1989)

(Case 146), that the power to grant bail is a judicial act which must be exercised by a judge. In *The People (AG) v O'Callaghan* (1966) (Case 153) the High Court enumerated certain matters which should be considered by a court when considering the question of bail: the seriousness of the charge and the nature of the evidence; the likely sentence; the likelihood of the commission of other offences while on bail; the possibility of disposing of evidence and of interfering with witnesses and jurors; the failure to answer to bail in the past; the fact that the defendant was caught red-handed; the objections of the police; and the possibility of a speedy trial. On appeal the Supreme Court held that the fundamental test in deciding whether to grant bail was the probability of the defendant evading justice. Many of the matters raised by the High Court went to deciding this central issue except the one which allowed the consideration that further offences might be committed if bail was granted. In the opinion of Ó Dálaigh CJ:

> the reasoning underlying this submission was a denial of the whole basis of our legal system. It transcends respect for the requirement that a man shall be considered innocent until he is found guilty and seeks to punish him in respect of offences neither completed nor attempted. I say 'punish', for the deprivation of liberty must be considered a punishment unless it can be required to ensure that an accused person will stand his trial when called upon.

The failure to grant bail would amount to a form of preventative justice which had no place in our legal system and was quite alien to the true purpose of bail. The Supreme Court decided that the probability that the accused, if released on bail, would commit crime was not a reason to refuse bail. The Supreme Court in the *Director of Public Prosecutions v Ryan* (1989) emphasised that the decision in *O'Callaghan*'s case should be upheld and should not be departed from.

Bail is usually set by the court before which the defendant appears though this jurisdiction is reserved to the High Court under the *Criminal Procedure Act 1967*, section 29, in cases of treason, usurping the functions of government, obstruction of government, obstruction of the President, certain offences under the *Official Secrets Act 1963*, and murder, attempted murder, conspiracy to murder or piracy. That same Act, section 31 of the 1967 Act, permits a person brought in custody to a garda station to be released on bail.

A statute which purported to exclude the right of the High Court to grant bail in *In re McAllister* (1973) (Case 96) was contrary to Article 34.3.1° of the Constitution. It was decided by the Supreme Court, in *The People (AG) v Gilliland* (1986), that the test for granting bail in extradition cases should not differ from that in ordinary criminal cases.

Bail must not be fixed at a figure so large as would in effect amount to a denial of bail and in consequence lead to inevitable imprisonment of the accused person. It is common when a court is granting bail to attach conditions, e.g. reporting to the local garda station at regular times. The Supreme Court decided, in *L'Henryenat v Attorney General* (1983) (Case 92), that security ordered to be lodged, in return for the release prior to the trial of a fishing vessel which it was alleged had been engaged in illegal fishing, did not amount to additional and excessive bail to ensure the attendance at the trial of the master of the vessel.

Imprisonment

A common form of detention is imprisonment while undergoing a lawful sentence. Once a court imposes a sentence which must be of definite duration the function of the court is at an end. The length of time which a person spends in prison is a matter which under the constitutional doctrine of the separation of powers rests entirely with the executive. While a court will sentence a person to a particular prison it is not an unwarrantable intrusion into the judicial domain for a statute to permit the executive to alter the place of detention: see *The State (Boyle) v Governor of Military Detention Barracks* (1980) (Case 178).

Where a person is found not guilty but insane a statute which permitted that person to be detained at the pleasure of the executive was not, in *Director of Public Prosecutions v Gallagher* (1991) (Case 54), an invasion of the judicial domain.

An individual, convicted and sentenced to imprisonment, does not as a consequence lose every constitutional right. According to the Supreme Court, in *The State (McDonagh) v Frawley* (1978), many normal constitutional rights are abrogated or suspended while a person is held as a prisoner pursuant to a lawful warrant. The obvious right suspended is that of personal liberty. But what rights remain unimpaired by the imprisonment? We will see, from the decided cases, that the rights which may be exercised by a prisoner are those which do not depend on the continuation of liberty and which are compatible with the reasonable requirements of the prison service, or which do not impose unreasonable demands on it.

One right which is retained is the right to bodily integrity. In *The State (C.) v Frawley* (1976) (Case 183), according to Finlay P in the High Court:

> when the executive, in exercise of what I take to be its constitutional right and duty, imprisons an individual in pursuance of a lawful warrant of a court, then it seems to me to be a logical extension of the principle laid down in *Ryan v Attorney General* (Case 171) that it may not, without justification or necessity, expose the health of that person to risk or danger.

In both the *McDonagh* and *C.* cases the prisoners concerned unsuccessfully complained of inadequate medical facilities in prisons. A prisoner, in *The State (Richardson) v Governor of Mountjoy Prison* (1980) (Case 200), successfully complained to the High Court that the toilet facilities were a danger to her health. The prisoner was not ordered to be released; the prison authorities were given an opportunity to upgrade the conditions.

The High Court held, in *The State (Gallagher) v Governor of Portlaoise Prison* (1987), that the diminution of the constitutional rights of the prisoner's family was clearly envisaged by the Constitution which recognised the requirement for the trial of offences and the imposition of punishments which had consequential effects in relation to any rights associated with convicted persons. The Supreme Court, in *Murray v Attorney General* (1991) (Case 127), held that the right to procreate of a married couple, protected by Article 40.3 of the Constitution, where both were serving long prison sentences, could be restricted as a reasonable consequence of the State's power to imprison. But in *Kearney v Minister for Justice* (1986) (Case 85) it was decided that while the right of a prisoner to communicate, or be communicated with, was not absolute in that prison security required that correspondence could be scrutinised, the unauthorised interference with letters to the prisoner was a breach of his constitutional right to communicate and nominal damages were awarded for that breach.

Where a convicted prisoner was in breach of a temporary release the High Court, in *Cunningham v Governor of Mountjoy Prison* (1985), held that a subsequent rearrest and return to custody to serve the remainder of the sentence was unlawful because a period of seven months was allowed to elapse between the two events which, in the absence of explanation, was unfair.

Where a person is convicted in the District Court and a sentence is affirmed on appeal in the Circuit Court it is a common practice that the warrant does not issue immediately. The High Court held, in *Dutton v O'Donnell* (1989), that in such cases unreasonable delay in the issue and execution of such warrants might breach the convicted person's constitutional right to fair procedures. In that case a delay, without explanation, of four and a half months between the withdrawal of the appeal and the issue of the committal warrant was considered excessive and the arrest on foot of the warrant was held to be unlawful.

Internment without Trial
A possible deprivation of liberty is internment without trial though this form of detention has not been resorted to by the executive in recent years. Indeterminate internment without trial was found unconstitutional in *The State (Burke) v Lennon* (1940) (Case 181) though after a minor amendment to the impugned law, the Bill was referred to the former Supreme Court,

which decided that the law was not repugnant to the Constitution: *Article 26 and the Offences Against the State (Amendment) Bill 1940* (Case 10).

Internment without trial is a form of preventative detention disliked by the Supreme Court in *The People (AG) v O'Callaghan* (1966) (Case 153) (see page 202), which laid down the principles to be applied when bail applications are being decided. One judge, Walsh J, thought that internment without trial could only be used:

> in the most extraordinary circumstances carefully spelled out by the Oireachtas and then only to secure the preservation of the State in a time of national emergency or in some situation akin to that.

For reasons explained on page 50 the Supreme Court may not feel bound by the decisions of the former Supreme Court, or that the provisions of Article 34.3.3° of the Constitution, which provide that the validity of a law the Bill of which was referred to the Supreme Court could not be challenged again, were applicable to Bills referred to the former Supreme Court. Internment without trial could yet face constitutional challenge.

Apart from objections to internment without trial on constitutional grounds, its administration may be difficult following a change of judicial attitude on the scope of judicial intervention in the review of administrative action. The former Supreme Court, in *Article 26 and the Offences Against the State (Amendment) Bill 1940* (Case 10), per Sullivan CJ, said:

> the only essential preliminary to the exercise by a Minister of the powers ... is that he should have formed opinions on the matters specifically mentioned in the section. The validity of such opinions is not a matter that could be questioned in any court.

A similar conclusion was reached, on the point that the courts could not review a decision to intern, in In *re Ó Láighléis* (1960) (Case 144) by the former Supreme Court. But in *The State (Lynch) v Cooney* (1982) (Case 191) this judicial practice was reversed. Speaking of the relevant statute,[6] admittedly not the *Offences Against the State (Amendment) Act 1940*, the Supreme Court held it was satisfied that the statute did not exclude review by the courts and that any opinion formed by the Minister thereunder must be one which is bona fide held and factually sustainable and not unreasonable. Henchy J stated:

> it is to be presumed that when Parliament conferred the power, it intended it to be exercised only in a manner that would be in conformity with the Constitution and within the limitations of the power as it is to be gathered from the statutory scheme or design. This means, amongst other things, not only that the power must be exercised in good faith, but that the opinion

or other subjective conclusion set as a precondition for the valid exercise of the power must be reached by a route that does not make the exercise unlawful — such as by misinterpreting the law, or by misapplying it through taking into consideration irrelevant matters of fact, or through ignoring relevant matters. Otherwise, the exercise of the power will be held to be invalid for being *ultra vires*.

To justify a particular internment the Minister making the decision might, in legal proceedings, be called on to expose the evidence on which the decision was based. The possible requirement of having to justify an internment order may, among other things, be a disincentive to introducing this form of detention.

Incarceration because of Mental Illness

Another form of detention is the indefinite holding in preventative custody of persons of unsound mind under the *Mental Treatment Act 1945*. The value of such a law was accepted by the former Supreme Court in *In re Philip Clarke* (1950) (Case 36) where O'Byrne J explained:

the impugned legislation is of a paternal character, clearly intended for the care and custody of persons suspected to be suffering from mental infirmity and for the safety and well being of the public generally ... We do not see how the common good would be promoted or the dignity and freedom of the individual assured by allowing persons, alleged to be suffering from such infirmity, to remain at large to the possible danger to themselves or others.

The necessity for having some judicial determination before a person could be detained under that law was rejected in that case though a different conclusion might be reached if the matter was judicially reviewed anew.

The *Mental Treatment Act 1945*, section 260, requires an intending plaintiff to obtain leave of the court before instituting any proceedings in respect of acts purporting to have been done pursuant to the Act. Such leave shall not be granted unless the court is satisfied that there are substantial grounds for contending that the person against whom the proceedings are to be brought acted in bad faith or without reasonable care. The Supreme Court ruled in *Murphy v Greene* (1991) that to comply with the section an intending plaintiff must establish, as a matter of probability, the existence of facts constituting substantial grounds for contending that the proposed defendant acted in bad faith or without reasonable care.

Imprisonment for Debt

Imprisonment for debt continues to exist as part of our law. Under the *Enforcement of Court Orders Act 1926*, as amended, a procedure is available whereby a debtor against whom judgment has been given, and who has no goods to be seized in execution, may be examined in the District Court and ordered to pay by instalment. On default in the instalments an application for the arrest and imprisonment of the debtor may be sought, which can only be granted for a period of up to three months, if the District Court is satisfied that the failure to pay was due, not to inability, but to wilful refusal or culpable neglect.

Extradition
An individual may be arrested for the purpose of extradition. In *The State (Quinn) v Ryan* (1965) (Case 199) the Supreme Court struck down a statute which empowered the removal of an individual, wanted in Britain for a crime, out of this jurisdiction without an opportunity given to that individual to have recourse to the courts in this country to question that arrest or procedure. Effectively this judgment caused extradition to cease but only temporarily. To remedy this lacuna in our laws, the *Extradition Act 1965* and amendments were enacted. Under its provisions an individual wanted in another country must be given a judicial hearing before the extradition can take place.

The Act sets two types of procedures in extradition matters: one for extraditions between Ireland and the United Kingdom (Part III), and another for extraditions between Ireland and other countries (Part II). While the general law and procedures are similar there are important differences. We will discuss extradition between Ireland and the United Kingdom first.

Where a judicial authority in the United Kingdom issues a warrant applying for the arrest of a person accused or convicted of an offence in the United Kingdom, which is an indictable offence, or an offence punishable on summary conviction by imprisonment for a maximum period of at least six months, the Commissioner of the Garda Síochána on the production of the warrant and, where it appears that the person named or described in the warrant may be found in the State, endorses the warrant for execution. *Shannon v Attorney General* (1984) (Case 174) decided that this endorsement by the Commissioner was an administrative, as distinct from a judicial, function. Likewise, the High Court decided, in *Wheeler v Culligan* (1989) (Case 213), that the power granted to the Attorney General to direct the Commissioner of the Garda Síochána not to execute a warrant on the ground of insufficiency of evidence was procedural rather than judicial in nature.

The warrant may be executed by any member of the Garda Síochána and the person arrested must be brought before the District Court. The District Court makes an order for the delivery of that person at some convenient point of departure from the State into the custody of a member of a police force of the place in which the warrant was issued for conveyance to that place. It was decided by the High Court, in *The State (McFadden) v Governor of*

Mountjoy Prison (1981) (Case 193) that an arrested person must be afforded fair procedures: (a) a copy of the warrant should be given, (b) the person should be informed that legal representation is permissible, and (c) that an adjournment was available for the purpose of obtaining legal representation or advice. An extradition order shall not be made if it appears to the District Court that the offence specified in the warrant does not correspond with any offence under the laws of this State, which is an indictable offence or is punished on summary conviction by imprisonment for a maximum period of at least six months. Where the court does not make an extradition order the arrested person must be discharged.

Should the court make an extradition order the individual concerned shall not, without his or her consent, be delivered up for extradition until the expiration of fifteen days from the date of the order. The court, on the making of the order, must inform the individual to be extradited of the right to make an application to the High Court for release under section 50 of the Act. The individual must not be delivered up for extradition pending the outcome of that appeal, or the outcome of an application under Article 40.4.2° of the Constitution. An individual ordered to be extradited shall be released if a direction is given by the High Court, and on appeal by the Supreme Court, that the offence to which the warrant relates is:

1. a political offence, or an offence connected with a political offence (this matter is discussed in fuller detail a little later).
2. an offence under military law which is not an offence under ordinary criminal law.
3. a revenue offence. The High Court held, in *McDonald v McMahon* (1989), that these words referred to an offence in connection with taxes or duties in relation to any place outside the State and that the fees charged for the renewal of Irish passports by an Irish embassy abroad did not constitute taxes or duties.
4. there are substantial reasons for believing that the individual, if removed from the State, would be prosecuted or detained for a political offence, or an offence connected with a political offence, or an offence under military law which is not an offence under ordinary criminal law.
5. the offence specified in the warrant does not correspond with any offence under the law of the State which is an indictable offence, or is punishable on summary conviction by imprisonment for a maximum period of at least six months.

Where the individual is not to be delivered up for extradition within one month of the order being made the High Court, on application by or on behalf of that individual, may, unless reasonable cause be shown for the delay, order that individual to be discharged.

The constitutionality of Part III was challenged in *Shannon v Attorney General* (1984) (Case 174) on the ground that the law, procedure and practice relating to the interrogation, detention or trial of a person in Northern Ireland would, on their due application, subject the person to what would be less than his entitlement under Article 40.3 of the Constitution in a corresponding prosecution in this State. While the Supreme Court rejected the claim on the facts as proven, Henchy J warned:

> the presumption is that the *Extradition Act 1965* will not be operated in such a manner as to violate the constitutional rights of those affected by its operation. Thus, if it were shown in a particular case that the provisions of Part III of the Act were being used for a purpose, or for a manner, inconsistent with such constitutional rights, the courts would be bound to refuse to give effect to Part III.

To reach a conclusion on whether to extradite or not it would be necessary to balance a number of factors, including the nature of the constitutional right involved, the consequence of an invasion of it, the capacity of the courts to afford further protection of the right, and the extent of the risk of invasion. On the balancing of these and other factors in each case the courts must conclude whether its intervention to protect a constitutional right is required and, if so, in what form.

The Supreme Court ruled, in *Finucane v McMahon* (1990) and *Clarke v McMahon* (1990), that it was necessary to intervene to protect constitutional rights and the form such protection took was to prevent the extraditions because there was a probable risk that if extradited to Northern Ireland the parties would be assaulted or injured by the illegal actions of prison staff while in custody. The court's primary obligation was the duty to prevent such invasions of rights and it was not a sufficient discharge of that duty for the court to rely on the vindication of those rights by compensation after they had been invaded. On the other hand, in *Ellis v O'Dea* (1990), the Supreme Court ruled that on the evidence presented the extradition to Britain could not be prevented because a risk had not been established that the plaintiff would be tried or prosecuted or that investigations would be conducted in a manner which would be inconsistent with the reasonable standards of a fair trial required by the Constitution.

We will now examine the procedures, under Part II of the Act, for extraditions between Ireland and other countries. This part of the Act may be applied by government order in two types of situations. First, where by an international agreement or convention to which the State is a party an arrangement is made with another country for the surrender by each country to the other of persons wanted for prosecution or punishment: this was the method used for implementing a Treaty of Extradition between Ireland and the United States of America, which Treaty was declared inoperable in *The State (Gilliland) v Governor of Mountjoy Prison* (1987) (Case 188) on the ground that, since it involved a charge on public funds, it had not been approved by Dáil Éireann under Article 29.5.2° of the Constitution.[7] Second, where the government is satisfied that reciprocal facilities to that effect will be afforded by another country: this was the method used for implementing Part II with regard to the Commonwealth of Australia — the government made the order on 26 October 1984, and on the same day the Governor General of Australia made regulations, entitled *Extradition (Republic of Ireland) Regulations* which applied their relevant law.

A request for the extradition of an individual must be made in writing, and communicated, together with the appropriate documents, by a diplomatic agent of the requesting country to the Minister for Justice. Should the Minister receive a request for the extradition of a named individual, the Minister by order signifies that request to the District Court, which issues a warrant for the arrest of that individual. Where the District Court is satisfied that (a) the extradition of that individual has been duly requested, and (b) that Part II applies in relation to the requesting country, and (c) extradition of the individual is not prohibited by Part II, and (d) the appropriate documents are produced, the court must make an order committing that person to a prison there to await the order of the Minister for Justice for his or her extradition. The court must, on the making of the committal order, inform the individual that he or she will not be surrendered, unless by consent, until after the expiry of fifteen days from the date of the order, and informs the individual of the provisions of Article 40.4.2° of the Constitution.

Extradition shall be granted under Part II only in respect of an offence which is punishable under the laws of the requesting country, and of the State, by imprisonment for a minimum period of at least one year or by a more severe penalty.

If there has been a conviction and sentence in the requesting country, imprisonment for a period of at least four months or a more severe penalty must have been imposed.

Extradition shall not be granted:

1. for an offence which is a political offence, or an offence connected with a political offence (this is discussed fully later);
2. if there are substantial grounds for believing that a request for extradition for an ordinary criminal offence has been made for the purpose of prosecuting or punishing a person on account of his race, religion, nationality or political opinion;
3. for military offences which are not offences under ordinary criminal law;
4. for revenue offences;

5. where the offence for which it is requested is regarded, under the law of the State, as having been committed in the State;
6. where a prosecution is pending in the State against the individual for the offence for which extradition is requested;
7. where final judgment has been passed by the State, or in a third country, on the individual in respect of the offence for which extradition is requested;
8. where according to the law of either the requesting country, or the State, the individual has become immune from prosecution or punishment by reason of the lapse of time;
9. the offence is punishable by death under the law of the requesting country but is of a category for which the death penalty is not provided for by the law of the State, or is not generally carried out, unless the requesting country gives such assurances as the Minister for Justice considers sufficient that the death penalty will not be carried out;
10. where the individual shall not be charged, sentenced or detained for any offence committed prior to surrender, other than that for which the extradition is requested;
11. unless sufficient evidence is produced where the extradition provisions require the production by the requesting country of evidence as to the commission by the individual of the offence;
12. where provision is not made by the law of the requesting country, or by the extradition agreement, that that country shall not surrender the individual to another country.

The Minister for Justice may, if the individual is not released by the High Court, by order direct the individual to be surrendered to such other person as in the Minister's opinion is duly authorised by the requesting country to receive that individual.

Most litigation under the *Extradition Act 1965* has centred on the question as to what constitutes a political offence, or an offence connected with a political offence. As will be seen from the decisions in these cases a clear definition of either does not emerge. The approach taken by the courts is to consider whether the facts presented in each individual case fall within either category without offering a definition of what constitutes a political offence or an offence connected with a political offence.

The first of these cases was *Bourke v Attorney General* (1972) where the Supreme Court held that the aiding of a convicted spy to escape from prison, while not a political offence, was an offence connected with a political offence. In *McGlinchey v Wren* (1982), while the claim that the offence was political — that of the murder of an elderly postmistress in the course of an armed robbery — was withdrawn in the Supreme Court, O'Higgins CJ said:

all that can be said with authority in this case is that ... this offence could not be said to be either a political offence or an offence connected with a political offence. Whether a contrary conclusion would be reached in different circumstances would depend on the particular circumstances and on whether those particular circumstances showed that the person charged was at the relevant time engaged, either directly or indirectly, in what reasonable, civilised people would regard as political activity.

It was claimed, in *Shannon v Fanning* (1984), that the offences of murdering two former Northern Ireland politicians were political offences. The Supreme Court rejected this claim. O'Higgins CJ, speaking for the majority, defined a political offence thus:

in my view it follows that what constitutes a political offence falls to be determined in each case having regard to the act done and the facts and circumstances which surrounded its commission — the onus being on the person claiming the political exception to establish that the offence ... comes within its protection ... the circumstances (as so disclosed) of the murders in question here were so brutal, cowardly and callous that it would be a distortion of language if they were to be accorded the status of political offences or offences connected with political offences.

Hederman J, in a separate judgment, said:

in my view the nature of the plaintiff's claim cannot be judged in the light of the assessment of the acts themselves, divorced from any circumstances involving him or divorced from any motivation on his part ... it is my opinion that the decisive criterion to determine whether an ordinary criminal offence becomes a relative political offence is whether the perpetrator acted with a political motive or for a political purpose.

McCarthy J, also in a separate judgment, said:

in my opinion ... the objective determination of whether or not an offence charged is a political offence, or an offence connected with a political offence ... should primarily rest upon an assessment of three factors:
1. the true motivation of the individual or individuals committing the offence. I do not share the view that, in order to assess motive, the individual charged must admit his involvement in the crime.
2. the true nature of the offence itself.
3. the identity of the victim or victims.

A claim in *Quinn v Wren* (1985) was made that a forgery offence, committed on behalf of the Irish National Liberation Army, a proscribed organisation,[8] was a political offence or an offence connected with a political offence. Again the claim was rejected. Finlay CJ said:

the plaintiff states that he committed the offence charged for the purposes of the INLA, the aims and objectives of which are the establishment of a 32 county workers' republic by force of arms. The achievement of that objective necessarily and inevitably involves the destruction and setting aside of the Constitution by means expressly or impliedly prohibited by it: see Articles 15.6 and 39. To interpret the words 'political offence' ... so as to grant immunity or protection to a person charged with an offence directly intended to further that objective would be to give to the section [50 of the 1965 Act] a patently unconstitutional construction. This court cannot, it seems to me, interpret an Act of the Oireachtas as having the intention to grant immunity from extradition to a person charged with an offence the admitted purpose of which is to further or facilitate the overthrow of the Constitution and the organs of State thereby.

The claim was made in *Russell v Fanning* (1988) that various offences arising out of a prison escape were political in that the plaintiff took part as a member of the Irish Republican Army, a proscribed organisation, for the purpose of carrying on the campaign for the ending of British rule in Northern Ireland. The Supreme Court, in rejecting the claim, felt bound by its own decision in *Quinn v Wren*. Finlay CJ held:

the objectives for which ... the attack was made on [a police officer] and the objectives which were a factor in the escape ... from the prison were to achieve the reintegration of the national territory by force of arms. The plaintiff states that he is a member of an organisation, the Provisional IRA, which intends to carry out the task. The Constitution and in particular Article 6 ... make it quite clear that, subject to the provisions of the Constitution, decisions as to the method by which the national territory is to be integrated are matters for the Government subject to the control of Dáil Éireann, and that the carrying out of these decisions is exercisable only by or on the authority of the organs of State established by the Constitution. Any person or group of persons is, of course entitled to advocate a particular policy of reintegration, whether that is or is not consistent with the existing Government policy from time to time. For a person or a group of persons, however, to take over or seek to take over the carrying out of a policy of reintegration decided upon by himself or themselves without the authority of the organs of State established by the Constitution is to subvert the Constitution and to usurp the functions of Government. In my view, 'political offence' within the meaning of section 50 of the *Extradition Act 1965*, cannot be construed so as to grant immunity to a person who by his own admission has, in respect of the matters with which he is charged, that objective. This ground of appeal must fail.

The Supreme Court, in *Finucane v McMahon* (1990), refused to follow its own decision in *Russell v Fanning*. In this case the plaintiff claimed to be a member of the IRA and the offences relating to escaping from custody in Northern Ireland were directed against the British Army in an attempt to end British rule in Northern Ireland and that he did not have as an objective the subversion of the Constitution or the usurpation of the organs of State established by the Constitution. In holding the offences to be political, Walsh J, speaking for a majority of the Supreme Court, said:

> I am of opinion that the court cannot draw the inference that it was the intention of the Oireachtas that the provisions relating to the political exemption in the *Extradition Act 1965* should not apply to persons charged with politically motivated offences of violence when the objective of such offences was to secure the ultimate unity of the country ... the fact that the policy or activities followed by persons acting outside the jurisdiction of the State is opposed to or contrary to the policy adopted by the Government of Ireland in relation to the unity of the country is not ... sufficient to equate it to the policy to overthrow this State or to subvert the Constitution ... There may be matters in international affairs including warlike activities in respect of which the Government of this State has a particular interest or a particular policy including that under Article 29 of the Constitution, of seeking to promote the peaceful settlement of international disputes. But that in itself would not be sufficient to enable the courts to deprive anybody who involves himself in the same dispute, in a manner opposed to the general government policy and who becomes a fugitive in this State, of the benefit of the statutory provisions dealing with the political exemption.

It can be seen from these cases that the courts have attempted to define the expressions 'political offence' or 'an offence connected with a political offence' in some restricted manner without a clear or easy definition emerging.

The *Extradition (European Convention on the Suppression of Terrorism) Act 1987* provides that certain offences are not to be regarded as political. No offence shall be regarded as a political offence or an offence connected with a political offence if the court, or the Minister for Justice, having taken into due consideration any particularly serious aspects of the offence is of opinion that the offence cannot properly be regarded as political or connected with a political offence. In deciding this question consideration may be given to the fact that the act in issue created a collective danger to the life, physical integrity or liberty of persons, or that it affected persons foreign to the motives behind it, or that cruel or vicious means were used in the commission of the offence. While this statute applies to all offences particular mention is made of: (a) offences involving the unlawful seizure of aircrafts or unlawful acts against the safety of civil aviation; (b) serious offences involving an attack against the life, physical integrity or liberty of an internationally protected person, such as a head of State, a head of government or an agent of an international organisation; (c) an offence involving kidnapping, the taking of a hostage or serious false imprisonment; (d) an offence involving the use of an explosive or an automatic firearm, if such endangers persons (in *Sloan v Culligan* (1991) the Supreme Court construed this offence to mean a present use with a present danger to persons only and did not include a possession with the intention for future use endangering persons); and (e) an attempt to commit any of these offences.

The Supreme Court in *The People (AG) v Gilliland* (1986) decided that in considering the question of bail in extradition cases, where for example the individual was awaiting the outcome of High Court proceedings, that the test was that applicable in all bail applications — whether the party resisting bail has satisfied the court that there was a likelihood that the individual seeking bail would abscond.

AN ORDER UNDER ARTICLE 40.4.2° OF THE CONSTITUTION

Speedy Remedy for Unlawful Detention
At common law a detention was tested, as to its legality, by the writ of habeas corpus. The process was swift and relatively informal. A procedure, similar though not identical, contained in Article 40.4.2° of the Constitution, probably subsumes the common law remedy. It declares that upon complaint being made by, or on behalf of, any person to the High Court, and any and every judge thereof, that such person is unlawfully detained, the High Court, and any judge to whom such complaint is made, must inquire into the complaint and *may* order the person in whose custody such person is detained to produce the body of such person before the High Court and to certify in writing the grounds of that detention. The High Court must, after the body of such person has been produced, and after giving the person in whose custody he or she is detained an opportunity of justifying the detention, order the release of such person unless satisfied that that person is being detained in accordance with law.

This speedy procedure for testing the legality of an arrest or detention has been used in a variety of different types of situations: suspects in garda custody,[9] prisoners in custody,[10] patients in hospitals,[11] children in residential care[12] and in the custody of parents and others, and persons about to be deported.[13]

This jurisdiction is vested in the High Court: no other court can exercise this jurisdiction, save the Supreme Court on appeal from the High Court.

This principle was emphasised by the Supreme Court in *Keating v Governor of Mountjoy Prison* (1990) where McCarthy J stated:

> the holding of such an enquiry is constitutionally the role of the High Court. Article 40.4.2° expressly contemplates the complaint of lawful detention being made to the High Court or any judge thereof... it would clearly be an unwarrantable and unlawful usurpation of the constitutional role of the High Court if any inferior court were to embark upon such an enquiry with a view to holding that a person was being unlawfully detained and ordering his release. The District Court has no such function. In the course of a hearing a justice of the District Court or a judge of the Circuit Court, in an appropriate case, is bound to enquire into the circumstances under which particular evidence was obtained and may rule against the admission of such evidence if satisfied that it was obtained in circumstances involving a breach of constitutional rights such as to taint the evidence itself. It is, however... wholly inconsistent with the constitutional rule of the High Court that... a District Justice should embark upon the constitutional enquiry as to the validity of detention.

It is unusual in law for one individual to be allowed to litigate on behalf of another. The making of an application under Article 40.4.2° is one such exception which permits a complaint to be made by, or on behalf of, any person. Such exceptions are to be seen in *The State (Burke) v Lennon* (1940) (Case 181) where a brother of the person detained brought the application, and in *The State (Quinn) v Ryan* (1965) (Case 199) where the solicitor of a person released by the High Court was allowed to bring a fresh application after that person had again been detained and removed out of the jurisdiction.

Because the word 'may' is used in Article 40.4.2°, there is no obligation on the High Court to order the production of the detained person before the court. It was decided by the Supreme Court, in *The State (Woods) v Kelly* (1969), that this was merely an enabling power and that an order for release can be made where the person is not before the court. The High Court decided in *The State (Gallagher) v Governor of Portlaoise Prison* (1987) that since there was no requirement in that particular case to hear arguments from the State it was not necessary to have the applicant in court to respond to any submission or argument made by the State.

Two Stage Procedure

The procedure under Article 40.4.2° is that the person complaining of the unlawful detention applies *ex parte** to the High Court for a conditional order directing the person causing the detention to justify that detention in writing. Where that person fails to justify the detention the conditional order is made absolute and the High Court orders the release of the detained person.

Occasionally the detained person is released after the making of the conditional order. In that event the jurisdiction of the High Court is at an end. The released person is left to pursue any other appropriate legal remedies.

The High Court cannot make an absolute order in the first instance, without giving the person, in whose custody the detained person is alleged to be, an opportunity to be heard. The Supreme Court so decided in *The State (Rogers) v Galvin* (1983) (Case 201). Henchy J explained the procedure thus:

> Article 40.4.2° postulates two stages of enquiry before the detained person may be released. First, there is to be an order, if the court thinks it necessary, that the body of the detained person be produced in court on a named day and that the detainer certify in writing the grounds of detention. So much of the court proceedings may be *ex parte*. Secondly, upon the actual or notional production of the body on the named day, the detainer is to have the further opportunity, in the light of all the then available evidential material, of justifying the detention. It is only then, if the detainer fails to satisfy the court that the detention is 'in accordance with law' ... that release from custody may be ordered.

Multiple Applications

Can a person, having obtained a conditional order which is not made absolute, go from judge to judge of the High Court until one judge is found who upholds the complaint, or until the membership of the High Court has been exhausted? This point was decided by the former Supreme Court in *The State (Dowling) v Kingston* (1937), where an individual, refused an absolute order by the majority of a three-judge High Court, later renewed the application before the judge who had decided in his favour. This judge refused to reconsider the matter and, on appeal, it was held that once the law had been declared by a competent court that decision was binding on the individual members of that court. Murnaghan J drew an important distinction when he held:

> there is no right to apply to a judge after the High Court has pronounced the detention to be legal. It is quite a different matter ... to say that the refusal of a judge to grant the first *ex parte* application prevents an application to another judge. In such a case the detention has not been declared to be in accordance with law.

But should new grounds be subsequently advanced that the detention is unlawful, after a determination has been made, the Supreme Court held in the *Application of Woods* (1970) that the High Court was under a constitutional obligation to consider the application anew.

Consequences of Release

Article 40.4.2° of the Constitution declares in unambiguous terms that once the High Court concludes that the individual is detained unlawfully the release of that individual must be ordered. Does the making of such an order preclude a fresh detention? The answer is no. An illustration that an initial release by the High Court does not grant an immunity from re-arrest on the same matter subsequently is the case of *The State (McFadden) v Governor of Mountjoy Prison* (1981) (Case 193) where the High Court held that a person, arrested on foot of an extradition warrant, had been denied fair procedures both on arrest and in the subsequent hearing in the District Court. On the person's re-arrest some time later it was argued that this arrest was also unlawful, though the High Court, in *The State (McFadden) v Governor of Mountjoy Prison (No. 2)* (1981), held the second arrest to be lawful.

The point could be argued that before a second arrest can be lawfully effected the released person must be really and truly free. An immediate re-arrest may be tainted with the original illegality in that the High Court might hold that no actual release had taken place. In *The State (Trimbole) v Governor of Mountjoy Prison* (1985) (Case 204), McCarthy J, in the Supreme Court, said:

> during the course of the argument, the question was canvassed as to whether or not the prosecutor could be validly arrested and extradited upon a fresh warrant . . . from Australia. [His] counsel expressly conceded that such an arrest and extradition would be valid. That is not to say that such arrest and extradition might not be challenged; for myself, I would like to make it clear that the views that I have expressed are not to be taken as any indication that the prosecutor is now seven weeks after his release free from extradition from this country.

Appeal to the Supreme Court

At common law it was the tradition that the State would not appeal the release of a person that had been ordered as a result of a habeas corpus hearing. This rule was confirmed by the former Supreme Court in *The State (Burke) v Lennon* (1940) (Case 181), though in *The State (Browne) v Feran* (1967) (Case 180) the present Supreme Court ruled that, unless such an appeal was prohibited by statute law, an appeal lay by virtue of Article 34.4.3° of the Constitution (see page 121). The Supreme Court ruled in *The State (Trimbole) v Governor of Mountjoy Prison* (1985) (Case 204) that once the High Court ordered a release under Article 40.4.2° of the Constitution the Supreme Court could not put a stay on that order so as to prevent the release pending the hearing of the appeal. The court did accept that it could, after hearing the appeal and overruling the High Court, order the re-arrest of the person concerned.

Where the body of a person alleged to be unlawfully detained is produced before the High Court, and that court is satisfied that such person is being detained in accordance with a law but that such law is invalid having regard to the provisions of the Constitution, the High Court must refer the question of the validity of such law to the Supreme Court by way of case stated, and may admit the individual to bail (Article 40.4.3°). This sub-article was added to the Constitution by ordinary legislation after the unforeseen decision of the High Court in *The State (Burke) v Lennon* (1940) (Case 181). The Supreme Court held in *The State (Sheerin) v Kennedy* (1966) (Case 203) that this provision applied only to post-constitutional statutes. Instances of this jurisdiction being invoked are *In re Doyle, an infant* (1955) (Case 56, see page 257) and *The State (Gilliland) v Governor of Mountjoy Prison* (1987) (Case 188, see page 105).

Non-application of Article 40.4.2° of the Constitution
Article 40.4.6° declares that the procedure for testing the validity of a detention, contained in Article 40.4.2°, cannot be invoked to prohibit, control, or interfere with any act of the defence forces during the existence of a state of war or armed rebellion (see page 54).

RIGHT TO LIFE

Right to Continuance of Life
Probably the greatest right of all is the right of the living to the continuance of that life. Where the exercise of this right is extinguished all other rights and protections are superfluous. The deliberate taking of human life can occur in different situations such as murder, self-defence, provocation and the quelling of armed rebellion. The deliberate taking of human life by the State by way of execution has been abolished.

It was hinted that the right to life was one of the unspecified constitutional rights. The High Court, in *Conroy v Attorney General* (1965) (Case 38), per Kenny J, said:

> every individual, as an individual, had certain inherent rights of which the right of life is the most fundamental.

Right to Life of the Unborn
Another fundamental right is the right to life of the unborn. This right has now been expressly acknowledged in Article 40.3.3° of the Constitution by the *Eighth Amendment to the Constitution (Pro-Life) Act 1983* which declares that the State acknowledges the right to life of the unborn and, with due regard

to the equal right to life of the mother, guarantees in its laws to respect, and, as far as practicable, by its laws to defend and vindicate that right.

Which right prevails when the two rights are in conflict falls to be decided in particular cases. The only such case was the *Attorney General v X.* (1992) (Case 16) where it was accepted that the risk that a mother might commit suicide must be taken into account when reconciling the right of the unborn to life and the right of the mother to life. Finlay CJ concluded:

> that the proper test to be applied is that if it is established as a matter of probability that there is a real and substantial risk to the life, as distinct from the health, of the mother which can only be avoided by the termination of her pregnancy, such termination is permissible, having regard to the true interpretation of Article 40.3.3° of the Constitution.

Assistance in the Destruction of the Life of the Unborn

It is neither unconstitutional nor unlawful to discuss abortion though it is unconstitutional to assist in the ultimate destruction of the life of the unborn by abortion. The Supreme Court held in *Attorney General (Society for the Protection of Unborn Children (Ireland) Ltd) v Open Door Counselling Ltd* (1989) (Case 16a) that the counselling of pregnant women within this jurisdiction to travel abroad to obtain an abortion,[14] or to obtain further advice on abortion within that foreign jurisdiction, was unconstitutional having regard to Article 40.3.3° of the Constitution. The court granted an injunction to prevent such activities. Finlay CJ said:

> the essential issues in this case do not in any way depend upon the plaintiff establishing that the defendant was advising or encouraging the procuring of abortions. The essential issue ... having regard to the nature of the guarantees contained in Article 40.3.3° of the Constitution is the issue as to whether the ... admitted activities were assisting pregnant women within the jurisdiction to travel outside that jurisdiction in order to have an abortion. To put the matter in another way, the issue and the question of fact to be determined is: was it thus assisting in the destruction of the life of the unborn? I am satisfied beyond doubt that having regard to the admitted facts the defendant was assisting in the ultimate destruction of the life of the unborn by abortion in that it was helping the pregnant woman who had decided upon that option to get in touch with a clinic in Great Britain which would provide the service of abortion.

The Supreme Court also held that there was thus no implied or unenumerated constitutional right to information about the availability of a service of abortion outside the State which, if availed of, would have the direct consequence of destroying the expressly guaranteed constitutional right to life of the unborn.

The Supreme Court decision in that case must now be read subject to two amendments to the Constitution. The *Thirteenth Amendment of the Constitution Act 1992* provides that Article 40.3.3° of the Constitution shall not limit freedom to travel between the State and another State and the *Fourteenth Amendment of the Constitution Act 1992* provides that Article 40.3.3° of the Constitution shall not limit freedom to obtain or make available in the State, subject to such conditions as may be laid down by law, information relating to services lawfully available in another State.

The ambit of these new articles awaits judicial interpretation. The Supreme Court refused, in *Attorney General (Society for the Protection of Unborn Children (Ireland) Ltd) v Open Door Counselling Ltd* (1993), where the defendant sought to have an injunction which had been granted against it in the 1988 case (see above) lifted, to adjudicate on the interpretation of each of the new additions to Article 40.3.3° of the Constitution on the ground that the matter had neither arisen in nor been decided by the High Court, and because the provisions of the Constitution had not been in force or enacted at the time when the original case was determined.

The Defence of the Unborn's Right to Life

While it is a truism to say that the unborn cannot protect itself from activities which may prevent its right to life being exercised the question must be raised as to who is the proper party to do so. The obvious answer is the mother. But what is to happen in instances where the threat to the unborn comes from the mother?

The Supreme Court ruled in *Attorney General (Society for the Protection of Unborn Children Ltd) v Open Door Counselling Ltd* (1989) (Case 16a) that the jurisdiction of the courts could be invoked by a party who had a bona-fide concern and interest for the protection of the constitutionally guaranteed right to life of the unborn and that the courts, as the judicial organ of the State, would be failing in their duty as far as practicable to vindicate and defend that right if they were to refuse relief on the grounds that no particular pregnant woman who might be affected by the making of an order was represented before the courts. The court also ruled that the Attorney General as the holder of a high constitutional office was an especially appropriate person to invoke the jurisdiction of the courts in order to vindicate and defend this right. In the later case, the *Society for the Protection of Unborn Children Ltd v Coogan* (1990), the Supreme Court ruled that the Attorney General did not have the exclusive right to commence proceedings seeking to enforce compliance with the provisions of Article 40.3.3° of the Constitution. Any citizen showing a bona-fide concern and interest in the enforcement of the provisions may initiate an action seeking to enforce compliance with the article and that since the plaintiff was not in the position of being an officious or meddlesome intervenient in the matter it had sufficient *locus standi* to maintain the action without the intervention of the Attorney General.

RIGHT TO BODILY INTEGRITY

Personal Integrity
The right to bodily integrity was first expounded, as an implied constitutional right, in *Ryan v Attorney General* (1965) (Case 171). In the High Court Kenny J suggested it extended to:

> no mutilation of the body or any of its members may be carried out on any citizen under authority of the law except for the good of the whole body and that no process which is or may, as a matter of probability, be dangerous or harmful to the life or health of the citizens or any of them may be imposed (in the sense of being made compulsory) by an Act of the Oireachtas.

On the evidence presented in that case it was held that the fluoridation of the public water supply was not an interference with that right. The existence of the right was accepted in *The State (C.) v Frawley* (1976) (Case 183) and *The State (McDonagh) v Frawley* (1978), though in neither case was it breached. In *The State (Richardson) v Governor of Mountjoy Prison* (1980) (Case 200) this right was extended to include the right of a person in custody not to have his or her health endangered (for a fuller discussion of these cases see page 203).

The High Court held, in *D. v Ireland* (1992) (Case 47), that the crime of rape violated the victim's right to bodily integrity though it refused to award damages against the State for such a violation. Obviously the perpetrator was the party to be sued.

The Supreme Court ruled, in *Finucane v McMahon* (1990), that where a court was satisfied that there was a real danger that a person whose extradition was sought would suffer ill-treatment in breach of constitutional rights if delivered out of the jurisdiction, the extradition of such person must be refused (see page 209).

FREEDOM TO TRAVEL

Freedom of Movement
The right to personal liberty would be meaningless if there was no corollary of freedom of movement. This right is encompassed in the right to travel. It was suggested by the High Court, in *Ryan v Attorney General* (1965) (Case 171),

by Kenny J, that one of the unspecified constitutional rights was the right to free movement within the State and it was acknowledged in *Kane v Governor of Mountjoy Prison* (1988) that freedom of movement included the right to travel freely without overt or covert surveillance.

The ambit of this right was extended in *The State (K.M.) v Minister for Foreign Affairs* (1979) (Case 190) where the right to travel outside the State was firmly established. In the High Court Finlay P explained:

> the citizens of the State may have a right (arising from the Christian and democratic nature of the State — though not enumerated in the Constitution) to avail of such facilities without arbitrary or unjustified interference by the State. To put the matter more simply and more bluntly, it appears to me that, subject to the obvious conditions which may be required by public order and the common good of the State, a citizen has the right to a passport.

Obvious exceptions would be in time of war, or a debtor fleeing creditors, or a criminal fleeing from justice. The existence of this constitutional right was affirmed by the High Court in *Lennon v Ganley* (1981) where an injunction to restrain the Irish Rugby Football Union, who were organising a rugby tour of South Africa, from associating themselves with Ireland during the tour, was refused. O'Hanlon J said:

> the defendants and the players who are participating in the tour, have a prima facie constitutional right to travel abroad for the purpose of taking part in sporting fixtures in other countries as well as in Ireland if they wish to do so. They should only be restrained from exercising such right if it was in some way unlawful for them to act in the manner in which they seek to act.

Chapter 13

FREEDOM OF ASSOCIATION

A Social and Personal Need

Article 40.6.1° of the Constitution clearly acknowledges that man is a social being. It declares that the State guarantees to the citizen, subject to public order and morality, the right to form associations and unions. Ordinary social intercourse, which the individual finds so socially essential, is a constitutionally protected right. The citizen can associate for an infinite number of reasons. Personal relationships, infrequently considered under freedom of association, are central to the well-being of society. The right to marry, to have children and to form a family are examples of this personal right of association. Political, social, charitable, sporting, educational, religious and economic clubs, groups, unions and associations can be formed without the permission of or interference from the State or the organs of government.

The exercise of this right to associate by one group may lead to claims of discrimination by other groups who are excluded from associations formed by the first group. While those excluded may feel aggrieved, and the practice may be socially undesirable, this freedom to choose associates may be the price society must pay to benefit from the freedom of association. As with all other rights freedom of association is not an absolute right. Laws may be enacted for the regulation and control in the public interest of the exercise of this right[1] but such laws must contain no political, religious or class discrimination.

The Right of Dissociation

The right of association must imply the complementary right to dissociate. This was decided in two trade union cases but the principle has general application. The High Court and, on appeal the Supreme Court, in the *Educational Co. of Ireland v Fitzpatrick* (1961) (Case 63) declared this right to exist and to be protected from unlawful interference. Budd J explained:

> I hold ... that under the Constitution a citizen is free to join or not to join an association or union as he pleases. Further, that he cannot be deprived

of the right to join or not to join such associations as he pleases ... is tantamount to saying that he may not be compelled to join any association or union against his will.

An attempt by an employer to impose union membership on an existing employee, which was not a condition of employment when the contract of employment was made between the parties, is also an infringement of this right of dissociation. This was decided by the Supreme Court in *Meskell v CIE* (1973) (Case 117) where a scheme agreed between management and unions whereby employees would be dismissed, and re-employed on condition that they joined and remained members of a particular union, was held to be a conspiracy to deprive an individual of the constitutional right to dissociate.

A point as yet undecided by the courts is whether a condition in a new contract of employment that the employee must join and remain a member of a union, or a particular union, or refrain from union membership, is constitutional. This is a different point than in *Meskell*'s case because in that case the employee was dismissed under a contract which did not contain a compulsory union membership clause. An attempt by the employer subsequently and unilaterally to impose such a condition failed. To secure employment an individual may accept terms not otherwise acceptable and may wish to renege on some terms subsequently, either to resign from union membership completely, or to resign from the designated union and join another union which the employer will refuse to recognise. Such a situation arose in *Becton, Dickinson Ltd v Lee* (1973) though the affected employees pre-empted dismissal by withdrawing their labour and staging a strike, leaving the courts to decide the sole issue as to whether a trade dispute existed. The employer had agreed with a union that all craft employees would join and remain members of that union. Craft employees on entering employment signed an agreement to this effect, but once in employment refused to honour the commitment because they already belonged to a union and they did not wish to relinquish membership of it. When the employer refused to negotiate with the employees' existing union, the employees went on strike and picketed the place of employment. The employer sought an injunction to prevent the picketing. The constitutional point was not relevant but the differing views of two judges of the Supreme Court may give some indication of the answer to such question when it does arise. Walsh J said:

> I have assumed that the term in the contract of employment with regard to trade union membership is not one which would be held void. It is not necessary to express any opinion upon the question of how far, or in what circumstances, a person can contract out of a constitutional right; or to what extent such an agreement would be enforced.

Henchy J was inclined to the view that such a term in the contract was possible. He said:

> the question whether it is permissible under the Constitution to ensure by contract that a man must remain indefinitely a member of a particular union does not arise for decision in this case. All I find necessary to decide is that Article 40.6 is no impediment to providing by contract that membership of a particular union is to be a prerequisite for a particular employment.

From the cases it is clearly established that an individual cannot be compelled to associate. The question then arises as to whether an organisation must, and can be compelled by the courts to, accept into membership a person it does not want. That was the point which arose in *Tierney v Amalgamated Society of Woodworkers* (1959) where a union refused an application for membership. In refusing assistance to the plaintiff the High Court, per Budd J, said:

> it has heretofore been of the essence of a voluntary organisation that the members, and they alone, should decide who should be their fellow-members.

Clearly forcing an organisation to accept a particular person into membership infringes the existing members' freedom to dissociate. Organisations may lay down some criteria for membership which must be met by applicants before acceptance into membership can be obtained. Many organisations do have such rules. A nunnery may only accept women, a workingmen's club may only accept men. An association for the blind may only accept the blind, a horse breeders' association may only accept those who breed horses. Put another way organisations may discriminate on the grounds of religion, race, sex, ability, interest and on other grounds without any redress available to those denied membership. Law to prohibit such apparent discrimination might infringe the constitutional twin rights to associate and dissociate. An argument might be made that organisations which accept public funds should not have rules which permit discrimination.

In *Murphy v Stewart* (1973) (Case 125) one union was prepared to accept the plaintiff's membership but only if the union to which he already belonged gave its consent, which it would not give. The Supreme Court in a rather unsatisfactory decision held that it was not the refusal to agree to the transfer that was the real issue, but the refusal of the new union to accept the plaintiff into membership. It was decided by the High Court in *Abbott v Irish Transport & General Workers Union* (1980) (Case 2) that there was no constitutional right of negotiation and that the court could not compel an employer to negotiate with a union of the employee's choice where the employer refused voluntarily to do so.

Public Order

The Constitution permits a limitation on the freedom of association on the ground of public order. There are common law and statutory limitations imposed on the exercise of this right. In the absence of judicial decision it cannot be said with any degree of certainty that all, or any, of these limitations are constitutional.

There are statutory limitations imposed on associations which threaten to undermine the authority or security of the State. The *Offences Against the State Act 1939* defines an unlawful organisation as one which promotes treason, or which advocates by force the alteration of the Constitution, or which maintains an armed force without constitutional authority, or encourages the commission of criminal offences, or promotes the attainment of any particular object by violent or unlawful means, or encourages the non-payment of taxation. The Government may by order declare an organisation to be an unlawful one[2] and, though this suppression order need not be laid before the Houses of the Oireachtas, a person claiming to be a member of a suppressed organisation had thirty days to apply to the High Court for a declaration, known as a declaration of legality, that such organisation is not an unlawful organisation. The applicant must give evidence and submit to cross-examination. Once the High Court makes a declaration of legality the suppression order becomes null and void.

It is an offence to belong to an unlawful organisation, and the *Offences Against the State (Amendment) Act 1972*, section 3, provides a special method of establishing the fact of such membership to the satisfaction of the court. Where a garda officer not below the rank of chief superintendent, in giving evidence on such a charge, states that he or she believes the accused at the material time was a member of an unlawful organisation, that statement shall be evidence of that fact. This section only operates when Special Criminal Courts are in existence. The practice has been to acquit should the person charged deny membership. This section was unsuccessfully challenged as to its constitutionality in *O'Leary v Attorney General* (1991) (Case 145).

The law of conspiracy is another limitation on the exercise of freedom of association. It is a common law misdemeanour for two, or more persons, to do an unlawful act, or to do a lawful act by unlawful means. It is a civil wrong where two or more persons combine together for the purpose of damaging another's trade or business, or if they agree to perform an unlawful act and that other person is damaged by that unlawful act. The law of conspiracy has been extended to include a conspiracy to deprive an individual of constitutional rights. This wrong first surfaced in *Meskell v CIE* (1973) (Case 117) where an employer conspired with trade unions to deprive an employee of the right to dissociate, a case discussed earlier.

Much of the sting in the law of conspiracy at common law was removed when trade unions were given statutory protections. How far, if at all, the Oireachtas can regulate the number of trade unions was litigated on constitutional grounds in the *National Union of Railwaymen v Sullivan* (1947) (Case 129). The Supreme Court struck down the legislation. Murnaghan J explained:

> it purports to limit the right of the citizen to join one or more prescribed organisations ... any such limitation does undoubtedly deprive the citizen of a free choice of the persons with whom he shall associate. Both logically and practically, to deprive a person of the choice of the persons with whom he will associate, is not a control of the exercise of the right of association, but a denial of the right altogether.

The *Defence Act 1954* prohibits members of the permanent defence forces from joining, remaining in, or subscribing to any political organisation or society, or any secret society, though under the *Defence (Amendment) Act 1990* they may form and belong to representative associations. The *Garda Síochána Act 1924*, as amended, prohibits members of the Garda Síochána from being members of a trade union though a representative body may be established to promote the welfare and efficiency of its members, but must not concern itself with matters of discipline and promotion. These representative bodies must be independent of and unassociated with any body, or person, outside of the Garda Síochána. This restriction on freedom of association was challenged, but upheld, in *Aughey v Attorney General* (1989) (Case 17). In the Supreme Court, Walsh J concluded:

> the statute concentrated on areas of particular sensitivity in a police force. If these areas became the subject of multi-union or multi-association agitation or industrial action by members of the Garda Síochána it would be a matter of grave public concern and public interest particularly because of the fact that the Garda Síochána is a unitary national police force. In the light of these considerations it cannot be said that [the statutory provisions are] an unreasonable or a disproportionate regulation of the exercise of the right guaranteed by the Constitution, nor can it be said to strike at the roots of that constitutionally guaranteed right namely, the right to form associations and unions.

In the commercial field there are restrictions on the right to associate. The *Companies Act 1963*, section 376, as amended, provides that no partnership of more than twenty persons can be formed for the purpose of any business that has for its object the acquisition of gain, except in the cases of solicitors, accountants and bankers. A private registered company must have at least two members and not more than fifty members generally, whereas a public registered company must have at least seven members. A challenge was made in the *Private Motorists Provident Society Ltd v Attorney General* (1983) (Case 167) to a statute that prohibited the plaintiff company from carrying on a banking business, as it had done prior to the enactment of the statute, on the ground that it infringed the right of association. In rejecting the claim, the Supreme Court held that the exercise of such a right was not prevented by a law which limited and controlled in the public interest what such an association may do.

There are few instances where statute actually attempts to impose association. The *Unfair Dismissals Act 1977* is one such example. It empowers the Employment Appeals Tribunal to order the reinstatement or re-engagement of an employee who has been unfairly dismissed. An employer is thus restricted in the exercise of the freedom to dissociate, and this law may be unconstitutional. Would compulsory military service be a breach of this constitutional right on the same ground, or could such forced association be justified on the ground that the common good, the defence of the State, required such association?

Morality
There are a number of instances where the law restricts freedom of association on the ground of morality. Certain close blood relatives cannot marry: such marriage is void in the eyes of the law. Sexual relations are forbidden between different classes of persons. Incest is forbidden, as is intercourse with persons under the age of 17 years. A distinction must be drawn between the mere fact of association and engaging in certain types of activity. This was emphasised in *Norris v Attorney General* (1984) (Case 130) where the criminalisation of certain sexual conduct was alleged to infringe freedom of association. This claim was rejected by the Supreme Court in that to associate with others possessed of a similar attitude to sexual morals was not an offence though to associate with others for the purpose of engaging in forbidden sexual activities would be an offence.[3]

Chapter 14

FREEDOM OF ASSEMBLY

A Social and Human Right

Man as a social being needs the company of other humans. The Constitution in Article 40.6.1° acknowledges this basic human necessity by declaring that the citizen has the right to assemble peaceably and without arms. The obvious assembly is a man and a woman in marriage together with children within the family. Article 41 acknowledges the family as the natural primary and fundamental unit group of society and as a moral institution, the possessor of inalienable and imprescriptible rights antecedent and superior to all positive law. Often when enumerating constitutional rights the most obvious are neglected. Individuals are thus constitutionally entitled to form families and other personal relationships.

Freedom of assembly is usually considered in a different light, in the sense that individuals can congregate together for all kinds of purposes. The remainder of this chapter concentrates on this aspect of this constitutional right.

Meetings can broadly be divided into three types. Into the first go private meetings in private places, and the law rarely attempts to regulate such assemblies. But on occasion it does. For example, meetings of registered companies must be in accordance with the *Companies Act 1963*, as amended, and the formal meetings of other bodies may be regulated by their rules, which may be judicially enforced in appropriate circumstances. Apart from the criminal law, the law of nuisance and planning and other safety regulations, individuals can make use of their property as they please. The holding of meetings in private is not the concern of any public authority, including the Gardaí. No permission is required from any executive authority to hold private meetings in private places.

Into the second category of meetings go public meetings in private places. Here again there are very few legal controls. Provided the legal rules about trespass, defamation and proper behaviour, fire and safety regulations are adhered to, the holders of the meetings and those attending are subject to no legal restraints and need no permission from the executive arm of government. In some instances, in order to carry on a business, the private place in which individuals may meet may need a licence. Public houses and public dance halls are examples.

The third category of meetings are processions and meetings held in public places. It is in this category of meetings that some legal restraints are felt. A public place is an open space to which the public have access for the time being whether on payment or not. Many of the restraints on the exercise of this right are of common law origin and probably survive the enactment of the Constitution. Some of these restraints are considered later.

The Constitution protects freedom of assembly subject to the needs of public order and morality. We will look at the restraints under these two broad headings, though under the second there will be very little to say.

Public Order

Most public processions are lawful because they simply consist of individuals exercising their legal right to move along the highway. The common law permits that activity alone on the public highway.[1] The public highway exists for the movement of persons thereon from one private premises to another. A public procession is merely a collective body of individuals using the highway, though a procession may amount to an obstruction of the highway, which is a criminal offence. The practical test in this regard is whether an unreasonable use is made of the highway and this, it seems, may include a procession. Before holding a public procession garda permission, or any other permission, is not necessary but notice of the route facilitates the Gardaí in the management of traffic, may protect those taking part in the procession and may assist to retain the support of the public at large because the purpose of the procession may be to highlight certain matters.

The holding of a meeting on the public highway is not in itself a criminal offence though there is no unrestricted right to hold such meetings. It may constitute an obstruction of the highway, both for the speakers and the listeners, or it may be conduct likely to lead to a breach of the peace — which means that there must be a reasonable belief that the behaviour in question would lead to a disturbance involving physical force. It is an offence under the *Public Meeting Act 1908* to unlawfully attempt to break up a public meeting.

But a meeting on a public highway which is not initially unlawful may become so in a number of ways. An *unlawful assembly* means an assembly of three or more persons in order to commit a crime, or in order to do some legal or illegal act together, which endangers public peace or makes firm and courageous people fear a breach of the peace. *Riot* is defined as a tumultuous disturbance by three or more persons who have assembled in order to carry out some common purpose, and to help one another by force if necessary against anyone who opposes them, and then to do what they have planned using enough force or violence to alarm at least one person of reasonable firmness. The difference between unlawful and riotous assembly is that the moment persons in a crowd, however peaceful their original intentions, come together to act for some common purpose in such a way as to make reasonable individuals fear a breach of the peace, the assembly becomes unlawful. It becomes riotous when alarming force or violence is used and anyone who actively encourages such an assembly by words, signs or actions or by participation is guilty of riotous assembly.

A *rout* is a disturbance of the peace by persons who intend to do some act, which if they had succeeded, would amount to riot but who failed to achieve their purpose. An *affray* is a fight between two or more persons who fight in the presence of others who were neither encouraging nor participating and some of whom were frightened by the fighting.

Those acting to disperse an unlawful assembly may use no more force than is necessary in the particular circumstances. In *Lynch v Fitzgerald* (1938) the father of a youth, killed by a bullet fired by a Garda in suppressing a riot, sued for damages. The classical explanation of the law in this regard was given by Hanna J in the High Court:

> it is an invariable rule that the degree of force to be used must always be moderate and proportioned to the circumstances of the case, and the end to be attained. Hence it is that arms ... must be used with the greatest of care, and the greatest pain must be exercised to avoid the infliction of fatal injuries ... a gun should never be used, or used with any specified degree of force, if there is any doubt as to the necessity.

It is an offence under section 27 of the *Offences Against the State Act 1939* to hold a public meeting for the purpose of supporting, aiding, abetting or encouraging an unlawful organisation. If a member of the Garda Síochána, not below the rank of chief superintendent, is of opinion that such a meeting is to be held he may, either by notice to the organisers or by publishing in a manner reasonably calculated to come to the knowledge of the organisers, prohibit that meeting. Following the principles established in *The State (Lynch) v Cooney* (1982) (Case 191, see page 236), such administrative decision must be bona fide and made on factual grounds that are sustainable and reasonable. An aggrieved party may apply to the High Court for an order annulling such prohibition.

It is an offence under section 28 of the *Offences Against the State Act 1939* for any public meeting or procession to be held in any public street or unenclosed place within one-half mile of any building in which either or both Houses of the Oireachtas are sitting, or about to sit. This offence is only committed if the procession or meeting has been prohibited by a member of the Gardaí not below the rank of chief superintendent and a garda calls on those taking part to disperse. Presumably the garda making the prohibition order must not act unreasonably or capriciously.

Under section 4 of the *Offences Against the State (Amendment) Act 1972* any meeting, procession or demonstration intended or directly or indirectly likely to influence any court, person or authority concerned with the institution, conduct or defence of any civil or criminal proceedings, including a party or witness, as to whether or how the proceedings should be instituted, conducted, continued or defended, or as to what should be their outcome, constitutes an interference with the course of justice and is unlawful.

Picketing is in law a 'watching and besetting' and is a criminal offence under the *Conspiracy and Protection of Property Act 1875*. But picketing in furtherance of a trade dispute is exempt from criminal and civil liability under section 11 of the *Industrial Relations Act 1990*.[2] The immunity conferred by this statute is confined to authorised trade unions holding a negotiation licence and depends on two factors: the existence of a trade dispute, and that the picketing is solely for the purpose of peacefully obtaining or communicating information, or of peacefully persuading any person to work, or to abstain from working. Picketing for an unconstitutional purpose may be prohibited: see *Educational Co. of Ireland v Fitzpatrick* (1961) (Case 63 on page 224). In *Brendan Dunne Ltd v Fitzpatrick* (1958) (Case 24) Budd J, in the High Court, explained:

> if citizens in the course of assembly commit a breach of the peace or some other breach of the law, they thereby disturb public order, and their actions are not protected by the Constitution in respect of the breach of the law committed.

Morality

Legal interference with the right of assembly on the ground of morality is rare and usually merges into the complementary rights of freedom of association and freedom of expression. It is an offence to stage an obscene show, while it is not an offence to attend one. It is an offence to show in public a film not passed by the censor, whereas it is not an offence to attend such a film. Indecent conduct likely to lead to a breach of the peace is unlawful and can be punished.

Chapter 15

FREEDOM OF EXPRESSION

A Human and Social Need

An individual can self-express in an almost infinite number of ways. The writing of a song, the wearing of particular clothes, the playing of a sport, the landscaping of a garden, the choosing of a career and the cooking of a meal are some of the various forms of self-expression. Self-expression is a basic human and social need. It is one of the imperative aspects of personal liberty. Article 40.6.1° of the Constitution guarantees to citizens the right to express freely their convictions and opinions. The tendency to consider this right as merely encompassing the freedom of the press, or free speech, is to ignore the wider scope of the guarantee. Convictions and opinions can be expressed in more varied forms than simply the oral or written form. While most of this chapter will concentrate on these forms of communications, the reader must not lose sight of the wider meanings to be given to the exercise of this constitutional right.

An instance where the courts refused to suppress the publication of opinions, or put in a positive way where the courts upheld the right to exercise this freedom was in the *Attorney General for England and Wales v Brandon Book Publishers Ltd* (1987). There it was argued that a deceased member of the British intelligence service, whose memoirs were to be published by the defendants, had acted in breach of the principle of confidentiality which existed between employer and employee. The High Court refused to grant an injunction against the book's publication. Carroll J held:

> any consideration of the question of preventing publication of material of public interest must be viewed in the light of the Constitution. Article 40.6.1° guarantees liberty for the exercise of the right of citizens to express freely their convictions and opinions subject to public order and morality. In the expansion of that, the Article refers to the organs of public opinion 'preserving their rightful liberty of expression' provided it is not used to undermine public order or morality or the authority of the State. There is no question of public order or morality or the authority of the State being

undermined here. Therefore . . . there is, prima facie, a constitutional right to publish information and the onus rests on the plaintiff to establish . . . that the constitutional right of the defendant should not be exercised.

The Right to Communicate

The right to express freely convictions and opinions contains, by implication, the complementary right of having those convictions and opinions communicated to and received by other individuals. This constitutional right of freedom of expression would be useless if, for example, the State, having permitted the individual to publish a newspaper, ordered that all copies of the newspaper were to be sold only to the State. The expression of convictions and opinions is only meaningful in the context of the ability of those exercising this right to inform and influence others. Freedom of expression has as much to do with the freedom to hear the opinions of others as it has with the right to propagate one's own convictions.

The implied constitutional right to communicate was first acknowledged in the *Attorney General v Paperlink Ltd* (1984) (Case 12). In the High Court, Costello J explained:

> it seems to me that as the act of communication is the exercise of such a basic human faculty that a right to communicate must inhere in the citizen by virtue of his human personality and must be guaranteed by the Constitution . . . The exercise of the right can take many forms and the right to express freely convictions and opinions is expressly provided for in Article 40.6.1°. But the activity which the defendants say is inhibited in this case is that of communication by letter and as this act may involve the communication of information and not merely the expression of convictions and opinions I do not think that the constitutional provision dealing with the right to express convictions and opinions is the source of the citizen's right to communicate. I conclude that the very general and basic human right to communicate . . . must be one of those personal unspecified rights of the citizen protected by Article 40.3.1°.

Limitations on the Freedom of Expression

The limitations placed by the Constitution on freedom of expression are threefold: restrictions are imposed to protect the authority of the State, public order and morality. Difficulties arise in defining these restrictions and further complications arise from the fact that some of the currently accepted legal exceptions do not readily fall within any of the three classifications.

Apart from these different grounds for limiting freedom of expression, the State uses different methods of suppressing opinions. Pure, or pre-publication, censorship operates when the authorities exercise a pre-publication veto. This kind of censorship is rare under our law but it does exist.[1] It is a method of censorship more redolent of wartime conditions. The second method of censorship is more common. Here the publications of opinions do not require a pre-publication official imprimatur. The banning follows publication. As a result a publication may be simply suppressed, or together with suppression, the possibility of prosecution, either criminal or civil, may follow. This is because views are presented which the law declares may not be presented, or which the executive power, regardless of the letter of the law, wishes to suppress. The third method of censorship is that of self-censorship. The authorities may create a climate in which it is dangerous to publish certain convictions and opinions. By manufacturing such a situation, the State forces the individual to perform the task of censor, which the authorities are reluctant to do openly. The State hopes to achieve its repressive aims in this way with a minimum of public odium. Undoubtedly instances can be pointed to where publication did not take place because of fear, or threat, of prosecution.

Authority of the State

The Constitution places on the State a duty to curtail freedom of expression in defence of the State. This defence of the existence and integrity of the State and its organs of government is an integral part of the business of government. The defence of the authority of the State was raised as justification for the action taken by the executive in *The State (Lynch) v Cooney* (1982) (Case 191). In upholding the legislation impugned the Supreme Court, per O'Higgins CJ, explained:

> it follows that the use of such organs of opinion for the purpose of securing or advocating support for organisations which seek by violence to overthrow the State or its institutions is a use which is prohibited by the Constitution. Therefore it is clearly the duty of the State to intervene to prevent broadcasts on radio or television which are aimed at such a result or which in any way would be likely to have the effect of promoting or inciting to crime or endangering the authority of the State.

The court upheld a decision of the relevant member of the government which ordered RTE to refrain from broadcasting certain electoral broadcasts by members of Provisional Sinn Féin. This restriction was justified on the ground that other members of the organisation had been convicted of certain offences, and others had said certain things on previous occasions. The fact that the broadcast to be made would not have contained any matter which challenged the authority of the State was deemed irrelevant. What was crucial was that the broadcast was intended to seek and rally support for the Sinn Féin organisation. The danger with this kind of decision is that by attempting to uphold the existence and integrity of the State, ideas or doctrines which are considered essential to its well-being are protected from criticism and views which are declared detrimental are proscribed.

The *Broadcasting Authority Act 1960*, as amended, permits the Minister for Communications to prohibit by order broadcasts of a particular matter, or any matter of a particular class, which in the Minister's opinion would be likely to promote or incite to crime or would tend to undermine the authority of the State. A number of such orders have been made.[2] The ministerial order directs RTE to refrain from broadcasting any matter by way of interview with a spokesman or spokesmen for any one or more of a number of listed organisations whether purporting to be a political party broadcast or not made by or on behalf of or advocating, offering or inviting support for such organisations or a broadcast by any person or persons representing, or purporting to represent such organisations. One of these ministerial orders was the subject of a challenge in *The State (Lynch) v Cooney* (1982) (Case 191), discussed in the previous paragraph. While accepting that such legislation was permissible, the Supreme Court held that the power to make the orders was not unfettered. The exercise of that power was open to judicial review and any opinion formed by the Minister must be bona fide held, be factually sustainable and be reasonable.

The exact scope of these orders was discussed in *O'Toole v RTE* (1992). RTE had refused to broadcast interviews with the plaintiff who was involved in a trade dispute solely on the ground that he was a member of Sinn Féin, one of the banned organisations. The Supreme Court ruled that RTE was wrong because the order was directed against a broadcast on behalf of Sinn Féin or by any person or persons purporting to represent that organisation and not directed against a broadcast by a particular person as an individual. While access to broadcasting time had to be regarded as a privilege and not a right, the Supreme Court held that a decision to single out a particular person or group of persons and to impose a blanket prohibition against his or their views on any topic whatever, expressed in their personal capacity and not as spokesman for or as representing any organisation, would have to be justified on very substantial grounds, which did not exist in the present case, having regard to the constitutional guarantees of freedom of expression contained in Article 40.6 of the Constitution and having regard to the dominant position of RTE in the field of radio and television.

The *Offences Against the State Act 1939* makes it unlawful to set up in type, print, publish, post, distribute, sell or offer for sale any document, which includes a book or magazine, containing anything incriminating, treasonable or seditious. It is unlawful for any person to send or contribute to any newspaper, or for the proprietor of any newspaper, to publish any communication which comes from an unlawful organisation. On conviction the court may order the forfeiture of the offending document and the printing machinery. Foreign newspapers which contain such offending material may by order of the Minister for Justice be seized and destroyed or may be prohibited from importation. It is unlawful for any person to be possessed of any treasonable, seditious or incriminating document or on premises or lands owned or occupied by him.

The central issue in the defence of the State is the issue of secrecy. The State has secrets and needs, it feels, to keep them. The *Official Secrets Act 1963* prohibits the communication of official information by any person unless authorised, or when the communication is made in the course of the duties of a holder of public office, or when it is a duty in the interest of the State to communicate it. There exists, in general, a mania in the public service in favour of secrecy. In recent years this veil of secrecy has been somewhat dented by judicial review of administrative action. The plea for State secrecy was greatly curtailed in *Murphy v Dublin Corporation* (1972) (Case 124) when the Supreme Court refused to allow a Minister to hide behind a blanket claim of executive privilege. This and other cases on the subject are discussed on page 107.

According to Article 40.6 the publication or utterance of seditious matter shall be punishable in accordance with law. *Sedition*, whether by spoken or written words or by conduct, is generally all endeavours which tend to promote public disorder but which fall short of treason. It is not a widely prosecuted offence because statute has created specific offences from some of its ingredients. It is an offence to cause disaffection in the Defence Forces, and in the Garda Síochána. It is an offence to have a sketch or model of a military establishment, or to wear a military uniform when not so entitled.

The *Offences Against the State (Amendment) Act 1972* makes it an offence to publish a statement, orally or in writing, which constitutes an interference with the course of justice.

CONTEMPT OF COURT

Definition of Contempt
The ambit of contempt of court was stated in *Keegan v de Búrca* (1973), in the Supreme Court, by Ó Dálaigh CJ:

> criminal contempt consists in behaviour calculated to prejudice the due course of justice, such as contempt *in facie curiae*,* words written or spoken or acts calculated to prejudice the due course of justice or disobedience to a writ of habeas corpus by the person to whom it is directed — to give but some examples of this class of contempt. Civil contempt usually

arises where there is a disobedience to an order of the court by a party to the proceedings and in which the court has generally no interest to interfere unless moved by the party for whose benefit the order was made. Criminal contempt is a common law misdemeanour and, as such, is punishable by both imprisonment and fine at discretion, that is to say, without statutory limit, its object is punitive. Civil contempt, on the other hand, is not punitive in its object but coercive in its purpose of compelling the party committed to comply with the order of the court, and the period of committal would be until such time as the order is complied with or until it is waived by the party for whose benefit the order was made.

Contempt in Facie Curiae

Contempt *in facie curiae* may consist of the refusal to answer questions lawfully put in court proceedings, as in *Keegan v de Búrca*. Journalists have no constitutional or legal immunity from being compelled to disclose information which comes their way in the course of their professional duties. This rule was explained in *In re Kevin O'Kelly* (1974) where a journalist, called to give evidence of conversations he had had with the accused, was punished for contempt when he refused to answer questions put to him by the prosecution. The Court of Criminal Appeal held that as far as the administration of justice was concerned the public had the right to every person's evidence except for those persons protected by a constitutional or legal privilege. Another common form of this contempt is disobedience of court orders. Thus in *Davern v Butler* (1927) it was contempt to disobey an order of the Master of the High Court to lodge accounts. It was a contempt to ignore an injunction which restrained interference with fishing rights in *Little v Cooper* (1937). Another example is *The State (Commins) v McRann* (1977) (Case 185). Refusal to obey an order of habeas corpus (see page 215) was, in *In re Earle* (1938), a contempt of court.

Contempt *in facie curiae* may be punished summarily by the court before which the contempt is committed. Where the contempt is criminal, the imprisonment must, where that is the form of punishment imposed, as was decided in *Keegan v de Búrca*, be for a definite period. With regard to the trial of civil contempt the High Court decided, in *The State (Commins) v McRann* (1977) (Case 185), that the matter may be disposed of summarily and that trial by jury is not available. The period of imprisonment may be of indefinite duration. That decision was approved of by the Supreme Court in *The State (H.) v Daly* (1977).

Sub Judice Contempt

It is a contempt of court to publish any matter which is *sub judice*:* under judicial consideration. The proposed publication of the offending matter may be restrained by injunction, or where the matter has been published the offending party may be fined and/or imprisoned, though in such instances an apology to the court may be sufficient.

The first requisite is that legal proceedings must have been initiated. This is illustrated in *The State (DPP) v Independent Newspapers Ltd* (1985) where a newspaper was cited for contempt for the publication of a report that the Director of Public Prosecutions intended to have an unnamed local authority member charged with certain sexual offences. The councillor's political party was mentioned though the local authority was not. The High Court refused to order attachment for contempt on the ground that no court had actual seisin of a charge.

Where legal proceedings have been initiated it is a contempt to make comments which are calculated or intended to interfere with those pending proceedings. What must be shown is a real risk of prejudice as opposed to a mere remote possibility of prejudice. In the *Attorney General v Cooke* (1924) remarks in a newspaper described picketing in a trade dispute as a disgrace, a menace to the peace, intimidatory and urged the executive to protect the public from such treatment. The publication took place the day after some of the picketers had been arrested and charged. The High Court, in dismissing the contempt charge, ruled that courts had to be careful, on the one hand, not to permit any comments to be made on pending proceedings which were calculated or intended to interfere with the proceedings, and on the other hand, not to interfere with the right and freedom of the press to comment on matters of public interest and concern.

Following the arrest and charge of a person with criminal offences, in *In re Malcolm McArthur* (1983), the Taoiseach of the day, at a press conference, inadvertently and in reply to a question, passed remarks which touched on that person's forthcoming trial. Immediately, the Government Information Service requested journalists not to publish the remarks. A newspaper published part of the contents of a letter sent to the Taoiseach by the accused and said further that the accused had written a letter to the former Attorney General. Another newspaper published a photograph of the accused. The High Court held that no contempt had been committed by the Taoiseach or by the newspaper which carried the report of the two letters, but the court held it was a contempt to publish the photograph of a person after the charge but before the trial.

In *Weeland v RTE* (1987) the plaintiff, a successful party in court proceedings which was made the subject matter of a television programme, sought an injunction to prevent its broadcast pending an appeal on the grounds that it was critical of the court judgment, it attempted to surround the judgment with a wall of criticism and innuendo, it advocated a result other than that sustained in the proceedings, and it prevented a fair hearing of the appeal because it made the presentation of his defence more difficult. The High Court ruled that although the programme was unbalanced it did not go beyond the acceptable limits of reasonable criticism and did not amount to contempt of court.

In *Desmond v Glackin and the Minister for Industry and Commerce* (1992) (Case 52) it was claimed that remarks made in a radio broadcast by the Minister exposed the plaintiff to public odium in relation to judicial review proceedings he had initiated. The plaintiff in affidavits had made serious allegations against the Minister not merely of mistakes of law in the manner in which he was interpreting the relevant statutory powers but of mala fides and improper motives in the manner in which the plaintiff was being treated. The High Court held that it was permissible to make such allegations and to seek to substantiate them in the course of the legal proceedings. But it seemed to conflict with some of the basic principles of fair play if those allegations could be delivered in open court on an *ex parte* application, and be duly reported on a nationwide basis accompanied by a commentary from the plaintiff's public relations advisers while denying the right to the Minister to reply immediately in equally forthright terms in defence of his own good name and reputation. An untrue newspaper report, in *Wong v Minister for Justice* (1992), which linked a party in judicial review proceedings to triad gangs of the Chinese underworld, a triad being an illegal criminal society, was derogatory of that party, exposed him to public obloquy and was prejudicial to the administration of justice. The High Court held that the administration of justice would suffer if a litigant in mid-trial was held up to such obloquy and if false reporting was the norm.

The same principles of contempt are applied where the trial has concluded and an appeal is pending though since appeals are heard by professional judges the courts are reluctant to prohibit comment on the matter. In *Cullen v Toibín* (1985) a person convicted of murder attempted to prevent the publication by a magazine of an account of the case based on the material supplied by the sole prosecution witness on the ground that the publication would prejudice the pending appeal. The Supreme Court held, that since the appeal was on a matter of law to be heard by professional judges, no prejudice could be caused.

Contempt of Scandalising the Court
The State (DPP) v Walsh (1981) (Case 187) decided that the contempt of scandalising a court was, in general, triable by jury. The Supreme Court divided on the issue. The minority held that justice could only be protected by swift action and that summary disposal was constitutionally permissible. The majority held there was prima facie a right to trial by jury where there were live and real issues of fact to be decided. In cases where there are no

live issues of fact to be tried the matter may be disposed of summarily by the High Court.

Prohibition on Reporting Legal Proceedings

There is a collection of statutes which prohibits, in one way or another, the publication of court proceedings. For example, the *Criminal Procedure Act 1967* prohibits the publication of evidence given at a preliminary investigation, which is a pre-trial procedure, except the name of the accused, the charge and the result. The *Criminal Law (Rape) Act 1981* prohibits, except in certain circumstances, the publication of the identity of the complainant in a sexual assault case, or the identity of the accused but only if acquitted. The *Official Secrets Act 1963* permits a court, when hearing cases under the statute, to hold that part of the case in camera. A whole variety of family law statutes, such as the *Guardianship of Infants Act 1964*, are heard in private.[3]

Public Order

It is an offence to use abusive or threatening language calculated to provoke or lead to a breach of the peace. Criminal libel is an offence: it consists of the writing or publishing of defamatory words about any living person, or words calculated or intended to provoke that person to wrath, or to expose that person to public hatred, contempt or ridicule, or to damage that person's reputation; also the publishing of a picture or effigy. Besides being an offence, a libel is a civil wrong, as is slander.[4] It is difficult to categorise both these civil wrongs under this heading though it can be done because the absence of some remedy might lead to self help, which the law discourages. Rightly they should both be encompassed within the constitutional right to one's good name.

In general a person can carry a poster displaying words or images, unless this is likely to lead to a breach of the peace: see *Brendan Dunne Ltd v Fitzpatrick* (Case 24). Some idea of the words which may be prevented is contained in the judgment of Walsh J in *E. I. Co. v Kennedy* (1968):

> the use of words such as 'scab' or 'blackleg' is historically so associated with social ostracism and physical violence as to be far beyond anything which might be described as mere rudeness or impoliteness and go beyond what is permitted by law. In the present context the reference made to the race or nationality of the employers could produce the same disorderly response.

Of course, a banner which contains defamatory words leaves the bearer open to a civil action and possible injunction to prevent repetition. Flyposting — that is, the sticking up of posters in public places — is now illegal and the offenders can be fined: *Litter Act 1982*. It is an offence, in general, to use a loudspeaker in a public place: *Local Government (Planning and Development Act) 1963*. In general it is not an offence to distribute literature in public free of charge, though it may be littering, and the person by doing so may obstruct the public highway. The sale of literature in a public street or on a public highway may require a casual trading licence.

Morality
According to Article 40.6, the publication or utterances of blasphemous or indecent matter is an offence which shall be punishable in accordance with law. *Blasphemy* and *blasphemous libel* consist of indecent and offensive attacks on Christianity or the scriptures or sacred persons or objects, calculated to outrage the feelings of the community. The mere denial of Christian teachings is not enough. There is no recorded conviction for these offences in this State in many years, though the offence survives.

Indecency means any act which offends modesty, causes scandal or injures the morals of the community. Any person who, at or near or in sight of any place along which the public habitually passes, commits any indecent act, commits an offence. It is an offence to show for gain or reward an indecent or profane performance. In the *Attorney General v Simpson* (1959) it was held that there must be an intention to deprave or corrupt those viewing the performance, in that instance *The Rose Tattoo* by Tennessee Williams. The prosecution failed because this essential element could not be proved. Any public sale, or exposure for sale, or exposure to public view of any indecent book, picture or print is an offence. Soliciting for prostitution in any public place is an offence.

Censorship of publications was established by the *Censorship of Publications Acts 1929 to 1967*, which established a Censorship of Publications Board of five persons, appointed by the Minister for Justice, which is empowered to prohibit the sale and distribution of any book which, in their opinion, is indecent or obscene, or which advocates the procurement of abortion. The board is required to examine any book in respect of which a complaint is made to it by any person, or which has been referred to them by a customs officer. It must take into account, in examining a book, the literary, artistic, scientific or historical merit or importance, and the general tenor of the book, the language in which it is written, the nature and extent of the circulation which, in its opinion, it is likely to have, the class of reader which, in its opinion, may reasonably be expected to read it, and any other matters relating to the book which appear to them to be relevant. An appeal may be made from an order of this board to an Appeal Board, also of five persons. The Censorship Board is also entitled to make prohibition orders in respect of periodicals which have usually or frequently been indecent or obscene, which advocate the procurement of abortions, or which have devoted an undue proportion of space to the publication of matter relating to crime. The application of these laws have lead to prohibition orders against the books of many authors of note, together with many works of pure pornography. The 1967 Act places a twelve-year time limit on the life of a prohibition order, though a publication de-banned in this way might be re-banned. It is an offence to sell, keep for sale or distribute a prohibited publication, though it is not an offence to possess a copy of a banned book or magazine. Before the making of a prohibition order the board *may* communicate with its author, editor or publisher.

In *Irish Family Planning v Ryan* (1979) the publishers of a family planning booklet challenged the making of a prohibition order on the ground that they should, in natural justice, have been informed before a prohibition order was made. The Supreme Court held that the direction to communicate was not mandatory but merely discretionary. In order to conclude whether this discretion had been exercised fairly the court examined the booklet. The court held that it reached out to those who might wish to be informed as to the different methods of contraception which were available and that far from being pornographic or lewdly commercial or pandering to prurient curiosity it simply aimed at giving factual information on a delicate topic as to which there was genuine concern. It espoused no cause; it advocated no course of conduct. In those circumstances it is not possible to hold that this book should have been banned for being 'indecent or obscene'. Since the board had not exercised its discretion properly the banning order was quashed. It transpired that the board in eight and a half years had never once communicated with an author, editor or publisher.

The censorship of films was established by the *Censorship of Films Acts 1923* to *1970* under which no film may be shown in public unless the Film Censor has granted a certificate that it is fit for showing. Should the censor refuse a certificate, any person affected may appeal to an Appeal Board. The censor may issue a certificate in respect of a film, parts of which he thinks unfit for public exhibition, where the owner of the film consents to the cutting of these parts. The censor may also issue a 'limited certificate' permitting the film to be shown in special places or to special audiences. The Film Censor may only refuse a certificate if of the opinion that the film is 'indecent, obscene or blasphemous, or because the exhibition thereof in public would tend to inculcate principles contrary to public morality or would be otherwise subversive of public morality'. The censor's certificate is not required unless the film is shown in public, so private societies and clubs which confine admission to their members are not obliged to obtain a certificate in respect of the films shown by them. Nor are films to be shown by individuals in their homes subject to censorship.

The *Video Recordings Act 1989* regulates, subject to certain exceptions, the sale, hire and supply of video recordings. The Film Censor will be obliged to issue a supply certificate to each video recording unless the work is unfit for viewing because it would be likely to cause or encourage persons to commit crimes, or would tend, by reason of the inclusion in it of any obscene or indecent matter, to deprave or corrupt persons who might view it, or it depicts acts of gross violence or cruelty towards humans or animals. The effect of the issue of a supply certificate is that video recordings of the work can be sold or otherwise supplied. Certain videos, those supplied neither for reward nor in the course of a business nor those designed only to provide a record of an event or occasion, are exempted supplies and need not be submitted to the Film Censor for a supply certificate.

There is no legislation for the censorship of stage plays though a prosecution may result should it be indecent or obscene, as was the allegation in *Attorney General v Simpson*. Nor is there legislation for the censorship of records or video tapes.

RELIGIOUS FREEDOM

Article 44.2.1° of the Constitution declares that freedom of conscience and the free profession and practice of religion are, subject to public order and morality, guaranteed to every citizen. According to Walsh J, in the Supreme Court, in *McGee v Attorney General* (1974) (Case 101):

> the meaning of Article 44.2.1° is that no person shall directly or indirectly be coerced or compelled to act contrary to his conscience in so far as the practice of religion is concerned, and subject to public order and morality, is free to profess and practise the religion of his choice in accordance with his conscience. Correlatively, he is free to have no religious beliefs or to abstain from the practice or profession of any religion.

This guarantee has not been the subject of any constitutional action. But some practices, such as polygamy, or compulsory military service, may be upheld or condemned under this Article.

Chapter 16
FAMILY RIGHTS

Marriage

Article 41.3.1° of the Constitution declares that the State pledges to guard with special care the institution of marriage, on which the family is founded and to protect it against attack. Neither the Constitution nor statute law defines marriage. The common law defined marriage as being 'the voluntary union for life of one man and one woman to the exclusion of all others'.[1] According to Costello J in *Murray v Attorney General* (1985) (Case 127) 'the concept and nature of marriage which [the Constitution] enshrines is derived from the Christian notion of a partnership based on an irrevocable personal consent, given by both spouses which establishes a unique and very special life-long relationship'.

These definitions of marriage may be too restrictive in a pluralist society. There are religions with adherents in the State which permit polygamy. The courts' response to a claim by a person charged with bigamy that his or her constitutional right to marry according to religious beliefs was being infringed might lead to a wider definition of marriage than the one currently held though this definition, Christian in character, would be hard to displace. An equally interesting question would be which of the spouses of such a deceased person would be the spouse for the purposes of the *Succession Act 1965.*[2]

The Right to Marry

The right to marry, while not expressly stated in the Constitution, is one of the implied personal rights suggested by Kenny J in the High Court, in *Ryan v Attorney General* (1965) (Case 171). As with other constitutional rights it is not absolute and there are legal restrictions on the grounds of age and blood relationship. Certain statutory formalities must be observed.

The Protection of Marriage

Article 41.3.1° was successfully pleaded in *Murphy v Attorney General* (1982) (Case 123) where it was claimed that parts of the income tax code attacked the institution of marriage because a married couple paid more income tax than two single persons living together and earning similar incomes. The Supreme Court accepted this contention. Kenny J said:

> the nature and potentially progressive extent of the burden . . . is such that, in the opinion of the court, it is a breach of the pledge by the State to guard with special care the institution of marriage.

Similarly, in *Hyland v Minister for Social Welfare* (1990) (Case 82), the Supreme Court decided that provisions of the social welfare code, which granted lesser benefits to a married couple and their child living together than to an unmarried couple with a child living together, penalised the married state. The administrative scheme which implemented a European Community directive dealing with payments to persons farming in disadvantaged areas was held to be invalid by the High Court in *Greene v Minister for Agriculture* (1990) because the imposition of burdens on married couples living together breached the constitutional pledge to guard with special care the institution of marriage.

This article defeated a claim by an illegitimate individual, in *O'B. v S.* (1984) (Case 132), who argued that succession law which excluded illegitimate children from inheriting on their fathers' intestacy was unconstitutional.[3] In the Supreme Court, Walsh J explained:

> the *Succession Act 1965* must be seen as a most important part of what might be generally referred to as family law . . . It can scarcely be doubted that the Act . . . was designed to strengthen the protection of the family as required by the Constitution and, for that purpose, to place members of a family based upon marriage in a more favourable position than other persons in relation to succession to property . . . Having regard to the constitutional guarantee relating to the family, the court cannot find that the differences created by the Act . . . are necessarily unreasonable, unjust or arbitrary.

Again, in *Norris v Attorney General* (1984) (Case 130), a challenge to laws which prohibited certain sexual acts, was partly unsuccessful because of the potential harm which the decriminalising of such acts would have on the institution of marriage. O'Higgins CJ, in the Supreme Court, explained:

> surely, a law which prohibits acts and conduct by male citizens of a kind known to be particularly harmful to the institution of marriage cannot be regarded as inconsistent with a Constitution containing such a provision.

Where a marriage is in difficulties, communications passing between the spouses and a marriage counsellor may be privileged on the ground that the State guarantees to protect marriage and the family, a principle decided by the High Court in *E. R. v J. R.* (1981) (Case 59) though the court held that the privilege could be waived by the mutual consent of the spouses.

The common law granted a right to a husband to sue for the loss of the consortium of his wife and denied a similar action to a wife who had lost the consortium of her husband. The Supreme Court ruled, in *McKinley v Minister for Defence* (1992) (Case 105), that this rule was in breach of the guarantee of equality contained in Article 40.1 of the Constitution. Instead of the court denying to the husband this right of action because of its inconsistency with Article 40.1 the simpler solution adopted by the court was to make the common law conform to the Constitution by a declaration that the established right of the husband continued to exist and that a wife was entitled to the exercise of the same right. The court emphasised the special place given to marriage in the Constitution which highlighted the need to afford equal rights to both spouses. This decision is in contrast to that in *The State (DPP) v Walsh* (1981) (Case 187) where the common law held that where a wife committed a crime in the presence of her husband it was presumed, until the contrary was proven, that she committed it under his duress, was contrary to Article 40.1. The Supreme Court merely decided that the rule did not survive the enactment of the Constitution. The consequence of this is that this defence is no longer available to wives. Had the court adopted the approach taken in *McKinley*'s case this defence would now be available to husbands with the peculiar consequence that where a husband and wife committed a crime together neither could be convicted because both could claim that each committed it under the duress of the other.

Prohibition on Divorce

Article 41.3.2° of the Constitution declares that no law shall be enacted providing for the grant of a dissolution of marriage. The expression 'dissolution of marriage' is not defined though it is taken to mean divorce *a vinculo matrimonii** which is a judicial declaration that a valid marriage is at an end. This prohibition does not prevent the courts from granting a decree of nullity which is a declaration that no valid marriage ever existed. The People, in 1986, rejected a proposal to substitute this sub-article with another which would have permitted divorce.[4] Even in situations which fall far short of divorce the courts are reluctant to acknowledge conduct which may be seen as encouraging or facilitating divorce. The High Court, in *Dalton v Dalton* (1982), refused to make a separation agreement a rule of court because the parties agreed to obtain a decree a vinculo.[5] To do so would have been to ask the court to lend its support to a course of conduct which was contrary to public policy within this jurisdiction.

Recognition of Foreign Divorces

The prohibition on the availability of divorce in this jurisdiction is absolute and clear. The very different question has arisen as to whether our courts should recognise decrees of divorce granted in foreign jurisdictions. In the *Bank of Ireland v Caffin* (1971) (Case 18) Kenny J, in the High Court, explained the law in this regard:

> in 1921 the courts of Ireland . . . recognised the validity of a decree of divorce *a vinculo* made by the courts of the country where the husband and wife were domiciled . . . the national parliament has not legislated on the matter . . . and the law as existing when the Constitution was passed was that a divorce effected by a foreign court of persons domiciled within its jurisdiction was regarded as valid in our jurisdiction.

In the later case of *Gaffney v Gaffney* (1975) this rule was confirmed by the Supreme Court, which refused recognition to a divorce decree because it was granted by a jurisdiction in which the parties were not domiciled (see page 26 for a discussion of domicile). It was decided by the High Court, in *L. B. v H. B.* (1980), that a foreign divorce obtained by fraud would not be recognised in this country.

The Supreme Court refused, in *K. D. (Otherwise C.) v M. C.* (1987), to consider the test of real and substantial connection as an alternative to domicile in this regard.

This common law rule that our courts would recognise a foreign divorce provided it had been obtained in a jurisdiction where both parties were domiciled has been altered by statute. Because of the rules relating to domicile the sole domicile considered was the domicile of the husband. The *Domicile and Recognition of Foreign Divorces Act 1986* provides that a foreign divorce will be recognised in this State if it is obtained in a jurisdiction where *either* spouse is domiciled at the time it was granted. Now that a married woman may, under the same statute, have a domicile independent of her husband our courts will recognise a divorce obtained by a wife provided she was domiciled in the jurisdiction which granted it. This statute only applied prospectively.[6]

The common law rule as to the dependent domicile of a wife came up for discussion on constitutional grounds in *W. v W.* (1992) (Case 209) where the recognition of foreign divorce obtained prior to the coming into effect of the *Domicile and Recognition of Foreign Divorces Act 1986* was discussed. While the Supreme Court decided that the rule of dependent domicile of a married woman ceased to be part of Irish law on the enactment of the Constitution because it breached Article 40.1 which guaranteed equality, the question arose as to what flowed from that decision. A declaration of repugnancy and non-survival of the rule would in general result in a demise of the common law rule. But the Supreme Court adopted a different approach. According to Egan J:

. . . the appropriate basis of recognition in these circumstances for divorces obtained prior to the [enactment of the *Domicile and Recognition of Foreign Divorces Act 1986*], which would be consistent both with the Constitution and with the general principles of international law, would be a recognition of a divorce, if granted by the courts, of a country in which either of the parties to a marriage was domiciled at the time of the proceedings for divorce.

Recognition of Foreign Ancillary Orders

The separate issue which has arisen is whether our courts should recognise foreign ancillary orders made consequent to the granting of decrees of divorce. The first case in this category is *Mayo-Perrott v Mayo-Perrott* (1958) (Case 114), where an action was brought in this country to recover the costs of a divorce case which had been heard in England. The action was dismissed by the former Supreme Court because, as Kingsmill Moore J explained:

> it cannot be doubted that the public policy of this country as reflected in the Constitution does not favour divorce *a vinculo* . . . it would fail to carry out public policy if, by a decree of its own courts, it gave assistance to the process of divorce by entertaining a suit for the costs of such proceedings. The debt which it is sought to enforce is one created by proceedings of a nature which could not be instituted in this country, proceedings the institution of which our public policy disapproves.

In *Mahon v Mahon* (1978) (Case 113) an ex-wife sued for the arrears of maintenance on foot of an order obtained in Britain. The High Court granted the order on the ground that the maintenance order was severable from the divorce. Hamilton J said:

> I accept unreservedly that if the recognition or enforcement of a maintenance order would have the effect of giving active assistance to facilitate in any way the effecting of a dissolution of marriage or to give assistance to the process of divorce that such recognition or enforcement would be contrary to public policy . . . in enforcing and recognising this maintenance order . . . it cannot be said that such enforcement or recognition is giving active or any assistance to facilitate in any way the effecting of a dissolution of marriage or is giving assistance to the process of divorce. It is merely providing for the maintenance of spouses and as such cannot be regarded as contrary to public policy.

An ex-wife, in *G. v G.* (1984) (Case 71) sued her ex-husband for maintenance for their child on foot of an American court order. The ex-husband resisted the claim, arguing that the order for maintenance was inseparable from an order for divorce. The maintenance order was made eighteen months before the divorce decree. Finlay P, in the High Court, in granting the relief claimed, said:

> the law of this country does not recognise divorce and will not aid it. It does, however, recognise and in recent years developed a strict and efficient code for the imposition of liability on a parent to maintain a child . . . a claim by a mother who has custody of a child against the child's father for a payment towards its maintenance is a form of action known to the courts of this country and regularly enforced by them.

But the court left open the question as to whether it would recognise the order for custody of a child which was granted to one of the parents for the first time, and as an integral part, of a decree for divorce in a foreign jurisdiction, and the maintenance order only commenced on the making of the decree for divorce.

The parties, in *Sachs v Standard Chartered Bank (Ireland) Ltd* (1987), domiciled in England, obtained a divorce there. The ex-husband was ordered to pay his ex-wife a lump sum in lieu of regular maintenance. The ex-wife sought to execute that order in this country against a bank which held deposits in the name of her ex-husband. In granting relief Finlay CJ, in the Supreme Court, explained:

> the provision of maintenance arising from the obligation of a spouse in a marriage to a dependent spouse is something recoverable within the law of this country and something for which ample provision has been made by relatively modern legislation. In these circumstances, it seems to me that not only should public policy not be deemed to prevent the enforcement of this judgment but that the requirements of public policy seem clearly to favour it.

The Family

Article 41.1 declares that the State recognises the family as the natural, primary and fundamental unit group of society, and as a moral institution possessing inalienable and imprescriptible rights, antecedent and superior to all positive law. The State guarantees to protect the family in its constitution and authority, as the necessary basis of social order and as indispensable to the welfare of the nation and the State. The family is not defined but judicial dicta confine it to the family founded on marriage. The first of these views was expressed in *The State (Nicolaou) v An Bord Uchtála* (1966) (Case 195) in the High Court by Henchy J:

> I am satisfied that no union or grouping of people is entitled to be designated a family for the purposes of the article if it is founded on any relationship other than that of marriage.

In the same case, in the Supreme Court, Walsh J explained:

> it is quite clear from the provisions of Article 41 . . . that the family referred to in this Article is the family which is founded on the institution of marriage . . . While it is quite true that unmarried persons cohabiting together and the children of their union may often be referred to as a family and have many, if not all, of the outward appearances of a family, and indeed for the purposes of a particular law be regarded as such, nevertheless so far as Article 41 is concerned the guarantees . . . are confined to families based upon marriage.

The marriage of the parents after the birth of a child, or children, renders the unit a family for the purposes of Article 41. In *In re J., an infant* (1966) Henchy J explained:

> in construing Article 41 . . . the first question to be decided is whether the father, mother and child together constitute a family. I am of opinion that they do. It is true that the child was born illegitimate and, therefore, outside a family, but by its parents' marriage it has clearly become a legitimate child of the marriage. I find it impossible to distinguish between the constitutional position of a child whose legitimacy stems from the fact that he was born the day after his parents were married, and that of a child whose legitimacy stems from the fact that his parents were married the day after he was born . . . The crucial fact in each case is that the child's legitimacy and consequent membership of the family are founded on the parents' marriage.

While it is a family founded on marriage that is constitutionally protected the question may arise what constitutes a family. Obviously husband, wife and children are the most usual family unit group. A widow, or widower, and children would also constitute a family. A deserted spouse and children are a family. Whether brothers and sisters, or grandparents and grandchildren constitute a family is less clear. They probably do in that their relationship stems from a marriage. In the High Court in *Murray v Attorney General* (1985) (Case 127), according to Costello J:

> a married couple without children can properly be described as a 'unit group' of society such as is referred to in this Article and the lifelong relationship to which each married person is committed is certainly a 'moral institution'. The words used in the article to describe the 'family' are therefore apt to describe both a married couple with children and a married couple without children.

The Constitution does not spell out all the inalienable and imprescriptible rights of the family. It leaves this task to the Oireachtas and the courts. According to Kenny J in *Ryan v Attorney General* (1965) (Case 171):

inalienable means that which cannot be transferred or given away while imprescriptible means that which cannot be lost by the passage of time or abandoned by non-exercise.

The High Court held in *H. v John Murphy & Sons Ltd* (1987) (Case 74) that Article 41 of the Constitution conferred on the family the right to protection from laws and from the deliberate acts of the State officials which attack or impair its constitution or authority. The Constitution did not confer on the family a right to protection from a negligent act committed by another which attacked or impaired its constitution or authority.

The Role of Woman and Mothers

Article 41.2 declares that in particular the State recognises that by her life within the home, woman gives to the State a support without which the common good cannot be achieved. The State shall, therefore, endeavour to ensure that the mother shall not be obliged by economic necessity to engage in labour to the neglect of her duties in the home. This article was called in aid, in *L. v L.* (1992) (Case 90), by a wife claiming a share in the family home which had been acquired solely by the husband. While the Supreme Court accepted that maintenance or alimony must be set by a court so as to avoid forcing the wife and mother by economic necessity to labour out of the home to the neglect of her duties in it there was no jurisdiction in the court capable of being exercised in pursuance of the sub-article to cover the transfer of any particular property right to the wife and mother.

Marital Privacy in Family Planning

One of the implied rights possessed by the family is the right to marital privacy in the matter of family planning. This was decided in *McGee v Attorney General* (1974) (Case 101) where a married woman complained that the prohibition on the importation of artificial contraceptives was a breach of this implied right to marital privacy. In acknowledging the existence of such a right, most of the members of the Supreme Court held that it was protected by Article 40.3.1° of the Constitution. One judge, Walsh J, based his judgment on family rights. He explained:

> it is a matter exclusively for the husband and wife to decide how many children they wish to have; it would be quite outside the competence of the State to dictate or prescribe the number of children which they might have or should have. In my view, the husband and the wife have a correlative right to agree to have no children . . . Article 41 of the Constitution guarantees to the husband and wife against any such invasion of their privacy by the State. If follows that the use of contraceptives by them within that marital privacy is equally guaranteed against such invasion.

254 Constitutional Law and Constitutional Rights in Ireland

Right of Family to Consort Together

In general circumstances members of a family have the constitutional right to consort together and to enjoy each other's company. Many of the express rights which belong to the family, such as guardianship and education, are based on this assumption. But this right may be curtailed, for example, where one of the family members is imprisoned (see *The State (Gallagher) v Governor of Portlaoise Prison* (1987) page 204), or where both parents are imprisoned (see *Murray v Attorney General* (1990) on page 256), or a barring order which excludes one spouse from the family home is in existence, or one or more of the children have been taken into State care. A father in *Cosgrove v Ireland* (1982) was awarded damages against the State because the Minister for Foreign Affairs granted passports for the children to the mother in disregard of the father's wishes and without a court order, which dispensed with such consent. The High Court ruled that the father's right to the joint guardianship of his children had been infringed.

One area where there has been some litigation is where one or both of the spouses, not citizens of the State, was either refused entry to the State, or faced deportation from the State. The first of these cases was *Abdelkefti v Minister for Justice* (1984) (Case 3). On the facts of that case the High Court held that refusal by the State to admit a non-citizen male, the husband of an Irish citizen, did not infringe any constitutional right of the wife. Barron J explained:

> the [non-citizen male] and his wife and their children have their home outside the jurisdiction and have no present intention of establishing a home within the State. The . . . wife wishes to travel to the State from time to time in order to visit her immediate family. When she does so, she wishes to do so in the company of her husband. In so far as the [wife's] claim is based upon the refusal by the [State] as being a denial of her personal rights under Article 40.3 of the Constitution, I do not regard the fulfilment of a desire to visit her immediate family in the company of her husband as being of such a fundamental nature as to be guaranteed by such constitutional provision. In so far as the [parties'] claim is based on rights protected by Article 41.1 of the Constitution, I can see nothing in the refusal by the [State] which could be said to weaken the family as an institution or to weaken its position in our society nor is there anything in such refusal which can be said to undermine the status of marriage.

In the *State (Bouzagou) v Station Sergeant of Fitzgibbon Street Garda Station* (1985) (Case 177) a non-citizen male, married to an Irish citizen, was refused entry into the State on the grounds that he had no visa and was unable to support himself. He claimed the benefit of the right to the society of his family. Rejecting the claim in the High Court, Barrington J explained:

the prosecutor's problem, however, is that he cannot automatically claim the rights guaranteed to the family under Article 41, because, in this case, unfortunately, the family is divided . . . The wife and children now live as a separate unit and, when the prosecutor was last in the country, had the protection of a barring order against him.

In these two cases non-citizen males, married to Irish citizens and the father of Irish citizens, were refused entry to the State. What is to happen where the non-citizen is resident in this State — can the non-citizen be deported? This point arose in *Pok Sun Shum v Ireland* (1985) (Case 166), where a non-citizen male was ordered to leave this country though given three months to settle his affairs. His wife claimed that she was entitled to the society of her husband within the State. Costello J, in the High Court, accepted the general pro-position that the wife was entitled to the society of her husband, but added:

I do not think that the rights given to the *family* are absolute, in the sense that they are not subject to some restrictions by the State and . . . restric-tions are, in fact, permitted by law, when husbands are imprisoned and parents of families are imprisoned and, undoubtedly, whilst protected under the Constitution, these are restrictions permitted for the common good on the exercise of its rights. It seems to me that the [*Aliens Act 1935*], and orders made under it are permissible restrictions and I cannot hold that they are unconstitutional.[7]

It may well be that with the reform of the law of citizenship, contained in the *Irish Nationality and Citizenship Act 1986*, discussed in detail on page 24, that many non-citizen spouses may opt for Irish citizenship and the prob-lems encountered in the above cases will not be repeated. But should the non-citizen spouse retain the existing citizenship the rules which these cases postulate will continue to be relevant. While these cases indicate that it was the husband who encountered difficulties there is no reason in principle why these rules should not be applied to non-citizen wives who retain existing citizenship and who refuse to adopt, or are ineligible for, Irish citizenship.

The question as to deportation where both the spouses were non-citizens and there were children of the marriage who were citizens arose in *Fajujonu v Minister for Justice* (1990) (Case 66). It was accepted by the Supreme Court that the parents and the children constituted a family within the meaning of the Constitution and that the children were entitled to the care, protection and society of their parents in the family group which was resident within the State. According to Walsh J:

in view of the fact that these are children of tender age, who require the society of their parents and when the parents have not been shown to have been in any way unfit or guilty of any matter which makes them unsuitable custodians to their children, to move to expel the parents in the particular circumstances of this case would . . . be inconsistent with the provisions of Article 41 of the Constitution guaranteeing the integrity of the family.

The Supreme Court accepted that the State could force a family constituted of non-citizens parents and children who are Irish citizens to leave the State only if, after due and proper consideration, it was satisfied that the interests of the common good and the protection of the State and society were so predominant and overwhelming as to justify such an interference with the rights of such a family under the Constitution.

Right to Procreate

The constitutional right to procreate by a married couple was acknowledged by the courts in *Murray v Attorney General* (1985) (Case 127). In the High Court Costello J explained:

by explicitly recognising and protecting this concept of the institution of marriage, it would follow that the right of each spouse to beget children is implicitly recognised and protected.

But again this right to procreate, like other constitutional rights, is not absolute, and in that case, the courts found that the restrictions placed on the spouses by the State, both convicted prisoners serving long prison sentences, were constitutionally permissible.

Family Rights in General

When understanding the ambit of family rights it is a mistake to equate these family rights with parental rights. Each member of the family is possessed of rights: the parents jointly, the parents individually and each of the children. In cases of dispute, as in other areas of constitutional law, difficulties arise in attempting to reconcile the various rights. Two broad principles which form the corner-stone of the law in this regard are relied on. According to Sullivan CJ, in the former Supreme Court, in *In re Frost, infants* (1947):

the first proposition, was that the court must regard the family as a unit, the control and management of which is vested in both parents while both survive.

The former Supreme Court rejected the argument that the rights of parents are absolute rights, the exercise of which cannot in any way be controlled by the courts. Again according to Sullivan CJ:

the second proposition was that a child has natural and imprescriptible rights recognised by the Constitution . . . the court has jurisdiction to control the exercise of parental rights, but in exercising that jurisdiction it must not act upon any principle which is repugnant to the Constitution.

The Supreme Court ruled in *Article 26 and the Adoption (No. 2) Bill 1987* (Case 4) that Article 42.5 should not be confined, having regard to the duty of parents towards their children, to the duty of merely providing education. Parents were obliged to cater for the other personal rights of the child.

Guardianship

The *Guardianship of Infants Act 1964*, as amended, gives statutory expression to these rules by providing that all matters concerning guardianship and custody must be decided on the basis of the welfare of the child and that parents have equal rights to and are joint guardians of their children. This legal right to joint guardianship was breached by the Minister for Foreign Affairs in *Cosgrove v Ireland* (1982) where passports were issued for children to a mother despite objections from the father. In the High Court, McWilliam J held:

> the passports should not have been issued without an application to the court being made by the wife and that this should have been told to the wife. Accordingly, in my view, the Department must share responsibility with the wife for the failure of the wife to obtain the consent of the court to sole custody of the children being had by her.

In relation to custody of children there are two broad types of cases: the first relates to disputes between parents, or a parent, and a stranger, though the latter may be a relative; and the second type are cases involving contests between parents. A full examination of this area of law is found in textbooks on family law[8] and passing mention is made here only in so far as the topic infringes on constitutional law.

In general, parents or a parent will be given custody against a stranger, or against the State but not in every case. In *In re O'Brien, an infant* (1954), a father who gave his daughter to her grandmother because of long-term illness, his wife — the child's mother — having died, had his daughter restored to him. O'Byrne J, in the former Supreme Court, said:

> the sanctity of the family and the enduring existence of parental authority seem to me to be guaranteed by these provisions [of the Constitution] and I consider that I am entitled to say that the framers of the Constitution considered, and enacted, that the best interests and happiness of the child would be served by its being a member of the parental household . . . the [grandmother] has failed to show that the father has failed in his duty to his child.

A law which permitted one parent to commit a child to care but which required the consent of both parents to release the child was deemed to be unconstitutional in *In re Doyle, an infant* (1955) (Case 56). The former Supreme Court, per Maguire CJ, said:

in the view of this court [Article 42.5] does not enable the legislature to take away the right of a parent who is in a position so to control the education of his child, where there is nothing culpable on the part of either parent or child.

This emphasis that the best place for the child is with its natural parents was again stressed in the modern case of *In re J.H. (Otherwise R.), an infant* (1985) (Case 83), which involved a dispute between adopting parents and the natural parents. In the Supreme Court, Finlay CJ stated:

I would therefore accept the contention that in this case section 3 of the *Guardianship of Infants Act 1964* must be construed as involving a constitutional presumption that the welfare of the child . . . is to be found within the family unless the court is satisfied on the evidence that there are compelling reasons why this cannot be achieved or unless the court is satisfied that the evidence establishes an exceptional case where the parents have failed to provide education for the child and to continue to fail to provide education for the child for moral or physical reasons.

In *W. v W.* (1980) (Case 208) the youngest child of a family of four was, almost from birth, cared for and in the custody of a couple, not the parents though with the consent of both parents. The parents' marriage irretrievably broke down and the mother, who suffered from mental illness, sought custody of the child when it was 4 years old. In the High Court, Ellis J explained:

there is no natural or prima facie right of a parent to custody of his child or her children but . . . there is a rule of prudence that in most cases the best place for a child is with its parent, but . . . there can be circumstances varying with each case (not necessarily amounting to intentional misconduct or behaviour), to which valid objection can be taken in the interests of the welfare of a child, whereby the parent can lose custody of the child not only to another contending parent but to a stranger.

The judge left the child with the strangers. In this exceptional case there were strong reasons why the welfare of the child demanded this result. The parents were separated, the child had spent four formative years in another household, the child was still of tender years and its natural mother suffered from mental illness.

Education and the Family
Article 42 of the Constitution declares that the primary and natural educator of the child is the family and the State guarantees to respect the inalienable right and duty of parents to provide, according to their means, for the religious and moral, intellectual, physical and social education of their children.

Parents are free to provide this education in their homes, or in private schools, or in schools recognised or established by the State. The State shall not oblige parents in violation of their conscience and lawful preference to send their children to schools established by the State, or to any particular type of school designated by the State. But, as guardian of the common good, the State may require children to receive a certain minimum of moral, intellectual and social education.

The meaning to be given to the word education has been discussed in a number of cases. In *Ryan v Attorney General* (1965) (Case 171) the High Court felt that the word was not used in a wide sense because since parents were free to provide this education in their homes or in schools established or recognised by the State, it must be of a scholastic nature. The Supreme Court thought that education was essentially the teaching and training of a child to make the best possible use of his or her inherent and potential capacities, physical, mental and moral. This definition was adopted by the High Court in *O'Donoghue v Minister for Health* (1993) (Case 140). Applying this definition to the facts in *Ryan*'s case, the Supreme Court held that to teach a child to minimise the dangers of dental decay by adequate brushing of teeth was physical education because it induced the use of the child's own resources. The High Court held, in *Landers v Attorney General* (1975) (Case 91), that the definition of education did not include the public singing career of a child between the age of 7 and 10 years. But the Supreme Court, in *Article 26 and the Adoption (No. 2) Bill 1987* (Case 4), favoured a wider meaning to be accorded the word. Finlay CJ said:

Article 42.5 of the Constitution should not . . . be construed as being confined, in its reference to the duty of parents towards their children, to the duty of providing education for them. In the exceptional cases envisaged by [Article 42.5] where a failure in duty has occurred, the State by appropriate means shall endeavour to supply the place of parents. This must necessarily involve supplying not only the parental duty to educate but also the parental duty to cater for the other personal rights of the child.

It comes as some surprise to many parents that they are under no constitutional obligation to send their children to school. On the contrary, parents have the express constitutional right to educate children in their own homes and in a manner considered wisest by the parents. The *School Attendance Acts 1926* to *1967* are misunderstood and are often misapplied. The State can only interfere with this parental right when a child is not receiving 'a certain minimum education'. The meaning and extent of this phrase was explained by the former Supreme Court in *Article 26 and the School Attendance Bill 1942* (Case 11), by Sullivan CJ:

we are of opinion that the State, acting in its legislative capacity through the Oireachtas, has power to define it . . . which expression, in the opinion of the court, indicates a minimum standard of elementary education of general application.

The court condemned a section which delegated this power of prescribing a minimum standard to the executive arm of government. To the present day the Oireachtas has not defined in legislation a minimum standard of education. It is therefore impossible for the courts to conclude that any child is not receiving education because the courts have no yardstick to judge such a standard by.

The former Supreme Court, in *In re Doyle, an infant* (1955) (Case 56), held that Article 42.2 of the Constitution expressly secured to parents the right to choose the nature of the education to be given to their children and the schools at which such education was to be provided and that this right was a continuing one. Parents were entitled to change and substitute schools as in their judgment they thought proper and to hold that a choice once made was binding for the period of a child's education would be a denial of such right.

Article 42.4 of the Constitution declares that the State shall provide for free primary education and shall endeavour to supplement and give reasonable aid to private and corporate educational initiative. It was clarified by the Supreme Court in *Crowley v Ireland* (1980) (Case 44) that the State's duty is to provide 'for' free primary education and not to provide it. In *Conway v INTO* (1991) (Case 39) an award of damages was made against a teachers' union who had unlawfully interfered with this constitutional right of a child to receive free primary education.

This obligation which rests on the State is towards all children whatever their capacities. The High Court held, in *O'Donoghue v Minister for Health* (1993) (Case 140), that the State had failed to fulfil this obligation towards a profoundly handicapped child.

There are, contrary to popular opinion, very few state-owned educational institutions in this country. Article 44.2.4° of the Constitution declares that legislation providing aid for schools must not discriminate between schools under the management of differing religious denominations, nor should such legislation affect prejudicially the right of any child to attend a school receiving public money without attending religious instruction at that school. Thus a child cannot be compelled to attend religious instruction at any school which receives public funds, whether directly by way of building or capitation grants, or indirectly by the payment of the teaching staff.

Religion and the Family

Under Article 42.1 of the Constitution parents have the right to decide on the religious upbringing of their children. Parents are free to instruct their children in the tenets of one religious denomination or in none. The State cannot interfere, in general, with the exercise of such right. Where parents agree to put that agreement into practice and continue in agreement there is never a difficulty from a legal perspective. In cases of disagreement between parents the courts may be requested to intervene to resolve the conflict. The conflict may arise where the parents cannot agree, which is rare, or more likely, the parents will have agreed, will have put that agreement into practice and some time later one parent may unilaterally wish to alter the religious upbringing of the children.

It is regrettable that this issue of choice of religious upbringing was, in the earlier cases, confused with custody rights. In those cases, such as *Tilson* (discussed later), it was presumed that the issues were identical. In fact the two issues are completely separate. It does not follow that the parent with custody can decide all issues affecting the welfare of the child without the consent of the other parent, or failing that, the consent of the court. Who decides on the religious upbringing of the children? In *In re Tilson, infants* (1951) (Case 206), Murnaghan J, in the former Supreme Court, explained:

> the true principle under our Constitution is this. The parents — father and mother — have a joint power and duty in respect of the religious education of their children. If they together make a decision and put it into practice it is not in the power of the father — nor is it in the power of the mother — to revoke such decision against the will of the other party . . . if a difference between father and mother leads to a situation in which the child is neglected, the State, through the courts, is to endeavour to supply the place of the parents.

There have been very few cases where disputes arose between parents, even separated parents, with regard to the religious upbringing of their children. In one such case, *H. v H.* (1976), the High Court decided, among other grounds, to grant custody of a 2-year-old boy, who had been baptised a Roman Catholic, to the father and not to the mother, who had formed an attachment with a person of the Jewish persuasion whom she proposed to marry, was receiving instruction in the Jewish faith and intended to alter the child's religion accordingly.

The State cannot dictate the religion in which parents are to instruct their children, and, it seems, neither can others. A direction in a will, in *Burke v Burke* (1951) (Case 28), as to the education of a child legatee* was set aside, though the gift remained valid because, according to Gavan Duffy P in the High Court, it:

would override the sacred parental authority and defy the parental right and duty of education under Article 42.

The provision in a will, in *In re Blake, deceased* (1955) (Case 21), that the children named to benefit should be brought up as Roman Catholics was declared void by the High Court as offending public policy because, as Dixon J explained, it was:

> an attempt to interfere with or fetter the right and duty guaranteed to parents by the Constitution to provide for the education of their children.

Adoption and the Family

The rules on family rights set out above could be taken to apply solely to the natural family, that is, parents married to each other and children of their blood, though this cannot be absolutely stated. We have already noted (page 251) and will do so again that constitutional family rights do not attach to extra-marital families. Are family rights protected by the Constitution diminished in any way where the family consists of a child, or children, not related by blood to the parental figures within that family? The answer seems to be no, subject to two provisos. The first is that the family must be founded on marriage in that the parental figures must be married to each other; and the second is that the child, or children, must have been adopted in accordance with law. There is no decided case law on this point.

The law permits adoption, the purpose of which is to vindicate two possible sets of rights. The first right to be vindicated is that of a married couple, who cannot beget children, to rear and have the company and society of children, in order to allow them to exercise parental rights protected under the Constitution. The second right to be vindicated is that all children should have the opportunity to belong to a family founded on marriage, the primary unit group of society. The effect of the making of a valid adoption order is that (a) the child acquires the rights of a natural child in relation to its adoptive parents; (b) the adoptive parents acquire the rights of natural parents in relation to the child adopted; and (c) the natural parents lose all rights to the adoptive parents in regard to the child.

The procedure is laid down by the *Adoption Act 1952*, as amended,[9] and is based on the consent of all the parties, except a very young child unable to give its consent. At present all children are, in general, eligible for adoption. Under the 1952 Act only orphans and illegitimate children were eligible for adoption. A proposal to extend this facility of adoption to all children, particularly legitimate children whose parents had failed in their duty towards their children, was referred to the Supreme Court in *Article 26 and the Adoption (No. 2) Bill 1987* (Case 4). The court upheld the measure as an example of the State's fulfilment of its obligation, as far as was practicable, to vindicate the personal rights of a child whose parents had failed in their duty. This obligation was fulfilled by providing a law which permitted, with safeguards, the incorporation of the child into an alternative family.

Adoption is only an alternative where the child is eligible for adoption and the statutory formalities have been observed. Before the final adoption order is made, the consent to the adoption may be withdrawn and this coupled with the marriage of the child's natural parents alters the circumstances considerably, in that parents and child constitute a family within the provisions of Article 41 of the Constitution. This occurred in *In re J. H. (Otherwise R.), an infant* (1985) (Case 83), where the natural parents sought the return of their child which had been placed for adoption. The Supreme Court ruled that the proper test in such cases was that the best interests of the child were served within the natural family unit except in exceptional circumstances.

Many of the adoption cases are concerned with the question of consent, and the consequences which flow from the withdrawal of such consent, as in *In re J. H., an infant*, already mentioned, and do not turn on the constitutionality of adoption itself.

Non-Marital Family

It has been made abundantly clear by judicial comments that the only family protected under the Constitution is the family founded on marriage. What rights, if any, have non-marital families? Superficially they appear to have the same rights as the constitutional family, though in essence such rights seem to flow from the personal rights possessed by the individuals under Article 40 rather than any collective rights protected under Article 41. Extramarital families may be treated differently under the law and such discriminations may be justified on the ground that the family founded on marriage must be granted protection by the State. This was the result in *O'B. v S.* (1984) (Case 132) where the Supreme Court upheld laws which did not grant like treatment to legitimate and illegitimate children as regards intestate succession on the ground that the laws were enacted by the State in furtherance of its duty to protect the family founded on marriage (and see page 246).

What particular personal rights do the parties to a non-marital family possess? Has the natural mother a constitutional right to the custody of her child? The Supreme Court, in *G. v An Bord Uchtála* (1980) (Case 70), ruled that the unmarried mother had a constitutional right to the custody and the control of the upbringing of her child. A consequence of that decision is that a mother, when giving a consent to the adoption of her child, is permanently alienating a constitutional right though this point has not been actually decided.

The natural father has fared much worse. In *The State (Nicolaou) v An Bord Uchtála* (1966) (Case 195) the natural father was, in the circumstances of that case, denied the right to be consulted before an adoption order was made in relation to his child. It must be stressed that this decision does not illustrate a general principle that a natural father has no rights in relation to his illegitimate child. Where he cares for and has custody of that child he may, in appropriate circumstances, repel the State, a stranger and even the mother from interfering with such custody because in such a case, as in all cases concerning children, the central and vital question is the best interests of the child.

The *Guardianship of Infants Act 1964* provides that the father of an illegitimate child may apply to the courts for access to his child. Section 12 of the *Status of Children Act 1987* amended the 1964 Act by inserting a section which provides that where the father and mother of a child are not married to each other the court may, on the father's application, appoint him a guardian of the child. In interpreting this section the Supreme Court ruled in *K. v W.* (1990) that the section did not confer on a natural father the right to be guardian of his child, nor did such a right exist under the Constitution. The section grants the natural father a right to apply to the court to be appointed guardian and in exercising its discretion the court must regard the welfare of the child as the first and paramount consideration.[10]

Constitutional Rights of Children

Children have both personal rights under Article 40 of the Constitution, which are available to other persons, and family rights protected under Article 41. It was pointed out by the Supreme Court in *Article 26 and the Adoption (No. 2) Bill 1987* (Case 4) that the rights of a child who is a member of a family include those rights referred to in Articles 40, 43 and 44, as well as those identified in Articles 41 and 42. Obviously children of a family are entitled to the society, care, guidance and protection of their parents and to have all the opportunities of participating to the full in family life. According to Henchy J, in the Supreme Court, in *G. v An Bord Uchtála* (1980) (Case 70):

> all children whether legitimate or illegitimate, share the common charac-
> teristic that they enter life without responsibility for their status and with
> an equal claim to what the Constitution expressly or impliedly postulates
> as the fundamental rights of children. Since Article 42 recognises the
> children of a marriage as having a natural and imprescriptible right (as
> the correlative of their parents' duty) to the provision for them of religious
> and moral, intellectual, physical and social education, a like personal
> right should be held to be impliedly accorded to the illegitimate child by
> Article 40.3.

Apart from according equal status to all children, O'Higgins CJ, in the same case, suggested some of these constitutional rights:

having been born, the child has the right to be fed and to live, to be reared and educated, to have the opportunity of working and of realising his or her full personality and dignity as a human being.

The primary duty of raising children rests with the parents jointly, if married, and on the mother, if the parents are unmarried. Where the parents fail to provide the child with the necessities of life the State must do so (Article 42.5). And a child, the possessor of constitutional rights, may vindicate these and may claim damages for their infringement. For example, in *Conway v INTO* (1991) (Case 39) the plaintiff recovered damages from a number of teachers' unions for the infringement of her constitutional right to free primary education. In *Wadda v Ireland* (1993) (Case 210) the High Court upheld the constitutionality of the *Child Abduction and Enforcement of Custody Orders Act 1991* because its provisions were in the interests of children by protecting them from the harmful effects of their wrongful removal from the State of their habitual residence, particularly by one parent in defiance of the wishes of the other parent.

The State is obliged, as far as practicable, to vindicate the personal rights of a child whose parents have failed in their duty towards that child.

There has been no litigation on when constitutionally a child becomes an adult. Presumably, the courts would be reluctant to displace the view taken by the Oireachtas in this regard. But the difficulty is that common law and statute do not lay down a uniform age as to when legal rights, and responsibilities, attach to the child. Criminal responsibility and tortious liability begins at 7, a person may take full-time employment at 15, may marry with consent at 16, and consent to sexual activity can be made at 17 years. Persons may vote at 18 and full adulthood does not arrive until 21 years of age when citizens can stand for election to Dáil Éireann (see page 76). The *Age of Majority Act 1985* has gone a long way towards reducing the age of adulthood, generally, to 18.

Chapter 17

PROPERTY RIGHTS

Property as an Institution

In Article 43 the State acknowledges that man, in virtue of his rational being, has the natural right antecedent to positive law to the private ownership of external goods and accordingly the State guarantees to pass no law attempting to abolish the right to private ownership, or the general right to transfer, bequeath and inherit property. The nature of this article was considered by the Supreme Court in *Blake v Attorney General* (1981) (Case 22) by O'Higgins CJ:

> it is an article directed to the State and to its attitude to these rights, which are declared to be antecedent to positive law. It does not deal with a citizen's right to a particular item of property ... such rights are dealt with in Article 40 under the heading 'Personal Rights' ... Under this Article the State is bound, in its laws, to respect and vindicate the personal rights of citizens. There exists, therefore, a double protection for the property rights of a citizen. As far as [the citizen] is concerned, the State cannot abolish or attempt to abolish the right of private ownership as an institution ... in addition [the citizen] has the further protection under Article 40 as to the exercise by him of his own property in particular items of property.

The Supreme Court rejected the claim in *O'B. v S.* (1984) (Case 132) that the absence from succession law of a right of illegitimate children to inherit on the intestacy of their father was an abolition of the right to inherit property protected by Article 43. Walsh J said:

> it appears to the court that the phrase 'and inherit property' must necessarily be related to the exercise of the power to transfer property by bequest and that what the State has guaranteed in the article is to pass no law attempting to abolish the general right to inherit property so bequeathed. That does not mean that the State may not, in appropriate cases, prevent the succession to property.

Property Rights as a Personal Right
In the High Court, Kenny J analysed the Constitution and the then few decided cases in *Central Dublin Development Association v Attorney General* (1975) (Case 33), and reached the following conclusions as to property rights:

(1) The right of private property is a personal right.
(2) In virtue of his rational being, man has a natural right to individual or private ownership of worldly wealth.
(3) This constitutional right consists of a bundle of rights most of which are founded on contract.
(4) The State cannot pass any law which abolishes all the bundle of rights which we call ownership, or the general right to transfer, bequeath and inherit property.
(5) The exercise of these rights ought to be regulated by the principles of social justice, and the State accordingly may, by law, restrict their exercise with a view to reconciling this with the demands of the common good.
(6) The courts have jurisdiction to inquire whether the restriction is in accordance with the principles of social justice and whether the legislation is necessary to reconcile this exercise with the demands of the common good.
(7) If any of the rights, which together constitute our conception of ownership, are abolished or restricted (as distinct from the abolition of all the rights), the absence of compensation for this restriction or abolition will make the Act, which does this, invalid if it is an unjust attack on property rights.

Property rights are emphatically personal rights protected by Article 40.3 of the Constitution. Should any particular law amount to an unjust attack on these rights, which will in each case be a subjective view, the absence of compensation will render the law invalid.

The Common Good
The State recognises that the exercise of property rights ought, in civil society, to be regulated by the principles of social justice, and accordingly the State may, as occasion requires, delimit by law the exercise of these rights with a view to reconciling their exercise with the exigencies of the common good (Article 43.2). There are innumerable instances of the curtailment of private property rights in our laws, as many as those which restrict personal liberty. Examples are an extensive range of taxation, price control, planning law, easements, nuisance, trespass, various compulsory purchase procedures, restrictions on premises as regards safety, possession of certain

substances as a criminal offence, and the necessity to be licensed. The reader must not assume that each of these restrictions is in fact constitutionally permissible because, as the case law shows, many statutory provisions which were in force for years were eventually successfully challenged.

The case law will be considered under common headings rather than chronologically.

Interference with Contractual Rights

Both common law and statute make great inroads on the freedom to contract. Some such restrictions have been challenged as to their constitutionality. In the first case, the *Pigs Marketing Board v Donnelly (Dublin) Ltd* (1939) (Case 165), the High Court was asked to rule on a measure which interfered with contractual rights. Hanna J said:

> the days of *laissez faire* are at an end and this is recognised in Article 43.2.2° ... This law does not abolish private ownership in pigs and bacon, it only delimits the exercise of these rights by the persons in whom they are vested.

The court had earlier examined the purpose of the legislation and accepted that the pigs and bacon industry was of great importance to the national economy, not alone by providing a staple article of food but also because it was an industry which both in home consumption and export was of considerable value. *Blake v Attorney General* (1981) (Case 22) saw a challenge to statutes which interfered with the contractual relationship between certain landlords and tenants, by restricting recovery of the premises and prohibited rent increases. Giving the judgment of the Supreme Court in striking down these legislative measures O'Higgins CJ explained:

> it is, therefore, apparent that in this legislation rent control is applied only to some houses and dwellings and not to others, that the basis for the selection is not related to the needs of the tenants, to the financial or economic resources of the landlords, or to any established social necessity and, since the legislation is now not limited in duration, is not associated with any particular temporary or emergency situation. Such legislation, to escape the description of being unfair and unjust, would require some adequate compensatory factor for those whose rights are so arbitrarily and detrimentally affected.

The special security of tenure was also condemned. O'Higgins CJ explained:

> in the view of the court, a restriction to this extent of a landlord's right to obtain possession of rented premises is not in itself constitutionally invalid, provided the restriction is made on a basis that is not unconstitutionally

unfair or oppressive, or has not due regard both to the personal property rights of the landlord and the rights that should be accorded to tenants, having regard to the common good. However, the restriction on the right to recover the possession ... is not distinguishable, or capable of being saved, by such considerations. It is an integral part of the arbitrary and unfair statutory scheme whereby tenants of controlled dwellings are singled out for specially favourable treatment, both as to rent and as to the right to retain possession, regardless of whether they have any social or financial need for such preferential treatment and regardless of whether the landlords have the ability to bear the burden of providing such preferential treatment.

An attempt to soften the effects of this decision was struck down by the Supreme Court in *Article 26 and the Housing (Private Rented Dwellings) Bill 1981* (Case 9) for the same reasons.

In deciding whether a statute, which interferes with contractual rights, has retrospective or prospective effect the better view is that it should be interpreted in such a way as not to apply to contracts entered into before the statute was passed. This was the view expressed in *Hamilton v Hamilton* (1982), in the Supreme Court, by O'Higgins CJ:

> when one considers that this is an Act of the Oireachtas, the proposition that it was intended to affect and frustrate pre-existing contractual rights becomes unstatable. Were this legislation to have the effect contended for, it would constitute an unjust attack upon and a failure by the State to vindicate the property rights [of one of the defendants], and of others similarly situated, and would constitute a clear infringement of ... Article 40.3.2° of the Constitution.

Confiscation of Property

There are many instances of laws which permit the confiscation of goods. The *Fisheries (Consolidation) Act 1959*, as amended, permits the confiscation of illegally caught fish, fishing gear and, on a second conviction, the boat. The question arose in *Attorney General v Southern Industrial Trust* (1960) (Case 13) as to whether a statute could be constitutionally justified which conferred a power to confiscate a particular piece of property and to divest a person of its ownership, without compensation, particularly one who had not committed any breach of the law with regard to that property. In the High Court, Davitt P said:

> I do not think it can be reasonably contended that the customs code, severe and unpopular though it may seem to those who have most evidence of it as transgressors, has not been enacted with a view to the promotion of the

common good, nor do I think that it can be contended that a person who takes the risk of illegally importing or exporting his own property has any reasonable cause to complain of injustice if it is forfeited in consequence of his offence.

With regard to the seizing of an innocent person's property the court held that the customs code, by providing a method for the mitigation of penalties, was an attempt to reconcile the rights of innocent owners on the one hand, and the exigencies of the common good on the other.

A statue, with adequate safeguards, which permitted the seizing of monies standing in a bank account which belonged to an unlawful organisation was held to be constitutional by the High Court in *Clancy v Ireland* (1989) (Case 35).

Restrictions on the Use of Private Property

Our laws place numerous restrictions on the use to which property may be put. A typical example is the planning law which was challenged in *Central Dublin Development Association v Attorney General* (1975) (Case 33) where the nature of the legislation was examined. In the High Court Kenny J held:

if there is to be planning development someone must decide whether new or altered buildings are to be allowed in a specific place and whether land should be retained as an unbuilt space. The very nature of town and regional planning requires restriction ... Town and regional planning is an attempt to reconcile the exercise of property rights with the demands of the common good.

The Supreme Court ruled in *Pine Valley Developments Ltd v Minister for the Environment* (1987) that the grant of outline planning permission was not intended as a limitation of the owner's property rights but rather as an enlargement and enhancement of these rights. The purchase of the lands by the plaintiff company for development purposes had to be seen as a speculative risk, and the subsequent invalidity in a legal action of the Minister's decision to grant permission, although probably contributing towards a diminution in value of those lands, could not be seen as an unjust attack on the plaintiff company's property rights.

Another restriction placed by statute on the owner's use and enjoyment of property is the national monuments code. This code was challenged in *O'Callaghan v Commissioners of Public Works* (1985) (Case 138) on the grounds that the preservation order, made in that case, was unlimited in time and not counterbalanced by the State's requirement to pay compensation, and that it was made without affording the landowner any prior notice, or any opportunity for review or appeal against the order. Giving the judgment of the Supreme Court, which upheld the legislation, O'Higgins CJ explained:

it cannot be doubted that the common good requires that national monuments which are the prized relics of the past should require to be preserved as part of the history of our people. Clearly, where damage to such monuments is the probable result of unrestricted interference by the owners or other persons, a conflict arises between the exigencies of the common good and the exercise of property rights. This is particularly so where, as in this case, the interference initiated by the owner involves the ploughing and consequent destruction of that which constitutes the monument. In the view of the court this legislation has been enacted in discharge by the State of its duty under Article 43.2. The legislation is not arbitrary or selective. It applies to all national monuments wherever situated and whoever owns them. Its purpose is to preserve in the national interests each such monument by prohibiting any action which may damage or destroy the same. The exercise of the property rights guaranteed in Article 43.1.2° ought to be regulated by the principles of social justice, as defined in Article 43.2.2°.

Regulation of Licences

Many activities can only be carried on by way of a licence granted by the State. Matters pertaining to such licences are governed by statute and have generated a considerable body of law, some in the constitutional field. As a general principle the courts regard the possession of a licence as a property right.

The loss of a licence following breaches of the law under which the licence was issued was not considered to be an unjust attack on property rights in *The State (Pheasantry Ltd) v Donnelly* (1982) (Case 198) where the owner of a restaurant forfeited a wine licence on conviction of breaches of the licensing laws. In the High Court Carroll J explained:

the licence is a privilege granted by statute and regulated for the public good. It is *ab initio* subject to various conditions, one of which is the inherent possibility of automatic forfeiture ... If the conditions necessary for statutory forfeiture are fulfilled, this is brought about through the [owner's] own fault. There is no constitutional right to a liquor licence or a renewal thereof. There are only such rights as are given by statute subject to limitations and conditions prescribed by statute. A person applying for a licence knows, or ought to know, that it can be forfeited in certain events. When those events occur, [the owner] cannot be heard to complain.

Where a person is possessed of a licence it is possible that the issue of additional licences to others may diminish the commercial value of that licence. In such circumstances is the issue of the additional licences an unjust attack on property rights. This was the point in *Hempenstall v Minister for the Environment* (1992) (Case 79) where it was argued that the issue of further licences would result in a diminution in the value of property rights. That contention was rejected by the High Court. Costello J explained:

> property rights arising in licences created by law ... are subject to the conditions created by law and to an implied condition that the law may change those conditions. Changes brought about by law may enhance the value of those property rights ... or they may diminish them ... But an amendment of the law which by changing the conditions under which a licence is held reduces the commercial value of the licence cannot be regarded as an attack on the property rights in the licence — it is the consequence of the implied condition which is an inherent part of the property right in the licence.

Compulsory Acquisition of Property

There are a number of instances where an individual's land or premises may be compulsorily acquired, usually for the purpose of public utility, against the wishes of the individual, even with compensation. The powers exercised under such a statute were challenged in *O'Brien v Bord na Móna* (1983) (Case 133) on the grounds that the absence of a statutory duty on the defendant to give notice of the intention to make a compulsory purchase order, and the absence of an appeal were in breach of property rights protected by Article 40.3. Holding that the powers were administrative in nature, the Supreme Court upheld the statute on the ground that it was enacted for the common good. O'Higgins CJ explained:

> it is clear that the purpose of the statute was to make available the considerable natural resources of turf in the State in the best possible fashion for the use of the nation. Both in terms of the statute itself and indeed of the events which have since occurred in the development of the activities and work of Bord na Móna it is clear that the dominant method by which the overall purpose was to be achieved and has been achieved was by the acquisition of boglands ... and the working of them by Bord na Móna itself so as to produce turf and turf products. It seems clear that it was by this procedure that a major source of energy was intended to be and has in fact been harnessed for the use of society in general ... The statue must, therefore, be viewed as constituting a decision that the common good requires that bogland should be available for compulsory acquisition.

While some statutes permit the absolute acquisition of property others permit a partial interference with property which amounts, in law, to a burden on the land. Such a statute, which permitted the compulsory erecting of pylons on and cables across land, was challenged in *ESB v Gormley* (1985) (Case 65) on the ground that the *ex gratia** payment was not sufficient compensation and offended Article 40.3.2° of the Constitution. In holding the statute unconstitutional the Supreme Court, per Finlay CJ, said:

[the statute] must be interpreted as granting to the plaintiff a power compulsorily to impose a burdensome right over the land ... Having regard to the social benefits of electricity and its contribution to the economic welfare of the State, the uncontradicted evidence adduced in this case of necessity for and value of this transmission line to the national supply system leads to an inescapable conclusion that the power to lay it compulsorily is a requirement of the common good ... On the evidence, the plaintiff in the laying of this transmission line does not in fact pay compensation which it asserts is reasonable ... It must be concluded that the imposition of a statutory obligation to pay compensation which in the absence of agreement fell in any particular case to be independently assessed could not impose an additional cost on the plaintiff in the erection of this line which would be inconsistent with social justice or with the requirements of the common good.

Where property is taken compulsorily, what form should the compensation take? Must it be money or could it be, as in *Dreher v Irish Land Commission* (1984) (Case 58), land bonds? The Supreme Court held that the payment in bonds which carried interest, as distinct from monetary compensation, was not an unjust attack on property rights. In the Supreme Court, Walsh J said:

the State in exercising its powers under Article 43 must act in accordance with the requirements of social justice but clearly what is social justice in any particular case must depend on the circumstances of the case ... I think it is clear that any State action thus authorised by Article 43 of the Constitution and conforms to that Article cannot by definition be unjust for the purpose of Article 43.3.2°. It may well be that in some particular cases social justice may not require the payment of any compensation upon a compulsory acquisition that can be justified by the State as being required by the exigencies of the common good. It is not suggested that the present case is one such [case] ... The effect of the section is then that the price of the land is to be paid for in land bonds which were to be issued at a rate which made them as near as could be reasonably achieved equal in actual value to the price fixed. Thus [the section] cannot be read as creating any reasonably avoidable injustice or indeed any real injustice.

Taxation

Taxation is a major restriction on private property rights. In *Brennan v Attorney General* (1984) (Case 25) a challenge was made to the valuation system on which agricultural rates were assessed. The Supreme Court struck down the legislation. Giving the judgment of the court, O'Higgins CJ stated:

> with regard to Article 40.3 the court is of opinion that the ... complaints that this Article has not been observed are justified and should be upheld ... The evidence and the facts ... [were] that the use of the 1852 valuations was continued as a basis for agricultural rates, long after the lack of uniformity, inconsistencies and anomalies had been established and, long after methods of agricultural production had drastically changed. This in itself was an unjust attack on the property rights of those who ... found themselves with poor land paying more than their neighbours with better land. When this injustice had become obvious the State had a duty to take action in protection of the right involved. This it failed to do. In continuing ... the same system without revision or review the State again, in the opinion of the court, failed to protect the property rights of those adversely affected by the system from further unjust attack. In the assessment of a tax such as a county rate reasonable uniformity of valuation appears essential to justice. If such reasonable uniformity is lacking the inevitable result will be that some ratepayer is required to pay more than his fair share ought to be. This necessarily involves an attack upon his property rights which by definition becomes unjust. The plaintiffs have established such injustice in this particular case.

A qualified tax on residential property was challenged, and upheld, by the Supreme Court in *Madigan v Attorney General* (1986) (Case 110). O'Higgins CJ explained:

> so far as the courts are concerned this is a tax measure. As such it necessarily interferes with the property rights of affected citizens. However, such interference cannot be challenged as being unjust on that account, if what has been done can be regarded as action by the State in accordance with the principles of social justice and having regard to the exigencies of the common good as envisaged by Article 43.2 of the Constitution ... While people so affected might feel that they had genuine grounds for complaint against and opposition to the tax they could not challenge its validity because they had difficulty in paying.

There was a similar result in *Browne v Attorney General* (1991) (Case 26) where provisions which imposed an income tax burden on benefits in kind was in issue. In the High Court Murphy J said:

> in the context that all tax is burdensome and understandably resented as such, there does not seem to be any objection in principle to the imposition of tax on the availability of an asset any more than one could successfully object to its imposition on ownership or possession of assets.

In that case the challenge to the *Income Tax Act 1967* raised an interesting point as to how far legislation which, it was conceded, was constitutional at the time of its enactment might become unconstitutional as a result of the inroads of inflation. It was accepted that the category of employees whose emoluments exceeded £15,000 per annum in 1967 represented a reasonable cutting off point when the law was enacted: in that year the plaintiff earned £800. The High Court suggested that the challenge to the legislation on this point would have to be made on the basis that the Oireachtas, by failing to repeal or amend the statute so as to reflect the changes in money values brought about by inflation, was a failure to vindicate constitutional rights. Such an argument failed in *Cafolla v Attorney General* (1985) (Case 30, see page 280) on its particular facts. It was not necessary for the High Court to explore that particular question because it would only have arisen in the event of the challenge to law being successful and the Revenue Commissioners being forced to rely on earlier provisions which apply to benefits in kind generally.

Succession Rights

The question arose in *O'B. v S.* (1984) (Case 132) whether the absence from succession law of a right of illegitimate children to inherit on their fathers' intestacy was a failure by the State to protect property rights under Article 40.3.2° of the Constitution. The Supreme Court held that it was not. Walsh J said:

> the court has already decided that no such right was vested in the defendant [an illegitimate child] under Article 43 and to that extent, therefore, that ground of the claim based on Article 40.3, must fail. If the defendant had a vested right to property under [the law] then, of course, it would be a right falling to be defended and vindicated under Article 40.3.

Entry on Premises

Many statutes grant to persons, who have no legal interest in the property, powers of entry on to that property. As a precondition to the exercise of many of these powers there must be some intervention, such as the necessity to obtain a search warrant, by an authority other than the party seeking the entry. Invariably the authority granting the warrant must be satisfied as to certain matters as a precondition to the issue of the search warrant. It was held by the High Court, in *Ryan v O'Callaghan* (1987) (Case 172), that the issue of a search warrant in such circumstances was an administrative rather than a judicial act.

The issue of a search warrant was challenged, in *Berkeley v Edwards* (1988), on the ground that the Peace Commissioner issuing the warrant could not have been satisfied by the information on oath from a garda that there were reasonable grounds for suspecting that an offence under the *Larceny Act 1916* had been committed. The High Court held that the information on oath by a garda that he was making enquiries into a specific larceny, that he had reasonable cause for suspicion that all or some of the stolen property would be found in the premises to be searched, and that the suspicion was based on information he had received and which he believed, was sufficient to make it appear to the Peace Commissioner that there was reasonable cause to believe that stolen property would be found on the premises to be searched. But in *Byrne v Grey* (1988) a search warrant issued by a Peace Commissioner, under the *Misuse of Drugs Act 1977*, as amended, was held to be invalid because the Peace Commissioner issuing the warrant had not personally been satisfied that there was reasonable ground for suspicion. The High Court held that the Peace Commissioner was not entitled to rely on a sworn averment by a garda that the garda had reasonable grounds for suspicion.

A power of entry without judicial intervention granted under a statute was challenged in *Abbey Films Ltd v Attorney General* (1981) (Case 1). The High Court held that entry into premises could be authorised by the Oireachtas in a manner other than by an order of a court or a warrant. On appeal to the Supreme Court, Kenny J held:

> the ... powers are those of entry, requiring the production of books and taking copies or extracts from these. None of these powers affects 'the right of private ownership or the general right to transfer, bequeath, and inherit property' referred to in Article 43.1.2° of the Constitution. The powers of entry and inspection which are given ... do not infringe those constitutional rights in any way.

Where an arrest is made on private property under a statutory power which provides wide powers of arrest the courts may limit the scope of the power. For example, such powers may not be exercisable on private property. In *DPP v McCreesh* (1992) the Gardaí had followed the defendant's car for some distance which turned into the defendant's driveway. The Gardaí entered the driveway and after a brief discussion formed the opinion that the defendant was driving with excessive alcohol. The section provided that a member of the Garda Síochána may arrest without warrant a person who in the member's opinion is committing or had committed an offence. When the Gardaí informed the driver that they were going to arrest him he informed them that they were on private property and requested them to leave. They arrested the defendant and at his trial the question arose whether the arrest was lawful. The Supreme Court held it was not. Hederman J explained:

if it had been intended by the Oireachtas to confer on a member of the Gardaí the power to make inroads on the property rights of citizens which are recognised and protected by the common law, and to enter on private property against the will of the owner and there arrest the owner, express provision should have been made for such in the [statute].

Where the entry on to the premises is in breach of constitutional rights evidence obtained as a result of that breach may be admitted where the breach is inadvertent: see *The People (AG) v O'Brien* (1965) (Case 152, page 197), or be rejected where the breach is conscious and deliberate: see *The People (DPP) v Kenny* (1990) (Case 158, page 199).

Where the entry on to the premises is unlawful the entrant is a trespasser and evidence obtained after an illegal entry may be inadmissible at a subsequent trial: see *Director of Public Prosecutions v McMahon* (1986) (page 201). In that case the Gardaí were involved in a covert operation against the proprietor of premises they had entered with a view to ascertaining whether there was any evidence on the premises with which they could charge the proprietor with a criminal offence. On the other hand where Gardaí enter premises in the course of routine inquiries to ask for information the Gardaí cannot be treated as trespassers. In *Minister for Justice v Wang Zhu Jie* (1991) Gardaí in plain clothes entered a restaurant for the purpose of making routine inquiries in relation to the enforcement of the *Aliens Act 1935*. On entering they were approached by the defendant, dressed as a waiter, who pointed to a table, asked 'how many?' and indicated that he was going to offer them a place at a table in the restaurant. One of the Gardaí produced his identification and after a brief conversation arrested the defendant. At a subsequent trial the question arose whether the Gardaí were trespassers. If they were the arrest was unlawful and the prosecution would fail. In the High Court, Costello J explained:

it seems to me there must be hundreds of occasions every week in which members of An Garda Síochána enter premises asking for information in the course of their ordinary law enforcement duties and it would be an extraordinary situation for the court to hold that, because they had not express permission before entering premises making routine inquiries, they then entered as trespassers ... the reality is that owners of premises have a duty to co-operate with members of An Garda Síochána in the enforcement of the law ... members of the public who own property and premises impliedly allow members of An Garda Síochána to come on to their property to make inquiries and that the Gardaí are entitled to assume that they are allowed to come on to premises in the ordinary course of their duties as law enforcement officers. That situation can alter, however, if the proprietor indicates to the garda authorities that he does not wish the garda officers to enter the premises.

The Right to Earn a Livelihood

One of the unspecified personal rights in Article 40.3 is the right to earn a livelihood though as with all constitutional rights it is not absolute. The existence of this right does not impose a duty on the State either to provide employment, or to provide for employment. The ambit of the right extends to a willingness by the courts to protect from unlawful attack an individual's employment and unlawful obstruction in the quest for employment.

The right was first acknowledged in *Murtagh Properties Ltd v Cleary* (1972) (Case 128) where a demand, backed by a threat of a picket, was made that women should not be employed in any capacity solely because they were women.[1] This picket was prevented by injunction because, as Kenny J in the High Court explained:

> the plaintiffs contended that the Constitution recognises a right to earn a livelihood without discrimination of sex, though they conceded that an employer was entitled to refuse to employ anyone for any reason. They then said that this right is infringed when an employer who is willing to employ a female is prevented from doing so by a union whose objection is solely on the ground of sex . . . a demand backed by a threat of a picket that women should not be employed at all in any capacity because they are women (and not because the work is unsuitable for them or too difficult or too dangerous) is a breach of this right . . . the purpose of the threat of the picket is to compel the employers to dismiss the bar waitresses solely because they are women, and this is a breach of their constitutional rights.

The right to earn a livelihood was accepted by the Supreme Court as a constitutional right in *Murphy v Stewart* (1973) (Case 125) where Walsh J stated:

> it has been submitted in this court . . . that among the unspecified personal rights guaranteed by the Constitution is the right to work: I accept that proposition. The question of whether that right is being infringed or not must depend upon the particular circumstances of any given case: if the right to work was reserved exclusively to members of a trade union which held a monopoly in this field and the trade union was abusing the monopoly in such a way as to effectively prevent the exercise of a person's constitutional right to work, the question of compelling that union to accept the person concerned into membership (or, indeed, of breaking the monopoly) would fall to be considered for the purpose of vindicating the right to work.

A scheme by a trade union which provided for the compulsory retirement of casual dockers at 65 years of age was not considered by the High Court, in *Rogers v Irish Transport & General Workers Union* (1978) (Case 170), to be an infringement of this right. Finlay P explained:

compulsory retirement at the age of 65 in various forms of employment and walks of life, in particular associated with pension rights, are a common feature of a very great number of activities in this country ... It seems to me that the provision of such compulsory retirement coupled with pension rights is in accordance with and not in conflict with the directive of social policy recognising and acknowledging the right of persons to earn a livelihood

Interference with the right to earn a livelihood might come in the form of a law which prevents the carrying on of a particular type of commercial activity. This was the claim in *Private Motorists Provident Society Ltd v Attorney General* (1983) (Case 167), where it was alleged that the statutory prohibition of operating a banking business was in breach of property rights. The Supreme Court rejected that claim. O'Higgins CJ stated:

the prohibition contained in the impugned section is not an expropriation of the business of the society or of the property rights of its shareholders. It is a regulation and control of the range of business which the society may lawfully transact. The Oireachtas is bound to legislate having regard to the requirements of the common good. It is clear ... on the evidence ... that the regulation and control effected by the legislation was reasonable, and was in accordance with the public interest and with the requirements of the common good. It cannot, therefore, be regarded as an unjust attack on property rights.

Another example of restrictions placed on the carrying on of a particular type of commercial activity is the case of *Hand v Dublin Corporation* (1991) (Case 75). The challenge was to restrictions placed on casual trading which it was claimed amounted to an interference with the right to earn a livelihood. Griffin J explained:

in the opinion of the court the Oireachtas has to legislate for the control and regulation of casual trading in a public place to which the public have access as of right ... it is open to the Oireachtas to provide for strict control and regulation of that trading having regard to the exigencies of the common good. This the Oireachtas has done ... where a person engaged in casual trading has been convicted of an offence under the [*Casual Trading Act 1980*], it is neither unjust nor unreasonable to deprive that person of the right to obtain a licence under the Act by reason of his having been convicted of a second or further offence under the Act.

Where the law requires a business activity to be licensed a person who complies with the law by obtaining a licence may prevent others who are unlicensed from engaging in the activity particularly where it can be shown that the activities of the unlicensed operator interfered with the right of the licensed operator to earn a livelihood. This was decided in *Parsons v Kavanagh* (1990) (Case 150) where O'Hanlon J, in the High Court, said:

> I take the view ... that the constitutional right to earn one's livelihood by any lawful means carries with it the entitlement to be protected against any unlawful activity on the part of another person ... which materially impairs or infringes that right.

A statute which grants a business monopoly to one party will effectively prevent others from carrying on a similar business. Such a statute, which granted a monopoly to the post office to carry letters, was challenged in *Attorney General v Paperlink Ltd* (1984) (Case 12). The High Court held, that while the State had a duty by its laws to protect from unjust attack the personal rights of the defendants to earn a livelihood, the postal monopoly did not constitute such an attack. Any ideological preference for private enterprise deducible from the Constitution did not require the State, in legal proceedings, to justify the existence of a public monopoly. On a further point, Costello J held:

> obviously, it is not in the public interest that a service supplied by a department of State is administered inefficiently. But this does not mean that the Act under which it is supplied is unconstitutional. The ineffi- ciency of a public service may be an argument for amending or repealing the Act ... but it cannot mean that the provisions of a statute are thereby rendered unconstitutional.

Statute may render certain activities criminal. Gaming is one of these activities which is regulated by law. It was claimed in *Cafolla v Attorney General* (1985) (Case 30) that the restrictions placed on the monetary limit as to stake and prize money from gaming machines in amusement halls, valid when the law was enacted, now, because of inflation and other matters, infringed the right to earn a livelihood. The Supreme Court rejected this claim. Finlay CJ said:

> the statutory provisions ... clearly indicate a continuing view on the part of the Oireachtas ... that the exigencies of the common good required a strict control on the provision of facilities for gaming in amusement halls ... If instead of exercising a right absolutely to prohibit the use of [the fruit machine] the legislature permits it, subject even to a very rigid restriction which makes both the use of the machine unattractive and the profitability of its operation small or minimal, that cannot be inconsistent with the Constitution.

A statute, which provided that a person convicted of one of a range of criminal offences by a Special Criminal Court was to forfeit employment funded either centrally or locally, a consequence which did not flow where a person was convicted of a similar offence in an ordinary court, was ruled to be invalid. The Supreme Court held, in *Cox v Attorney General* (1991) (Case 42), that such wide and discriminate consequence was an unjust attack on the constitutional right of that person to earn a livelihood. Finlay CJ stated:

> the court is satisfied that the State is entitled, for the protection of public peace and order, and for the maintenance and stability of its own authority, by its laws to provide onerous and far-reaching penalties and forfeitures imposed as a major deterrent to the commission of crimes threatening such peace and order and State authority, and is also entitled to ensure as far as practicable that amongst those involved in the carrying out of the functions of the State, there is not included persons who commit such crimes. The State must in its laws, as far as practicable, in pursuing these objectives, continue to protect the constitutional rights of the citizens ... it has been established to the satisfaction of the court that notwithstanding the fundamental interests of the State which the section seeks to protect, the provisions of the section fail as far as practicable to protect the constitutional rights of the citizen and are, accordingly, impermissibly wide and indiscriminate.

Where parties enter into an employment contract and one party refuses to release the other party from the obligations of the contract where that other party seeks better conditions elsewhere the High Court ruled, in *Egan v Minister for Defence* (1988) (Case 64), that such a refusal did not breach the other party's constitutional right to earn a livelihood.

The Right to Litigate

Like the right to earn a livelihood, the right to litigate is often stated in very broad terms which are not supported by either the Constitution or judicial decision. There are two instances where the Constitution expressly acknowledges the right to have recourse to the courts. The first of these is the right to apply to the High Court under Article 40.4.2° of the Constitution to question a particular detention (see page 221). Speaking of this Article in the Supreme Court, in *The State (Quinn) v Ryan* (1965) (Case 199), Walsh J said:

> that right to apply to the High Court or any judge thereof is conferred on every person who wishes to challenge the legality of his detention. It must follow that any law which makes it possible to frustrate that right must necessarily be invalid having regard to that provision of the Constitution.

The second of these express rights to litigate is contained in Article 34.3.2° which declares that the jurisdiction of the High Court, and on appeal the

Supreme Court, shall extend to the question of the validity of any law having regard to the provisions of the Constitution.

The question was raised, in *Macauley v Minister for Posts and Telegraphs* (1966) (Case 97), whether there was an unrestricted right of access to the High Court to vindicate a legal, as distinct from a constitutional right. Kenny J held that, in the case before the court, there was. He declared:

> that there is a right to have recourse to the High Court to defend and vindicate a legal right and that it is one of the personal rights of the citizen included in the general guarantee in Article 40.3 seems to me to be a necessary inference from Article 34.3.1 of the Constitution.

But Kenny J left open the question whether it was possible under the Constitution to confer *exclusive* jurisdiction in any justiciable matter on any court other than the High Court. This point has since been litigated in a number of cases (see page 122) without final conclusion.

There can only be a right to litigate under the Constitution if some legal or constitutional right is infringed. There are many instances where the law does not grant a remedy against a perceived wrong. The Oireachtas may abolish causes of action. A consequence of this is that one individual may be able to sue before the Act comes into effect, which another person cannot sue once the Act is in effect.[2]

The courts will not tolerate inference by the legislature which infringes on actions pending in the courts because such actions contravene the doctrine of the separation of powers. This was emphatically held by the former Supreme Court in *Buckley v Attorney General* (1950) (Case 27), per O'Byrne J:

> there is another ground on which, in our view, the Act contravenes the Constitution. We have already referred to the distribution of powers effected by Article 6. The effect of that Article and of Articles 34 to 37, inclusive, is to vest in the courts the exclusive right to determine justiciable controversies between citizens or between a citizen or citizens ... and the State. In bringing these proceedings the plaintiff was exercising a constitutional right and she was, and is, entitled to have the matter in dispute determined by the judicial organ of the State. The substantial effect of the Act is that the dispute is determined by the Oireachtas and the court is required and directed by the Oireachtas to dismiss the plaintiff's claim without any hearing and without forming any opinion as to the rights of the respective parties to the dispute.

In that instance the statute was enacted in relation to a particular case. What is the consequence of the enactment of a statute which will apply to the generality of cases but which effects one particular case which is then pending?

This problem was touched on in *Hamilton v Hamilton* (1982) and the solution was suggested, in the Supreme Court, by Henchy J:

> if the effect of [the statute] was to extinguish or to stultify [a litigant's] constitutional right to pursue his pending claim for specific performance (a claim which the High Court ... has formally declared to be good in law), the Act would be unconstitutional to that extent. However, as the Act enjoys a presumption of constitutionality, and as it makes no reference (either expressly or by necessary implication) to pending proceedings such as [these], I would hold that it must be read as having no bearing on such proceedings.

The *Statute of Limitations 1957*, and other related statutes, have come under judicial scrutiny as a possible infringement of the right to litigate. In the first of these *O'Brien v Keogh* (1972) (Case 134), a law which gave a minor, in the custody of his parents, a shorter period of time to bring an action for personal injuries than a minor not in parental custody, was rejected by the Supreme Court as an attack on such minor's property rights. The correctness of this decision was questioned in *Moynihan v Greensmyth* (1977) (Case 120), where the Supreme Court upheld a section which barred certain claims if not made within a two-year period. The court thought this period reasonable having regard to other parties' right to have the issue resolved speedily. The failure of the statute to provide a different period for minors was not an unjust attack on their property rights. The difference between the two cases is that in *Moynihan v Greensmyth* the statutory provision applied to all whereas in *O'Brien v Keogh* more favourable conditions were granted to some minors without any justification.

The requirement to pay fees in order to litigate was referred to in *In re J.C.* (1985) where an alleged destitute claimed a denial of access to the courts on this ground. While holding against the applicant on the facts, Barrington J, in the High Court, speculated:

> that despite our existing system of civil legal aid, a case might arise where the High Court would have jurisdiction to dispense with the payment of stamp duty or court fees by a litigant as the only means of vindicating his rights.

The same issue arose in *Mac Gairbhith v Attorney General* (1991) and while holding that the expense of stamp duty as a cost in litigation had not impeded the plaintiff, O'Hanlon J said:

> these charges levied by the State are the price the citizen has to pay for access to the courts where his rights under the Constitution and the ordinary law are to be protected, and disputes are to be resolved between

parties in an orderly and acceptable manner. I have no doubt that the frightening cost of litigation, made up in part of these heavy charges levied by the State, are a major deterrent to people who wish to have access to the courts established under the Constitution and may in many cases actually prevent parties from availing of rights nominally guaranteed to them under the Constitution.

The High Court rejected the contention that the plaintiff was prevented from gaining access to the courts by reason of the State's failure to provide a place, namely a law library, for the plaintiff to study the law of the country because the provision of a law library for the use and enlightenment of litigants was not a constitutional right.

There are few statutory restrictions on the right of access to the courts. One such limitation is contained in section 260 of the *Mental Treatment Act 1945*, discussed on page 206, which requires leave of the High Court before proceedings can be issued. Speaking in the Supreme Court, in *Murphy v Greene* (1991), on this section Finlay CJ said:

> section 260 is prima facie a curtailment of the constitutional right of every individual of access to the courts to the extent that it requires a pre-condition of leave of the court for the bringing . . . of a claim for damages for an asserted wrong. It seems reasonable, as was stated by O'Higgins CJ in *O'Dowd v North Western Health Board* (1983), that one of the reasons for this curtailment is to prevent a person who is or has been thought to be mentally ill from mounting a vexatious or frivolous action, or one based on imagined complaints. [This section] must be strictly construed in the sense that it must not be availed of except where it was essential to do so.

Property of Religious Denomination or Education Institution
Article 44.2.6° of the Constitution declares that the property of any religious denomination or any education institution shall not be diverted save for necessary works of public utility and on payment of compensation. This article has never been judicially considered.

Inviolability of Dwelling
Article 40.5 of the Constitution declares that the dwelling of every citizen is inviolable and shall not be forcibly entered save in accordance with law. In *The People (AG) v O'Brien* (1965) (Case 152) Walsh J, in the Supreme Court, attempted a definition of a dwelling:

> in a case where members of a family live together in the family home the house as a whole is for the purpose of the Constitution the dwelling of each member of the family. If a member of a family occupies a clearly defined

portion of the house apart from the other members of the family, then it may well be that the part not so occupied is no longer his dwelling and that the part he separately occupies is his dwelling as would be the case where a person not a member of the family occupied or was in possession of a clearly defined portion of the house.

The High Court in *Abbey Films Ltd v Attorney General* (1981) (Case 1) was not satisfied that office premises were a dwelling. A dwelling does not have to be a permanent structure: it can be of a temporary nature such as a caravan, house-boat or even a tent.

There are many instances where the law permits the dwelling to be entered. Many statutes provide for the issuing of search warrants such as searches for firearms, explosives, stolen property and drugs. Other officials have limited rights to enter the dwelling. The common law has a rule which provides that where a person under a claim of legality enters premises and then abuses the entry that person becomes a trespasser *ab initio*. The rules which apply to personal liberty, such as the strict construction of statutes which interfere with constitutional rights, will have a like application as regards dwellings.

One consequence of an unconstitutional entry is that evidence obtained as a result of a deliberate and conscious violation of the right of the inviolability of the dwelling must be excluded from evidence unless there are extraordinary circumstances. This was decided in the *O'Brien* case though on the facts there was no deliberate and conscious breach, merely a mistake. On the other hand the unlawful entry of a dwelling in *The People (DPP) v Kenny* (1990) (Case 158) resulted in the rejection of evidence obtained following a search (see page 199).

An arrest made as a result of the breach of this right to the inviolability of the dwelling is illegal. This was stressed in the *Director of Public Prosecutions v Gaffney* (1988), where Gardaí entered a dwelling without a warrant or invitation and made an arrest. In the Supreme Court Walsh J stated:

> the entry made by the Garda Síochána ... was not one authorised by law and was in breach of the constitutional guarantee of the inviolability of the dwelling of every citizen contained in Article 40.5 of the Constitution. Therefore the arrest effected on foot of that unlawful and unconstitutional entry was illegal.

This point was emphasised in *Director of Public Prosecutions v McCreesh* (1992) where Gardaí entered the driveway of a dwelling after following a motorist suspected of driving offences. Despite the motorist immediately informing the Gardaí that they were trespassers the Gardaí arrested the motorist. In the Supreme Court Hederman J said:

the arrest of the defendant was not a lawful arrest. If it were intended by the Oireachtas to confer on a member of the Garda Síochána the power to make inroads on the property rights of citizens which are recognised and protected by the common law, and to enter private property against the will of the owner and there arrest the owner, express provisions should have been made for such a power.

An arrest effected on the property of a stranger may be lawful. This was decided by the Supreme Court in *Director of Public Prosecutions v Forbes* (1993) where a person was arrested in the driveway of a dwelling owned by a stranger where he had fled from pursuing Gardaí. O'Flaherty J explained:

there is no question that the Gardaí were trespassers. It must be regarded as axiomatic that any householder gives an implied authority to a member of the Gardaí to come on to the forecourt of his premises to see the enforcement of the law or prevent a breach thereof ... this case is not concerned with any question of entering a dwelling-house and ... there is not ... any question of any form of implied waiver of any constitutional right. Further, like any implied authority, it is an implication which the evidence may, on occasion, rebut. Clearly, in this case the Gardaí were acting in the execution of their duties.

The major remedy for the breach of this constitutional right is an action for damages, a remedy available at common law for trespass.

The constitutional protection applies only to dwellings and not to other lands and premises which are not so used. It will be a question of fact in cases of dispute whether the premises are or are not dwellings. While the constitutional guarantee may not protect other types of lands and premises, an entry not in accordance with law is illegal and an action for damages may result. Evidence obtained as a result of a breach of the law may, at the discretion of the court, be admitted into evidence. This principle was restated in the *Director of Public Prosecutions v McMahon* (1987) by the Supreme Court in a case where Gardaí without the proper warrant visited licensed premises to ascertain whether breaches of the gaming laws were being committed (see page 201).

Part Three
CASES ON CONSTITUTIONAL LAW

This part contains in alphabetical order the major cases in constitutional law. Each case contains a statement of the facts together with the principle of constitutional law decided. Only the majority decision, which forms the judgment of the appropriate court, is given. Many of the cases decided issues of legal importance but these issues are, for the sake of clarity, omitted. The year given is when the case was first reported though the decision may have been delivered earlier.

CASE 1 ABBEY FILMS LTD v ATTORNEY GENERAL (1981)

The plaintiff company distributed films which were rented to exhibitors and two of its directors were directors of a company which owned forty cinemas. Complaints were made by independent cinema owners that they were unable to obtain a fair share of the best films for exhibition. The *Restrictive Practices Act 1972* empowered an investigation of any aspect of the supply or distribution of goods, or the supply of a service and section 15 empowered an authorised officer to enter business premises and require the production of documents and such information as the officer might reasonably request. An application could be made within seven days to the High Court for a declaration that the exigencies of the common good did not warrant the exercise of these powers. The plaintiff sought a declaration that this section was unconstitutional.

Held, by the Supreme Court, in rejecting the claim that the Oireachtas could impose on an accused the onus to establish a limited and specified matter in criminal cases, and that while the promotion of the common good was primarily the function of the Oireachtas there was nothing to prevent the Oireachtas from investing the courts with such jurisdiction. The powers of entry and inspection did not infringe private ownership.

CASE 2 ABBOTT v IRISH TRANSPORT & GENERAL WORKERS UNION (1980)

The plaintiff was a member of the ITGWU until he resigned and joined the Amalgamated Transport & General Workers Union. By that time this union had recruited a sizeable number of the staff in the plaintiff's place of employment though an equal number contained membership with the ITGWU. A dispute arose between the employer and the ATGWU. The employer decided not to negotiate with the ATGWU or any union other than the ITGWU in resolving the dispute because of the fear that the ITGWU would take industrial action. The plaintiff sought an order to compel his employer to negotiate with the trade union of his choice.

Held, by the High Court, that in the absence of a constitutional right of negotiation the employer could not be forced to negotiate with the trade union of the employee's choice.

CASE 3 ABDELKEFTI v MINISTER FOR JUSTICE (1984)

The plaintiff, an Irish citizen, married a Tunisian national in Ireland though the parties set up home outside the State. The plaintiff claimed, when her husband was refused entry to this State when the parties came on a visit, that she had a constitutional right to her husband's company whenever she entered and remained within the State.

Held, by the High Court, that the fulfilment of a desire of the plaintiff to visit her family in the company of her husband was not of such a fundamental nature as to be guaranteed by the Constitution. The refusal to permit the plaintiff's husband's entry did not weaken the family as an institution or undermine the status of marriage.[1]

CASE 4 ARTICLE 26 AND THE ADOPTION (NO. 2) BILL 1987

The *Adoption (No. 2) Bill 1987* intended to provide for the adoption of any child whose parents were deemed to have failed in their constitutional duty towards it by setting out the circumstances in which the High Court would be empowered to make an order dispensing with the consent of a parent or guardian. The failure of parents in their duty towards a child must be total in character, arise from physical or moral reasons, continue for more than one year and must be shown to have amounted to an abandonment of all parental rights over the child. If there was any likelihood that before the child reached the age of 18 years the parents would resume the discharge of their duties no order could be made. The President, pursuant to Article 26.1.1° of the Constitution, referred the Bill to the Supreme Court.

Held, by the Supreme Court, in advising the President that the Bill was constitutional, that the State was obliged, as far as practicable, to vindicate the personal rights of a child whose parents had failed in their duty towards that child.

It was constitutionally permissible for a statute to restore to any member of an individual family constitutional rights of which it was deprived by a method which disturbed or altered the constitution of that family having regard to the nature of the family as a unit group possessing inalienable and imprescriptible rights. The guarantees afforded to the institution of the family by the Constitution, with their consequent benefit to the children of a family, could not be construed in such a way that on the failure of that benefit it cannot be replaced where the circumstances demanded by incorporating the child within an alternative family.

CASE 5 ARTICLE 26 AND THE CRIMINAL LAW (JURISDICTION) BILL 1975

The Oireachtas passed the *Criminal Law (Jurisdiction) Bill 1975*, which proposed, *inter alia*, that a person who commits certain offences outside the jurisdiction of the State could, if apprehended here, be tried and punished in the same way as if the offence had been committed within the jurisdiction. The President, pursuant to Article 26.1.1° of the Constitution, referred the Bill to the Supreme Court.

Held, by the Supreme Court, in advising the President that the Bill was constitutional, that Ireland, being a sovereign State, had the full power through the Oireachtas to legislate with extra-territorial effect in accordance with the accepted principles of international law.

CASE 6 ARTICLE 26 AND THE ELECTORAL (AMENDMENT) BILL 1961

Following the High Court decision that the *Electoral (Amendment) Act 1959* was invalid, in *O'Donovan v Attorney General* (Case 141), the Oireachtas enacted the *Electoral (Amendment) Bill 1961* which revised the constituencies. The 1956 census figures were used notwithstanding the near completion of the 1961 census. The President, pursuant to Article 26.1.1° of the Constitution, referred the Bill to the Supreme Court.

Held, by the Supreme Court, in advising the President that the Bill was constitutional, that the constitutional requirement that the constituencies must be revised every twelve years having regard to the population, as ascertained at the last preceding census, meant the last preceding completed census. The Constitution recognised that an exact parity in the ratio between members of Dáil Éireann and the population of each constituency is not required and what was practical was a matter primarily for the Oireachtas. While the court would not lay down a figure above or below which a deviation from the national average would not be permitted it reserved the right to interfere where the divergencies from the national average were such as to indicate that the requirements of the Constitution had been ignored.[2]

CASE 7 ARTICLE 26 AND THE ELECTORAL (AMENDMENT) BILL 1983

The Oireachtas enacted the *Electoral (Amendment) Bill 1983* which contained provisions entitling British citizens to vote in Dáil Éireann elections. The President, pursuant to Article 26.1.1° of the Constitution, referred the Bill to the Supreme Court.

Held, by the Supreme Court, in advising the President that the Bill was repugnant to the Constitution, that the right to vote at elections for members of Dáil Éireann conferred on every citizen by Article 16 was a right which was restricted to citizens who formed part of the People of Ireland.[3]

CASE 8 ARTICLE 26 AND THE EMERGENCY POWERS BILL 1976

The Houses of the Oireachtas on 1 September 1976, invoking Article 28.3.3° of the Constitution, resolved that arising out of the armed conflict taking place in Northern Ireland a national emergency existed affecting the vital interest of the State. Later that month, the *Emergency Powers Bill 1976* was enacted, which was stated to be 'for the purpose of securing the public safety and the preservation of the State in time of armed conflict'. The Bill permitted detention without charge for a period of seven days. The President, pursuant to Article 26.1.1° of the Constitution, referred the Bill to the Supreme Court.

Held, by the Supreme Court, in advising the President that the Bill was constitutional, that once it was established that the procedural requirements affecting a Bill to which Article 28.3.3° applied had been satisfied, the provisions of that sub-article prevented any part of the Constitution being invoked to invalidate such a Bill. There was a presumption that the facts stated in the resolutions were correct and such presumption in this instance had not been displaced. Therefore the court had no jurisdiction to declare the Bill, or any part of it, repugnant to the Constitution.[4]

CASE 9 ARTICLE 26 AND THE HOUSING (PRIVATE RENTED DWELLINGS) BILL 1981

Some sections of the *Rent Restrictions Act 1960* were declared unconstitutional in *Blake v Attorney General* (1981) (Case 22). To deal with the resulting situation the *Housing (Private Rented Dwellings) Bill* was enacted which provided a measure of security for the tenants of certain dwellings, a reasonable return for landlords and the eventual termination of the tenants' possession of such dwellings. The District Court could determine the gross rent which was defined as the rent which a willing tenant not already in occupation would give and a willing landlord would take for the dwelling. Section 9 provided that tenants, from the years 1982 to 1985, would be required to pay only a proportion of the difference between the rent payable when the Bill came into operation and the rent fixed by the District Court. The President, pursuant to Article 26.1.1° of the Constitution, referred the Bill to the Supreme Court.

Held, by the Supreme Court, in advising the President that the Bill was repugnant to the Constitution, that the effect of the rebates permitted by section 9, whereby landlords were to receive an amount which was less than the just and proper rent was, in the absence of any constitutionally permitted justification, an unjust attack on property rights contrary to Article 40.3.2° of the Constitution.

CASE 10   ARTICLE 26 AND THE OFFENCES AGAINST THE STATE (AMENDMENT) BILL 1940

The High Court, in *The State (Burke) v Lennon* (1940) (Case 181), declared a section of the *Offences Against the State Act 1939* unconstitutional. Resulting from that decision this Bill was enacted. Section 4 provided that whenever a member of the Government is of opinion that any particular person is engaged in activities which are prejudicial to the preservation of public peace and order, or to the security of the State, the Minister may by warrant order the arrest and detention of such person. The President, pursuant to Article 26.1.1° of the Constitution, referred the Bill to the Supreme Court.

Held, by a majority of the Supreme Court, in advising the President that the Bill was constitutional, that the power given to a Minister was not a power to administer justice and did not contravene Article 34 of the Constitution which provided that justice must be administered in courts. This detention was not in the nature of a punishment but of preventative justice, being a precautionary measure taken for the purposes of preserving the public peace and order and security of the State. Nor did it contravene Article 38 of the Constitution which provides that no person be tried on any criminal charge save in due course of law.

CASE 11   ARTICLE 26 AND THE SCHOOL ATTENDANCE BILL 1942

The *School Attendance Bill 1942* had as its purpose the further and better provision for ensuring school attendance by children. Section 4 provided that a child was not deemed to be receiving suitable education unless such education, and the manner in which the child was receiving it, had been certified by the Minister for Education to be suitable. The President, pursuant to Article 26.1.1° of the Constitution, referred section 4 of the Bill to the Supreme Court.

Held, by the Supreme Court, in advising the President that section 4 was repugnant to the Constitution, that the Minister might require a higher standard of education than could properly be prescribed as a minimum standard under Article 42.3.2° of the Constitution. The standard contemplated by the section might vary from child to child and accordingly was not such a standard of general application as the Constitution contemplated. Furthermore the requirement as to the manner in which a child was receiving education was not warranted by the Constitution.

CASE 12 ATTORNEY GENERAL v PAPERLINK LTD (1984)

The *Post Office Act 1908*, as amended, granted the Minister for Posts and Telegraphs the monopoly of conveying letters. The Attorney General sought an injunction against the company when it began to operate a courier service conveying letters. The directors of the company challenged the constitutionality of the statute on the grounds that it infringed the right to communicate freely and that it interfered with the right to earn a livelihood.

Held, by the High Court, that while there was both a constitutional right to communicate under Article 40.3.1°, and a constitutional right to earn a livelihood under Article 40.3.2°, neither was absolute and the provisions of this statute providing a State monopoly were a permissible regulation of both rights by law.

CASE 13 ATTORNEY GENERAL v SOUTHERN INDUSTRIAL TRUST LTD (1960)

The defendant company financed the purchase of a car on hire-purchase. The hirer exported the car and on re-importation it was seized by the customs. When the Attorney General brought proceedings to forfeit the car it was alleged by the defendant that the *Customs (Temporary Provisions) Act 1945* was unconstitutional in so far as it purported to authorise the forfeiture of an innocent party's goods.

Held, by the Supreme Court, that the common good at times required that an innocent person's goods or property be forfeited to the State and in such cases the provisions of the Constitution were not violated.

CASE 14 ATTORNEY GENERAL v TRIBUNAL OF INQUIRY INTO THE BEEF PROCESSING INDUSTRY (1993)

The Houses of the Oireachtas adopted resolutions that a Tribunal of Inquiry be established to inquire into certain matters of urgent public importance. During the course of evidence by a former member of the government the tribunal indicated an intention to raise questions concerning the details of discussions which took place at certain Government meetings. The Attorney General objected to the asking of those questions on the ground that, having regard to the provisions of the Constitution, discussions between members of the Government meeting together for the purpose of making decisions were absolutely confidential and that the contents of such discussions could not be inquired into by the tribunal.

Held, by the Supreme Court, that while Dáil Éireann had the ultimate sanction and control over the Government by virtue of Article 28.10 of the Constitution the separation of powers demanded that whilst the Government retained the support of Dáil Éireann a claim of confidentiality was justified with regard to discussions at Government meetings from the provisions in Article 28.2 dealing with collective authority and collective responsibility. It followed that the Houses of the Oireachtas could not by resolutions appoint some outside agent to inquire into matters of public importance and clothe that inquiry with a much greater power and a fundamentally different power than that possessed by Dáil Éireann.

CASE 15 ATTORNEY GENERAL v HAMILTON (1993)

The Houses of the Oireachtas adopted resolutions that a Tribunal of Inquiry be established to inquire into certain matters of public importance following allegations made in Dáil Éireann and in a television programme. The members of Dáil Éireann who had made the original allegations made written statements to the Tribunal of Inquiry and later appeared as witnesses. The question arose whether the privilege granted to members of the Oireachtas by Article 15.13 of the Constitution that the members of each House of the Oireachtas shall not, in respect of any utterance in either House, be amenable to any court or any authority other than the House itself, extended to the written statements submitted to the Tribunal of Inquiry.

Held, by the Supreme Court, that if the members of Dáil Éireann were questioned on their written statements submitted to the Tribunal of Inquiry they would, in reality, be questioned on their utterances in Dáil Éireann because the statements were merely a reiteration of such utterances. The furnishing of statements could not be employed to circumvent the constitutional privilege that members of Dáil Éireann enjoy. If a member of Dáil Éireann was disciplined for failing to elaborate on what was in such a statement that member would, in reality, be punished because of the utterances in Dáil Éireann and that would be in direct breach of the constitutional immunity contained in Article 15.13 of the Constitution.

CASE 16 ATTORNEY GENERAL v X. (1992)

A 14-year-old girl was pregnant and after careful consideration her parents reached a decision that she should travel out of the State to undergo an abortion. The parents informed the Garda Síochána and inquired from them whether any particular process was available for testing the aborted foetus to provide evidence for the subsequent trial of a person charged with having sexual intercourse with the girl which was a criminal offence because of her young age. The Gardaí submitted that inquiry to the Director of Public Prosecutions who in turn communicated with the Attorney General. The Attorney General applied to the High Court for an interim injunction restraining the girl and her parents from leaving the State and from arranging or carrying out a termination of the pregnancy. At the time that order was made the parties had left the State and were arranging for the abortion. On being informed of the order the parties returned. At a later hearing the court held that while there was a risk that the girl might take her own life that risk was much less and of a different order of magnitude than the certainty that the life of the unborn would be terminated. Having regard to the rights of the mother the duty to protect the life of the unborn as required under Article 40.3.3° required the High Court to grant a permanent injunction. The parties appealed.

Held, by the Supreme Court in setting aside the order of the High Court, that the proper test to be applied was that if it was established as a matter of probability that there was a real and substantial risk to the life as distinct from the health of the mother which could only be avoided by the termination of her pregnancy that such termination was permissible having regard to the true interpretation of Article 40.3.3°of the Constitution. The court ruled that the parties had satisfied the test and established as a matter of probability that there was a real and substantial risk to the life of the mother by self-destruction which could only be avoided by termination of the pregnancy.

CASE 16a ATTORNEY GENERAL (SOCIETY FOR THE PROTECTION OF UNBORN CHILDREN (IRELAND) LTD) v OPEN DOOR COUNSELLING LTD (1989)

As a result of proceedings instituted by the plaintiff the High Court granted a declaration that the activities of the defendant in counselling pregnant women within the jurisdiction of this State to travel abroad to obtain an abortion, or to obtain further advice on abortion within that foreign jurisdiction, was unlawful having regard to Article 40.3.3° of the Constitution and granted an injunction accordingly. The defendant appealed.

Held, by the Supreme Court, that where the jurisdiction of the courts is invoked by a party who has a bona-fide concern and interest for the protection of the constitutionally guaranteed right to life of the unborn the courts would be failing in their duty if they were to refuse relief on the ground that no particular pregnant woman who might be affected by the making of the order was represented before the courts. The Attorney General, as the holder of high constitutional office, was an especially appropriate person to invoke the jurisdiction of the court in order to vindicate and defend the constitutionally guaranteed right to life of the unborn. The defendant was assisting in the ultimate destruction of the life of the unborn by abortion which was contrary to Article 40.3.3° of the Constitution. No implied or unenumerated constitutional right to information about the availability of a service of abortion outside the State existed. If such a right did exist and was availed of it would have the direct consequence of destroying the expressly guaranteed right to life of the unborn.[5]

CASE 17 AUGHEY v IRELAND (1989)

The *Garda Síochána Act 1924*, as amended, provided for the establishment of associations for the various ranks of the Garda Síochána below the rank of surgeon for the purpose of representing members of the Garda Síochána in all matters affecting their welfare and efficiency. Every association so established shall be independent of, and unassociated with, any body or person outside the Garda Síochána. It was also provided that it was not lawful for a member of the Garda Síochána to be, or become, a member of any trade union or of any association established other than an association established under this statute of which the objects were to control or influence the pay, pensions or conditions of service of any police force. The plaintiff member of the Garda Síochána sought a declaration that this prohibition was an unconstitutional interference with freedom of association.

Held, by the Supreme Court, in dismissing the action, that while the statute did not prohibit members of the Garda Síochána forming or becoming members of a trade union or any other association provided that the objects were not 'to control or influence pay, pensions, or conditions of service of themselves or any police force', the statutory exclusion of such objects from any association or union of members of the Garda Síochána amounted to a permissible regulation and control of the constitutional right to form associations because the excluded areas were of particular sensitivity in a police force and of serious public interest.

CASE 18 BANK OF IRELAND v CAFFIN (1971)

The testator married in England in 1928, and in 1956 an English court granted him a divorce. Later he came to live in Ireland and married. On his death the question arose as to which of his 'widows' was the spouse for the purposes of the *Succession Act 1965* which provides that should a testator leave a spouse and no children the spouse is entitled as of right to one half of the estate.

Held, by the High Court, that prior to the establishment of the Irish Free State in 1921 the courts in Ireland had applied the common law rule that recognised a decree of divorce *a vinculo matrimonii* pronounced by a court of a foreign country in which both parties were then domiciled. Since this rule was not inconsistent with the Constitution of the Irish Free State or the Constitution of Ireland it continued in force. Accordingly, the spouse of the marriage celebrated in Ireland was the spouse for the purposes of succession law.[6]

CASE 19 BEAMISH AND CRAWFORD LTD v CROWLEY (1969)

The plaintiff was a brewer in Cork and owned the defendant's licensed premises. A term of the tenancy provided that the licensee only sell alcohol supplied by the brewer. When an injunction was sought to prevent the defendant breaching the tenancy it was pleaded that the alcohol supplied was not of merchantable quality. The plaintiff served notice that the trial be held in Dublin to which the defendant objected.

Held, by the Supreme Court, in directing that the trial be held in Cork, that the possibility of adverse publicity was not to be taken into consideration since the Constitution provided, apart from certain exceptions, that publicity was inseparable from the administration of justice.

CASE 20 BEECHAMS GROUP LTD v BRISTOL MEYERS CO.
(1983)

An appeal was made to the High Court from a decision of the Controller of Patents. It sought to bring a further appeal to the Supreme Court. The *Patents Act 1964* permitted appeals on questions of law under certain sections of that statute but not under the section in question.

Held, by the Supreme Court, that no appeal lay. It was open to the Oireachtas, by virtue of Article 34.4.3° of the Constitution, to curtail the appellate jurisdiction of the Supreme Court provided this was done in clear and unambiguous language.

CASE 21 IN RE BLAKE, DECEASED (1955)

The testator bequeathed a legacy in trust towards the maintenance and education of grandchildren provided they were reared as Roman Catholics.

Held, by the High Court, that the condition on which the trust legacy was given was contrary to public policy and was void in that it attempted to restrict the right and duty of parents to educate their children as guaranteed in Article 42 of the Constitution.

CASE 22 BLAKE v ATTORNEY GENERAL (1982)

The plaintiff was the landlord of premises to which the *Rent Restrictions (Amendment) Act 1960*, as amended, applied. These statutes restricted any increase in the rent and restricted the recovery of 'controlled dwellings'. The plaintiff claimed these provisions constituted an unjust attack on property rights contrary to Article 40.3.2° of the Constitution.

Held, by the Supreme Court, in finding these provisions unconstitutional, that the prohibition on increases in rent was a restriction of the property rights of one group of citizens for the benefit of another group of citizens which was done without compensation and without regard to the financial capacity, or the financial needs, of either group. The legislation gave no opportunity for rent review and provided no limitation on the period of restriction. The restriction on the landlord's right to recover possession of controlled dwellings was also condemned an an unjust attack on the landlord's property rights.[7]

CASE 23 BOLAND v AN TAOISEACH (1974)

A conference was held between the Irish and British Governments. In an issued communiqué the Irish Government fully accepted and solemnly declared that there could be no change in the status of Northern Ireland until a majority of the people of Northern Ireland desired a change in that status. A formal agreement, incorporating this statement, was to be signed later and registered with the United Nations. The plaintiff sought an injunction to restrain the government from implementing the communiqué and from entering into any agreement which would, it was claimed, limit the exercise of sovereignty over any portion of the national territory, or which would prejudice the right of the Oireachtas and Government of Ireland to exercise jurisdiction over the whole of the national territory.

Held, by the Supreme Court, in refusing the injunction, that this declaration of the government owed its existence to an exercise of the executive power of government and that the courts had no power under the Constitution, because of the doctrine of the separation of powers, to review the stated policy of the government.

CASE 24 BRENDAN DUNNE LTD v FITZPATRICK (1958)

The plaintiff carried on business and agreed with staff to open late on occasional evenings. When members of a trade union, objecting to the late openings, picketed the premises and paraded in an adjacent street with placards an injunction to prevent the picketing was sought.

Held, by the High Court, though deciding the case on other grounds, that the action in parading around with placards was not protected by Article 40.6.1° of the Constitution because the right to freely express convictions and opinions could only be exercised subject to there being no risk of a breach of the public peace.

CASE 25 BRENNAN v ATTORNEY GENERAL (1984)

The plaintiff owned a farm with a rateable valuation. This valuation was made under the *Valuation Acts 1852–1864* by reference to the average price of certain crops in the years 1849–1852 and once made could not be altered. The valuation determined the liability for various local taxes. The plaintiff claimed this method of valuation was unconstitutional.

Held, by the Supreme Court, that the use of the 1852 valuation long after the lack of uniformity, inconsistencies and anomalies had been established and methods of agricultural production had changed, was an unjust attack on the plaintiff's property rights in that the plaintiff with poor land was paying more than neighbours with better land. The absence of any review procedure was a further unjust attack on property rights. In the assessment of local taxes reasonable uniformity of valuation was essential to justice.

CASE 26 BROWNE v ATTORNEY GENERAL (1991)

Sections 117 and 120 of the *Income Tax Act 1967* provide, subject to numerous qualifications and refinements, that income tax is payable by the beneficiary on expenses incurred by a body corporate on the provision for certain classes of employees of living or other accommodation, of entertainment, of domestic or other services or of other benefits or facilities of whatever nature save to the extent that the expense so incurred related wholly, exclusively and necessarily to the performance by the employee of the duties of employment. These provisions applied only to employees whose employment for a particular year of assessment was £15,000 or more. Section 4 of the *Finance Act 1982* provides that every employee to whom a motor car is entrusted for the purposes of his employer's business and who is not effectively prohibited from using it for his private purpose was liable to tax annually on a sum which, subject to a variety of adjustments and refinements, is equal to one-fifth of the original market value of the car. This section applies to all employees to whom a car is made available by reason of their employment without reference to the amount of their annual emoluments. The plaintiff was a sales representative whose nature of work and terms of employment involved him in calling at regular intervals on customers or potential customers scattered throughout a wide area which, for all practical purposes, made the use of a motor car essential. He was provided with a motor car by his employer and was permitted to use this car otherwise than for the employer's business. The plaintiff on being taxed for this benefit challenged the constitutionality of these provisions on the ground that it interfered with the right to earn a livelihood and the tax was ill targeted, discriminatory and arbitrary.

Held, by the High Court, in dismissing the claim, that the tax charged did not impede the constitutional right to earn a livelihood in that it was not imposed on a business activity but on the availability of a car for private use. If the tax on benefits appeared to create an unusual burden for the parties then those who created the circumstances, in this case the employer, and not the legislation are answerable for any resulting injustice. It was the special circumstances of the individuals or the particular arrangements which created the anomalies that appeared to exist. These circumstances were not a ground for condemning the legislation as being unconstitutional.

CASE 27 BUCKLEY v ATTORNEY GENERAL (1950)

The trustees of Sinn Féin, unable to determine the ownership of certain monies, lodged these in the High Court. The plaintiff brought an action seeking the payment of these monies. While the action was pending in the courts the Oireachtas enacted the *Sinn Féin Funds Act 1947*, which provided, *inter alia*, that the action should be stayed, and that the High Court, on an application made on behalf of the Attorney General, make an order dismissing the action and directing that the monies be disposed of in the manner laid down by the statute.

Held, by the Supreme Court, in declaring the statute unconstitutional as an unwarrantable interference by the Oireachtas with the operation of the courts in a purely judicial domain, and as such contrary to the constitutional doctrine of the separation of powers. It also infringed the right to private property. While the Oireachtas may delimit property rights when the common good requires, it was open to the courts to review any such delimitation.

CASE 28 BURKE v BURKE (1951)

The testatrix left property on trust for the maintenance, education in Ireland and upbringing as a Roman Catholic of a named minor. The selection of a Roman Catholic school to be attended by the minor was in the absolute discretion of the trustees.

Held, by the High Court, that the direction regarding the selection of the school was null and void since it abrogated parental authority and the right and duty of education guaranteed to the family under Article 42 of the Constitution.

CASE 29 BYRNE v IRELAND (1972)

The plaintiff was injured by reason of a subsidence of a footpath where a trench had been excavated and refilled by persons employed in the Department of Posts and Telegraphs. An action for negligence was brought against 'Ireland' and the Attorney General.

Held, by the Supreme Court, that the former immunity from action enjoyed by the crown did not transfer to the State in Ireland after 1922 and therefore was not continued by the Constitution of Ireland. Under the Constitution, the State is a juristic person vicariously liable for the wrongful acts of its servants committed in the course of their employment.

CASE 30 CAFOLLA v ATTORNEY GENERAL (1985)

The plaintiff was a licensed amusement caterer and was convicted of exceed-ing the stake limits as permitted by section 14 of the *Gaming and Lotteries Act 1956*, as amended. When challenging the constitutionality of the section it was accepted that the imposition of limits on the stake to be wagered and the prizes to be won was constitutionally valid when enacted, but due to events such as inflation which had occurred since the law was enacted, the section then operated to infringe the plaintiff's constitutional right to earn a livelihood.

Held, by the Supreme Court, in upholding the section, that the provisions that the common good required a strict control on the provisions of facilities for gaming in amusement halls.

CASE 31 CAHILL v SUTTON (1980)

When the plaintiff sued the defendant for damages for negligence for per-sonal injuries it was pleaded that the action was barred by section 11 of the *Statute of Limitations 1957* in that it had been commenced after the expiration of three years from the date on which the alleged negligence had occurred. The plaintiff then challenged the constitutionality of the section on the ground that it contained no exception in favour of an injured person who did not become aware of the facts on which a claim could be based until after the expiry of the limitation period, or until a short time before its expiry. A successful challenge would not benefit the plaintiff because it was admitted that she had always known all the facts necessary to enable her to institute proceedings.

Held, by the Supreme Court, in dismissing the action, that as the plaintiff's challenge was based solely on the absence of statutory provisions which, if present, would not be applicable to the facts of her claim, she could not establish that any right of hers had been infringed or was threatened by the absence of such provision. Accordingly, the plaintiff had failed to establish the *locus standi* necessary to invoke the jurisdiction of the courts to deter-mine the validity of a law having regard to the provisions of the Constitution.

CASE 32 CASHMAN v ATTORNEY GENERAL (1990)

The *Betting Act 1931* provides for a register of bookmaking offices. A licensed bookmaker applied for a certificate that his premises were suitable for regis-tration. The plaintiff objected on the ground that there were already an excessive number of registered premises in the district. The application was refused and the bookmaker appealed to the District Court. The statute provided that on the appeal the Garda Superintendent and the Revenue Commissioners and no other person shall be entitled to be heard in opposition to the appeal. Because the plaintiff could neither be heard nor adduce evidence at the appeal he claimed that the statutory provision was inconsistent with the Constitution as being an impermissible interference in the judicial domain.

Held, by the High Court, that the restriction imposed on the District Court by limiting the persons who may be heard was an impermissible interference in the judicial domain by the legislature. While the deletion from the section of the words 'no other person' would not grant the plaintiff a statutory right to be heard, it would leave to the District Court a jurisdiction to determine what rights, if any, it would accord to the plaintiff on the hearing of the appeal.

CASE 33 CENTRAL DUBLIN DEVELOPMENT ASSOCIATION v ATTORNEY GENERAL (1975)

The *Local Government (Planning and Development) Act 1963* makes provision, in the interest of the common good, for the proper planning and development of cities, towns and other areas. A planning authority is obliged to make a plan for its area and permission is necessary for any development. The plaintiffs challenged the constitutionality of the statute on the grounds that it constituted an unjust attack on property rights.

Held, by the High Court, that good urban planning was essential for the common good and that the statute was not an unjust attack on property rights. Any opinion of the planning authorities could be reviewed by the courts.

CASE 34 CITYVIEW PRESS LTD v AN CHOMHAIRLE OILIÚNA (1980)

An Comhairle Oiliúna (AnCo) was established by the *Industrial Training Authority Act 1967* for the better training of persons in industry. Section 21 empowered the authority, for the purposes of meeting its expenses, to impose a levy on employers in designated industries. A levy was made on the plaintiff company, an employer in the printing industry. The section was challenged on the ground that the power to impose a levy was an unconstitutional delegation of legislative power to an executive body.

Held, by the Supreme Court, that the section was not an unconstitutional delegation of legislative power in contravention of Article 15 of the Constitution. The section contained a clear declaration of legislative policy by the

Oireachtas and provided each House of the Oireachtas with an opportunity to annul a levy order.

CASE 35 CLANCY v IRELAND (1989)

The *Offences Against the State (Amendment) Act 1985* provides machinery whereby the Minister for Justice, when of opinion that money held in a bank account is the property of an unlawful organisation, may without prior notice to the account holder freeze the money and cause it to be paid into the High Court. An unlawful organisation includes organisations which encourage or advocate the commission of treason, which raise or maintain a military or armed force in contravention of the Constitution or which seek to procure a change in the Constitution by force, violence or other unconstitutional means. A person claiming to be the owner of such money may apply within six months to the High Court for a direction that the money, together with interest and compensation for any loss, be paid to him. Where the court is satisfied that that person is the owner it can make an order accordingly. In such proceedings the onus of proof is on the applicant. Where no application is brought, or where such an application is dismissed, the Minister may apply *ex parte* to the High Court for an order directing that the money be paid to the State. The Minister for Justice, acting under the powers contained in the statute, ordered a bank to pay money standing to the credit of a particular account into the High Court to be dealt with pursuant to the provisions of the statute. The plaintiff claimed to be the owner of such money and challenged the constitutionality of the statute.

Held, by the High Court, that the statutory scheme did not amount to confiscation of the property. The provision of a fair hearing and the payment of compensation rebutted the suggestion that the statute was an unjust attack on private property. The statute constituted a permissible delimitation of property rights in the interests of the common good.

CASE 36 IN RE PHILIP CLARKE (1950)

The *Mental Treatment Act 1945*, section 165, provides that where a garda is of opinion that a person of unsound mind should be placed under care and control, the garda may take such person into custody and apply to the authorised medical officer for that person's reception into the appropriate mental hospital. When the applicant was taken into custody and detained in a mental hospital he argued that the section was contrary to Article 40.4.1° of the Constitution on the ground that there was no judicial intervention between his arrest and subsequent detention.

Held, by the Supreme Court, in upholding the constitutionality of the section, that it was of a paternal character designed for the protection of the individual and the promotion of the common good. The examination by responsible medical officers with the least possible delay satisfied every reasonable requirement.

CASE 37 CONDON v MINISTER FOR LABOUR (1981)

The plaintiff was a member of an association of bank officials who refused to be bound by the terms of voluntary national wage agreements. The association concluded a separate agreement with the banks. The *Regulations of Banks (Remuneration and Conditions of Employment) (Temporary Provisions) Act 1975* was enacted and could be brought into effect, and expire, by ministerial order. After the statute was activated an order prohibiting the payment by the banks of the increases was made. The plaintiff challenged the constitutionality of the Act as being contrary to Articles 34, 40 and 43 of the Constitution. While this action was pending the statute expired due to ministerial order and at the trial of the action it was argued that the plaintiff's claim disclosed no cause of action, owing to the expiry of the statute.

Held, by the Supreme Court, that where at the commencement of an action the plaintiff had a cause of action based on the validity of a statute, the expiry of the statute before the hearing of the action did not affect the exercise by the High Court, and on appeal the Supreme Court, of its constitutional power to review the statute unless the court is satisfied that a similar statute will not be introduced.

CASE 38 CONROY v ATTORNEY GENERAL (1965)

The plaintiff was convicted of the summary offence of drunken driving contrary to section 49 of the *Road Traffic Act 1961*. The penalty on conviction was imprisonment not exceeding six months, and/or a fine not exceeding £100, and the disqualification from holding a driving licence for a specified period. The plaintiff claimed that the section did not create a minor offence which could be tried summarily but was one which must be tried by jury in accordance with Article 38.5 of the Constitution.

Held, by the Supreme Court, that such penalties were not so severe as to exclude the offence from the category of minor offences which could be tried in a summary manner without a jury. The disqualification from driving was not in the nature of a punishment but the withdrawal of a right granted by the statute.

CASE 39 CONWAY v IRISH NATIONAL TEACHERS' ORGANISATION (1991)

All teachers, save one, of three national schools in a parish withdrew their services because of a trade dispute. The teachers' trade union issued a directive to their members in adjoining schools not to enrol pupils from any of the three schools at which the trade dispute existed. The plaintiff, a pupil at one of the affected schools, was prevented from having education for almost a year. She sued the teachers' union for damages for breach of her constitutional right to free primary education under Article 42.4 of the Constitution.

Held, by the Supreme Court, in awarding £7,500 damages, that the year's loss of schooling for the plaintiff who had a high degree of intelligence was detrimental and infringed her constitutional right to free primary education. The court awarded an additional sum of exemplary damages because the intended consequence of the trade union's act was the direct deprivation of the plaintiff of her constitutional right.

CASE 40 COSTELLO v DIRECTOR OF PUBLIC PROSECUTIONS (1984)

The plaintiff was charged before the District Court with two indictable offences. The District Justice conducted a preliminary investigation of those charges and being of opinion that there was insufficient evidence, discharged the plaintiff. When the Director of Public Prosecutions, in exercise of powers conferred by section 62 of the *Courts of Justice Act 1936*, directed that the plaintiff be sent forward for trial by jury on the same charges, the plaintiff challenged the constitutionality of the section on the ground that it offended the doctrine of the separation of powers.

Held, by the Supreme Court, in striking down the section, that when the District Justice was conducting a preliminary investigation the judicial power of the State was being exercised. The effect of the section was to render a judicial determination nugatory and accordingly the section constituted an unwarrantable interference by the executive in the judicial domain.[8]

CASE 41 COWAN v ATTORNEY GENERAL (1961)

An election petition to have the plaintiff's election to a local authority declared invalid was brought on the ground that he was disqualified by law in that at the time he was an undischarged bankrupt. The High Court assigned a practising barrister to be the election court to try the petition. The plaintiff claimed that the relevant statutory provisions, under which the election court was established, infringed Article 37 of the Constitution.

Held, by the High Court, in declaring the sections of the relevant law unconstitutional, that the election court was not exercising limited powers and functions because it might make findings which would affect in the most profound and far-reaching way the lives, liberties, fortunes and reputations of those against whom they were exercised. Also, because it might exercise criminal jurisdiction, it violated Article 37 of the Constitution.

CASE 42 COX v IRELAND (1991)

Section 34 of the *Offences Against the State Act 1939* provided that whenever a person was convicted by a Special Criminal Court of a scheduled offence and held an office or employment remunerated out of the Central Fund or monies provided by the Oireachtas or monies raised by local taxation, such person on such conviction shall forfeit such office or employment. Such person also forfeits a pension funded in the same way. Every person so convicted was disqualified for holding within seven years after the date of such conviction any such office or employment. The plaintiff, a qualified vocational teacher paid out of public funds, was convicted of scheduled offences by a Special Criminal Court. On his release the board of management of the school would have re-employed him in his original position but for the Minister for Education's enforcement of this section. Thus the plaintiff's post was vacated, he was ineligible for re-employment at that school or any school funded by the State for seven years from the date of his conviction, his pension and other such rights and expectations were forfeited and he lost his right to pay-related social insurance benefits for a like period. The plaintiff challenged the constitutionality of this section on the grounds that it was an unjust attack on his right to earn a livelihood and on his property rights.

Held, by the Supreme Court, that notwithstanding the fundamental interest of the State which the section sought to protect, the State was required by its laws as far as was practicable in pursuing those objectives, to continue to protect the constitutional rights of the citizens. Because of the wide and discriminate nature of the section the court ruled that it failed as far as was practicable to protect the constitutional rights of the citizen and was therefore invalid.

CASE 43 CROTTY v AN TAOISEACH (1987)

The *European Communities Act 1986* purported to amend the *European Communities Act 1972* by enacting into domestic law portions of a Treaty entitled the 'Single European Act'. The plaintiff contended that Article 29.4.3° of the Constitution did not authorise the ratification by the State of these provisions of the Single European Act which were intended to amend the three treaties which established the European Communities.

Held, by the Supreme Court, that Article 29.4.3° of the Constitution must be construed as an authorisation given by the State not only to join the three Communities as they existed in 1973, when the State first became a member, but also to join in amendments of these treaties so long as such amendments did not alter the essential scope or objectives of the Communities. An examination of these amendments concluded that they were within the original aims and objectives of the Communities, and as such were within the permitted authorisation contained in Article 29.4.3° of the Constitution.

Dáil Éireann approved the Single European Act, a Treaty, the purpose of which was to amend and supplement the three treaties on which the European Communities were founded. Title III of the Single European Act intended to place on a formal basis co-operation between the member states in the field of foreign policy. On ratification each member state's foreign policy would move from a national to a European level. The plaintiff sought to injunct the Government from ratifying this Treaty.

Held, by the Supreme Court, that in the conduct of the State's external relations, as in the exercise of the executive power in other regards, the Government is not immune from judicial control should it act in a manner or for a purpose which is inconsistent with the Constitution. Any attempt by the Government to make a binding commitment to alienate in whole, or in part, to other states the conduct of foreign relations, would be an unconstitutional diminution of sovereignty as being inconsistent with the Government's duty, conferred on it by Article 29.4, to conduct those relations in accordance with Article 5 and Article 6 of the Constitution. The injunction was granted.[9]

CASE 44 CROWLEY v IRELAND (1980)

All teachers, save one, of three national schools in a parish withdrew their services because of a trade dispute. The Department of Education arranged buses to bring children affected by the dispute to and from schools in neighbouring parishes. The plaintiff, a schoolchild affected by the dispute, was dissatisfied with these alternative arrangements and sought an order directing the provision of free primary education within the parish in accordance with Article 42.4 of the Constitution.

Held, by the Supreme Court, that while Article 42.4 conferred on the plaintiff a right to receive free primary education the sole obligation on the State was to 'provide for' such education and not to supply it. The evidence established that the State had not failed in its duty in this regard and the action was dismissed.

CASE 45 CULLEN v ATTORNEY GENERAL (1979)

The *Road Traffic Act 1961* created the summary offence of driving without insurance. On conviction, section 57 empowered the District Court, in addition to any other punishment, to fine the defendant a sum of damages which were to be paid to injured parties. The plaintiff was convicted of driving without insurance and the court awarded the injured party £606. The plaintiff challenged the section on the ground that the offence it created was not a minor offence within the provisions of Article 38.2 of the Constitution.

Held, by the High Court, that since the section did not limit the amount of the damages which could be imposed it could not constitute a minor offence which could be tried by a court of summary jurisdiction.

CASE 46 CURTIS v ATTORNEY GENERAL (1985)

Section 34 of the *Finance Act 1963* provided that, in the event of a party charged with fraudulent evasion of customs duties challenging the estimated value of the goods, the subject of the charge, he must give notice of such challenge to the prosecution. The District Court conducting the preliminary investigation in the matter must determine the value of the goods and such valuation was final and not appealable. At the subsequent trial by jury the value so determined was conclusive. The plaintiff was charged with this offence and the total estimated value of the goods was £31,000. If convicted, the plaintiff would be liable to be fined treble the value of the goods. The plaintiff challenged the statute on the ground that it offended Article 38 of the Constitution.

Held, by the High Court, is striking down the section, that the role of the jury in a trial on indictment was to determine disputed issues of fact. Since the issue of the value of the goods was material as to whether the accused had the necessary fraudulent intent the preclusion of the jury from determining such issue was in breach of Article 38. It was also invalid to assign an issue of fact for determination to the District Court in relation to an offence which was not minor. There was an absence of fair procedures in that a court on appeal against conviction and punishment would be precluded from reducing a fine because the value was unappealable.

CASE 47 D. v IRELAND (1922)

The plaintiff was raped and the perpetrator was convicted and sentenced to eighteen years' imprisonment. The plaintiff claimed that she had a right to be compensated by the State under Article 40.3.2° of the Constitution in respect of the injuries and pain which she suffered. The claim was opposed on the ground that the State had vindicated the plaintiff's rights by seeking to prevent crime, by punishing wrongdoers and by providing a civil remedy to the victim against the wrongdoer: to seek to impose an obligation to pay compensation for personal injuries by a criminal would make the State an insurer.

Held, by the High Court, in dismissing the claim, that the plaintiff had failed to establish a constitutional right to compensation from the State for injuries caused by a criminal.

CASE 48 DEATON v ATTORNEY GENERAL (1963)

The plaintiff was charged with smuggling offences contrary to section 186 of the *Customs (Consolidation) Act 1876* which empowered the Revenue Commissioners to elect between alternative penalties: either forfeiture of treble the value of the goods, including the duty payable thereon, or £100. The plaintiff claimed the section breached the doctrine of the separation of powers.

Held, by the Supreme Court, in deciding for the plaintiff, that the selection of punishment is an integral part of the administration of justice and as such cannot be committed to the hands of the executive as the section purported to do.

CASE 49 DE BÚRCA v ATTORNEY GENERAL (1976)

A list of jurors prepared under the *Juries Act 1927* consisted of ratepayers in a district and were persons aged between 21 and 65 years with land or premises with a rateable valuation in excess of a prescribed minimum. Women ratepayers had to apply to be included. The plaintiff was returned for trial by jury on criminal charges and before the trial challenged the statute as to its constitutionality.

Held, by the Supreme Court, that the exclusion of non-ratepaying citizens from a jurors' list was an invidious discrimination which offended Article 40.1 of the Constitution. A jury drawn from a panel so formed offended Article 38.5 of the Constitution by reason of its lack of representativeness. The conditional exclusion of women, which was based on sex alone, was an invidious discrimination and the virtual elimination of women from jury service resulted in a similar unrepresentativeness.[10]

CASE 50 DEIGHAN v HEARNE (1990)

The plaintiff was assessed for income tax for a number of years in which he failed to make tax returns. He neither appealed these assessments nor did he seek to extend the time to appeal.The Collector General issued a certificate to the appropriate authority and a notice of seizure of the plaintiff's goods was issued. The plaintiff challenged sections 184, 416 and 485 of the *Income Tax Act 1967* on the grounds that the exercise of such powers were an administration of justice and that they were harsh and unnecessarily stringent.

Held, by the Supreme Court, that the power to make an assessment in default of a return did not impose any binding liability unless and until it became final and conclusive by reason of the failure to appeal. Since there was no justiciable controversy between the plaintiff and the tax authorities the exercise of the challenged powers was not an administration of justice which was reserved to courts under Article 34 of the Constitution. Having regard to the rights of a taxpayer at various stages in the procedure the code was not unduly harsh as to amount to a failure to protect the rights of an individual under Article 40.3 of the Constitution.

CASE 51 DENNEHY v MINISTER FOR SOCIAL WELFARE (1984)

The plaintiff, a married man with two children, was deserted by his wife. Following the desertion he applied for payment, under the *Social Welfare (Consolidation) Act 1981*, as a deserted spouse. When this was refused, on the ground that it was payable only to deserted wives, the plaintiff challenged the statute on the ground that to provide a wife with a benefit which was not available to a husband, in the same circumstances, was an invidious discrimination contrary to Article 40.1 of the Constitution.

Held, by the High Court, in rejecting the claim, that the statute did not invidiously discriminate against the deserted husband but was a justifiable discrimination in favour of deserted wives on the ground of social function.[11]

CASE 52 DESMOND v GLACKIN AND THE MINISTER FOR INDUSTRY AND COMMERCE (1992)

Section 10(5) of the *Companies Act 1990* provides that if any person refuses to produce to the inspectors any book or document or refuses to attend before the inspectors when required so to do or refuses to answer any question which is put to him by the inspectors with respect to the affairs of the company, the inspectors may certify the refusal to the court and the court may thereupon inquire into the case, and after hearing any witness who may be produced against or on behalf of the alleged offender and any statement which may be offered in evidence punish the offender in like manner as if he had been guilty of contempt of court. The plaintiff had an interest in a company which was being investigated by the defendant. When the plaintiff attended before the inspector he refused to answer certain questions because he believed that the questions were outside the scope of the inquiry and the defendant certified his refusal to the High Court. The plaintiff challenged the constitutionality of the section.

Held, by the Supreme Court, that the High Court was inquiring into and hearing a matter which was criminal in character and that having regard to the punishment which could be imposed, imprisonment or fine without limit, that the summary manner of disposal of the matter was in conflict with the requirement of Article 38.5 of the Constitution which provided for a jury trial. The court severed the unconstitutional words from the section, i.e. 'punish the offender in like manner as if he had been guilty of contempt of court'.

CASE 53 DILLANE v ATTORNEY GENERAL (1980)

The plaintiff appeared in the District Court on road traffic offences. When the prosecuting garda withdrew the summonses, the plaintiff applied for costs which were refused. Rule 67 of the District Court Rules 1948 states that a District Justice has a general power to award costs and witnesses' expenses against any party to proceedings but may not make such award against, *inter alios*, a member of the Garda Síochána acting in the discharge of his duties as a police officer. The plaintiff challenged the constitutionality of this rule.

Held, by the Supreme Court, that the discrimination in favour of a member of the Garda Síochána was justified under Article 40.1 of the Constitution on the ground of social function. The rule did not violate any property right because the eligibility for costs could not be enumerated as one of the property rights protected by the Constitution.

CASE 54 DIRECTOR OF PUBLIC PROSECUTIONS v GALLAGHER (1991)

In the Central Criminal Court a jury returned a special verdict as provided for in the *Trial of Lunatics Act 1883* that the defendant was guilty of the murder charged against him but that he was insane at the time. The court ordered that he be detained until further order. Some months later when the defendant applied to be released the court ordered that the defendant be detained in the Central Mental Hospital until the pleasure of the Government of Ireland was known. The defendant claimed that the statute was constitutionally vulnerable as a purported exercise by the executive arm of government of a judicial power.

Held, by the Supreme Court, in dismissing the claim, that once the verdict was delivered and the order of detention was made the function of the court was discharged. The functions given to the executive by the statute, to care for the insane person and the protection of the common good, were not judicial in nature.

CASE 55 DOOLEY v ATTORNEY GENERAL (1977)

The *Prohibition of Forcible Entry and Occupation Act 1971* provides that a person who forcibly enters land or premises is guilty of an offence unless he is the owner, or if not the owner, he does not interfere with the use and enjoyment of the land or premises, or he enters in pursuance of a bona-fide claim of right. Owner is defined as the lawful occupier, or every person lawfully entitled to the immediate use and enjoyment of unoccupied land or premises, or any person having an estate or interest in the land or premises. When the plaintiff was charged with an offence under the statute she claimed that some of its sections contravened Article 40.1 of the Constitution.

Held, by the Supreme Court, in rejecting the claim, that the sections did not invidiously discriminate between owners and landless persons contrary to Article 40.1 of the Constitution in that the exclusion of the owner from the application of these sections excluded only the person in lawful occupation or the persons entitled to the occupation. All other persons, whether having, or not having, an estate or interest in the land or premises, were amenable to these sections.

CASE 56 IN RE DOYLE, AN INFANT (1955)

Section 10 of the *Children Act 1941* authorised the District Court to send a child to an industrial school where the parents were unable to provide for its support. Before making the order the court must be satisfied that the child's parents consented or that one of them consented and the consent of the other could be dispensed with by reason of that parent's mental incapacity, desertion or imprisonment. If the parents satisfied the Minister for Education that they were able to support the child the Minister was obliged to order its discharge. Unemployed and deserted by his wife, the father of a child consented to an order being made to take the child into care. The consent of the mother was dispensed with. When the father's circumstances improved later in the year he applied to the Minister to discharge the child which was refused because both parents were not consenting to the application. The father challenged the constitutionality of the section.

Held, by the Supreme Court, that the common law principle that a parent could not be bound by any agreement which had the effect of depriving the parent of the right to the control and custody of his/her child was preserved by Article 42 of the Constitution. Accordingly, section 10 was repugnant to the Constitution because it purported to permit a parent to deprive himself/ herself of the control of his/her child.

CASE 57 DRAPER v ATTORNEY GENERAL (1984)

The plaintiff, a citizen of Ireland entitled to vote at general elections for members of Dáil Éireann, suffered from multiple sclerosis and, because of her chronic physical disability, was unable to travel to a polling station to cast her vote at such elections. The plaintiff claimed that alternative facilities to enable her to vote in such elections should be provided.

Held, by the Supreme Court, in rejecting the claim, that having regard to the obligation of secrecy, the need to prevent electoral abuses and other requirements of the common good, the relevant law provided a reasonable regulation of such elections. The failure to provide facilities to enable the plaintiff to vote at these elections did not amount to an interference by the State in the exercise of the right to vote declared in Article 16.1.2° of the Constitution. Nor did that failure constitute a breach by the State of Article 40.1 relating to the equality of citizens before the law in that the provisions actually made were not unreasonable, unjust or arbitrary.[13]

CASE 58 DREHER v IRISH LAND COMMISSION (1984)

The Land Commission compulsorily acquired the lands of the plaintiff. The *Land Bond Act 1934* provided that an amount equal to the market value of the land was payable only in land bonds, as compensation. The plaintiff did not want land bonds and challenged the constitutionality of the statute.

Held, by the Supreme Court, in upholding the statute, that it formed an important branch of our social legislation and that compensation by disposable land bonds which carried a fair rate of interest could not be said to be an unjust attack on property rights protected by Article 40.3 of the Constitution.

CASE 59 E. R. v J. R. (1981)

A priest acted as marriage counsellor to spouses and claimed privilege in respect of communications made to him in that capacity when legal proceedings between the spouses were at hearing.

Held, by the High Court, that having regard to the guarantee contained in Article 41 of the Constitution that the State must protect the family, communications made to a minister of religion acting as a marriage counsellor are privileged. That privilege belonged to the spouses, and not to the minister of religion, and may be waived by the mutual consent of the spouses.

CASE 60 EAMONN ANDREWS PRODUCTIONS LTD v GAIETY THEATRE ENTERPRISES LTD (1973)

The plaintiff company was granted a new tenancy in premises owned by the defendant company by the Circuit Court pursuant to the *Landlord and Tenant Act 1931*. The defendant company appealed to the High Court which dismissed the appeal. Section 39 of the *Courts of Justice Act 1936* provides that the decision of the High Court on an appeal under this section of the Act shall be final and conclusive and not appealable. Section 39 of the 1936 Act was re-enacted by section 48 of the *Courts (Supplemental Provisions) Act 1961*. When the defendant company appealed to the Supreme Court it argued that the coming into effect of Article 34.4.3° of the Constitution was to cause section 39 to cease to be operative and it was not captured by section 48 of the 1961 Act.

Held, by the Supreme Court, that a decision of the High Court which determines an appeal from the Circuit Court cannot be the subject of an appeal to the Supreme Court because section 39 of the *Courts of Justice Act 1936* as re-enacted by section 48 of the *Courts (Supplemental Provisions) Act 1961* constituted a valid exception to the appellate jurisdiction of the Supreme Court in accordance with Article 34.4.3° of the Constitution.

CASE 61 EAST DONEGAL CO-OPERATIVE LIVESTOCK MART LTD v ATTORNEY GENERAL (1970)

The *Livestock Marts Act 1967* made the selling of livestock by auction an offence unless by licence. Section 3 enabled the Minister for Agriculture to grant or refuse a licence at his discretion, to attach conditions, and to revoke a licence where the holder committed an offence under the statute. Section 4 enabled the Minister to exempt from the provisions of the statute the conduct of any particular business, or business of any particular class. The plaintiffs challenged these sections as to their constitutionality.

Held, by the Supreme Court, that section 3 was constitutional on the ground that it must be presumed all proceedings, procedures, discretions and adjudications which were permitted by the Act were intended by the Oireachtas to be conducted in accordance with the principles of constitutional justice which required that the Minister should (a) consider every case on its merits, (b) should consider the submissions of any applicant or licensee, and (c) ensure that an opportunity be given to controvert any case that was made in favour of the course that the Minister intended to adopt. The court held section 4 unconstitutional in that the power of the Oireachtas under Article 40.1 of the Constitution to have due regard to the differences of capacity and social function in its legislation could not be delegated so as to exempt a particular individual from the operations of the statute.

CASE 62 ECCLES v IRELAND (1985)

The *Offences Against the State Act 1939*, which permitted the establishment of Special Criminal Courts in certain circumstances, provides that members of such courts are appointed and removable at will by the Government and that every member of such tribunal be paid such remuneration and allowances as was deemed proper. The plaintiff was convicted of capital murder by a Special Criminal Court and claimed that his trial was not in due course of law and in breach of Article 38.1 of the Constitution because such tribunal lacked judicial independence.

Held, by the Supreme Court, in rejecting the claim, that while a Special Criminal Court did not attract the express guarantees of judicial independence contained in Article 35 of the Constitution, it possessed, derived from the Constitution, a guarantee of independence in the carrying out of its functions. Any attempt by the executive to interfere with the judicial independence of that tribunal in the trial of a person charged before it would be an attempt to frustrate the constitutional right of such person to a trial in due course of law and would be prevented, or corrected, by the ordinary courts, such as the High Court and Supreme Court, established under the Constitution.

CASE 63 EDUCATIONAL CO. OF IRELAND v FITZPATRICK (1961)

Some employees of the company were trade union members and others were not. When the union members failed to persuade the others to join a union they endeavoured to force the company to compel these employees, by the threat of dismissal if necessary, to join a union. When this failed the union members withdrew their labour and picketed the company's premises. The company sought an injunction to prevent the picketing.

Held, by the Supreme Court, that while there was a trade dispute in existence, the provisions of the *Trade Disputes Act 1906*, which permitted peaceful picketing in furtherance of a trade dispute, could not be used to coerce persons to join a trade union against their will. The picketing was therefore unlawful and the injunction to prevent it was granted.

CASE 64 EGAN v MINISTER FOR DEFENCE (1988)

The plaintiff, an officer with twenty-four years' service in the permanent Defence Forces, held the rank of commandant and was a pilot in the Air Corps. The plaintiff contemplated retirement and the possibility of obtaining civilian employment. He was offered a post in private industry with emoluments greater that those enjoyed as a serving officer. If the plaintiff was allowed to retire he would receive a lump sum gratuity and a pension. The *Defence Act 1954* provides that officers such as the plaintiff may, with the permission of the Minister for Defence, retire. When the plaintiff sought permission to retire it was refused and he claimed, *inter alia*, that the statute which empowered the refusal to retire early to take up civilian employment was unconstitutional because it violated the fundamental right of an individual to use one's labour as one sees fit.

Held, by the High Court, in rejecting the plaintiff's claim, that the constitutional right postulated by the plaintiff could not exist in the circumstances of this case because he had entered into a voluntary agreement to serve in the permanent Defence Forces until retirement. Accordingly, the right to transfer his labour did not arise until the period of service ended by efflux of time or when given permission to retire early. The plaintiff had not sought to resign from the Defence Forces but to retire prematurely from it. This was not a right but a concession which, if granted, carried with it substantial financial advantages.

CASE 65 ESB v GORMLEY (1985)

The plaintiffs proposed to compulsorily erect three pylons on the defendant's lands, pursuant to the *Electricity (Supply) Act 1927*, as amended. In exercising its powers the plaintiffs made *ex gratia* payments in compensation. When the plaintiffs sought an injunction to restrain the defendant from preventing entry to the land, the defendant challenged the statute as an unjust attack on property rights.

Held, by the Supreme Court, in finding for the defendant, that while the provision of a national electricity supply and the consequential compulsory powers were a requirement of the common good, an *ex gratia* payment of compensation in an amount determined by the plaintiffs did not amount to a protection by the State against an unjust attack on the property rights of the defendant within Article 40.3 of the Constitution since it was clear that the provision of a procedure for compensation which could be independently assessed was practicable.[14]

CASE 66 FAJUJONU v MINISTER FOR JUSTICE (1990)

The plaintiff, a citizen of Nigeria, married a citizen of Morocco before they came to live in the State. After taking up residence three children were born: each was a citizen of Ireland. The plaintiff sought to restrain the defendant from prohibiting the plaintiff from residing in the State or taking any further action against him under the *Aliens Act 1935* or, in the alternative, that that statute was inconsistent with the provisions of the Constitution.

Held, by the Supreme Court, that where a non-citizen has resided for an appreciable time in the State and has become a member of a family unit within the State which consisted of children who are citizens those children, as citizens, have a constitutional right to the company and care of their parents within a family unit and generally that is a right which these citizens would be entitled to exercise within the State. While the parents who are not citizens cannot claim any constitutional right of a particular kind to remain in Ireland by reason of their having as members of their family children born in Ireland who are citizens, they are entitled to assert a choice of residence on behalf of their children, in the interest of those children. The court was satisfied that the State, pursuant to the powers contained in the statute, could force the family so constituted to leave the State provided, after due and proper consideration, the State was satisfied that the interests of the common good and the protections of the State and its society justified an interference with what is clearly a constitutional right. The discretion vested in the defendant could only be exercised with a full recognition of the fundamental nature of the constitutional rights of the family and any reason which would justify the removal of this family, consisting of five persons, three of whom were citizens, against the apparent will of the entire family, from the State must be a grave and substantial one associated with the common good.

CASE 67 FINN v ATTORNEY GENERAL (1983)

The plaintiff, prior to the submission of a proposal in a referendum held pursuant to Article 46.2 of the Constitution to the People for a decision, claimed that the proposal was repugnant to the Constitution.

Held, by the Supreme Court, that the provisions of Article 34.3 of the Constitution, which confers on the High Court and, on appeal, the Supreme Court, the jurisdiction to adjudicate on the validity of any law does not extend to a Bill expressed to be one to amend the Constitution which has been passed, or deemed to have been passed, by both Houses of the Oireachtas.

CASE 68 FISHER v IRISH LAND COMMISSION (1948)

The plaintiff was the yearly tenant of an extensive holding vested in the Land Commission. When the commission took steps to resume the holding, with compensation, the plaintiff challenged the constitutionality of that procedure.

Held, by the Supreme Court, that the provisions of the *Land Act 1923* which authorised the resumption for specific purposes of holdings vested in the Land Commission was purely an administrative act, and while all concerned were bound to act judicially, they were not administering justice contrary to Article 34 of the Constitution.

CASE 69 FOLEY v IRISH LAND COMMISSION (1952)

The plaintiff signed an agreement with the Land Commission for the purchase of land. A dwelling house was built on it and the commission, on learning that the plaintiff had not taken up permanent residence in it, warned that unless he did so they would consider retaking the land. When the plaintiff failed to take up residence, the commission demanded possession and he challenged the constitutionality of section 2 of the *Land Act 1923* which permitted the direction of the Land Commission as to residence.

Held, by the Supreme Court, in upholding the section, that the condition as to residence was not an abolition of private property within the meaning of Article 43.1.2° but a delimitation of these rights with a view to reconciling their existence with the common good and in accordance with the principles of social justice.

CASE 70 G. v AN BORD UCHTÁLA (1980)

A guardian of a child is entitled to that child's custody and proceedings may be taken by the guardian for the restoration of such custody. An adoption order cannot be made without the consent of the child's guardian, which consent may be withdrawn at any time before the adoption order is made. Where a consent has been refused, or withdrawn, the adopters may apply to the High Court which may under section 3 of the *Adoption Act 1974*, if it is satisfied that it is in the child's best interest, make an order giving custody to the applicant and may authorise An Bord Uchtála (the Adoption Board) to dispense with such consent. The mother of an illegitimate child is that child's guardian. The unmarried plaintiff gave birth to a daughter. While in hospital she was advised to place her child for adoption and when the child was two months old she placed it with an adoption society and signed a consent. Later, when her parents agreed to help rear the child, the mother withdrew her consent. In the meantime the child had been placed with a married couple. The mother issued proceedings to have her child restored to her and the married couple sought an order dispensing with the mother's consent.

Held, by the Supreme Court, that the mother had a natural right to the custody of her child, such right being a personal right under Article 40.3 of the Constitution. Such right was not absolute in that the child had a natural right to have its welfare safeguarded which was also a personal right within Article 40.3. The test in deciding an application under the statute was whether the mother had refused, or withdrawn, her consent capriciously or irresponsibly, or whether the welfare of the child overwhelmingly demanded that an order under the section be made. In finding for the mother the court held that the welfare of the child did not require that she should remain in the custody of the married couple and that the mother's consent had not been withdrawn capriciously or irresponsibly.

CASE 71 G. v G. (1984)

The parties, married in Ireland, went to live in the United States of America. In April 1978 the wife filed in the Massachusetts courts a petition for divorce. In February 1979 the wife, in separate proceedings, sought maintenance for a child of the marriage which was granted in April 1979. In accordance with the standard practice of the Massachusetts courts, the divorce decree, dated

May 1980, contained an order directing the husband to make maintenance payments in support of the child. The parties returned separately to this country. When the ex-wife claimed arrears of maintenance in the High Court the ex-husband contended that such proceedings were tantamount to implementing divorce and were in violation of Article 41.3 of the Constitution.

Held, by the High Court, in giving judgment for the ex-wife, that the order directing payment of maintenance for the child was the product of proceedings which were distinct from the divorce proceedings, notwithstanding the incorporation of that maintenance relief in the decree of divorce and that, accordingly, the provisions of Article 41 of the Constitution did not preclude the granting of the relief sought.

CASE 72 GLAVIN v GOVERNOR OF MOUNTJOY PRISON (1991)

The plaintiff was charged in the District Court with an indictable offence and following a preliminary examination was returned for trial by jury to the Circuit Court. He pleaded guilty and was sentenced to imprisonment. It subsequently transpired that the District Justice who had conducted the preliminary examination had continued in office after the date of his retirement: see *Shelly v Mahon* (Case 175). The plaintiff sought his release on the ground that the order sending him forward for trial and all the subsequent proceedings in the Circuit Court were null and void.

Held, by the Supreme Court, in ordering the plaintiff's release, that a trial in due course of law meant a trial in compliance with the law as it existed at the time the trial took place and that this extended not only to the trial on indictment but to all steps required by law as a preliminary to such trial. Every accused person had a constitutional right to have a preliminary examination in the District Court conducted by a judge duly appointed in accordance with the provisions of the Constitution.

CASE 73 GOODMAN INTERNATIONAL v TRIBUNAL OF INQUIRY INTO THE BEEF PROCESSING INDUSTRY (1992)

The Houses of the Oireachtas adopted resolutions that a Tribunal of Inquiry be established to inquire into certain matters of urgent public importance. The plaintiff company, because the matters being investigated impinged on its activities, claimed that the Houses of the Oireachtas in so acting had breached the Constitution in that the resolutions directed the tribunal to inquire into allegations of criminal conduct in that it provided for the trial of persons on criminal charges otherwise than in due course of law and without a jury contrary to Article 38; that in so far as the tribunal was to inquire into matters which were or could be the subject of civil litigation the resolutions were in breach of Article 34 in that they purported to direct the administration of justice otherwise than by courts established by law by judges appointed in the manner provided by the Constitution; and that coupled with the inquisitorial nature of the Tribunal the resolutions constituted a failure by the State to protect as best it may from unjust attack and to vindicate the good name and property rights of the plaintiff company in breach of Article 40 of the Constitution.

Held, by the Supreme Court, in dismissing the challenge, that an inquiry conducted as these resolutions provided, into the question as to whether criminal acts had been committed, even to the extent of inquiring whether criminal acts had been committed by a named person or persons and the reporting of the truth or falsity of such allegations to the Oireachtas, could not be construed or deemed a trial on a criminal charge within the meaning of Article 38, because the essential of a trial of a criminal offence is that it is done before a court or a judge which has the power to punish in the event of a guilty verdict. The inquiry to be held by this Tribunal had not that feature: it was a simple fact-finding operation reporting to the Oireachtas. The submission under Article 34 failed because it was not part, and never has been part, of the function of the judiciary in our system of law to make a finding of fact, in effect, *in vacuo*, and to report it to the Oireachtas. A finding by the tribunal either of the truth or falsity of any particular allegation which might be the subject matter of existing or potential litigation formed no part of the material on which a court who had to decide that litigation could rely. With regard to the State's failure to protect the good name and property rights the court had to assume, until the contrary was established, that the tribunal would conduct its affairs in accordance with fair procedures and the argument that the publicity attendant on the proceedings of the tribunal would make it impossible for the plaintiff company to have a fair trial by a jury on a criminal charge in the future did not invalidate the resolutions or proceedings before the tribunal: that was a matter to be determined later when criminal proceedings were initiated.

CASE 74 H. v JOHN MURPHY & SONS LTD (1987)

A father of a young family suffered severe personal injuries in the course of his employment with the defendant for which he received compensation. Due to the severe nature of his injuries the father was made a ward of court. The children, suing through their mother, claimed that their family rights protected by the Constitution had been breached and sought damages for the loss of non-pecuniary benefits which the father of a family bestows on his children.

Held, by the High Court, that while Article 41.1 of the Constitution confers on the family the right to protection from legislation and from the deliberate acts of State officials which attack or impair its constitution or authority, it does not confer on the family any right to protection from a negligent act which attacks or impairs its constitution or authority. While Article 42.1 impliedly confers on the children of a family the right to be educated by their father it does not confer on such children any right to protection from a negligent act which interferes with such a right.

CASE 75 HAND v DUBLIN CORPORATION (1991)

The *Casual Trading Act 1980* provides that no person shall engage in casual trading in a casual trading area unless the holder of a casual trading licence issued by the Minister for the Environment and a casual trading permit issued by the appropriate local authority. Section 4(6) of the statute provides that the Minister shall not grant a casual trading licence to a person who has been convicted of two or more relevant offences within a five-year period calculated in accordance with the statute. The plaintiff was a street trader and while at one time was the holder of the licence and permit was no longer the holder of these documents because of a dispute between the parties in the course of which the plaintiff had been successfully prosecuted at least twice under the statute and as a consequence had been refused a licence. The plaintiff claimed that section 4(6) of the statute was unconstitutional in that the penalty imposed, which had the effect of depriving her of earning a living, was a punishment out of proportion having regard to the nature of the offence.

Held, by the Supreme Court, that it was permissible for the Oireachtas to provide for strict control and regulation of casual trading in public places to which the public had access, as of right, having regard to the common good. The court was of opinion that where a person who engaged in casual trading had been convicted of an offence under the Act it was neither unjust nor unreasonable to deprive that person of the right to obtain a licence by reason of a conviction for a second or further offence. Since the plaintiff had failed to establish that the impugned section was an unjust attack on rights protected by the Constitution the action should be dismissed.

CASE 76 HARDY v IRELAND (1993)

Section 4(1) of the *Explosive Substances Act 1883* provides that any person who knowingly has in his possession any explosive substance under such circumstances as to give rise to a reasonable suspicion that he does not have it for a lawful object shall unless he can show that he had it for a lawful object be guilty of felony. The plaintiff was convicted of an offence under the section and challenged its constitutionality on the ground that the effect of the section was to infringe the right of an accused person to be presumed innocent and that it placed a burden on him to prove his innocence which infringed Article 38.1 of the Constitution.

Held, by the Supreme Court, in dismissing the claim, that all facts, including the facts on which the suspicion was based, must be proved beyond reasonable doubt and that if the court of trial had a doubt about the fact or inference or suspicion drawn from such facts the court had an obligation to give the benefit of such doubt to the accused and acquit him.

CASE 77 IN RE HAUGHEY (1971)

Dáil Éireann ordered the Committee of Public Accounts to examine the expenditure of a certain grant-in-aid. Section 3 of the *Committee of Public Accounts of Dáil Éireann (Privileges and Procedure) Act 1970* provides that if a witness before the committee should refuse to answer any question to which the committee might legally require an answer the committee might certify that fact to the High Court which could punish that person as if guilty of contempt of that court. The applicant was called as a witness, made a statement and refused to answer any questions because hearsay evidence containing serious allegations had been made against him by another witness which he was given no opportunity to rebut. The committee certified an offence had been committed and the High Court sentenced him to six months' imprisonment. The applicant appealed.

Held, by the Supreme Court, that the conviction and sentence should be quashed. The offence created by the statute was not the offence of contempt of court but an ordinary offence which because of the unlimited nature of the penalty authorised was not a minor offence within Article 38.2 of the Constitution and must be tried by jury. The role of the applicant before the committee was not that of a witness but was that of a party accused of serious offences, whose conduct had become the subject matter of inquiry and, accordingly, the applicant should have been accorded the right to cross-examine, by counsel if he so desired, his accusers and to address, again by counsel, the committee in his defence in accordance with the rights guaranteed by Article 40.3 of the Constitution.

CASE 78 HEANEY v MINISTER FOR FINANCE (1986)

The Minister for Finance was the administrator of the Prize Bond Lottery, established by the *Finance (Miscellaneous) Act 1956*, under which scheme redeemable bonds purchased for £5 participated in periodic draws for prizes. The plaintiff purchased a bond in 1961 and proved that £5 in 1961 was equivalent to £50 at current values. He claimed that it was unfair that bonds currently purchased for £5 should have the same chance of winning a prize as his long-standing investment.

Held, by the High Court, in dismissing the claim, that the plaintiff had suffered no injustice in that his bond had participated in many past draws and that it was a fallacy to compare his position with that of current purchasers. It did not seem appropriate to consider the matter under Article 40.1 of the Constitution in that the guarantee of equality was confined to citizens as human persons and did not extend to any trade, pursuit or other lawful activity in which the citizen might be involved.

CASE 79 HEMPENSTALL v MINISTER FOR THE ENVIRONMENT (1993)

In 1991 the defendant made regulations under the *Road Traffic Acts* which prohibited the issue of new licences to hackney owners. The following year the defendant made further regulations which repealed the previous regulations and which did not contain a similar prohibition on the issue of new licences. The plaintiff hackney owner claimed that by repealing the 1991 regulations the defendant had infringed the plaintiff's constitutionally protected property rights in that the unrestricted licensing of hackney cabs would have an immediate and devastating effect on his business.

Held, by the High Court in dismissing the action, that an amendment of the law which changes the conditions under which a licence is held and which, as a result, reduces the value of the licence, cannot be regarded as an attack on property rights because the possibility of change is one of the implied conditions which is an inherent part of the right in the licence, and that a change in the law which has the effect of reducing values cannot in itself amount to an infringement of constitutionally protected property rights. The plaintiff could not satisfy the court on the balance of probabilities that the effect contended for would result from the change in the law.

CASE 80 HOLOHAN v DONOHOE (1986)

The plaintiff was awarded damages for personal injuries by a jury in the High Court. The defendant appealed and argued that the Supreme Court had jurisdiction to substitute its own assessment of damages for that of the jury. The plaintiff argued that, should the Supreme Court consider the damages excessive, its jurisdiction was confined to ordering a new trial in the High Court.

Held, by the Supreme Court, in varying the amount of the High Court award, that the court had, by virtue of Article 34.4.3° of the Constitution and in the absence of clear statutory provisions to the contrary, jurisdiction to substitute its own assessment of damages in an appropriate case.

CASE 81 HOWARD v COMMISSIONERS OF PUBLIC WORKS (1993)

The plaintiff claimed that planning permission was needed for the building by the defendants of a visitors' centre in a high amenity area. The defendants argued that the provisions of the *Local Government (Planning and Development) Act 1963*, which required persons seeking to undertake a development within the meaning of these statutes to obtain planning permission from the appropriate authorities, did not apply to the defendants by reason of their being exempted from the application of that statute as a State authority. The Supreme Court raised the question whether the presumption against the application of a general statute to the State or to State authorities, unless the statute expressly or by necessary implication applied to them, was a principle of our law which survived the decision in *Byrne v Ireland* (1972) (Case 29).

Held, by the Supreme Court, that there was no principle deriving from the Constitution or from the common law which presumed that the general statute does not apply to the State or which presumed that a general statute applied to the State. In endeavouring to ascertain whether the State was bound by the statute the principle was to apply the ordinary rules of statutory interpretation and without any presumption either way seek to ascertain the true meaning of the statute.

CASE 82 HYLAND v MINISTER FOR SOCIAL WELFARE (1990)

The plaintiff was a married man with one child. Both spouses were drawing social welfare. By virtue of the *Social Welfare (No. 2) Act 1985* the amounts of such social welfare payments to which the plaintiff and his wife were entitled were less than the amounts payable to a single man and a single woman and their child living together. The plaintiff claimed that this provision breached Article 41.3.1° of the Constitution.

Held, by the Supreme Court, that the sole reason for the application of the impugned provision to the plaintiff and his wife when it did not apply to other persons with similar entitlements was the fact of their marriage. This penalised the married state and amounted to a failure by the State to guard with special care the institution of marriage on which the family was founded and to protect it against attack as was required by Article 41.3.1° of the Constitution.

CASE 83 IN RE J. H. (OTHERWISE R.), AN INFANT (1985)

The natural mother of a child placed it for adoption. The adopting parents applied to adopt the child and commenced proceedings under the *Adoption Act 1974* to dispense with the consent of the mother to the making of an adoption order. In the meantime, the mother married the child's father and the couple sought custody of the child.

Held, by the Supreme Court, that on the marriage of the parents the child had acquired rights under the Constitution as a member of a family. The State could not supplant the parental role of providing, under Article 42.5, for the child's education except in exceptional circumstances arising from a parental failure for moral or physical reasons. In a contest between the parents of a legitimate child, constituting a family, and persons other than the parents as to custody of the child the provisions of the *Guardianship of Infants Act 1964* are not the sole criterion for the determination of such issue. In the absence of exceptional circumstances that statute must be construed as involving a constitutional presumption that the welfare of the child was to be found within the family.

CASE 83a J. v DELAP (1989)

The *Children Act 1908*, sections 57 and 65, provide that a young person found guilty of a criminal offence may be detained by order of the District Court in a reformatory school for not less than two years and not more than four years which shall expire not later than his nineteenth birthday. The plaintiff, ordered to be detained in a reformatory until he attained the age of 19 years, which amounted to a period of three years and four months, claimed that this offence was non-minor and that Article 38.5 of the Constitution had been breached.

Held, by the High Court, that the reform school, staffed by teachers and others qualified in social work and having no connection with the prison service, had as its primary purpose the provision of long-term training and educational facilities to help young offenders make a new start in life and acquire a useful place in society. It was not intended as a place of punishment or a place of detention for short-term prisoners. An obligation to remain in such a place did not convert such a school into a penal institution analogous to a prison, nor could the period spent there be regarded as a period of imprisonment in the penal sense of that term.

CASE 84 KEADY v COMMISSIONER OF AN GARDA SÍOCHÁNA (1992)

The plaintiff, when a member of the Garda Síochána, was charged with obtaining public funds by false pretences. A *nolle prosequi** was entered with regard to these offences. Later disciplinary proceedings under the *Garda Síochána (Discipline) Regulations 1971* were instituted arising out of the same facts which had led to the criminal charges. An inquiry was held, at which the plaintiff was represented, which decided that the plaintiff was guilty of the majority of the charges and so reported to the Commissioner of the Garda Síochána who dismissed the plaintiff from the force. The plaintiff challenged the decision on the ground that the subject matter of the alleged breaches of discipline constituted criminal matters and that the hearing, determination and the imposition of the penalty of dismissal did not constitute limited functions and powers of a judicial nature envisaged by Article 37 of the Constitution and that accordingly these regulations were invalid.

Held, by the Supreme Court, that the inquiry related to breaches of discipline which could not be regarded as criminal matters within the meaning of Article 37. What was involved was a decision relating to a disciplinary matter in an important branch of the public service and that was an administrative matter rather than a judicial matter. The Garda Síochána could not properly carry out its essential function of preserving law and order unless there was an entitlement in the Commissioner to enforce discipline which necessarily involved the ulimate sanction of dismissal from the force for sufficiently grave breaches of discipline.

CASE 85 KEARNEY v MINISTER FOR JUSTICE (1986)

Rule 63 of the Rules for the Government of Prisons 1947 provides that every letter to and from a prisoner should be read, and if found objectionable, should be censored or withheld. The plaintiff was a prisoner and claimed that this rule was an unconstitutional infringement of his right to communicate and claimed damages for the breach of this constitutional right in that certain letters that had been addressed to him had been unduly delayed in delivery.

Held, by the High Court, in acknowledging the existence of a constitutional right to communicate, that where the State lawfully exercised its power to deprive a citizen of the constitutional right to liberty, the restriction on the right to communicate contained in the rule was reasonably justified on the ground of prison security. The non-delivery of certain letters, due to the unauthorised actions of a prison officer, was an infringement of the plaintiff's constitutional right to communicate and £25 damages was awarded as compensation.

CASE 86 KENNEDY v HEARNE (1988)

Section 7 of the *Finance Act 1968* makes provision for the estimation by the Revenue Commissioners of unpaid tax and for the recovery of such tax where, after notification, the taxpayer has not required a claim of non-liability to be referred to the Appeal Commissioners, or where the taxpayer has not furnished a declaration of the amount which the taxpayer is liable to remit, together with payment thereof. Another statute applies this section to the recovery of tax for which an employer is liable and section 485 of the *Income Tax Act 1967* provides for the issuing of a certificate to the county registrar or sheriff of the county in which the defaulting taxpayer resides or carries on a business and for the subsequent seizure of the goods of such person. The Revenue Commissioners estimated the amount of unpaid tax due by the plaintiff in respect of employees. The plaintiff did not exercise, within the statutory period, the rights accorded under section 7 and the tax accordingly became recoverable. However, at a later date, the plaintiff made a declaration of liability, together with payment of the amount due, but at that time the computerised machinery of enforcement had been set in motion. A section 485 notice was subsequently served on the plaintiff demanding payment and threatening distraint. The notice was withdrawn after the plaintiff obtained an order from the High Court preventing further action by the sheriff. The plaintiff challenged the constitutionality of section 7 claiming that permitting the use of section 485 procedures involved the determination of a justiciable controversy, namely whether the taxpayer was in default by the Revenue Commissioners and/or Collector General, which amounted to an administration of justice contrary to Article 34 of the Constitution.

Held, by the Supreme Court, that one of the features of a justiciable controversy was that two parties are contesting some matter, whether of fact or of law, with conflicting or contradicting assertions concerning it. In the proceedings envisaged by section 7 no such contest arose because there was not at the date of the issue of the certificate a controversy about whether any tax had been paid in which the Collector General decided in favour of one contender against the other. An amount of tax had been paid but knowledge of its payment had not been transmitted to the Collector General due to the error in the computer's operation. The court was satisfied that the decision by the Collector General that the tax had not been paid did not impose a liability on the taxpayer or affect any of his rights. What was capable of imposing a liability or affecting rights was the fact of default in payment of a levied tax.

CASE 87 KENNEDY v IRELAND (1987)

By authority of a warrant issued by the Minister for Justice the plaintiff's telephone was tapped for a number of months. Some time later the Minister issued a public statement admitting the tapping with the acknowledgment that there had been no justification for it. The plaintiff brought an action for damages.

Held, by the High Court, that the right to privacy was one of the personal rights of the citizen which flowed from the Christian and democratic nature of the State, was constitutionally protected, and included the right to hold private telephone conversations without deliberate, conscious and unjustified intrusion by the State. This right was not an unqualified one but was subject to the constitutional rights of others, the requirements of public order, public morality and the common good. The tapping of the plaintiff's telephone had been deliberate, conscious and unjustified, and was an actionable infringement of constitutional rights. While the reputation of the plaintiff had been vindicated by the statement of the Minister for Justice the damage suffered had been aggravated by the fact that the tapping had been done by the organ of the State which was constitutionally obliged to defend rights.

CASE 88 KING v ATTORNEY GENERAL (1981)

One of the offences created by section 4 of the *Vagrancy Act 1824* was that of being a suspected person or reputed thief loitering in a public place with the intent to commit a felony. The *Prevention of Crimes Act 1871* provided that in proving the intent it was not necessary to show that the person charged was guilty of any particular act, or acts, if his or her known character could be proved. The plaintiff was convicted of this offence and challenged these provisions as to their constitutionality.

Held, by the Supreme Court, that the offence conflicted with Article 38.1 of the Constitution in that it allowed evidence of the known character of a person to be used in proving guilt on another charge, which was contrary to our concept of justice. Further it offended Article 40.1 in that a suspected person could be prevented from doing certain ordinary lawful acts in a public place, which were perfectly lawful for other citizens to do.

CASE 89 KOSTAN v IRELAND (1978)

The plaintiff, the Bulgarian master of a fishing vessel, was convicted of illegal fishing and fined £100. In accordance with the mandatory provisions of section 221 of the *Fisheries (Consolidation) Act 1959* the District Court ordered the forfeiture of the fish and fishing gear, which was valued at £102,000. The plaintiff claimed that the offence was not a minor one.

Held, by the High Court, that having regard to the punishment involving the loss of property to this value the offence could not be regarded as a minor one in accordance with Article 38.2 of the Constitution. The court rejected the argument that the loss of the fish and gear was a secondary consequence of conviction. The forfeiture was a primary or direct punishment intended to be a penalty and a direct consequence of conviction.[15]

CASE 90 L. v L. (1991)

The parties were married in 1968 and the husband purchased a family home in 1970. The marriage deteriorated and the wife, under the *Married Women's Status Act 1957*, claimed that the husband held a moiety of his interest in the family home in trust for her.

Held, by the Supreme Court, that to extend the common law doctrine of resulting trust which applied, where one spouse made contributions towards the acquisition of a family home, to situations where one spouse made neither direct nor indirect contribution towards the acquisition of a family home, would not be to develop the doctrine but to introduce a new one and to do so would be a usurpation by the judicial power of the role of the legislature. The court ruled that it had no jurisdiction to award to a wife and mother any particular interest in the family home in pursuance of Article 41.2 of the Constitution.

CASE 91 LANDERS v ATTORNEY GENERAL (1975)

An 8-year-old boy, with an exceptional musical talent, was offered large sums of money to perform publicly. The family, after providing adequate safeguards, agreed. Some engagements were performed on licensed premises and the father, convicted of allowing a child under the age of 14 years to perform on licensed premises, challenged the constitutionality of section 2 of the *Prevention of Cruelty to Children Act 1904*.

Held, by the High Court, in dismissing the claim, that the purpose of the statute was the protection of children of tender years from exploitation and was not an attack on the right to choose a career contained in Article 40.3, or an attack on family rights contained in Article 41, in that public appearances were outside the scope of family authority. Because the prevention of the exploitation of young children was for the common good, it was not an attack on property rights.

CASE 92 L'HENRYENAT v ATTORNEY GENERAL (1983)

The plaintiff, the French master of a fishing vessel, was arrested for illegal fishing and released on bail. The *Fisheries (Consolidation) Act 1959*, as amended, provided that the District Court may authorise the release of a fishing vessel on condition that security was furnished. The plaintiff challenged the statute on the ground that the requirement as to security was an additional bail and was unfair having regard to the constitutional right to liberty.

Held, by the Supreme Court, in dismissing the claim, that the law was obviously intended to ease the position of owners or masters of fishing vessels who may have legal proceedings pending over a significant period of time and that the requirement as to security could not be regarded as additional bail or as unfair in that it was not conditional on, or in any way connected with, the granting of bail to the master of the vessel.

CASE 93 LOFTUS v ATTORNEY GENERAL (1979)

The *Electoral Act 1963*, section 13, states that the Registrar of Political Parties shall register any political party which applies for registration provided it is a genuine political party organised to contest a Dáil Éireann or a local election. The consequence of registration enables the name of the candidate's party to be inserted after the candidate's name on the ballot paper. Otherwise a candidate may have the words 'Non-Party' inserted. On the plaintiff's application to have a political party registered being rejected, a challenge as to the section's constitutionality was made.

Held, by the Supreme Court, that the right to have a political party registered was not a personal right within Article 40.3 of the Constitution. The prevention of the name of a candidate's political party from appearing on the ballot paper was not an infringement of the right of association guaranteed by Article 40.6.1°. The discrimination made by the statute, which allowed automatic registration to parties represented in Dáil Éireann when the statute was enacted, was not an invidious discrimination contrary to Article 40.1 of the Constitution.

CASE 94 M. v AN BORD UCHTÁLA (1975)

The *Adoption Act 1952* provided that the adoption order must not be made unless the applicants were the same religion as the child and, if the child was illegitimate, the same religion as the mother. The plaintiffs were married, the husband being a Roman Catholic and the wife a member of the Church of England. The wife, before the marriage, had a child of which the husband was not the father. The child was being reared as a Roman Catholic. When the couple applied to adopt the child they were refused on the ground that the provisions regarding religion were not satisfied.

Held, by the High Court, that these provisions were contrary to Article 44.2.3° of the Constitution in that they imposed disabilities and made discriminations on the ground of religious profession or belief.[16]

CASE 95 M. v THE MEDICAL COUNCIL (1984)

The *Medical Practitioners Act 1978* permitted the Medical Council, through its Fitness to Practise Committee, to investigate professional misconduct against a doctor. Should the Council, after due investigation, conclude that a doctor's name be erased from the medical register the doctor may apply to the High Court to have such decision cancelled. If no such application is made the Council may apply to the High Court for an order affirming its decision. The findings of the committee, and the decision of the Council, may be made public where the doctor is found guilty of professional misconduct. An inquiry was held into the plaintiff's conduct and when the Council decided that the plaintiff's name should be erased from the medical register the plaintiff challenged the constitutionality of the statute.

Held, by the High Court, that since the exercise of the power to recommend erasure by the Medical Council was not final and binding it was not an administration of justice contrary to Article 34.1 of the Constitution. The powers to advise, admonish or censure a doctor were limited powers of a judicial nature permitted within Article 37. Since the onus of proof in establishing misconduct was on the Council, and the doctor had adequate rights to be heard, the procedures were not unfair. The common good required the publication of facts concerning a person who carries out duties, or follows a profession, which may affect the public, and therefore the publication of misconduct was not an unjust attack on the good name of a doctor contrary to Article 40.3.2° of the Constitution.

CASE 96 IN RE McALLISTER (1973)

The *Bankrupt and Insolvent (Ireland) Act 1857* provided that it was lawful for a court in bankruptcy proceedings, where a person did not fully answer any lawful question, to commit that person to prison, there to remain without bail, until he subjects himself to the court. During bankruptcy proceedings the High Court was asked to commit the applicant to prison who objected, on constitutional grounds, contending that he was entitled to trial by jury under Article 38.5 of the Constitution and that the statute purported to exclude from the High Court the power to grant bail.

Held, by the High Court, in committing the applicant to prison, that the procedure was not a trial of a criminal charge. But the words 'without bail' which purported to exclude the jurisdiction of the High Court to grant bail were inconsistent with Article 34.3.1° of the Constitution.

CASE 97 MACAULAY v MINISTER FOR POSTS AND TELEGRAPHS (1966)

The *Ministers and Secretaries Act 1924* provided that the *fiat* (permission) of the Attorney General had to be obtained before legal proceedings could be validly instituted in the High Court against a Minister of State. The plaintiff intended to commence proceedings against the defendant for breach of contract and while the *fiat* was applied for, it was never formally refused, nor was it forthcoming. On the issue of proceedings without the *fiat* the defendant claimed that the proceedings could not be validly maintained.

Held, by the High Court, that Article 40.3.1° of the Constitution implied a personal right in the citizen to have recourse to the High Court to assert and vindicate a legal right and that the procedure of seeking a *fiat* infringed that right to litigate and was unconstitutional.

CASE 98 IN RE MacCURTAIN (1941)

A Special Criminal Court was established under Part V of the *Offences Against the State Act 1939* which provisions were activated by a Government declaration under that Act. The applicant was convicted by a Special Criminal Court of murder and sentenced to death. This tribunal sat in a military barracks and was composed of officers of the Defence Forces. The applicant challenged the constitutionality of the Act.

Held, by the Supreme Court, that section 35 of the statute which authorised the Government to determine the question of the inadequacy of the ordinary courts was not invalid having regard to Article 38.3.1° of the Constitution. That tribunal, notwithstanding that all its members were military officers, was not a military court but a lawfully constituted Special Criminal Court.

CASE 99 McDAID v SHEEHY (1991)

The plaintiff was convicted of an excise offence under the *Imposition of Duties (No. 221) (Excise Duties) Order 1975* which had been made by the Government in exercise of powers conferred by the *Imposition of Duties Act 1957*. This order was confirmed by the *Finance Act 1976*. The plaintiff claimed that the 1957 Act was unconstitutional because it provided an impermissible delegation of legislative powers by the Oireachtas to the executive, that the statutory instrument was thereby invalid and he sought to have the conviction quashed.

Held, by the Supreme Court, that the 1957 order was constitutionally valid by virtue of the intervening statutory provisions of the *Finance Act 1976*. The court would not pronounce on the constitutionality of the *Imposition of Duties Act 1957* because it was settled jurisprudence of the Supreme Court not to pronounce on the constitutional validity of laws when such pronouncement would be of no benefit to the parties to the action.

CASE 100 McDONALD v BORD NA GCON (1965)

The *Greyhound Industry Act 1957* empowered Bord na gCon (the Greyhound Board), under section 47, to exclude a person from being on any greyhound track or at any public sale of greyhounds. The plaintiff appeared to alter a material document and was summoned to a meeting of a committee of the board which investigated the charge. On the making of an exclusion order the plaintiff challenged the constitutionality of the section.

Held, by the Supreme Court, in dismissing the claim, that the committee, while bound to act judicially, was not exercising powers of a judicial nature within the meaning of Article 37 of the Constitution.

CASE 101 McGEE v ATTORNEY GENERAL (1974)

The *Criminal Law (Amendment) Act 1935*, section 17, prohibited the sale or importation for sale of artificial contraceptives. When the plaintiff attempted to import these devices they were seized by the customs. The plaintiff, a married woman with four children, who had been informed by her doctor that another pregnancy would have serious results and might endanger her life, challenged the constitutionality of the section .

Held, by the Supreme Court, that the section was an unjustified invasion of the plaintiff's personal right to privacy in her marital affairs contrary to Article 40.3.1° of the Constitution.[17]

CASE 102 McGIMPSEY v IRELAND (1990)

The plaintiff sought a declaration that the Anglo-Irish Agreement signed by the Irish and United Kingdom Governments in November 1985 was unconstitutional in that the recognition of the existing constitutional arrangement in respect of Northern Ireland violated Articles 2 and 3 of the Constitution and that the agreement fettered the power of the Government to conduct the external relations of the State under Articles 28 and 29 of the Constitution.

Held, by the Supreme Court, that the Anglo Irish Agreement was not inconsistent with the Constitution in that the only reasonable construction of the agreement was that it constituted a recognition of the *de facto* situation in Northern Ireland and that it did so expressly without abandoning the claim to the re-integration of the national territory. The agreement did not fetter the power of the Government to conduct the external relations of the State in a manner contrary to Article 29 of the Constitution.

CASE 103 McGLINCHEY v IRELAND (1990)

The plaintiff was extradited to Northern Ireland, tried and convicted though on appeal the conviction was set aside. He was then extradited to the State where he was convicted and sentenced to a term of imprisonment. Being apprehensive that on his release another application to extradite him to Northern Ireland would be made he challenged the constitutionality of Part III of the *Extradition Act 1965* and the *Extradition (Amendment) Act 1987* on the ground that these statutes did not contain adequate safeguards which would ensure that the arrest and detention of suspects, and extradition orders made in respect of them, would not take place in respect of warrants which were invalidly issued in Northern Ireland. It was also argued that the Constitution did not permit the Oireachtas to recognise by its laws the legal efficacy of laws enacted for Northern Ireland which had not been enacted by the Oireachtas.

Held, by the High Court, that the *Extradition Act 1965* contained safeguards in that it specifically allowed time for the institution of habeas corpus proceedings in the High Court in which the validity of warrants could be challenged. The *Extradition (Amendment) Act 1987* contained further safe-guards in that the Attorney General was now interposed at the beginning of the extradition process. The Attorney General was required to consider whether there was a clear intention to prosecute the person named in the warrant and whether such intention was founded on the existence of sufficient evidence. The court held that until the national territory had been rein-tegrated the Constitution imposed a limit on the powers of the Oireachtas to make laws for the national territory: until that time it could only legislate for part of the national territory. There was no constitutional restriction on the Oireachtas which would prohibit it from recognising the legal efficacy of laws enacted for Northern Ireland either by the parliament of Northern Ireland, the parliament of the United Kingdom, or by ministerial order pursuant to delegated powers and the lawfulness of authorities established by such laws.

CASE 104 IN RE McGRATH AND HARTE (1941)

In pursuance of Article 51, which provided that the Constitution, except cer-tain articles including Article 51, could be amended by the Oireachtas within a three-year period after the date on which the first President entered into office, the *First Amendment of the Constitution Act 1939* was passed. It altered, *inter alia*, Article 28.3 of the Constitution. A military court was established under the *Emergency Powers (Amendment) Act 1940*, which permitted the trial of persons charged with certain offences. The applicants were convicted of murder and challenged the constitutionality of various matters.

Held, by the Supreme Court, that the amendment of the Constitution had been within the powers of the Oireachtas. The provisions of Article 25.2.1° which provide that the President shall not sign a Bill until the lapse of five days does not apply to a Bill to amend the Constitution. It was not necessary to recite the resolution declaring a state of emergency in a statute provided the statute was expressed to be for the purpose of securing the public safety and the preservation of the State in time of war.

CASE 105 McKINLEY v MINISTER FOR DEFENCE (1992)

The plaintiff, a married woman whose husband was a serving member of the Defence Forces, alleged that by reason of the defendant's negligence her husband has been seriously injured in an explosion. Her husband's injuries rendered him sterile and impotent and when she sued the defendant for dam-ages for the loss and impairment of her consortium and servitium it was resisted on the basis that the common law right to claim damages for loss of consortium and servitium was a right confined to a husband claiming for such loss arising from injury to his wife and that no corresponding right in the common law existed in a wife to claim in respect of injuries to her husband. The plaintiff claimed that this right should be extended to her which would cure the inequality.

Held, by the Supreme Court, that this common law right being confined to a husband and not available to a wife offended against the guarantee of equality contained in Article 40.1 of the Constitution. Having regard to the constitutional protection of the family and marriage on which it is founded the court ruled that where a common law rule offended against the principle of equality in a marriage relationship the solution was to identify and declare the equality by positive rather than negative action. Therefore since a husband's right of action in respect of such an action was recognised, so also should that of the wife in respect of her husband.

CASE 106 McLOUGHLIN v TUITE (1989)

The Inspector of Taxes issued a notice to the plaintiff requiring him to prepare and deliver returns of income for certain years. When the plaintiff failed to make these returns he was sued, under section 500 of the *Income Tax Act 1967*, for a penalty of £500 for each year, making a total of £5,500. The plaintiff challenged the constitutionality of the section on the ground that the penalty was punitive in nature and that he had not been afforded a trial in accordance with Article 38 of the Constitution.

Held, by the High Court, that the Oireachtas intended to create a non-criminal penalty recoverable in civil proceedings. The absence of the vocabulary of the criminal law, the power to sue in civil proceedings without the sanction of imprisonment for non-payment and the continuation of the liability after death were indications of this intent.

CASE 107 McMAHON v ATTORNEY GENERAL (1972)

Article 16.1.4° of the Constitution provides that voting at Dáil Éireann elections must be by secret ballot. The procedure according to the *Electoral Act 1923* was that the voter's number on the register of electors was marked on the counterfoil of the ballot paper immediately before that paper was delivered to the voter. The counterfoil and ballot paper contained an identical number. The plaintiff challenged this procedure on the ground that it was not secret in that by matching the counterfoil to the marked ballot paper it was possible to ascertain how the voter had voted.

Held, by the Supreme Court, in finding for the plaintiff, that the words secret ballot meant a ballot which is completely and inviolably secret.[18]

CASE 108 McMAHON v LEAHY (1984)

The plaintiff, with four others, escaped from lawful custody in Northern Ireland, and came to live in the State. In 1975, when the four other escapees were arrested within the State on extradition warrants each claimed successfully that the escape was a political offence, or an offence connected with a political offence, and was released by the High Court. In 1983, when the plaintiff was arrested on foot of an extradition warrant which alleged that he had escaped from custody in Northern Ireland he claimed the offence was a political offence or an offence connected with a political offence.

Held, by the Supreme Court, that the plaintiff's escape from custody in Northern Ireland did not differ from the other four escapees and that since the State had either acquiesced in, or had opposed unsuccessfully, the release of the other four escapees on the ground that the offence was a political offence, or an offence connected with a political offence, Article 40.1 of the Constitution, which declared that all citizens, as human persons, were to be held equal before the law, would be applied to prevent the State from contraverting the plaintiff's claim.

CASE 109 MADDEN v IRELAND (1980)

The Land Commission set in motion the statutory procedure for the compulsory acquisition of the plaintiff's farm for the relief of congestion by publishing a certificate by the lay commissioners that the land was so required. A provisional list was published which stated that the land would vest in the Land Commission on the appointed day if not excluded in consequence of a valid objection. Objections to the provisional list were heard by the lay commissioners with an appeal on a question of law, or of value, to the appeal tribunal whose decision was final subject only to an appeal to the Supreme Court. The plaintiff's objection was disallowed and the price of the land, equal to the market value, was fixed at £128,000. The plaintiff appealed and the appeal tribunal refixed the price at £233,600 which would be paid in land bonds. The plaintiff claimed that in hearing an objection to the provisional list the lay commissioners were deciding justiciable controversies and that the lay commissioners and the appeal tribunal when fixing the market value of the land were exercising judicial power in contravention of Article 34 of the Constitution.

Held, by the High Court, that the functions of the lay commissioners were administrative in nature rather than judicial and though the fixing of the price was a judicial power it was limited in nature and as such was permitted to be exercised by persons or bodies other than courts under Article 37 of the Constitution.

CASE 110 MADIGAN v ATTORNEY GENERAL (1986)

The *Finance Act 1983* imposed a residential property tax on persons owning and occupying dwellings with an aggregate net market value exceeding £65,000. The tax was levied at the rate of 1½ per cent on the amount by which the net market value exceeded that amount. Exempted from the tax were persons whose aggregate household income did not exceed £20,000. To the owner's income was added the income of persons normally resident with the owner. The plaintiff claimed these provisions were unconstitutional as offending personal privacy and property rights contained in Article 40 and family rights contained in Article 41 of the Constitution.

Held, by the Supreme Court, in rejecting the challenge, that when examining the constitutionality of a taxation measure the court will not enquire into the policy or effectiveness of the law but will recognise the duty of the State to impose taxation which necessarily interferes with the property rights of affected individuals. If a tax measure produces hardship a difficulty in making payment is not a sufficient ground for challenging its validity. A tax on the occupation of property does not infringe any personal right to equality contained in Article 40.1, nor was the tax, imposed with reference to a high market value, unfair or an unjust attack on property rights. In providing for an aggregation of incomes, the State was merely recognising the reality that members of a common household generally contribute to the expenses of the home and such a provision did not amount to an invasion of privacy.

CASE 111 MAGEE v CULLIGAN (1992)

Section 3 of the *Extradition (European Convention on the Suppression of Terrorism) Act 1987* provides that no offence for which a person has been convicted outside the State shall be regarded as a political offence in relation to any warrant for the arrest of a person, issued after the commencement of the Act, where the offence involves the use of an explosive or an automatic firearm if such use endangers persons. Section 1(4) provides that the Act applies whether the offence was committed or alleged to have been committed before or after the passing of the Act. The plaintiff, convicted in

Northern Ireland of murder and attempted murder by the use of an automatic firearm in 1981, escaped from custody there and was arrested in this State and an order for his extradition was made in 1989 by a District Justice who was then holding office for one year pursuant to a warrant of appointment issued by the President in accordance with section 51(1) of the *Courts of Justice Act 1936* as applied by section 48 of the *Courts (Supplemental Provisions) Act 1961*. The plaintiff challenged the constitutionality of section 1(4) of the 1987 Act as contrary to Article 15.5 of the Constitution and section 51(1) of the 1936 Act as contrary to Articles 34 and 35 of the Constitution.

Held, by the Supreme Court, that section 1(4) of the 1987 Act merely made a statutory amendment to a developing jurisdiction concerning the definition of a political offence and did not declare any act to be an infringement of the law and therefore did not declare any act to be an infringement of the law which was not so at the date of the commencement of the Act. The court was satisfied that section 51(1) of the 1936 Act was an exercise by the Oireachtas of the express right to regulate by law the number of judges and their terms of appointment contained in Article 36 of the Constitution and that the appointment of judges of the District Court for fixed short periods was not inconsistent with any provision of the Constitution, nor did it in any way interfere with or limit their constitutionally guaranteed independence.

CASE 112 MAHER v ATTORNEY GENERAL (1973)

The plaintiff was charged with drunken driving, and in the course of the trial the prosecution produced a certificate which, by virtue of the *Road Traffic Act 1968*, section 44, was deemed conclusive evidence of the amount of alcohol in the blood at the time the specimen of blood was taken. The plaintiff was convicted and challenged the constitutionality of the section on the ground that it infringed the separation of powers.

Held, by the Supreme Court, that by giving the certificate this quality of conclusiveness the Oireachtas had invalidly impinged on the exercise of the judicial power and therefore the section was invalid.[19]

CASE 113 MAHON v MAHON (1978)

The parties, married in Ireland, emigrated to England and divorced there. Six years later the ex-wife obtained a maintenance order, and on the parties' separate return to this country, she sought to enforce this order in the High Court which her ex-husband resisted on the ground that since it had been obtained in consequence of a divorce it would be contrary to public policy, as enshrined in the prohibition on divorce in Article 41.3.2° of the Constitution, to enforce it.

Held, by the High Court, in enforcing the order, that the recognition of the maintenance order, which merely provided for the maintenance of spouses, gave no assistance to the process of divorce and was not contrary to public policy.

CASE 114 MAYO-PERROTT v MAYO-PERROTT (1958)

The plaintiff obtained a decree of divorce *a vinculo matrimonii* and an order for the costs of these proceedings against the defendant in England. The defendant came to live in Ireland and the plaintiff sought to enforce the judgment for the costs of the divorce proceedings in the High Court.

Held, by the Supreme Court, that the public policy of this country as reflected in the Constitution did not favour divorce *a vinculo* and since the order for costs was not severable from the divorce the action was dismissed. The courts of this State would not give assistance to the process of divorce by entertaining an action for the costs of such proceedings.

CASE 115 MEAGHER v MINISTER FOR AGRICULTURE (1993)

Section 3(2) of the *European Communities Act 1972* states that regulations (statutory instruments) made under this section may contain incidental, supplementary and consequential provisions as appears to the Minister making the regulations to be necessary for the purposes of the regulations (including provisions repealing, amending or applying, with or without modification, other law, exclusive of this Act). The defendant made regulations which amended a statute. When this regulation was enforced against the plaintiff it was claimed that this power to amend a statute was an impermissible delegation of legislative power. The defendant claimed that the making of the regulation was an act done or a measure adopted by the State necessitated by the obligations of membership of the European Communities and was in accordance with Article 29.4 of the Constitution.

Held, by the Supreme Court, that the power given to make regulations in the form in which it was contained in the section was necessitated by the obligations of membership by the State of the European Communities and was therefore, by virtue of Article 29.4 of the Constitution, immune from constitutional challenge.

CASE 116 MELLING v Ó MATHGHAMHNA (1962)

The plaintiff was charged with the summary offence of smuggling. Under section 186 of the *Customs (Consolidation) Act 1876* the Revenue Commissioners elected to press for a penalty of £100. The plaintiff claimed that this offence, having regard to the punishment, was not a minor offence under Article 38.2 of the Constitution.

Held, by the Supreme Court, that an offence which attracted such a penalty was a minor offence which could be tried summarily under Article 38.2 of the Constitution.

CASE 117 MESKELL v CIE (1973)

The company agreed, following negotiations with four trade unions, to terminate the employment contracts of some employees and to offer each employee immediate re-employment on almost identical terms. As a special and additional term the employee must become, and remain at all times, a member of one of the four unions. The plaintiff's contract of employment was terminated and he was not re-employed as he refused to accept the new contract containing the special condition. At the date of dismissal the plaintiff had been employed by the company for fifteen years and had been a member of one of the four unions. The plaintiff sued the company for damages for breach of his constitutional rights.

Held, by the Supreme Court, in finding for the plaintiff, that this attempt to coerce the plaintiff into abandoning his constitutional right to dissociate was a violation of the Constitution and the plaintiff was entitled to damages for such violation.

CASE 118 MINISTER FOR JUSTICE v WANG ZHU JIE (1991)

Section 52 of the *Courts (Supplemental Provisions) Act 1961* provides that an appeal shall lie by leave of the High Court to the Supreme Court from every determination of the High Court on a question of law referred to the High Court. In a case which originated as a consultative case stated from the District Court to the High Court, that court refused leave to appeal its decision to the Supreme Court. The defendant sought leave to appeal from the Supreme Court on the ground that the refusal to grant leave was a decision of the High Court which in itself was appealable under Article 34.4.3° of the Constitution.

Held, by the Supreme Court, that the section provided a regulated right of appeal which is subject to the final discretion of the judge of the High Court answering the consultative case stated and must be construed as effecting an exception to the absolute right of appeal from decisions of the High Court to the Supreme Court provided for in Article 34.4.3° of the Constitution.

CASE 119 IN RE MORELLI (1968)

Having decided a probate matter the High Court awarded costs to one party out of the estate in dispute and made no order as to the costs of the other party. When the party not awarded costs appealed to the Supreme Court it was contended by the other party that it had been the practice not to appeal on the issue of costs without leave of the trial judge.

Held, by the Supreme Court, in deciding that an appeal lay, that this rule of practice would impose a restriction on the exercise of its appellate juris- diction prescribed by Article 34.4.3° of the Constitution.

CASE 120 MOYNIHAN v GREENSMYTH (1977)

The *Civil Liability Act 1961*, section 9, provides that proceedings cannot be commenced against the estate of a deceased person unless begun within a two- year period of the death. In August 1966 a motor car driven by the deceased, in which the plaintiff was a passenger, was involved in a collision and as a result the deceased died. In August 1969 the plaintiff sued the deceased's estate for negligence and when the defendant pleaded that the action was barred by virtue of the section the plaintiff challenged its constitutionality.

Held, by the Supreme Court, that there was no failure to protect from unjust attack the property rights of the plaintiff, guaranteed by Article 40.3.2° of the Constitution, in that the State owed a duty to individuals interested in the early completion of the administration of the estates of deceased persons.

CASE 121 MUCKLEY v IRELAND (1985)

Following the decision of the Supreme Court in *Murphy v Attorney General* (Case 123) the Oireachtas enacted the *Finance Act 1980*, section 21, which provided that married persons who in previous years had not paid the appropriate tax, liable under the sections of the *Income Tax Act 1967* which had been impugned in *Murphy*'s case, would be obliged to pay the same amount as if these invalid sections had been valid during those years. The plaintiffs, a married couple, challenged the section as to its constitutionality.

Held, by the Supreme Court, in striking down the section, that it contained the same fatal flaw as those sections impugned in the *Murphy* case, which imposed a greater burden of taxation on married couples than on unmarried couples living together and was therefore an attack on the institution of marriage which the State was bound to protect under Article 41.3.1° of the Constitution.

CASE 122 MULLOY v MINISTER FOR EDUCATION (1975)

The Minister for Education established a scheme for the payment of salary increments to secondary schoolteachers with teaching service abroad by lay teachers treated as teaching service under the scheme. The plaintiff, a priest and a secondary schoolteacher with teaching experience abroad, had his teaching experience abroad ignored when having his incremental salary adjusted.

Held, by the Supreme Court, that the rule restricting the scheme to lay secondary schoolteachers was repugnant to Article 44.2.3° of the Constitution wherein the State guaranteed not to make any discrimination on the ground of religious status.

CASE 123 MURPHY v ATTORNEY GENERAL (1982)

The plaintiffs, a married couple, claimed that sections 192 to 197 of the *Income Tax Act 1967*, which aggregated their incomes for the purpose of assessment of liability to income tax, thus attracting a higher rate of tax, in comparison to an unmarried couple living together, infringed Articles 40 and 41 of the Constitution.

Held, by the Supreme Court, that the sections were unconstitutional because the nature and potentially progressive extent of the burden created was a breach of the pledge contained in Article 41.3.1° of the Constitution by the State to guard with special care the institution of marriage. Article 40.1 of the Constitution was not infringed in that the unequal treatment for income tax purposes between a married couple living together and an unmarried couple living together was justified by the differences in social function between the two groups.[20]

CASE 124 MURPHY v DUBLIN CORPORATION (1972)

The plaintiff owned land over which a compulsory purchase order was made. The plaintiff objected and the report of a public inquiry which was held was

made to the Minister for Local Government. When the plaintiff issued proceedings to invalidate the purchase order and sought production of the report
the Minister refused on the ground of public policy and being contrary to
the public interest.

Held, by the Supreme Court, that if the Minister's claim was based on
executive privilege a conflict existed between the interests of the State in the
exercise of the executive power of the State and the interest of the State in
the administration of justice and that conflict had to be resolved by the High
Court which was charged with the administration of justice under the
Constitution. The document, if necessary, would be inspected by that court
and once it was proved that the document was relevant, the onus of establishing that the document should not be produced was on the party making
that claim.

CASE 125 MURPHY v STEWART (1973)

The plaintiff wished to change trade unions. The second union agreed to
accept his membership provided the first union had no objection. However,
the first union did object. The plaintiff claimed that the refusal of the first
union to give consent to the transfer was an infringement of the right of
association guaranteed by Article 40.6.1° of the Constitution.

Held, by the Supreme Court, that the refusal of one union to consent to
the plaintiff's transfer to another union was not an infringement of the right
to form associations and unions.

CASE 126 MURPHY v WALLACE (1990)

The plaintiff was convicted of a number of betting offences and fined. When
the fine remained unpaid a warrant authorising distraint against his goods
was issued which was returned endorsed 'without the means to pay'. A
warrant was then sought for the arrest of the plaintiff under section 90 of the
Excise Management Act 1890 which empowered the Revenue Commissioners
to apply for the arrest of the person in default. That person was to remain in
prison until the fine was paid, or until such person was ordered to be liberated
or discharged by the Revenue Commissioners. Section 76 of the *Courts of
Justice Act 1936* limited the length of time during which such person may be
committed to prison to six months. The plaintiff challenged the constitutionality
of the section on the ground that it granted to the Revenue Commissioners, as
part of the executive, and not to the District Court, a discretion as to the length
of time during which a person committed to prison could be detained.

Held, by the High Court, that the existence of the discretion was fatal to the validity of the power. Granting such a discretion to an arm of the executive was a breach of the separation of powers.

CASE 127 MURRAY v ATTORNEY GENERAL (1991)

The plaintiff husband and wife were serving sentences of life imprisonment. They had no children and claimed that the absence of the facilities to procreate within prison was a denial of their constitutional right as a married couple to beget children. By the time of their possible release the wife would be unlikely to be able to conceive a child.

Held, by the Supreme Court, that while the plaintiffs constituted a family and had the right to procreate under Article 40.3 of the Constitution the deprivation of a prisoner's liberty by the State resulted in the deprivation of many other constitutionally protected rights. The provision of facilities within the prison to enable prisoners to exercise conjugal rights would place unreasonable demands on the prison service. The length of time which a person sentenced to imprisonment for life spent in custody was a matter which under the constitutional doctrine of the separation of powers rested entirely with the executive.

CASE 128 MURTAGH PROPERTIES LTD v CLEARY (1972)

When the plaintiff publican employed some part-time waitresses the trade union representing bar waiters objected to the employment of women and pickets were placed on the premises. The plaintiff sought an injunction to prevent the picketing.

Held, by the High Court, in granting the injunction, that although the picketing was in furtherance of a trade dispute it was unlawful in that its purpose was to compel the dismissal of the bar waitresses in breach of their personal right to earn a livelihood which was enshrined in Article 40.3 of the Constitution.

CASE 129 NATIONAL UNION OF RAILWAYMEN v SULLIVAN
(1947)

The *Trade Union Act 1941*, Part III, established a trade union tribunal with power, on the application of any trade union claiming to organise a majority of the employees of a particular class in a business, to grant a determination that such trade union alone should have the right to organise employees of that class. Where such determination remained unrevoked no other union could accept as a new member any employee of that class. When a trade union applied to the tribunal the plaintiff, a rival trade union, claimed that Part III was unconstitutional.

Held, by the Supreme Court, that Part III of the statute, by purporting to deprive individuals of the choice of persons with whom they might associate was at variance with the emphatic assertion in Article 40.6.1° of the Constitution of the citizens' right to form associations and unions.

CASE 130 NORRIS v ATTORNEY GENERAL (1984)

The *Offences Against the Person Act 1861*, sections 61 and 62, and the *Criminal Law (Amendment) Act 1885*, section 11, provided for the criminalisation and punishment of certain sexual acts. The plaintiff, a homosexual, challenged their constitutionality.

Held, by the Supreme Court, that there was no invidious discrimination under Article 40.1 in that the legislature could prohibit certain sexual conduct between males while not prohibiting the same sexual conduct between females. Freedom of association under Article 40.6.1° of the Constitution was not infringed. Because of the Christian nature of the State, and on the ground that the deliberate practice of homosexuality was morally wrong, damaging to the health of the individual and the public and potentially harmful to the institution of marriage, there was, in such circumstances, no constitutional right to sexual privacy.[21]

CASE 131 NORTHAMPTON COUNTY COUNCIL v A. B. F. (1982)

An English local authority sought the return to its custody of a child who had been removed by its father from England. Both parents were British citizens, had married and were domiciled there, where the child had been born. The father took the child to this country because it was proposed to have her legally adopted, which was permissible under English law, but which was against the wishes of the father.

Held, by the High Court, in refusing the order sought, that to grant it would have been a breach of Article 41 of the Constitution which recognised the family as the natural, primary and fundamental group of society. It was inconceivable that, because of his British nationality, the father of the child could not rely on the recognition of the family for the purpose of enforcing his rights as the lawful father.

CASE 132   O'B. v S. (1984)

The deceased while alive had a permanent personal relationship with a married woman. There was a child of that relationship whom the deceased had supported, reared and educated. The deceased was survived by that child, with whom he had lived, and two sisters and a brother. He died intestate.* The *Succession Act 1965* provides that if an intestate dies, leaving neither spouse nor issue nor parents, the estate is distributed between brothers and sisters equally. In such circumstances the child of the deceased was not entitled to any portion of the estate.

Held, by the Supreme Court, that the right of intestate succession was not a personal right within Article 40.3 of the Constitution and that the discrimination in favour of legitimate issue was justified by Article 41 of the Constitution as the statute was designed to strengthen the protection of the family founded on marriage.[22]

CASE 133   O'BRIEN v BORD NA MÓNA (1983)

The *Turf Development Act 1946* empowered the board to acquire compulsorily certain lands. When the board sought to acquire some of the plaintiff's land, he challenged the constitutionality of the statute on the ground that the board was exercising judicial powers.

Held, by the Supreme Court, that the board in making a decision to acquire land was not acting judicially but administratively in that the purpose of the statute was to permit the acquisition and development of bogland for the common good.

CASE 134   O'BRIEN v KEOGH (1972)

The *Statute of Limitations 1957* provides that an action for negligence resulting in personal injury must be commenced within three years. Section 49 of the statute permitted a minor to bring an action within three years of reaching majority but this exception did not apply if the minor was in the custody of a parent. The plaintiff, a minor in the custody of his parents, suffered personal injuries in 1963 and when legal proceedings were commenced in 1968 the defendant claimed they were statute-barred. The plaintiff challenged the constitutionality of the section.

Held, by the Supreme Court, that the section failed to protect and vindicate the property rights of the plaintiff, which included the right to litigate and was contrary to the guarantee contained in Article 40.3.2° of the Constitution.

The section did not conflict with the guarantee of equality in Article 40.1 in that the purpose of the section was an attempt to establish equality between the two groups.

CASE 135 O'BRIEN v MANUFACTURING ENGINEERING CO. LTD (1973)

The *Workmens Compensation Act 1934*, as amended, permitted a workman injured by an employer's negligence to claim compensation under the statute or to take legal proceedings. Should a workman claim compensation and wish to sue it must be done within one year. The plaintiff, injured in 1963, accepted compensation, and on commencing legal proceedings against his employer in 1966 was met with the defence that the claim was statute-barred. The plaintiff challenged the constitutionality of the statute.

Held, by the Supreme Court, that the statute did not discriminate against the plaintiff in that it gave the advantage of drawing compensation while giving the opportunity to take legal proceedings. The one-year period was not unreasonably short and did not offend Article 40.1 of the Constitution.[23]

CASE 136 O'BYRNE v MINISTER FOR FINANCE (1959)

A judge while in office paid income tax. The plaintiff, as executrix of his estate, claimed that these deductions were an attack on judicial independence and contrary to Article 35.5 of the Constitution.

Held, by the Supreme Court, that the purpose of Article 35.5 of the Constitution was to safeguard the independence of the judiciary from the control of the executive and not to exempt the remuneration of judges from taxation common to all. To require a judge to pay taxes on income on the same basis as other individuals was not an attack on judicial independence.

CASE 137 O'CALLAGHAN v ATTORNEY GENERAL (1993)

The plaintiff was convicted by a jury in a criminal trial on a majority verdict of ten to two. When his appeal against conviction failed he challenged the constitutionality of section 25 of the *Criminal Justice Act 1984* on the grounds that a unanimous verdict of a jury was an indispensable feature of the right to trial in due course of law and to the right to jury trial and it was not within the competence of the Oireachtas to provide for majority jury verdicts in criminal cases.

Held, by the Supreme Court, in dismissing the action, that the essential feature of a trial by jury was the imposition between the accused and the prosecution of a reasonable cross-section of persons who bring their experience and common sense to bear in resolving the issue of the guilt or innocence of the accused. A requirement of unanimity was not essential.

CASE 138   O'CALLAGHAN v COMMISSIONERS OF PUBLIC WORKS (1985)

When the plaintiff, the owner of land which included a prehistoric promontory listed for preservation under section 8 of the *National Monuments (Amendment) Act 1954*, employed contractors to plough part of the area occupied by the fort, the commissioners made a preservation order the effect of which was to prohibit extensive activities being carried out on the site. The plaintiff claimed that the section was an unjust attack on property rights in that there was no provision for the payment of compensation to owners of lands on which national monuments stood.

Held, by the Supreme Court, in rejecting the claim, that the property rights guaranteed by Article 40.3 of the Constitution were subject to regulation with reference to the common good, which plainly required that national monuments be preserved, and to social justice, which may or may not, according to circumstances, require the payment of compensation.

CASE 139   O'CALLAGHAN v IRELAND (1993)

Section 23 of the *Misuse of Drugs Act 1977* provides that where a member of the Garda Síochána with reasonable cause suspects that a person is in possession of a controlled drug he may without a warrant search the person and if he considered it necessary for the purpose to detain that person for such time as is reasonably necessary for making the search and may require that person to accompany him to a garda station for the purpose of being so searched at the station. A member of the Garda Síochána in exercise of these powers attempted to search the plaintiff and when he resisted was charged with the unlawful assault of a peace officer in the due execution of his duty. The plaintiff challenged the constitutionality of the section on the ground that this power of search was unprecedented and created a situation where the citizen's rights were uncertain and that the absence of clear directions as to the manner in which the search was to be carried out rendered the power unconstitutional.

Held, by the Supreme Court, in dismissing the case, that given the extent of the problem created by the misuse of drugs the Oireachtas was entitled to encroach on the personal rights of the citizen to the extent specified in the section if it was necessary to combat the problem. While an abuse of the power might taint any evidence obtained as a result of this abuse the mere fact that the power was capable of being exercised in an improper manner did not render the power of search unconstitutional.

CASE 140 O'DONOGHUE v MINISTER FOR HEALTH (1993)

The plaintiff, an 8-year-old boy with profound mental and physical disability, spent only six hours a week in educational institutions funded by the State. When he claimed, through his mother, that the State had failed to honour its obligation, contained in Article 42.4 of the Constitution, to provide for free primary education for him it was argued that, because of his disability, the plaintiff was ineducable, that scholastic education would be of no benefit to him and that all that could be done was to make his life more tolerable by attempting to train him in the basics of bodily function and movement.

Held, by the High Court, that there was a constitutional obligation imposed on the State by the provisions of Article 42.4 of the Constitution to provide for free basic elementary education for all children and that this involved giving each child such advice, instruction and teaching as would enable the child to make the best possible use of his or her inherent and potential capacities, physical, mental and moral, however limited these capacities may be. The State had failed in that duty towards the plaintiff who, on the evidence presented, was educable. The court awarded damages as recoupment of the expenses incurred by the plaintiff's mother in an effort to make good the default on the part of the State.

CASE 141 O'DONOVAN v ATTORNEY GENERAL (1961)

The *Electoral (Amendment) Act 1959* purported to revise the constituencies and the number of members to be returned to Dáil Éireann from each such constituency. The plaintiff claimed that this statute was unconstitutional.

Held, by the High Court, that the statute offended Article 16.2.3° of the Constitution in that it departed substantially from the ratio of members of Dáil Éireann to the population thus causing grave inequalities of representation for which no justification or genuine administrative difficulty existed. It offended Article 16.2.4° because when revising the constituencies the Oireachtas did not have due regard to the changes in the distribution of population.[24]

CASE 142 IN RE O'FARRELL (1960)

The *Solicitors Act 1954* empowered a disciplinary committee of the Law Society, on hearing a complaint against a solicitor, to strike the name of that solicitor from the roll of solicitors. On being so struck off, the plaintiff challenged the constitutionality of this power.

Held, by the Supreme Court, that the power to strike a solicitor off the roll of solicitors was an administration of justice in that the infliction of such a severe penalty was a matter calling for the exercise of the judicial power of the State. To entrust this power to persons other than judges was an interference with the proper administration of justice, which was reserved to courts established under the Constitution.[25]

CASE 143 O'G. v ATTORNEY GENERAL (1985)

The plaintiff and his wife obtained custody of a child in expectation of the making of an adoption order once the consent of the child's mother had been obtained. Before the making of the adoption order the plaintiff's wife died. Under section 5 of the *Adoption Act 1974*, the plaintiff as a childless widower was no longer a person in whose favour an adoption order could be made. Had the plaintiff had another child in his custody his right to an adoption order would have been subject, according to the same section, to renewed consent from the child's mother. The plaintiff claimed that the section was invalid having regard to Article 40.1 of the Constitution.

Held, by the High Court, in holding for the plaintiff, that the ineligibility of a childless widower to adopt a child already in his custody was unreasonable and unjust and the section was invalid as offending Article 40.1 of the Constitution. The requirement of a renewed consent was similarly invalid.[26]

CASE 143a O'KEEFFE v FERRIS (1993)

The plaintiff was a director of a private company which was hopelessly insolvent. By special resolution it was resolved that the company be wound up voluntarily. The defendant was appointed liquidator and instituted proceedings against the plaintiff under section 297 of the *Companies Act 1963* which provides that if in the course of the winding-up of a company it appears that any business of the company was carried on with intent to defraud creditors or any fraudulent purpose the court may, if it thinks proper so to do, declare that any person who was knowingly a party to the carrying on of the business in the manner aforesaid shall be personally liable, without any limitation of liability, for all or any of the debts or other liabilities of the company as the court may direct. The plaintiff challenged the constitutionality of the section claiming that it was criminal in nature.

Held, by the High Court, that the Oireachtas clearly intended to create a civil offence which could be invoked so as to recover compensation from a group of wrongdoers for the benefit of those who were wronged. It was the clear intention that this should be a civil remedy and the section had achieved that purpose.

CASE 144 IN RE Ó LAIGHLÉIS (1960)

The applicant was interned without trial under section 4 of the *Offences Against the State (Amendment) Act 1940* and claimed his detention was contrary to the European Convention on Human Rights.

Held, by the Supreme Court, that the European Convention on Human Rights was not part of the domestic law of the State because the Oireachtas, in accordance with Article 29.6 of the Constitution, had not determined that the convention be part of the domestic law. The primacy of domestic legislation was not displaced by the State becoming a party to the convention, nor was the executive estopped in the courts from relying on the domestic law.[27]

CASE 145 O'LEARY v ATTORNEY GENERAL (1991)

Section 21 of the *Offences Against the State Act 1939* provides that it shall not be lawful for a person to be a member of an unlawful organisation. Section 24 of the Act provides that on the trial of a person charged with such offence proof to the satisfaction of the court that an incriminating document relating to the said organisation was found on such person or in his possession or on lands or in premises owned or occupied by him or under his control shall, without more ado, be evidence until the contrary is proved that such person was a member of the said organisation. Section 3(2) of the *Offences Against the State (Amendment) Act 1972* provides that where an officer of the Garda Síochána, not below the rank of chief superintendent, in giving evidence in such a trial, states that he believes that the accused was at a material time a member of an unlawful organisation, the statement shall be evidence that he was then such a member. The plaintiff was charged with membership of an unlawful organisation and being in possession of incriminating documents, a number of posters showing the picture of a man in paramilitary uniform brandishing a rifle and with the words 'IRA calls the shots' prominently displayed on them. At the trial a chief superintendent swore that it was his belief that on a stated date the accused was a member of an unlawful organisation known as the IRA. The plaintiff was convicted and challenged the constitutionality of section 24 of the 1939 Act and section 3(2) of the 1972 Act on the ground that they infringed the presumption of innocence which was a constitutionally protected right.

Held, by the High Court, that while every accused in every criminal trial enjoyed a constitutionally protected right to the presumption of innocence neither section infringed this right. As regards section 24 of the 1939 Act the court of trial had to evaluate and assess the significance of the evidence of possession and if it had a reasonable doubt as to the accused's membership of an unlawful organisation it must dismiss the charge even in the absence of exculpatory evidence. What section 3(2) of the 1972 Act did was to make admissible in evidence statements of belief which would otherwise be inadmissible. Like other evidence it had to be weighted and considered. The section could not be construed as meaning that the court of trial must convict the accused in the absence of exculpatory evidence. The accused need not give evidence and may ask the court to hold that the evidence did not establish beyond a reasonable doubt that he was a member of an unlawful organisation: should the court agree, the accused must be acquitted.

CASE 146 O'MAHONY v MELIA (1990)

The plaintiff was arrested and brought to a garda station where he was charged with a criminal offence before a Peace Commissioner who remanded him in custody to a sitting of the District Court the next day. The Peace Commissioner exercised this function by virtue of section 15 of the *Criminal Justice Act 1951*, as substituted by section 26 of the *Criminal Justice Act 1984*. The plaintiff claimed this power conferred on a Peace Commissioner to admit persons to bail or to remand in custody involved the administration of justice. Since a Peace Commissioner was neither a judge nor a court the exercise of this function was invalid having regard to Article 34.1 of the Constitution.

Held, by the High Court, that the power to hear evidence and to exercise a discretion as to whether a person should be remanded in custody or on bail was a judicial act and not an administrative act. Since a Peace Commissioner was not a judge this function as conferred by the statute was invalid having regard to the provisions of Article 34.1 of the Constitution.

CASE 147 O'MALLEY v AN TAOISEACH (1990)

The plaintiff sought an injunction to restrain the defendant from advising the President to dissolve Dáil Éireann unless and until further legislation was passed by the Oireachtas and was in force which revised Dáil Éireann constituencies to ensure compliance with the provisions of Article 16 of the Constitution. Statistical evidence disclosed substantial variations from the national average and that there were differences between the representation afforded to different constituencies.

Held, by the High Court, that the Oireachtas is obliged to revise the constituencies when a census return disclosed major changes in the distribution of the population and that the obligation placed on the Oireachtas by Article 16.2.4° was not discharged by a revision of the constituencies once every twelve years. The court was satisfied that the Oireachtas was in breach of its constitutional obligation to revise the constituencies particularly when the last census disclosed a major change in the distribution of population and the fact that the ratio between the number of members to be elected at any time for each constituency and the population of each constituency as ascertained at the last preceding census was not so far as was practicable the same throughout the country. The constitutional duty of dissolving Dáil Éireann is vested in the President (Article 13.2.1°), who is not answerable to any court for the exercise and performance of this duty (Article 13.8). The constitutional duty of advising the President on this matter is vested in the Taoiseach and the courts have no jurisdiction to place any impediment between the President and his or her constitutional adviser in this matter, which is solely the prerogative of the President.

CASE 148 O'REILLY v MINISTER FOR THE ENVIRONMENT
(1986)

The *Electoral Act 1963*, section 16, provides that each ballot paper in Dáil Éireann elections must contain a list of the candidates arranged alphabetically in the order of their surnames. The plaintiff, intending to present himself as a candidate at the next general election, claimed that the system of alphabetical listing was unfair and unjust and contrary to Article 40.1 of the Constitution.

Held, by the High Court, in rejecting the claim, that the alphabetical system of listing candidates constituted a reasonable regulation of elections to Dáil Éireann.

CASE 149 O'SHEA v DIRECTOR OF PUBLIC PROSECUTIONS
(1989)

The plaintiff was charged with receiving stolen property, pleaded not guilty and elected for trial by jury. A preliminary examination took place and the

District Justice made an order sending him forward for trial at the next sitting of the Circuit Court. When the indictment was preferred in the Circuit Court it consisted of two counts, namely, burglary and receiving, this latter count being different to the original charge. These counts were inserted by the Director of Public Prosecutions in exercise of the power contained in section 18 of the *Criminal Procedure Act 1967*, and were founded on the documents and exhibits considered by the District Justice at the preliminary examination. The plaintiff claimed that this power which permitted the inclusion of charges either in substitution for, or in addition to, charges for which an accused had been sent forward for trial constituted an invasion of the judicial domain, was contrary to the separation of powers and was invalid having regard to the provisions of the Constitution.

Held, by the Supreme Court, that the section was not capable of being operated to render nugatory the fundamental decision of the District Justice which was to the effect that having regard to the facts contained in the documents and exhibits the accused should be sent forward for trial. The substitution of counts in the indictment pursuant to the section was not in any conflict with the order made by the District Justice. By substituting or adding a count the Director of Public Prosecutions was not purporting to determine any issue between the People and the accused, but was merely providing the vehicle for the determination of such issues by the jury. Therefore the challenge against the constitutional validity of the section based on an alleged invasion of the judicial domain failed.

CASE 150 PARSONS v KAVANAGH (1990)

The plaintiff, operating a passenger bus service pursuant to a licence issued under the *Road Traffic Acts 1932–33*, sought an injunction to prevent the defendant who did not have the required licence from operating a similar bus service on the same route.

Held, by the High Court, in granting the injunction, that having regard to the provisions of the Constitution the right to earn a livelihood by any lawful means carried with it the entitlement to be protected against any unlawful activity on the part of another which materially impaired or infringed that right.

CASE 151 THE PEOPLE (ATTORNEY GENERAL) v CONMEY (1975)

The defendant was convicted in the Central Criminal Court, which is the High Court dealing with criminal matters, and appealed to the Court of Criminal

Appeal, which was a statutory right. When the appeal was dismissed he appealed to the Supreme Court and raised the question whether an appeal lay from the Central Criminal Court directly to the Supreme Court.

Held, by the Supreme Court, that by virtue of Article 34.4.3° of the Constitution, the Supreme Court had appellate jurisdiction from all decisions of the High Court unless prohibited by statute. No law prevented an appeal from the Central Criminal Court but in this case no appeal lay because the defendant had already exercised the right of appeal to the Court of Criminal Appeal.

CASE 152 THE PEOPLE (ATTORNEY GENERAL) v O'BRIEN (1965)

Members of the Gardaí, on foot of a search warrant which contained the incorrect address, raided the defendant's home. On conviction he appealed on the ground that the production at his trial of property found during the search should not have been allowed in that it was obtained without a valid search warrant and was in violation of Article 40.5 of the Constitution.

Held, by the Supreme Court, in dismissing the appeal, that the mistake in the warrant was an oversight. Had it been proved that the evidence had been obtained as the result of a deliberate and conscious violation of the constitutional rights of the defendant it would have been excluded in the absence of extraordinary excusing circumstances.

CASE 153 THE PEOPLE (ATTORNEY GENERAL) v O'CALLAGHAN (1966)

The defendant was returned for trial on various charges and was refused bail in the High Court on the ground that he would, if granted bail, interfere with witnesses.

Held, by the Supreme Court, in granting bail, that there was not sufficient evidence that the defendant would interfere with witnesses, nor could bail be refused merely on the likelihood of the commission of further offences while on bail because to do so would be to acknowledge a form of preventive justice unknown to our legal system.

CASE 154 THE PEOPLE (DIRECTOR OF PUBLIC PROSECUTIONS) v FARRELL (1978)

The *Offences Against the State Act 1939*, section 30, permits the arrest and detention of a person on suspicion of having committed certain offences for twenty-four hours. An order to extend this period for a further twenty-four hours must be made by an officer of the Garda Síochána not below the rank of chief superintendent, but this power may be exercised by a superintendent so authorised by the garda commissioner. The defendant's conviction was based on incriminatory statements made during the extended period of detention.

Held, by the Court of Criminal Appeal, in quashing the conviction, that since there was no evidence of the superintendent's authority to extend the defendant's detention for a further twenty-four hours, the statements were made while he was unlawfully detained and in deliberate and conscious breach of the constitutional right to personal liberty and should be excluded from evidence.

CASE 155 THE PEOPLE (DIRECTOR OF PUBLIC PROSECUTIONS) v GALLAGHER (1991)

At a trial the jury, by virtue of the *Trial of Lunatics Act 1883*, returned a special verdict that the defendant was guilty of the act charged but was insane at the time. The court ordered him to be detained in the Central Mental Hospital until the pleasure of the Government of Ireland was known. The defendant claimed that this exercise by the executive of a judicial power, that of setting a person at liberty, was constitutionally vulnerable.

Held, by the Supreme Court, in rejecting the claim, that the special verdict was an acquittal and since the trial was concluded the court did not pronounce a sentence. The role of the court was to order the detention of the person in a safe place until the executive, armed with both the knowledge and resources to deal with the problem, decided on the future disposition of the person. The executive could, when satisfied that having regard to the mental health of the person it was for public and private considerations safe, order his release

CASE 156 THE PEOPLE (DIRECTOR OF PUBLIC PROSECUTIONS) v HEALY (1990)

The defendant was arrested under section 30 of the *Offences Against the State Act 1939* on suspicion of being in unlawful possession of a firearm. He was interviewed at length by Gardaí and eventually agreed to make a statement which was inculpatory. The admissibility of this statement was challenged at his trial on the ground that prior to its completion a solicitor retained by the defendant's family had arrived at the garda station and requested an interview with the defendant. The solicitor was not permitted to see the defendant, nor was the defendant informed of the solicitor's presence in the station until after the completion and signing of the statement. The trial judge ruled that the defendant had, without any excuse, been denied a right of instant access to his solicitor and ruled the confession inadmissible. Since that was the sole evidence against the defendant he was acquitted and the Director of Public Prosecutions appealed.

Held, by the Supreme Court, that such an important and fundamental standard of fairness in the administration of justice as the right of access to a lawyer must be deemed a constitutional right. In this case the postponement of both the defendant's access to the solicitor and the informing of the defendant of the presence of the solicitor until after the completion of the statement was both a deliberate and conscious violation of the defendant's constitutional right and also a complete failure to observe reasonable standards of fairness in the procedure of the interrogation. The appeal was dismissed.

CASE 157 THE PEOPLE (DIRECTOR OF PUBLIC PROSECUTIONS) v HIGGINS (1985)

The defendant was arrested on a Sunday evening on suspicion of dangerous driving. The sergeant in charge of the station to which he was brought communicated with other garda stations informing them that the defendant was in custody should any Gardaí attached to these stations wish to interview him on suspicion of being involved in other crimes. Later that evening Gardaí from another station arrived and interviewed the defendant. The defendant made incriminatory statements in relation to other offences. The defendant was not charged but was detained in custody and brought before the District Court the following morning and charged with dangerous driving. Later he was charged with the other offences and, at his trial, it was argued that the incriminatory statements were made at a time when the defendant was unlawfully detained.

Held, by the Supreme Court, in quashing the conviction, that at the time the statements were made the defendant was not detained for the purpose of being charged or brought before a court but specifically for the purpose of being interviewed. He was therefore unlawfully detained and, to the knowledge of the Gardaí concerned, detained in deliberate and conscious violation of his constitutional right to personal liberty.

CASE 158 THE PEOPLE (DIRECTOR OF PUBLIC PROSECUTIONS) v KENNY (1990)

Members of the Garda Síochána, carrying out surveillance of a premises in which the accused was residing, observed activity which appeared to constitute trafficking in drugs. A search warrant, obtained from a Peace Commissioner pursuant to section 26 of the *Misuse of Drugs Act 1977* in respect of the premises, was brought and failing to gain entry by demand the Gardaí made a forcible entry and found the accused on the premises with a quantity of controlled drugs for which the accused took responsibility. In granting the warrant the Peace Commissioner had not independently decided that a search warrant was justified but accepted without question the suspicions of the Gardaí, a course of action which rendered the warrant invalid (see *Byrne v Grey* on page 276). The Court of Criminal Appeal upheld the accused's conviction but allowed an appeal to the Supreme Court on a point of law which was whether the forcible entry of the accused's home by members of the Garda Síochána on foot of an invalid search warrant constituted a deliberate and conscious violation of the accused's constitutional right to the inviolability of his dwelling such as to render the evidence found in the search inadmissible at the accused's trial.

Held, by the Supreme Court, that evidence obtained by the invasion of the constitutional rights of a citizen must be excluded unless a court was satisfied that either the act constituting the breach of constitutional rights was committed unintentionally or accidentally, or was satisfied that there were extraordinary excusing circumstances which justified the admission of the evidence. Since, in this case, the actions of the Gardaí were neither unintentional nor accidental, the conviction must be quashed.

CASE 159 THE PEOPLE (DIRECTOR OF PUBLIC PROSECUTIONS) v LYNCH (1981)

The defendant voluntarily went to a garda station to make a statement. After making the statement he was detained overnight, subjected to successive bouts of questioning by different groups of Gardaí and was not given an opportunity to sleep or rest. Following this interrogation the defendant made an incriminatory statement which was admitted as evidence at his trial and he was convicted.

Held, by the Supreme Court, in quashing the conviction, that since the defendant was not at liberty to leave the station he was in fact under arrest. Once under arrest he should have been charged and brought before a court. Failure to do so rendered his continued detention unlawful and unconstitutional at the time the statement was made. The statement ought to have been excluded from evidence.

CASE 160 THE PEOPLE (DIRECTOR OF PUBLIC PROSECUTIONS) v MADDEN (1977)

The defendant was arrested under the *Offences Against the State Act 1939*, section 30, which permits detention without charge, on suspicion of committing certain offences, for twenty-four hours. Shortly before this period was due to expire the defendant began to make an incriminatory statement which was not completed until three hours after the twenty-four hours had expired. This statement was admitted in evidence and, on conviction, the defendant appealed.

Held, by the Court of Criminal Appeal, in quashing the conviction, that because the statement was completed after the expiration of the period of lawful detention the defendant was then in unlawful custody which was a deliberate and conscious breach of his constitutional right to personal liberty and the statement ought to have been excluded from evidence.

CASE 161 THE PEOPLE (DIRECTOR OF PUBLIC PROSECUTIONS) v O'LOUGHLIN (1979)

The defendant, after the Gardaí found some stolen machinery on his land, went voluntarily to the garda station so that the Gardaí might confirm his explanation. Some hours after the explanation was found to be false, the defendant made an incriminating statement. On conviction, after this statement was admitted into evidence, the defendant appealed.

Held, by the Court of Criminal Appeal, in quashing the conviction, that from the time the Gardaí realised that the explanation was false the defendant's detention was unlawful in that he had neither been charged nor released. This detention amounted to a deliberate and conscious breach of his constitutional right to personal liberty and the statement should not have been admitted in evidence.

CASE 162 THE PEOPLE (DIRECTOR OF PUBLIC PROSECUTIONS) v O'SHEA (1982)

The defendant at his trial by jury in the Central Criminal Court was acquitted by the direction of the judge. The DPP appealed to the Supreme Court thus raising the question whether an appeal lies from a verdict of not guilty recorded by a jury at the direction of the trial judge.

Held, by the Supreme Court, that an appeal lay by virtue of Article 34.4.3° of the Constitution which grants to the Supreme Court jurisdiction to hear all appeals from the High Court unless curtailed expressly and unambiguously by statute law.

CASE 163 THE PEOPLE (DIRECTOR OF PUBLIC PROSECUTIONS) v QUILLIGAN (1992)

In the investigation of a crime the Gardaí arrested the defendant under section 30 of the *Offences Against the State Act 1939* which permits the Gardaí to detain a person without charge on suspicion of having committed one of a range of offences for an initial period of twenty-four hours which may be extended to forty-eight hours. The defendant was convicted and on appeal to the Supreme Court challenged the constitutionality of the section on the ground that the right to liberty was insufficiently respected and defended as was required by Article 40.3.2° of the Constitution.

Held, by the Supreme Court, that having regard to the protections afforded by the Constitution and the courts to a person so arrested the challenge failed as it had not been established that section 30 constituted a failure by the State, as far as was practicable, by its laws to defend and vindicate the personal right of immediate liberty of the citizen.

CASE 164 THE PEOPLE (DIRECTOR OF PUBLIC PROSECUTIONS) v SHAW (1982)

The defendant was arrested late on a Sunday evening and shortly after his arrest was suspected of involvement in the disappearance of two women. He was not brought before a court until the following Thursday evening. While in custody he made incriminatory statements which were admitted in evidence and, on conviction, he appealed.

Held, by the Supreme Court, in dismissing the appeal, that while there had been a deliberate and conscious breach of the defendant's constitutional right to liberty by his not being charged as soon as was practicable, or released, there existed extraordinary excusing circumstances in that attempts were being made to vindicate the right to life of another person.

CASE 165 PIGS MARKETING BOARD v DONNELLY (DUBLIN) LTD (1939)

The plaintiffs were empowered by statute to fix the price of pig-meat and the defendant, as a processor of pig-meat, was prohibited from purchasing pigs at prices other than those fixed: should it do so, it would be liable to the plaintiffs for the difference. On being sued for monies by the plaintiffs the defendant challenged the constitutionality of this power on the ground that it infringed property rights.

Held, by the High Court, that legislation interfering with trade competition, or with contractual rights, or with proprietary rights, was not *per se* unconstitutional.

CASE 166 POK SUN SHUM v IRELAND (1985)

The plaintiff, born in China and having lived in Hong Kong, came to Ireland in 1978 and observed the requirements of the *Aliens Act 1935*. Following a serious criminal incident the plaintiff's permission to remain as an alien was not continued, and in the same year he married an Irish citizen and later became the father of three children born in this country. The plaintiff claimed that, having regard to the rights guaranteed in Articles 40, 41 and 42 of the Constitution, the Minister for Justice had not the power to control or prohibit the departure, entry, re-entry and duration of stay of the plaintiff in this jurisdiction and that the plaintiff's wife had a constitutional right to the society of her husband within the State.

Held, by the High Court, in dismissing the claim, that the rights guaranteed to the family under Article 41 of the Constitution were not absolute and that restrictions for the common good, including the right to control aliens, were permissible. Since a power of deportation was not unconstitutional the fact that the plaintiff was married to a citizen did not in any way curtail or alter that power.[28]

CASE 167 PRIVATE MOTORISTS PROVIDENT SOCIETY LTD v ATTORNEY GENERAL (1983)

The plaintiff carried on a banking business which consisted in taking deposits from, and making loans to, members. Deposits grew to £135 million. The *Industrial and Provident Societies (Amendment) Act 1978* prohibited industrial and provident societies from accepting or holding deposits after the end of a period of five years commencing at the passing of the statute. The plaintiff challenged the constitutionality of the statute.

Held, by the Supreme Court, in rejecting the claim, that the statute, far from expropriating the business of the plaintiff, was a regulation and control of the range of business which it could carry out and was not contrary to Article 40.3 of the Constitution in that it was for the common good. Nor was it contrary to Article 40.6.1° which guaranteed freedom of association.

CASE 168 QUINN'S SUPERMARKET LTD v ATTORNEY GENERAL (1972)

The plaintiff company was prosecuted for keeping a meat shop open on a weekday evening contrary to a statutory order. Meat shops which sold kosher meat were exempt from the order. The plaintiff challenged the constitutionality of the order.

Held, by the Supreme Court, by exempting kosher meat shops the statutory order contained a discrimination on the ground of religious profession, belief or status and was contrary to Article 44.2.3° of the Constitution.

CASE 169 R. v R. (1984)

The plaintiff claimed various reliefs under the *Guardianship of Infants Act 1964*, the *Family Law (Maintenance of Spouses and Children) Act 1976* and the *Family Law (Protection of Spouses and Children) Act 1981*. When the first two statutes were enacted jurisdiction was conferred on the High Court but by the *Courts Act 1981* jurisdiction was confined to the Circuit and District Courts. The third statute conferred jurisdiction on the same courts. The plaintiff claimed that if the effect of these statutes was to restrict or remove the jurisdiction of the High Court to hear these claims they were unconstitutional.

Held, by the High Court, that having regard to the provisions of Article 34.3 of the Constitution the Oireachtas could establish, in addition to the High Court, other courts of first instance and to determine their jurisdiction. It was not competent for the Oireachtas to create a new judicial jurisdiction and withhold it from the High Court, nor could it reduce, restrict or terminate any jurisdiction of the High Court. Where concurrent jurisdiction existed the High Court could not be compelled to provide a person, as a constitutional right, with access to the High Court in lieu of recourse to the other court of first instance established by law which possessed the jurisdiction sought to be invoked.

CASE 170 ROGERS v IRISH TRANSPORT & GENERAL WORKERS UNION (1978)

The defendant trade union, at a meeting of one of its branches of which the plaintiff was a member, resolved that members of the branch on attaining the age of 65 years should compulsorily retire with a pension. The plaintiff had reached the age of 65 years and had, for thirty-four years, been a casual docker. He claimed that the resolution was invalid as an infringement of his constitutional right to earn a livelihood,

Held, by the High Court, in rejecting the claim, that compulsory retirement coupled with pension rights was not an infringement of the constitutional right to earn a livelihood. The retirement age of 65 years was common both in the public and private sectors and could not be regarded as unfair or unreasonable.

CASE 171 RYAN v ATTORNEY GENERAL (1965)

The *Health (Fluoridation of Water Supplies) Act 1960* imposed an obligation on a health authority to arrange for the fluoridation of water supplied to the public. The plaintiff, a mother of five children, whose home was connected to a public piped water supply, claimed that some provisions of the statute were unconstitutional.

Held, by the Supreme Court, that the right to bodily integrity was an implied constitutional right under Article 40.3.2° of the Constitution. That right was not infringed by the addition of fluoride to drinking water, nor was there any infringement of the rights guaranteed to the family under Article 41.1.2° of the Constitution.

CASE 172 RYAN v O'CALLAGHAN (1987)

The *Larceny Act 1916*, section 42(1), provides that if it appears from information on oath before a justice of the peace that there is reasonable cause to believe that any person has in his custody or possession or on his premises any property whatsoever, with respect to which any offence against this statute has been committed, the justice may grant a warrant to search for and seize that property. The power of a Peace Commissioner to issue a search warrant is derived from the *Courts of Justice Act 1924*, section 88. The defendant, a Peace Commissioner, having received sworn information from a member of the Garda Síochána, issued a search warrant relating to the plaintiff's premises. Property was found therein and the plaintiff, while awaiting trial on a larceny charge, challenged the constitutionality of these statutes and argued that a Peace Commissioner, in exercising this power to issue a warrant which authorised the entry and search of the dwelling house of a citizen, was exercising judicial power in a criminal matter which is a function lawfully exercisable only by judges appointed under the Constitution.

Held, by the High Court, in dismissing the case, that it was in the interest of the common good that a simple procedure should be readily available to the Gardaí to obtain search warrants in appropriate cases. The statutory procedure contained important protections for the public in that the investigating garda must swear an information that reasonable cause exists for suspecting that stolen property is to be found at the premises to be searched and a Peace Commissioner, an independent person unconnected with criminal investigations, must be satisfied that it is right and proper to issue the warrant. The issue of a search warrant prior to the commencement of a prosecution is part of the process of criminal investigation and is executive rather than judicial in nature.

CASE 173 S. v S. (1983)

The plaintiff gave birth to a child which was not that of her husband. She sought, with the agreement both of the child's father and of her husband, to have the child registered in the name of its father which was refused. She then sought an order of the High Court directing the Registrar General of Births and Deaths to register such birth accordingly.

Held, by the High Court, in granting the order, that the common law rule which prohibited the admission of evidence by a wife that a child born to her during wedlock was not the child of her husband was inconsistent with the right to fair procedures guaranteed by the Constitution and was calculated to defeat the due administration of justice.

CASE 174 SHANNON v ATTORNEY GENERAL (1984)

The plaintiff, whose extradition to Northern Ireland was ordered by the District Court, challenged the constitutionality of the *Extradition Act 1965*, Part III, which deals with extradition to the United Kingdom on the ground that the legal procedures in operation in Northern Ireland were unfair and unjust and that the endorsement of warrants by the Commissioner of the Garda Síochána was an administration of justice.

Held, by the Supreme Court, that while there were some differences between criminal procedures in Northern Ireland and this State, the evidence did not show that the procedures in Northern Ireland fell short of the minimum requirements for criminal trials in this State though the court reserved the right to refuse to give effect to Part III if it was to be used for a purpose inconsistent with the citizen's constitutional rights. The endorsement of warrants by the Garda Commissioner was merely procedural and was not an administration of justice within Article 34.1 of the Constitution since the ultimate delivery of a person out of the State was under the control of the courts.

CASE 175 SHELLY v MAHON (1990)

The defendant had been a judge of the District Court from 1976 until reaching the age of 65 years in 1984. There was statutory power to continue in office after reaching that age provided the requisite approval was obtained before the age of 65 years was reached which the defendant failed to obtain. Because of an oversight it was assumed that he would not reach retiring age until 1985. Approval for extending his period of office, based on that mistaken assumption, was obtained for a number of years. These were null and void because the defendant had ceased to be a judge for almost one year before the first approval had been obtained. On a date in 1987 he purported to convict the plaintiff of a road traffic offence. The Oireachtas enacted the *Courts (No. 2) Act 1988* which permitted the extension of the defendant's age of retirement to be retrospectively made in certain circumstances and to provide for certain validations. The statute provides that if any validation conflicts with a constitutional right of any person the validation shall be subject to such limitation as is necessary to secure that it does not so conflict but shall be otherwise of full force and effect. The plaintiff challenged the purported conviction.

Held, by the Supreme Court, that the prosecution of offences in accordance with the Constitution could not be conducted anywhere except in a court whose existence was authorised by the Constitution and presided over by a judge appointed in accordance with the requirements of the Constitution. The plaintiff never had the benefit of a trial before a lawfully appointed judge. The contention that as a result of the statute the absence of a trial was cured was to accept that the Oireachtas could by statute try and convict a person for a criminal offence was clearly contrary to Article 38.1 of the Constitution which provided that no person should be tried on any criminal charge save in due course of law.

CASE 176 SOMJEE v MINISTER FOR JUSTICE (1981)

The plaintiff, a Pakistani national, married an Irish citizen. The *Irish Nationality and Citizenship Act 1956*, section 8, provided an almost automatic conferment of citizenship on non-citizen women who marry Irish citizens whereas there were no similar provisions available to non-citizen males. The plaintiff claimed that this differentiation constituted an inequality before the law contrary to Article 40.1 of the Constitution.

Held, by the High Court, that the section did not create an invidious discrimination but a diversity of arrangements which were not contrary to Article 40.1 of the Constitution.[29]

CASE 177 THE STATE (BOUZAGOU) v STATION SERGEANT OF FITZGIBBON ST GARDA STATION (1985)

The prosecutor, a Moroccan national, married an Irish citizen in this country, was the father of two children born here, and had resided here for eight years until he left. On arrival back in Ireland he was refused leave to enter on the ground that he could not support himself and was detained pending his deportation. Inquiries revealed that domestic problems existed between the prosecutor and his wife, that he had been convicted of assaulting her and that she had obtained a barring order against him some months before he left the jurisdiction. The prosecutor sought his release, *inter alia*, on the ground that his family rights had been infringed.

Held, by the High Court, in refusing relief, that the prosecutor could not claim the rights guaranteed to the family under Article 41 of the Constitution because the prosecutor's family was divided and his wife and children were living as a separate unit.[30]

CASE 178 THE STATE (BOYLE) v GOVERNOR OF MILITARY DETENTION BARRACKS (1980)

The *Prisons Act 1972*, section 2, empowered the Minister for Justice in stated circumstances to direct the transfer of a named prisoner from civilian custody to military custody. The prosecutor, serving a prison sentence, was transferred from civilian detention to military custody and challenged the constitutionality of the section on the ground that the powers given to the Minister were judicial in nature in that when exercised they resulted in a different form of punishment being imposed than that imposed by the courts and thus infringed the doctrine of the separation of powers.

Held, by the Supreme Court, that the powers were administrative in nature and the section did not authorise the imposition of any punishment other than that which was in accordance with the sentence imposed by the courts.

CASE 179 THE STATE (BOYLE) v NEYLON (1987)

Section 31 of the *Courts Act 1981* provides for the transfer of the trial of a person charged with an indictable offence from the Circuit Court before which that person is triable to the Dublin Circuit Court. The prosecutor was transferred for trial from the Wicklow Circuit Court to the Dublin Circuit Court. He pleaded guilty and was sentenced to terms of imprisonment. He challenged the constitutionality of the section on the ground that the Dublin

Circuit Court had no jurisdiction to try him because Article 34.3.4° of the Constitution had been breached in that he had not been tried by a court of local and limited jurisdiction.

Held, by the Supreme Court, in dismissing the case, that while the purpose of the provisions of Article 34.3.4° for 'courts of local and limited jurisdiction' was the convenience of litigants the achievement of that aim was left to the Oireachtas. While the provision of local venues for the exercise of the Circuit Court jurisdiction fulfils the objective of the Article the Oireachtas may properly provide that another locality would be a more appropriate venue in certain cases.

CASE 180 THE STATE (BROWNE) v FERAN (1967)

The prosecutor had been tried, convicted and sentenced to six months' imprisonment. The High Court, in proceedings under Article 40.4.2° of the Constitution, ordered his release and the respondents in those proceedings sought leave to appeal to the Supreme Court which was opposed by the prosecutor on the ground that no appeal lay against either the grant or refusal of an order under Article 40.4.2° in a criminal cause or matter.

Held, by the Supreme Court, that the appeal was maintainable in that Article 34.4.3° of the Constitution provides that an appeal lay to the Supreme Court from all decisions of the High Court save to the extent to which that appellate jurisdiction was restricted either by the Constitution or by statute, and that there was no relevant restriction.

CASE 181 THE STATE (BURKE) v LENNON (1940)

The *Offences Against the State Act 1939*, section 55, empowered a Minister of State to order the arrest and internment without trial of a person if satisfied that the person was engaged in activities calculated to prejudice the preservation of the peace, order or security of the State. The prosecutor contended that his arrest and internment were unconstitutional.

Held, by the High Court, that internment without trial did not respect the citizen's right to personal liberty guaranteed by Article 40.4, and that in signing a warrant under the section the Minister was administering justice, which was a judicial function confined to the courts established under the Constitution.[31]

CASE 182 THE STATE (BYRNE) v FRAWLEY (1978)

The prosecutor was being tried by jury when the decision of the Supreme Court in *de Búrca v Attorney General* (Case 49) was given. The prosecutor was convicted. Neither at the trial nor on appeal was any objection made to the method of the selection of the jury despite the fact that the counsel at his trial was involved in the *de Búrca* case. The prosecutor made an application under Article 40.4.2° of the Constitution.

Held, by the Supreme Court, that while the jury which tried the prosecutor was unlawful, for the reasons given in the *de Búrca* case, the prosecutor was precluded from asserting that such jury was constituted unlawfully in that he elected, with the knowledge of that decision, to accept the jury sworn at his trial, and by the fact that he made no complaint on appeal.

CASE 183 THE STATE (C.) v FRAWLEY (1976)

The prosecutor, a prisoner serving a term of imprisonment, had a sociopathic personality disturbance, was physically strong, was aggressive and hostile to any form of authority, made repeated attempts at escape and had a record of swallowing metal objects that had to be removed by surgery. As a result he was kept in solitary confinement and deprived of most of the equipment of an ordinary prisoner. The prosecutor sought his release.

Held, by the High Court, in dismissing the application, that the rigorous conditions were imposed to diminish the possibility of the prosecutor injuring himself and were not a breach of the implied right to bodily integrity.

CASE 184 THE STATE (C.) v MINISTER FOR JUSTICE (1967)

The prosecutor, charged and remanded in custody until a stated date, was removed to a mental hospital pursuant to the *Lunatic Asylums (Ireland) Act 1875*, section 13, on the direction of the Minister for Justice, thus preventing the court from exercising its jurisdiction in relation to the charge.

Held, by the Supreme Court, that the section of the statute constituted a legislative interference with an exercise of the judicial power to administer justice and offended the constitutional principle of the separation of powers.

CASE 185 THE STATE (COMMINS) v McRANN (1977)

The prosecutor, committed to prison for contempt of court in failing to obey a civil order of the Circuit Court, claimed that this contempt was a criminal charge, was non-minor and only triable by a jury by virtue of Article 38.5 of the Constitution.

Held, by the High Court, that even if it assumed that this contempt was a criminal offence to which Article 38.5 of the Constitution applied, the terms of Article 34 constituted a qualification on Article 38 which authorised the courts to adjudicate in a summary manner the issue of contempt and to impose sanctions in the event of disobedience to their orders.

CASE 186 THE STATE (CRAVEN) v FRAWLEY (1980)

The prosecutor, a youthful offender, was serving a sentence in borstal, where he was considered to be a bad influence on other prisoners. The Minister for Justice, under the *Prevention of Crimes Act 1908,* made an order commuting the balance of the term of detention in the borstal to a term of imprisonment, and ordered the prosecutor to be detained in a prison. The prosecutor claimed that the Minister was administering justice contrary to Article 34 of the Constitution.

Held, by the High Court, that the action of the Minister in changing the place of detention was an administrative act and not a judicial act which was confined to the courts under Article 34 of the Constitution.

CASE 187 THE STATE (DIRECTOR OF PUBLIC PROSECUTIONS) v WALSH (1981)

Following the convictions of two persons of capital murder by a Special Criminal Court and their sentencing to death, the defendant issued a statement referring to the Special Criminal Court as a sentencing tribunal which was published by a national newspaper. When cited for contempt in the High Court the defendant demanded a jury trial claiming this offence was non-minor.

Held, by the Supreme Court, that in proceedings for criminal contempt committed other than in the face of the court there is a prima-facie right, under Article 38.5 of the Constitution, to trial by jury. This is subject to the proviso that there are real issues of fact to be decided. Where the facts are admitted the matter can be disposed of summarily.

CASE 188 THE STATE (GILLILAND) v GOVERNOR OF MOUNTJOY PRISON (1987)

A Treaty of Extradition between Ireland and the United States of America was signed and subsequently ratified on behalf of Ireland by the Minister for

Foreign Affairs. The treaty was laid before both Houses of the Oireachtas but was not approved by Dáil Éireann. The prosecutor was arrested on a request from the Government of the United States of America. The District Court made an order for his extradition. The prosecutor applied to the High Court and that court, pursuant to Article 40.4.3° of the Constitution, stated a case for the opinion of the Supreme Court as to whether the State was bound by the Treaty by reason of the fact that it had not been approved by Dáil Éireann in accordance with Article 29.5.2° of the Constitution.

Held, by the Supreme Court, that since some of the provisions of the Treaty involved a charge on public funds, having regard to Article 29.5.2° of the Constitution, the State was not bound by the Treaty unless, and until, its terms were approved by Dáil Éireann.[32]

CASE 189 THE STATE (HEALY) v DONOGHUE (1976)

The *Criminal Justice (Legal Aid) Act 1962* provides that a court may, on an application being made to it, grant legal aid where the offence is grave and the means of the person charged are insufficient to enable him to obtain legal representation. The prosecutor, unable to obtain legal representation from his own resources, was charged but was not informed by the court of his right to apply for legal aid. He was convicted.

Held, by the Supreme Court, in quashing the conviction, that Article 38 of the Constitution, which requires a criminal trial to be conducted in due course of law, imported the requirements of fair procedures. Where an accused faces a serious charge, and by reason of lack of education requires the assistance of a qualified lawyer in the preparation and conduct of a defence, the administration of justice requires that the accused should be afforded the opportunity of obtaining such assistance at the expense of the State even though the accused had not applied for it.

CASE 190 THE STATE (K. M.) v MINISTER FOR FOREIGN AFFAIRS (1979)

The prosecutor, an unmarried citizen, gave birth to a child which was registered in the name of its father, a non-citizen. The parties did not intend to marry each other. Due to the inability of the mother to care for the child, and because it had inherited the father's racial characteristics, it was decided in the child's best interests to allow it to be reared by the father's parents in his native country. A passport application by the prosecutor was refused on the ground that the *Adoption Act 1952*, section 40, prohibited the removal from the State of an illegitimate child under one year unless it was for the purpose of residing with the mother outside the State.

Held, by the High Court, that subject to public order and the common good, every citizen had the implied right, under Article 40.3.2° of the Constitution, to travel outside the State. The prohibition in the section was unconstitutional, though where the exercise of that right by or on behalf of the child affected its welfare adversely, the courts would intervene to protect the welfare of the child.

CASE 191 THE STATE (LYNCH) v COONEY (1982)

In its coverage of a general election, RTE allowed time on television and radio for political broadcasts by political parties. To qualify for time a political party had to have at least seven candidates. In line with this policy Provisional Sinn Féin were allotted two minutes. The defendant, the Minister for Posts and Telegraphs, made an order under section 31 of the *Broadcasting Authority Act 1960*, as amended, restraining RTE from broadcasting any party political broadcast on behalf of Provisional Sinn Féin. The prosecutor, one of the candidates, challenged the constitutionality of the section.

Held, by the Supreme Court, in upholding the section, that the guarantee of expression in Article 40.6.1° of the Constitution was qualified in the interests of public order and morality. The use of the organs of public opinion for the purpose of securing or advocating support for organisations which seek by violence to overthrow the State, which Provisional Sinn Féin did, was a use prohibited by the Constitution and placed on the State the duty to ensure that these organs are not so used.

CASE 192 THE STATE (McELDOWNEY) v KELLEHER (1983)

The *Street and House-to-House Collections Act 1962* provides that the holding of a collection of money from the public in the public street, or from house to house, required a permit which was obtained from a chief super-intendent of the Garda Síochána of the locality in which it was intended to hold such a collection. A permit would not be granted if the proceeds were to be used for a number of objectionable purposes. An appeal from such refusal lay to the District Court. Section 13 provided that if a member of the Garda Síochána, not below the rank of inspector, stated on oath that he had reasonable grounds for believing that the proceeds of the collection would be used for an unlawful object, or contrary to public morality, such appeal must be dismissed. The prosecutor applied for a permit, was refused, appealed, and at the hearing a chief superintendent gave evidence that he believed the proceeds would be used for the benefit of an unlawful organisation. The prosecutor challenged the constitutionality of section 13.

Held, by the Supreme Court, in finding for the plaintiff, that the section constituted an impermissible invasion of the judicial power in that it required that a judicial controversy be decided in a particular manner and was in breach of the doctrine of the separation of powers.

CASE 193 THE STATE (McFADDEN) v GOVERNOR OF MOUNTJOY PRISON (1981)

The prosecutor, arrested on foot of an English warrant, was brought before the District Court where an extradition order was made. At no time was he given a copy of the warrant or asked if he wished to be legally represented or if he required an adjournment to obtain legal advice or representation. He claimed that these procedures were unfair.

Held, by the High Court, that in extradition proceedings, because the liberty of the person was in jeopardy, the person arrested ought to be given ample opportunity to prepare his case. The procedures in this case fell short of the constitutionally accepted standard of fairness.

CASE 194 THE STATE (MURRAY) v McRANN (1979)

While detained in prison the prosecutrix was charged with committing a breach of prison discipline by assaulting a prison officer. After a proper investigation she was punished in a manner authorised by the prison rules. She claimed that this power to punish for a criminal matter was unconstitutional in that such jurisdiction was reserved exclusively to the courts.

Held, by the High Court, that the exercise by the governor of the prison of these functions, on the breach of prison discipline, was not transformed into an exercise of the functions and powers relevant to a criminal matter, within Article 37 of the Constitution, by the fact that such breach happened also to be a criminal offence.

CASE 195 THE STATE (NICOLAOU) v AN BORD UCHTÁLA (1966)

The prosecutor was the father of a child and though he wanted to marry the mother she was unwilling. When the mother placed the child for adoption the prosecutor, who had not been consulted, challenged the constitutionality of the *Adoption Act 1952*.

Held, by the Supreme Court, that the statute, which permitted the making of an adoption order for an illegitimate child without first obtaining the consent of the father, was not contrary to Article 40.1 of the Constitution in that it could be upheld on the ground of social function. The father of an illegitimate child did not have a natural right to its custody which required protection under Article 40.3 and that the prosecutor could not plead any breach of family rights, contrary to Article 41, in that those rights were confined to the family founded on marriage.[33]

CASE 196 THE STATE (O'CONNELL) v FAWSITT (1986)

The prosecutor was returned for jury trial in July 1982. From then until July 1984 the prosecutor appeared at regular intervals before the Circuit Court but until that date his case was not listed for hearing. Finally, 6 November 1984 was fixed for trial. The prosecutor, who by that time had obtained employment in England, mistook the date of the hearing, and returned a week early. He was unable to remain in the jurisdiction until that date, and the matter was adjourned until January 1985. The prosecutor attended the court on that date, but there was a further series of adjournments until April 1985. The prosecutor applied for an order of prohibition.

Held, by the Supreme Court, in granting the order of prohibition, that Article 38.1 of the Constitution entitled an accused person to have criminal charges tried with reasonable expedition according to the circumstances of the case. Having regard to the prosecutor's position there was excessive and inexcusable delay in having the charges proceeded with, and in the circumstances a trial after such delay would not be one in due course of law.

CASE 197 THE STATE (O'ROURKE) v KELLY (1983)

The *Housing Act 1966*, section 62, authorises a housing authority to apply to the District Court for a warrant authorising possession to be taken by the authority of a dwelling and the warrant for recovery will be issued if a demand for possession has been duly made. The prosecutor, against whom a warrant of recovery was issued, challenged the constitutionality of the section on the ground that the legislature had interfered with the administration of justice in that the District Court was deprived of any discretion in determining an application under the section.

Held, by the Supreme Court, in rejecting the claim, that the mandatory issue of the warrant was dependent on proof of the circumstances specified in the section, that such legislative provision was within the competence of the Oireachtas and that therefore the section did not constitute an interference by the legislature in the judicial domain.

CASE 198 THE STATE (PHEASANTRY LTD) v DONNELLY (1982)

The *Intoxicating Liquor Act 1927*, section 28, provides that on recording a third conviction for a licensing offence the licence was forfeited and no new licence shall at any time be granted in respect of premises to which such licence attached. The prosecutor, the owner of licensed premises with four convictions, challenged the constitutionality of the section.

Held, by the High Court, in upholding the section, that the forfeiture of the licence was not a primary punishment, was not relevant in considering the gravity of the offence and that the offences were minor within the meaning of Article 38.2. The licence was a privilege granted by statute and, since the regulating of intoxicating liquor was for the common good, a person applying for a licence should know that it could be forfeited in certain events and should these occur it was not an unjust attack on property rights under Article 40.3 of the Constitution.

CASE 199 THE STATE (QUINN) v RYAN (1965)

The prosecutor, arrested and released on foot of a defective English warrant, on re-arrest was immediately removed from the jurisdiction under the provisions of the *Petty Sessions (Ireland) Act 1851*, section 29.

Held, by the Supreme Court, in holding the section unconstitutional, in that it prevented an arrested person from testing the validity of his arrest in the High Court in accordance with Article 40.4.3° of the Constitution.[34]

CASE 200 THE STATE (RICHARDSON) v GOVERNOR OF
MOUNTJOY PRISON (1980)

The prosecutrix was imprisoned and proved that prisoners in the mornings emptied chamber pots into a toilet and washed them in a cold water sink. Some prisoners emptied these pots into the sink, in which human waste had been found. The prosecutrix claimed that these facilities failed to protect her constitutional right to health and human dignity.

Held, by the High Court, that the State had failed in its duty under the Constitution to protect the prosecutrix's health and to provide her with appropriate facilities with which to maintain proper standards of hygiene and cleanliness.

CASE 201 THE STATE (ROGERS) v GALVIN (1983)

The prosecutor, while in the custody of the respondent, was charged before a Special Criminal Court. The presiding member, a judge of the High Court, acceded to a request by the prosecutor to hear an application under Article 40.4.2° of the Constitution. The solicitor representing the Director of Public Prosecutions called the respondent to give evidence. The High Court judge ordered the immediate release of the prosecutor. The respondent appealed.

Held, by the Supreme Court, in allowing the appeal, that the High Court judge had failed to discharge his obligation under Article 40.4.2° of the Constitution to give the respondent an opportunity to have legal advice and representation, or to fully present his side of the case, or to exercise his constitutional right to certify in writing the grounds of detention.

CASE 202 THE STATE (ROLLINSON) v KELLY (1984)

A bookmaker was convicted summarily of betting offences and was fined £500 on each offence by virtue of section 25 of the *Finance Act 1926*. He challenged the constitutionality of the section on the ground that these offences, having regard to the nature of the punishment, were not minor.

Held, by the Supreme Court, that having regard to the contemporary value of the sum of £500, these offences were minor offences within Article 38.2 of the Constitution and could be tried summarily.

CASE 203 THE STATE (SHEERIN) v KENNEDY (1966)

The prosecutor was convicted summarily and sentenced, by virtue of section 2 of the *Prevention of Crimes Act 1908*, to two years in St Patrick's Institution, a place for the detention of persons within the age group of 17 to 21 years.

Held, by the Supreme Court, that an offence which attracts the deprivation of liberty for such a period could not be regarded as minor under Article 38.2 of the Constitution and must be tried by a jury.

CASE 204 THE STATE (TRIMBOLE) v GOVERNOR OF MOUNTJOY PRISON (1985)

The Australian national was arrested under section 30 of the *Offences Against the State Act 1939* and the High Court, because of the abuse of the powers given under that section, ordered his release. On the same day, prior to the release by the High Court, the government applied Part III of the *Extradition Act 1965* to Australia with effect from that date. The prosecutor, on his release by the High Court, was arrested and detained in prison pending the exercise by the Minister for Justice of his powers under that statute. The prosecutor claimed his detention was unlawful and unconstitutional.

Held, by the Supreme Court, upholding the order of the High Court releasing the prosecutor, that the courts had a positive duty to protect the individual against the invasion of constitutional rights. Where such invasion occurs the courts would restore, as far as possible, the individual to the position he would have been in had his rights not been infringed. The courts would ensure, as far as possible, that those acting on behalf of the executive who deliberately and consciously violated the constitutional rights of the individual did not gain for themselves the planned results of that invasion. Since no genuine suspicion existed the arrest was a gross abuse of section 30 which amounted to a deliberate and conscious violation of the prosecutor's constitutional rights and that detention was tainted by the illegality of the original arrest.

CASE 205 THE STATE (WALSHE) v MURPHY (1981)

The *Courts of Justice Act 1936* provides that a practising barrister or solicitor of at least ten years' standing may be appointed to act as a justice of the District Court for a limited period. The defendant's practice as a barrister for eight years was followed by continual employment in the public service until his appointment as a justice of the District Court. When the defendant purported to convict the prosecutor of a road traffic offence the prosecutor sought to have that conviction quashed.

Held, by the High Court, that the validity of the conviction depended on the validity of the defendant's appointment and that at the date of that appointment as a temporary justice of the District Court the defendant had not been eligible because he had not practised as a barrister for an aggregate period of ten years and also because he had not been a practising barrister.

CASE 206 IN RE TILSON, INFANTS (1951)

The parties, of different religions, were married in a church of the wife's religion. The husband signed an ante-nuptial agreement that all children of the marriage would be reared in the wife's religion. The four children of the marriage were baptised in the wife's religion. When differences arose between the spouses, the husband placed the children in an institution of his religion, and the wife sought their custody.

Held, by the Supreme Court, in granting custody to the wife, that under the Constitution both parents have a joint power and duty in respect of the religion of their children. If they together make a decision and put it into practice it is not within the power of either parent to revoke such decision against the will of the other.

CASE 207 TORMEY v ATTORNEY GENERAL (1985)

The plaintiff was sent forward for trial by jury to the Circuit Court and he claimed that the prohibition on having his trial in any other court, but particularly the High Court, was a violation of Article 34.3.1° of the Constitution.

Held, by the Supreme Court, that Article 34.3.1° which grants to the High Court full original jurisdiction in all matters must be read in conjunction with Article 36(iii) which conferred a power on the Oireachtas to commit certain matters to the exclusive jurisdiction of other courts of first instance. In making certain offences triable in the Circuit Court, and excluding the jurisdiction of the High Court in such matters, the Oireachtas had not offended Article 34.3.1°. An accused person, tried in a court other than the High Court, retains the right to invoke the original jurisdiction of the High Court by way of *certiorari*, prohibition, mandamus and an application under Article 40.4.2° of the Constitution.

CASE 208 W. v W. (1980)

The parties were married and had four children. For some years prior to the birth of the last child the wife suffered from psychiatric illness which required both in- and out-patient care. When the last child was born, due to the mother's inability to cope with a baby, the parties gave the child to the husband's sister and her husband. Later the marriage broke down and in proceedings in the High Court for custody of the children the three elder children were given to the wife and the youngest child was left in the custody of her aunt. Later the wife sought to vary the order of the High Court and challenged the constitutionality of section 3 of the *Guardianship of Infants Act 1964* which provides that in guardianship proceedings the first and paramount consideration is the welfare of the child.

Held, by the High Court, in upholding the section, that where there was a conflict between the constitutional rights of a legitimate child and the prima-facie constitutional right of its mother to its custody the child's rights should prevail, even if its welfare was to found in the custody of a person outside the family, provided there was good and justifiable reason, on the evidence, of the mother's inability to provide for the child's welfare. In this case, having regard to the fact that the child was 6 years of age, had formed a relationship with her aunt and uncle, the mother's continued mental illness and her poor financial situation, the welfare of the child was best served by refusing to vary the custody order.

CASE 209 W. v W. (1992)

The plaintiff emigrated from Ireland to England in 1965 and acquired an English domicile. The marriage broke down and the plaintiff went to live in Australia for two years. She returned to Ireland in 1971 where she resumed her Irish domicile of origin and while resident here she petitioned for divorce in England which was not contested and was granted in 1972. The plaintiff married the defendant in Ireland in 1973. Difficulties arose in the marriage and the plaintiff sought a judicial separation and ancillary orders. The defendant argued that the parties were not legally married to each other because the plaintiff was not domiciled in England when the divorce proceedings had been initiated. Since that divorce could not be recognised in this State because of the common law rule that only divorces granted by the courts of the jurisdiction of the common domicile of the spouses would be recognised, the parties' marriage was invalid and the application for judicial separation and other reliefs were inappropriate. The question arose as to whether the rule that the domicile of a married woman was to be the same as that of her husband survived the enactment of the Constitution was contrary to Articles 40.1 and 41, and if the rule did not survive, what effect that decision would have in regard to the recognition of foreign divorces and what the correct rules to be applied would be in regard to such divorces and in particular to the present case.

Held, by the Supreme Court, that the common law rule as to a married woman's domicile of dependency offended Article 40.1 of the Constitution in that it clearly resulted in married women not being held equal with single women or with men, whether single or married, and this inequality had nothing to do with differences of capacity, physical and moral, or social function.

The appropriate rule is to recognise a divorce where granted by the courts of a country in which either of the parties to a marriage was domiciled at the time of the proceedings for divorce. Applying that rule to this case the divorce would be recognised, the subsequent marriage was valid and the courts had jurisdiction to hear the judicial separation proceedings.[35]

CASE 210 WADDA v IRELAND (1993)

The *Child Abduction and Enforcement of Custody Orders Act 1991* enacted the Hague Convention on the Civil Aspects of International Child Abduction into law, which has as its purpose the protection of children from the harmful effects of their wrongful removal from the States of their habitual residence. The plaintiff, the mother of a young child, was married to the father of the child and at all material times the parties were habitually resident in the United Kingdom. Differences arose between the parents and the mother removed the child to Ireland. When the father initiated proceedings under the Act the High Court concluded that the father was entitled to an order returning the child to the United Kingdom. The mother challenged the constitutionality of the statute on the grounds that it failed to protect and vindicate the personal rights of the child as an Irish citizen because it deprived the child of an adjudication by an Irish court as to custody, that it failed to ensure access to the courts established under the Constitution and wrongfully ousted the jurisdiction of those courts, and that it failed to protect the rights of the family.

   Held, by the High Court, in dismissing the action, that the statute by providing that the child should not be returned where there was a grave risk of exposing the child to physical or psychological harm or otherwise placing the child in an intolerable situation was a serious obstacle to the argument that implementation of the Convention in this State violated the personal rights of the child. In addition the return of the child may be refused if this breached the fundamental principles relating to the protection of human rights and fundamental freedoms which must, as regards this State, be the rights protected in Article 40 to Article 44 of the Constitution. Had the High Court which heard the case been satisfied that those fundamental principles would be infringed by the return of the child there was no doubt that the court would have refused to make the order.

CASE 211 WARD v KINAHAN ELECTRICAL LTD (1984)

The plaintiff claimed damages for personal injuries in the High Court and when the defendant applied to have the action transferred to the Circuit Court the plaintiff challenged the constitutionality of section 25 of the *Courts of Justice Act 1924*, as amended, on the ground that it offended Article 34.3.1° of the Constitution.

Held, by the High Court, in dismissing the claim, that Article 34.3.1° did not confer a universal right of recourse to the High Court, that Article 34.3.4° provides for the establishment of other courts of first instance which must be local and limited and Article 36 enables laws to be made for the distribution of jurisdiction. It followed that business which falls within the full jurisdiction of the High Court may be assigned, within the limits express and implied in the Constitution, to some other court. Therefore the provisions of the section which permitted the transfer to the Circuit Court of an action commenced in the High Court did not offend the Constitution.

CASE 212 WEBB v IRELAND (1988)

The plaintiff discovered on land an ancient chalice and other religious objects, known as the Derrynaflan Hoard, the relevant part of which was a national monument. He delivered the hoard into the custody of the National Museum with a letter which stated that it had been delivered 'to your care for the present and pending determination of the legal ownership thereof'. The National Museum promised that the plaintiff would be honourably treated. Despite negotiations the parties were unable to agree on a reward and the plaintiff issued proceedings to recover the hoard.

Held, by the Supreme Court, that a necessary ingredient of sovereignty of a modern state was that the State should be the owner of objects which constitute antiquities of importance which are discovered and have no known owner. The right of the prerogative of treasure trove known to the common law should be upheld as an inherent attribute of a sovereign state. The plaintiff was entitled to rely on a legitimate expectation that the State would make a reasonable reward and the court awarded £25,000.

CASE 213 WHEELER v CULLIGAN (1989)

Section 44 of the *Extradition Act 1965*, inserted by the *Extradition (Amendment) Act 1987*, empowered the Attorney General to give a direction to the Commissioner of the Garda Síochána not to enforce a warrant for execution. In exercising this power the Attorney General must form an opinion (a) as to whether there is a clear intention to prosecute the person named in the warrant for the offence specified in it, and (b) as to whether the intention to prosecute is founded on sufficient evidence. The plaintiff was arrested on foot of warrants issued in England and endorsed for execution by the Deputy Commissioner of the Garda Síochána. Orders for extradition were duly made by the District Court. The plaintiff challenged the constitutionality of the section on the ground that when the Attorney General exercised this power he was administering justice and, since he was not a judge, this was contrary to Article 34.1 of the Constitution.

Held, by the High Court, that just as the Attorney General is not administering justice when he weighs up evidence before deciding whether to prosecute or not in cases in which he is the prosecuting authority, so too the Attorney General, in weighing up information under the section, is not administering justice. In both instances the Attorney General is taking a procedural decision which is necessary to be taken before justice is subsequently administered in the courts.

NOTES

Chapter 1 (pp. 1–9).

1. K. C, Wheare, *Modern Constitutions*, London 1966.
2. The Preamble and Article 45 entitled 'Directive Principles of Social Policy': 'the Constitution . . . expresses not only legal norms but basic doctines of political and social theory', per O'Higgins CJ in *Article 26 and the Criminal Law (Jurisdiction) Bill 1975* (Case 5), and 'the Constitution is a political instrument as well as a legal document', per Costello J in *Attorney General v Paperlink Ltd* (Case 12).
3. Unlike the Constitution of Saorstát Éireann 1922 which was vetted by the British Government.
4. At a plebiscite held on 1 July 1937, 685,105 voted in favour and 526,945 against. The Constitution came into effect on 29 December 1937.
5. 'The Draft Constitution shall be submitted to a plebiscite of the people' — *Plebiscite (Draft Constitution) Act 1937*, section 2 (1). The Act was silent as to whether a simple, or other weighted majority, was necessary for its enactment.
6. 'Redolent as they are of the great papal encyclicals': per Gavan Duffy P in *In re Tilson, infants* (Case 206), though this marked leaning towards one Church had waned by *Ryan v Attorney General* (Case 171) where Kenny J referred to 'the Christian and democratic nature of the State'.
7. 'In the absence of convincing evidence that the Constitution 1937 does not reflect the moral views, and the political and social culture of the majority of the Irish people, I believe that it would be unnecessary, premature or unwise to repeal the Constitution or to alter it in any fundamental way' — Mary Redmond in 'Fundamental Rights in Irish Constitution Law' published in *Morality and the Law*, Dublin 1982.
8. Declan Costello, 'The Natural Law and the Constitution' in *Studies*, Vol. XLV, 403, and Vincent Grogan, 'The Constitution and the Natural Law', in *Christus Rex*, Vol. 8, 201.
9. '. . . it was also the fundamental charter of the new State meant to be read and understood by the educated layman, and, where the language is that of an ordinary educated layman, it would be wrong to attempt to divorce it from its plain and ordinary meaning', said Kingsmill Moore J in *In re Employers' Mutual Insurance* (1955) speaking of the 1922 Irish Free State Constitution.
10. The Supreme Court decided in *The State (Quinn) v Ryan* (Case 199) that in constitutional cases the court was not bound by its own previous decisions.
11. Byce, *Studies in History and Jurisprudence*, Vol. 1, Essay 3.
12. The Seanad rejected the *Third Amendment of the Constitution Bill 1958* but Dáil Éireann passed a resolution that the Bill was deemed to have passed both Houses of the Oireachtas. It was put to the People but was defeated: see Note 27 below.

13. The first President, Dr Douglas Hyde, entered into office on 25 June 1938. So the transitional period ended on 25 June 1941.
14. Signed and promulgated on 2 September 1939.
15. Signed and promulgated on 30 May 1941.
16. *Third Amendment of the Constitution Act 1972.* In favour: 1,041,890; Against: 211,891. Signed by the President on 8 June 1972.
17. *Fourth Amendment of the Constitution Act 1972.* In favour: 724,835; Against: 131,514. Signed by the President on 5 January 1973.
18. *Fifth Amendment of the Constitution Act 1972.* In favour: 721,003; Against: 133,430. Signed by the President on 5 January 1973.
19. *Seventh Amendment of the Constitution (Election of Members of Seanad Éireann by Institutions of Higher Education) Act 1979.* In favour: 552,600; Against: 45,484. Signed by the President on 3 August 1979.
20. *Sixth Amendment of the Constitution (Adoption) Act 1979.* In favour: 601,694; Against: 6,265. Signed by the President on 2 August 1979.
21. *Eighth Amendment of the Constitution (Pro-Life) Act 1983.* In favour: 841,233; Against: 416,136.
22. *Ninth Amendment of the Constitution Act 1984.* In favour: 726,310; Against: 168,712. Signed by the President on 2 August 1984.
23. *Tenth Amendment of the Constitution Act 1987.* In favour: 755,423; Against: 324,977.
24. *Eleventh Amendment of the Constitution Act 1992.* In favour: 1,001,076; Against: 448,655.
25. *Thirteenth Amendment of the Constitution Act 1992.* In favour: 1,035,308; Against: 624,059.
26. *Fourteenth Amendment of the Constitution Act 1992.* In favour: 992,833; Against: 665,106.
27. *Third Amendment of the Constitution Bill 1958.* In favour: 453,322; Against: 468,989.
28. *Fourth Amendment of the Constitution Bill 1968.* In favour: 423,496; Against 657,898.
29. *Third Amendment of the Constitution Bill 1968.* In favour: 424,185; Against: 656,803.
30. *Tenth Amendment of the Constitution Bill 1986.* In favour: 538,279; Against: 935,843.
31. *Twelfth Amendment of the Constitution Bill 1992.* In favour: 572,177; Against: 1,079,297
32. For example, see *O'Donovan v Attorney General* (Case 141) and *Crowley v Ireland* (Case 44).

Chapter 2 (pp. 10–13).
1. Signed on 15 November 1985.

Chapter 3 (pp. 14–37).
1. Signed on 26 December 1933.
2. *80 Hague Recueil*, 1952, 1.80–96.
3. *Principles of International Law*, Oxford 1979.
4. *Introduction to International Law*, London 1979, Chapter 5.
5. *A Manual of International Law*, 1976.
6. See Chapter 8, page 105.
7. *Third Amendment of the Constitution Act 1972.* In favour: 1,041,890; Against: 211,891.
8. See Chapter 16, Family Rights — the 'Recognition of Foreign Divorce and Ancillary Orders', page 255.
9. To date on which the Constitution of Saorstát Éireann came into effect.
10. Honorary citizenship was conferred on Sir Alfred Chester Beatty, a philanthropist who donated a library to the State; on Dr T. Herrema, a kidnap victim; and on Mr Tip O'Neill,

the one-time Speaker of the House of Representatives of the American Congress, and his wife.

11. See *Abdelkefti v Minister for Justice* (Case 3).
12. *Pok Sun Shum v Ireland* (Case 166).
13. *L'Esprit des Lois,* 1748, Book XI, Chapter 6.
14. Charles Louis de Secondat, Baron de la Brede et de Montesquieu (1689–1755).
15. This decision was given on 16 July 1973. On 26 July 1973 the President signed into law the *Road Traffic (Amendment) Act 1973* which enacted the impugned section. The words 'be sufficient evidence until the contrary is shown' were substituted for the offending word 'conclusive'.
16. For example, the *Courts Act 1981.*
17. For example, the *Criminal Procedure Act 1967.*
18. For example, the *Road Traffic Act 1961.*
19. For example, the *Civil Liability Act 1961.*
20. For example, the *Unfair Dismissals Act 1977.*
21. For example, the *Family Law Act 1981* abolished criminal conversation, enticement and harbouring of spouses.
22. For example, the *Courts-Martial Appeal Court Act 1983.*
23. For example, the *Courts (Supplemental Provisions) Act 1961*
24. This case was appealed but the former Supreme Court, for reasons explained in Chapter 9, did not consider the appeal.
25. Other similar cases — *The State (Pheasantry Ltd) v Donnelly* (Case 198) and *Cartmill v Ireland* — are discussed under 'Classification of Crimes' in Chapter 9 on page 138.
26. This question of executive privilege is considered fully later in Chapter 8 on page 107.
27. The Supreme Court refused to follow its own previous decision, which decided this point in a contrary manner, in *The State (Shanahan) v Attorney General.*
28. For further discussion on this distinction, see page 148.

Chapter 4 (pp. 37–61).
1. For example, the *Solicitors Act 1954.*
2. For example, the *Holiday (Employees) Act 1973.*
3. For example, the *Decimal Currency Act 1969.*
4. For example, the *Succession Act 1965.*
5. For example, Radio Telefís Éireann, by the *Broadcasting Act 1969,* as amended.
6. For example, the *Road Traffic Act 1961.*
7. For example, the *Criminal Procedures Act 1967.*
8. For example, the *Family Law Act 1981.*
9. Only used on two occasions: *Third Amendment of the Constitution Bill 1958,* and *Pawnbrokers Bill 1964.*
10. The *Road Traffic (Amendment) Act 1973* was passed within a couple of days.
11. This definition, found also in Article 35 of the Constitution of Saorstát Éireann, is originally to be found in the *Parliament Act 1911.*
12. The certificate of the Ceann Comhairle is omitted from Money Bills when enacted and printed.
13. For example, the *Domicile and Recognition of Foreign Divorces Act 1986* — three months after its enactment.
14. For example, the *Extradition (European Convention on the Suppression of Terrorism) Act 1987* — to come into operation on 1 December 1987.
15. For example, the *Criminal Justice Act 1984.*

16. A Money Bill and an Abridged Time Bill may be challenged under Article 34.3.2° of the Constitution. A Money Bill — the *Finance Act 1983* — was challenged in *Madigan v Attorney General* (Case 110).

17. All the referrals to date have been decided within the sixty days: details of the time span in each are given in Notes 20–26 below. Most were, it seems, given within a short period: the exception, the *Criminal Law (Jurisdiction) Bill 1975*, was given within a few days of the time-limit, probably because of serious disagreements among the judges of the Supreme Court.

18. The *Oireachtas Committee on the Constitution 1967*, par. 99, suggested that this prohibition should expire seven years after the decision.

19. *The State (Quinn) v Ryan* (Case 199).

20. Referred 8 January 1940 — decision 9 February 1940.

21. Referred date unknown — decision 15 April 1943.

22. Referred date unknown — decision 14 July 1961.

23. Referred 10 March 1976 — decision 6 May 1976.

24. Referred 24 September 1976 — decision 15 October 1976.

25. Referred 24 December 1981 — decision 19 February 1982.

26. Referred 21 December 1983 — decision 8 February 1984.

27. In favour: 726,310; Against: 168,712.

28. Referred date unknown — decision 26 July 1988.

29. In *In re McGrath and Harte* (Case 104) the former Supreme Court considered, though rejected the argument on alleged procedural defects. Anything short of constitutional defect, such as the absence of words of enactment, will not invalidate the law: *Halpin v Attorney General*.

30. Its scope was severely limited: see *The State (Hoey) v Garvey*.

31. A Tribunal of Inquiry, consisting of three judges, established under the *Tribunals of Inquiry Act 1921*, to investigate allegations against a Government member made by two members of Dáil Éireann, held that the privilege given by Article 15.13 was excluded in that the Tribunal was the instrument chosen by the Oireachtas to make the inquiry: Report of the Tribunal Appointed by the Taoiseach on 4 July 1975: Prl. 4745.

Chapter 5 (pp. 62–75)

1. There have been seven Presidents of Ireland: Douglas Hyde, 1938–45 — no election; Sean T. O'Kelly, 1945–59 — elected in 1945, agreed in 1952; Eamon de Valera, 1959–73 — elected both occasions; Erskine Childers, 1973–74 — elected and died in office; Cearbhall Ó Dalaigh, 1974–76 — agreed candidate, resigned from office; Patrick Hillery, 1976–1990 — agreed candidate in 1976 and 1983; Mary Robinson 1990–present — elected 1990.

2. No candidate has even been nominated in this manner.

3. Non-citizens who may vote in Dáil Éireann elections have no franchise in presidential elections.

4. Andrew Johnson (1865–69) was impeached by the House of Representatives but not by the Senate. Richard Nixon (1969–74) resigned after the House Committee on the Judiciary voted three articles of impeachment.

5. Also judges of the Circuit and District Courts: *Courts (Supplemental Provisions) Act 1961*.

6. The Council of State has only met on thirteen occasions since 1937.

7. Two meetings of the Council of State were held for this purpose.

8. Eleven meetings were held for this purpose, though Bills were only referred to the Supreme Court on nine occasions: see Chapter 4.

Chapter 6 (pp. 76–92).
1. For example, the *Gas Act 1976* and the *Broadcasting Authority Act 1960.*
2. The relevant Electoral Acts provided as follows: 1947 — 147; 1961 — 144; 1969 — 144; 1974 — 148; 1983 — 166.
3. In favour: 424,185; Against: 656,803.
4. The number of constituencies provided by the relevant Electoral Acts were as follows: 1947 — 40; 1961 — 38; 1969 — 42; 1974 — 42; 1983 — 41.
5. Formerly designated as the Minister for Local Government.
6. The members were a judge of the Supreme Court (now replaced by the President of the High Court), the Secretary of the Department of the Environment and the Clerk of Dáil Éireann.
7. In favour: 726,310; Against 168,712.
8. *Electoral (Amendment) (No. 2) Act 1986.*
9. Formerly designated as the Department for Posts and Telegraphs.
10. The curious feature of this case was that the plaintiff was not registered on an electoral register. Had he the necessary *locus standi*? See Chapter 9, page 124.
11. *Electoral (Amendment) Act 1972.*
12. *Prevention of Electoral Abuses Act 1982*, section 1.
13. *Electoral Amendment (No. 2) Act 1986.*
14. This is known as the 'Droop' quota, after H. R. Droop who first evolved it in 1872.
15. 1959: In favour: 453,322; Against 486,989. In 1968: In favour: 424,185; Against: 657,898.
16. 1943 and 1944.

Chapter 7 (pp. 91–97).
1. In favour: 552,600; Against 45,484.
2. Examples of some nominating bodies: Royal Irish Academy, Incorporated Law Society, Irish Medical Association, Irish Countrywomen's Association, Royal Dublin Society, Irish Congress of Trade Unions, Confederation of Irish Industry, Insurance Institute of Ireland, and Irish Hotels Federation.

Chapter 8 (pp. 98–110).
1. The *Comptroller and Auditor General (Amendment) Bill 1992* would repeal these statutes and this Bill would then contain the law on the matter.
2. *Tenth Amendment of the Constitution Act 1987.*
3. The High Court decision in *The State (McCaud) v Governor of Mountjoy Prison*, which held to the contrary, was impliedly overruled.
4. For example, the Vienna Convention on Diplomatic Relations is incorporated into the *Diplomatic Relations and Immunities Act 1967.* The *Child Abduction and Enforcement of Custody Orders Act 1991* incorporated the Hague Convention and the Luxemburg Convention: see *Wadda v Ireland* (Case 210).
5. Report dated April 1974. Irish members were Brian Walsh, Seamus Henchy (both judges of the Supreme Court), T. A. Doyle (later a judge of the High Court) and D. Quigley. British members were Robert Lowry, Lord Scarman, Kenneth Jones and J. B. Hutton.

Chapter 9 (pp. 111–149).
1. For example, *Legitimacy Declaration (Ireland) Act 1868, Children Act 1908, Illegitimate Children (Affiliation Orders) Act 1930, Legitimacy Act 1931, Finance Act 1949, Adoption Act 1952, Married Women's Status Act 1957, Courts (Supplemental Provisions) Act 1961, Official Secrets Act 1963, Guardianship of Infants Act 1964, Succession Act*

1965, Criminal Procedures Act 1967, Criminal Justice Act 1951, and the *Criminal Law (Rape) Act 1980*.

2. The granting of legal aid is such a function.
3. Article 13.9 of the Constitution.
4. Under the *Courts of Justice Act 1924* and the *Courts of Justice (District Court) Act 1946* the judges of the Circuit and District Courts are to hold judicial office on the same tenure as judges of the Supreme and High Courts.
5. In that case the appeal by the DPP was dismissed though in *The People (DPP) v Quilligan* [1986] ILRM 495 the appeal was allowed.
6. Section 7 of the *Courts (Supplemental Provisions) Act 1961*.
7. The successful party is usually awarded costs against the other party though this is not always so, as the courts have a discretion as to costs. For example, in *Norris v Attorney General* (Case 130), which established no constitutional right, the unsuccessful plaintiff was awarded costs against the State, whereas in *The State (DPP) v Walsh* (Case 187), which established a general right to trial by jury in cases of scandalising a court, though not in the instant case, the plaintiff was lumbered with not only his own but also the State's costs.
8. In *East Donegal Co-operative Livestock Mart Ltd v Attorney General* (Case 61) the plaintiff had not been refused a licence, or in *McMahon v Attorney General* (Case 107) where the plaintiff, alleging that the voting system was not secret, but neither voted nor was registered to vote.
9. *Rent Restrictions (Temporary Provisions) Act 1981* was enacted to last six months but was extended twice.
10. The *Housing (Private Rented Dwellings) Act 1982* was amended by the *Housing (Private Rented Dwellings) Act 1983*.
11. This case, concerned with the issue as to whether an adoption order was valid, must be distinguished from another case of the same name, *M. v An Bord Uchtála* (Case 94), which dealt with religious discrimination.
12. In 1968: In favour: 424,185; Against: 656,803.
13. In 1984: In favour: 726,310; Against: 168,712.
14. *The State (Shanahan) v Attorney General* [1964] IR 239.
15. Where the accused consents to being so tried, though certain offences must be tried on indictment.
16. See under 'Armed Rebellion' in Chapter 4, page 57.
17. For example, *The State (DPP) v Walsh* (Case 187).
18. The constitutional point had not been argued in the High Court. Following from this decision the *Solicitors Act 1960* was passed, which vested the High Court with the power to strike a solicitor from the roll.

Chapter 10 (pp. 150–164).
1. Salmond, *Jurisprudence*, London 1966, Chapter 27.
2. See Chapter 1, page 4.
3. In favour: 601,694; Against: 6,265.

Chapter 11 (pp. 165–176).
1. See 'Who Can Avail of Constitutional Rights' in Chapter 10, page 158.
2. See now *Juries Act 1976*, page 142.
3. *Adoption Act 1991* includes widowers.
4. This case also found that a person accused of scandalising a court was, in general, entitled to a trial by jury. See 'Trial of Offences' in Chapter 9, page 146.

5. But these provisions were struck down as an attack on property rights. See 'The Right to Litigate' in Chapter 17, page 281.
6. The challenged law in that case has been amended by *Irish Nationality and Citizenship Act 1986* which is discussed in Chapter 3 under 'Citizen of the State' on page 24.
7. The *Criminal Law (Sexual Offences) Act 1993* repealed these laws and provides the common age of consent for males and females of 17 years.
8. Deserted husbands may now avail of a Lone Parent Allowance.
9. See under 'Non-Marital Family' on page 263.
10. But the legislation was struck down as being an attack on marriage. See under 'Marriage' in Chapter 16 on page 252.
11. The *Status of Children Act 1987* now provides succession rights for illegitimate children.
12. See Note 16 in 'Cases on Constitutional Law'.

Chapter 12 (pp. 177–223).
1. Most notably the English case of *Christie v Leachinsky* [1947] A.C. 573.
2. This case was decided before the enactment of the *Criminal Justice Act 1984*, section 4, which also permits a period of detention.
3. See *Drunken Driving and the Law*, de Blacam, 1986.
4. Printed in the *Report of the Committee to Recommend Certain Safeguards for Persons in Custody and for Members of an Garda Síochána*, April 1978, presided over by Barra O Briain.
5. For example, *McCarrick v Leavy* and *The People (AG) v Cummins*.
6. The *Broadcasting Authority Act 1960*, section 31: see page 237.
7. Dáil Éireann approved this Treaty by motion on 25 November 1986.
8. Organisations may be proscribed under section 18 of the *Offences Against the State Act 1939*.
9. For example, *The State (Hoey) v Garvey*.
10. For example, *The State (McDonagh) v Frawley*.
11. For example, *In re Philip Clarke* (Case 36).
12. For example, *In re Tilson, infants* (Case 206).
13. For example, *The State (Bouzagou) v Station Sergeant of Fitzgibbon Street Garda Station* (Case 177).
14. Abortion is an offence contrary to the *Offences Against the Person Act 1861*.

Chapter 13 (pp. 224–229).
1. There can be no discrimination in the area of employment on the ground of sex or marital status: *Employment Equality Act 1977*.
2. For example, the Irish Republican Army was declared to be an unlawful organisation by the Offences Against the State (Suppression) Order (S.I. 162 of 1939) by the Minister for Justice under section 18 of the *Offences Against the State Act 1939*.
3. The *Criminal Law (Sexual Offences) Act 1993* provides a common age of consent of 17 years for both males and females as regards most sexual activities.

Chapter 14 (pp. 230–233)
1. Any other activity on the public highway may amount to a public nuisance and/or trespass.
2. This statute repealed and substantially re-enacted the *Trade Disputes Act 1904*.

Chapter 15 (pp. 234–245)
1. For example, the *Broadcasting Authority Act 1960*, as amended.
2. By the Broadcasting Authority Act 1960 (section 31) Order (S.I. 7 of 1977) members of the Irish Republican Army and Provisional Sinn Féin were banned, and by the

Broadcasting Authority Act 1960 (section 31) Order (S.I. 10 of 1978) members of the Ulster Defence Association were banned.
3. See Note 2, Chapter 9.
4. See *Law of Defamation in Ireland*, McDonald, Round Hall Press 1987.

Chapter 16 (pp. 246–265)
1. *Hyde v Hyde* (1868) LR 1 P & D 130.
2. A spouse has a legal right to a portion of the deceased spouse's estate.
3. The current law is contained in *Status of Children Act 1987* which does confer succession rights on illegitimate children.
4. In favour: 538,279; Against: 935,843.
5. The High Court later made the separation agreement a rule of court when the clause relating to divorce was deleted.
6. 2 October 1986.
7. A similar result was obtained in *Osheku v Ireland* [1987] ILRM 330.
8. *Family Law*, Shatter.
9. The latest statute is the *Adoption Act 1991*.
10. The case is currently before the European Court of Human Rights and a decision is awaited: *Keegan v Ireland*.

Chapter 17 (pp. 266–286).
1. See now the *Employment Equality Act 1977*.
2. For example, *Courts Act 1981* abolished the contractual wrong of breach of promise of marriage.

Cases in Constitutional Law (pp. 287–385).
1. The non-citizen in this case might now be able to avail of Irish citizenship under the provisions of the *Irish Nationality and Citizenship Act 1986* which is discussed under 'Citizen of the State' in Chapter 3 on page 24.
2. This statute has since been repealed and replaced by subsequent Electoral Acts.
3. The *Ninth Amendment of the Constitution Act 1984* incorporated into the Constitution (Article 16.2) just such a proposal and the appropriate legislation was enacted: see page 81.
4. This statute operated for one year only and was not renewed.
5. The *Thirteenth Amendment of the Constitution Act 1992* is relevant here: see page 221.
6. The current law, contained in the *Domicile and Recognition of Foreign Divorces Act 1986*, discussed under 'Domicile' in Chapter 3 on page 26, is that a foreign divorce will be recognised if either of the parties was domiciled in the jurisdiction which granted it.
7. The current law in this area is contained in the *Housing (Private Rented Dwellings) Act 1982*, as amended.
8. The Supreme Court failed to follow its own contrary decision in *The State (Shanahan) v Attorney General* (1964).
9. By the *Tenth Amendment of the Constitution Act 1987* the People permitted the State to ratify the Single European Act: see page 16.
10. The current law is contained in the *Juries Act 1976* which provides that citizens between the ages of 18 and 70 years, with stated exceptions, can serve on juries.
11. Deserted spouses, irrespective of gender, can now claim a Lone Parent's Allowance.
12. The case decided in 1985 was not printed in the law reports until 1989.
13. The current law is contained in the *Electoral (Amendment) (No. 2) Act 1986* which provides for the registration of special voters' lists of physically ill or physically disabled persons: see page 82.

14. The *Electricity (Supply) (Amendment) Act 1986* now provides that the owner or occupier of lands must be paid compensation where lines are laid across or attached to land or premises.
15. The *Fisheries (Amendment) Act 1978*, section 2, now provides that the District Court has jurisdiction to try summarily any offence under the Act if the District Justice is of opinion that the facts proved against the defendant so charged constitute a minor offence fit to be tried summarily, and the Attorney General consents and the defendant does not object to being tried summarily.
16. This case is cited as *J.M.G. v An Bord Uchtála* (1974) 109 ILTR 62. The *Adoption (Amendment) Act 1974*, section 4, now provides that an adoption order shall not be made in any case where the applicants, the child and its parents, or if the child is illegitimate, its mother, are not all of the same religion, unless every person whose consent to the making of the order is required knows the religion, if any, of each of the applicants when that person gives consent.
17. The *Health (Family Planning) Amendment Act 1993* is now the relevant law.
18. The *Electoral (Amendment) Act 1972*, section 1, now provides that the appropriate law which contains the words 'that such number [on the register of electors] shall be marked on the counterfoil' should be deleted.
19. The current law, the *Road Traffic (Amendment) Act 1993*, provides that the certificate shall, until the contrary be proven, be sufficient evidence.
20. As a consequence of this decision the *Finance Act 1980* was enacted, portion of which was declared unconstitutional in *Muckley v Ireland* (Case 121).
21. The *Criminal Law (Sexual Offences) Act 1993* provides a common age of consent of 17 years for both males and females.
22. The *Status of Children Act 1987* removed the disabilities which illegitimate persons suffered under the law.
23. The *Workmen's Compensation Acts 1934* to *1955*, as amended, have been replaced by the *Social Welfare (Occupational Injuries) Act 1966*.
24. As a consequence of this decision the *Electoral (Amendment) Bill 1961* was enacted which the President referred to the Supreme Court: see *Article 26 and the Electoral (Amendment) Bill 1961* (Case 6). While the court upheld its provisions it has since been repealed.
25. The *Solicitors (Amendment) Act 1960*, section 8, provides that where the Disciplinary Committee of the Law Society, after holding an inquiry into the conduct of a solicitor, makes a report which is brought before the High Court, that court may by order (a) strike the name of a solicitor off the roll, or (b) suspend the solicitor from practice, or (c) censure the solicitor.
26. The *Adoption Act 1991* contains the current law.
27. The applicant took the case unsuccessfully to the European Court of Human Rights, the first case by a private individual.
28. The comments in Note 1 apply also in this instance.
29. The comments in Note 1 apply also in this instance.
30. The comments in Note 1 apply also in this case though since the parties were not living together the non-citizen may not qualify for citizenship.
31. As a consequence of this case the *Offences Against the State (Amendment) Bill 1940* was enacted which was referred to the Supreme Court: see *Article 26 and the Offences Against the State (Amendment) Bill 1940* (Case 10). The court upheld the Bill which continues as an Act to form part of our statute law: see page 204.
32. Dáil Éireann approved this Treaty by motion on 25 November 1986. It was brought into effect by statutory instrument (S.I. 22 of 1987).

33. The point whether an unmarried father must be consulted before his child is placed for adoption, is before the European Court of Human Rights in *Keegan v Ireland*. This case when before the Irish courts was known as *K. v W.* and is mentioned on page 264.
34. The *Extradition Act 1965* is the current law. It is discussed in Chapter 12 on page 207.
35. The current law is contained in the *Domicile and Recognition of Foreign Divorces Act 1986* which only applied prospectively and could not have applied to this case because it occurred before this statute was enacted.

GLOSSARY

ab initio: from the beginning.

absolute privilege: the non-liability of a member of the Houses of the Oireachtas to any court, other than to the Houses of the Oireachtas, for words spoken within the Houses of the Oireachtas.

ad hoc: for this special purpose.

appellant: the party complaining to a superior court of an injustice done by an inferior one. The other party is styled the respondent.

appellate jurisdiction: the jurisdiction exercised by a court when hearing appeals from a lower court.

applicant: the party applying for a judicial review such as *certiorari* (q.v.), prohibition, *mandamus* (q.v.) or an order under Article 40.4.2° of the Constitution. Should a conditional order be granted the party is then styled the prosecutor (q.v.). The term applicant is also applied to those who apply for bail to the High Court and to those who apply to the Court of Criminal Appeal for leave to appeal. If leave is granted they are then styled appellants.

artificial person: term applied to a corporation or registered company to distinguish it from a natural person.

Árus an Uachtaráin: the President's house.

a vinculo matrimonii: from the bond of marriage.

bona fide: in good faith.

certiorari: a High Court order commanding proceedings to be removed from an inferior court or other tribunal into the High Court for review.

carte blanche: complete discretion or authority.

Case Stated: a statement of facts prepared by one court for the opinion of another on a point of law.

CJ: Chief Justice.

collateral proceeding: in constitutional matters where a challenge is not made directly to a statute but to some order or decision given under a statute.

common law: the body of law based on judicial decisions, as distinct from statute law.

consultative jurisdiction: the jurisdiction exercised by a superior court when advising an inferior court on a point of law.

corpus juris: a body of law, especially the laws of a nation or State.

de facto: in actual fact, really, actual.

defendant: a party sued in a civil action or charged with a minor criminal offence. A party charged with a serious crime may be styled the accused.

de jure: by right, rightful.

durante bello: during war or armed rebellion.

executive privilege: a communication prepared in the exercise of the executive function which is protected from disclosure in evidence in any criminal or civil proceeding.

ex gratia: as an act of grace.

ex officio: by virtue of one's office.

ex parte: on one side.

felony: a serious crime such as murder, rape and robbery.

first instance, court of: the court before which an action is first tried, thus distinguished from an appeal court.

former Supreme Court: the Supreme Court of Justice in existence from 1924 to 1961, replaced by the Supreme Court in 1961.

Garda Síochána: the civilian police force.

habeas corpus: the deliverance from illegal confinement. This was its common law term. Now the procedure is more properly entitled an order under Article 40.4.2° of the Constitution.

imprimatur: sanction, authority or approval.

in facie curiae: in the face of the court.

intestate: without making a will.

intra vires: within one's legal powers.

inter alia: among other things; *inter alios* among other persons.

inter arma silent leges: war silences the law.

Iris Oifigiúil: the official Government gazette, published bi-weekly, in which all constitutional and legally important announcements are made.

J: Mr/Mrs/Miss Justice, title of judges of the Supreme and High Courts.

justiciable: capable of being determined by a court of law.

lacuna: a gap or space.

legatee: a person to whom a legacy is bequeathed.

locus standi: signifies a right of appearance in a court of justice.

mandamus: a command issuing from the High Court and directed to any party or inferior court requiring it to do some particular act which pertains to its office and duty.

mens rea: criminal intent, guilty mind.

misdemeanour: an offence not amounting to a felony.

MR: Master of the Rolls (a judicial office existing prior to 1923).

obiter dictum: a thing said by the way, an incidental remark.

nolle prosequi: to be unwilling to prosecute. Its effect is to withdraw the cause of action.

Oireachtas: Parliament — a deliberative assembly.

original jurisdiction: the jurisdiction exercised by a court when hearing and determining an issue at first instance.

P: President of the High Court.

plaintiff: the party seeking relief in civil proceedings.

prima facie: on the first view, at first sight.

privilege: by which certain communications are protected from disclosure in legal proceedings.

prohibition: an order of the High Court forbidding an inferior court from proceeding in a case there pending.

prosecutor, prosecutrix: means properly any party who prosecutes any proceedings in a court of justice, but usage has confined it to denote the complainant in *certiorari*, prohibition and *mandamus* proceedings and in applications under Article 40.4.2° of the Constitution. The defending party is styled the respondent.

Saorstát Éireann: the Irish Free State.

seisin: is the feudal possession of freehold land but is applied generally to denote custody or control of legal proceedings.

quo warranto: originally a criminal information (the initiation of a criminal charge) for the wrongful use of a franchise, but is now a method of trying the existence of a civil right.

statutory instrument: a form of delegated legislation. Statute empowers a designated party to make statutory instruments, which are a form of law, in order to operate further.

sub judice: under consideration.

sui juris: a phrase used to denote a person who is under no disability affecting his or her legal powers to make a conveyance of property, to bind by contract and to sue and be sued: as opposed to a person wholly or partially under disability, such as minors, mentally disordered persons and prisoners.

Taoiseach: Prime Minister (first in order of rank, leader, chief).

Tánaiste: Deputy Prime Minister (second in order of rank, heir presumptive).

ultra vires: beyond one's legal powers.

INDEX